A Study Guide for Small Group Leaders

REVELATION

The return of Christ in power and glory

DON FANNING

Branches
PUBLICATIONS
Forest, Virginia

First Edition 2012
Second Edition 2018
Published by Branches Publications
2040 Downing Dr.
Pensacola, FL 32505

Branches Publications was started to publish missions and discipleship training tools to equip leaders and teachers to be strategic with their lives by equipping disciples with ministry tools to help them fulfill the Great Commission. More materials are available at www.branchespublications.com and tgcresources.com (The Great Commission Resources). A daily discipleship Bible study explaining the commands we are suppose to teach every disciple at www.walkinghisway.com.

© 2012 Copyright: Branches Publications
Don Fanning
Design: Krista Freeman
All rights reserved
ISBN: 978-0-9855812-2-0

All parts of this publications are protected by copyright. Any utilization outside the strict limits of the copyright law, without the permission of the publisher, is forbidden and liable to persecution. This applies in particular to reproductions, translations, microfilming, and storage and processing in electronic retrieval systems.

Other books by Don Fanning available through Branches Publications can be purchased online at www.branchespublications.com and Amazon.com:

What in the World is God Doing? - An Introduction to Missions
*Walking His Way: A Daily Devotional Bible Study on the Commands in the NT
*Ten Steps of Fruitful Discipleship
*Inductive Bible Study Methods
*Romans: A Study Guide for Small Group Leaders
*Titus: A manual for the church
*1, 2, 3 John: Know for Certain
*Spiritual Gifts: A Survey and Definition of the Spiritual Gifts
*Gifts for Today
*Methods of Inductive Bible Study

* These books are also available in Spanish.

CONTENTS

CHAPTER **PAGE**

Chapter	Page
1. Introduction and John's commission to write Revelation.	5
2. Letters to the Seven Churches of Asia, part 1	27
3. Letters to the Seven Churches of Asia, part 2	63
4. The heavenly scene	87
5. The Seven Sealed Scroll	103
6. Opening the Seven Sealed Scroll	117
7. The Saved out of the Tribulation	133
8. The Seventh Seal and the Seven Trumpets	147
9. Trumpet Judgments #5-6 and Woes # 1-2	155
10. The Little Book.	169
11. The Two witnesses and the 7th Trumpet	179
12. The woman and the man child	195
13. The Beast	215
14. The 144,000 and Groups of three angels	233
15. The Seven Last Plagues (Bowls)	253
16. Seven Bowls	265
17. Babylon, the Whore Religion	285
18. The Fall of Babylon	305
19. The Wedding of the Lamb and the Battle of Armageddon	325
20. The Millennial Reign of Christ	345
21. The New Heavens, New Earth, and New Jerusalem	365
22. The New World	385
Bibliography	401

Charts:

Seven Churches	28
Daniel's 70th Week	114
Seven-year Tribulation Chart	115

CHAPTER 1

INTRODUCTION AND JOHN'S COMMISSION TO WRITE REVELATION

"The purpose of the Book of Revelation is to 'unveil' the Lord Jesus in His sovereignty over creation and history by the description of the events, which will precede His Second Coming."

THE UNVEILING OF THE RETURN OF JESUS CHRIST

We can never imagine the inward desire of our Lord to reveal Himself to the world as the Creator, God-Man, Savior and Lord of Lords. For the past two thousand years Christ has given to His followers the task of making Him known in His grace to the ends of the earth, but a time is coming when He will reveal Himself in His wrath to all the world. The Revelation is singular because it is written to reveal the true identity and purpose of the living Lord Jesus Christ. This revelation comes from Jesus Himself as His self-revelation. The Holy Spirit revealed to the aging Apostle John the last inspired revelation that man would receive until He comes back to earth to reign in Person in the Kingdom of God. The Book of Revelation selectively reveals the prophetic description of the future times after A.D. 100 with a lengthy description of the events that will take place in the seven years immediately preceding the Second Advent [Daniel's 70th Week – Dan 9:24-27] and the millennial Kingdom after which will conclude with a final judgment and the beginning of eternity with a new heaven and new earth.

The dating of Revelation is deduced from the mention of being written on the island of Patmos (1:9) where John had been exiled during the reign of emperor Domitian who died in A.D. 96 according to the early church father Irenaeus. Thus the date of A.D. 81 to 96 is given by most conservative scholars for the writing of the text. Except for the persecutions under emperor Nero, who reigned from A.D. 54 to 68, there had been little persecution of the church until Domitian, who reigned from A.D. 81-96. At the writing of Revelation the persecution had only recently begun since martyrdoms were still few (2:13). Domitian elevated his position to divinity with the title *Domitian et Deus noster* ["Domitian Our Lord and God"]. Shrines for the worship of the emperor were everywhere, especially in Roman Asia, but no Christian who claimed Christ as Lord and God could possibly acknowledge the emperor as a god. Evidently John, as leader of the expanding church at Ephesus, had been challenged as to whether his loyalty be to Rome or to the Lord Jesus. His choice led to his exile on a prison island called Patmos.

New Testament canon of books were widely distributed during the time of persecution, and Revelation was included in Irenaeus' list of NT inspired books around A.D.180. In the early third century Origen of Alexandria may have used the same 27 books as modern NT editions. Throughout the third century Justin Martyr, Eusebius, Apollonius and Theophilus, bishop of Antioch, quoted this book as Holy Scripture. When the Church became the empire's state-church by the end of the 4th century, everyone had begun to think they were already in the millennium, so some began to question the inspiration of Revelation since it did not seem to fit their experience. The Augustinian Roman Catholic state-church three hundred years later rejected the premillennial view, common in the Early Church, by the 5th century. At that time they needed a biblical justification for their kingdom-like powers under Rome. In A.D. 380 by decree of the emperor everyone was forced to be a part of the state-church. This immediate success and exaltation of the church could only be explained if the kingdom promises were allegorized to appear like they were already fulfilled in a spiritual or quasi-literal millennium as the church of the empire.

Revelation is a self-declared book of prophecy (1:3; 22:7, 18, 19), which tends to use symbolic and apocalyptic writing style, designed to make the message unforgettable, but not confusing to the first century reader. The key to understanding such symbols is to compare the use of symbols within the Book of Revelation as well as examine how such symbols are used in Daniel, Ezekiel or other OT prophetic passages. The harmony of Scriptures included the use of similar symbols to illustrate the same concepts in earlier prophecies. Symbols or metaphors are not ambiguous or impossible to understand concepts. If that were true, it may have lead one to want to spiritualize a meaning of a symbol to fit their contemporary application. Rather, when God inspired the use of a symbol, He intended it to mean something specific to the readers of that time. Our task is to discover this original meaning, not to make up a meaning to fit our time. Prophecy is the disclosing of information that was not made known to the prophet by ordinary means; rather, it is the revelation of God's will and His message to the mind of a prophet who then proclaims and/or writes it down on a parchment, while being controlled by the inspiration of the Holy Spirit, with the result that what was written was precisely and verbally, the words that God wanted to be spoken through the last apostle to the churches.

HOW SHOULD THE BOOK OF REVELATION BE INTERPRETED?

Few NT books have such a variety of interpretations as the Book of Revelation. The correct principles of interpretation are vital for agreement and must be applied consistently throughout the NT. The variety of views has less to do with the symbolic text of the Book, than with the methods or principles followed to interpret the text itself. This study will follow the **literal method** of interpretation, that is, the Historical-linguistic-grammatical method, which led the Early

Church to a literal understanding of a thousand-year reign after the return of Christ (Rev. 20), called the premillennial view ["before-millennium"]. The plain meaning of the text for the first century audience is the same meaning for us today. This view sees the use of symbols to be explained in the context or elsewhere in the Bible as real events, places or persons.

Another approach is the **allegorical method** of interpretation as was used by Augustine (A.D. 354-430), which led to the *amillennial* view ["no-millennium"]. He wanted the references to the millennium to be an allegory for the Church age and he saw the Book in general as a narrative of the spiritual conflict between God and Satan in the present time. The church was in power with Rome, which seemed to demonstrate the kingdom power as describe in Revelation, but the prevalent view of Christ returning before the millennium had to be rejected. As a result this view sees every event, person and thing mentioned in the book to be a symbol of some truth or event to be determined. This method does not technically interpret the Scriptures, rather by ignoring the common meanings of prophetic words, it gives authority to the imagination and speculation of the interpreter to fit the text into contemporary events or thoughts.

FOUR INTERPRETATIONS FOR THE REVELATION:

The **Preterist view** [meaning "past" fulfillment] believes that the entire book was fulfilled in the early conflicts of the church in the first century, or at least by A.D. 312. This view denies any prophetic or predictive aspect of most of the book. It sees Armageddon as God's judgment on the Jews, which was carried out by the Roman army described as the "Beast." Rev. 5-11 is the church's victory over Judaism. Rev. 12-19 is the record of the church's victory over Rome. Rev. 20-22 is the record of the glory of the Church Age. All the different branches of this view agree that the events of the Book do not refer to specific events, but generalized ways that God is dealing with man.

The **Historical view** came out of the Middle Ages, which sees the Revelation as a picture of the entire history of the Church age between Christ's first and second coming. The Church would expand, despite persecution, until it dominated the entire world, but it would gradually become an apostate system, where real Christians would be persecuted. Luther, Isaac Newton, and many teachers of the postmillennial school of interpretation held this view. One of its difficulties is to have

INTRODUCTION AND HEAVENLY COMMISSION TO WRITE

any consistency in deciding which descriptions in Revelation refer to which event in history. Everyone says the events were fulfilled in their generation. Others combine the historical and the allegorical to bring out devotional or spiritual teachings from Revelation. There are more that fifty different major interpretations of the historical view of Revelation.

The **Futuristic view,** which has been adopted by many conservative writers, usually premillennialists, agrees that chapters 4-22 deal with future events that are unfulfilled until Christ raptures His church. Furthermore, most agree that chapters 4-18 describe the seven years just before the second Advent of Christ, often referred to as the Great Tribulation, which will be a worldwide persecution and unprecedented martyrdom. The futurist attempts to follow specific rules of interpretation of a literal or normal reading of the text according to grammatical, historical, linguistic rules of interpretation. Symbols are understood in the plain, normal meaning as they are used in biblical texts or common sense ("I am the door"). This leads one to a consistent interpretation, which often requires a considerable amount of biblical research.

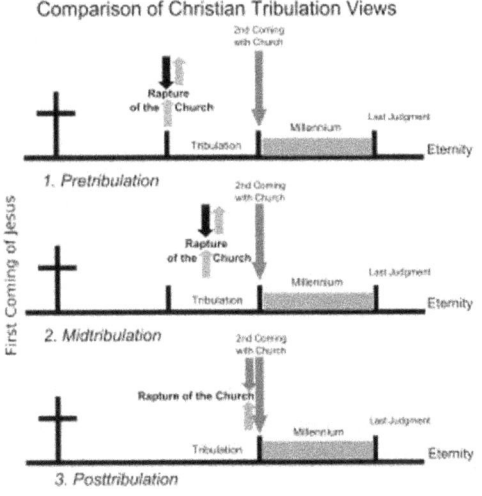

One of the major themes of the Revelation has to do with the millennium (six times in Rev 20 John refers to a "thousand-year" reign with Christ (vs. 2-7). Belief in a literal millennium is also called "chiliasm" (Greek, *chilioi*, "thousand"), which was condemned in the fourth century (Council of Constantinople, 381) and in the Nicaene Creed by the phrase, "whose kingdom shall have no end." There are three different views of the millennium:

Premillennialism: Christ returns before the millennium begins.
Amillennialism: there is no millennium, rather the Church Age is the figurative fulfillment of the millennium, which was popularized by Augustine – a Roman Catholic and the Reformers' Covenant Theology view.
Postmillennialism: Christ will return after a literal or figurative thousand years of Christian dominance in the world – a view popular in

the 19th century, then faded with the Civil War, then two World Wars. Toward the end of the 20th century this view has become popular in the Charismatic Kingdom-Now theology.

Finally there are three primary Premillennialist views of when the believers will be "caught up," or raptured, to be forever with the Lord. Some are **Pre-tribulationalists** who teach the rapture ocurrs before the beginning of the Tribulation period). Others are **Mid-tribulationalists** who see the rapture mid-way through the Tribulation (at the 3 ½ year point of the 7-years) Period, and **Postribulationalists** who see a rapture after the Tribulation Period just before the kingdom is established. This latter rapture view does not take people up to heaven, but rather transfers a glorified people directly into the Kingdom age at the end of the Tribulation period. If all believers are raptured at the end of the Tribulation, then no living believers would enter the millennium!

The purpose of the Book of Revelation is to "unveil" the Lord Jesus in His sovereignty over creation and history by the description of the events, which will precede His Second Coming (Rev 4-18), then a graphic description of the Second Coming event (Rev. 19), followed by the millennial reign of Christ (Rev 20), then the launching of the eternal state (Rev. 21-22).

These events will culminate the prophecies of the OT by explaining what the prophets had seen earlier. Such awareness should produce in the believer who believes this truth a sense of eminency that motivates a purposeful life and holiness.

The Book unfolds the "hidden power of lawlessness" that "was already at work" (2 Thes 2:7) though limited during the Church Age by the Holy Spirit, but will accelerate to a climax in the manifestation of the final Antichrist of the Revelation. The anti-Christian passion will crescendo into the Tribulation Period of persecution described in the Revelation. In spite of the opposition powers that will be manifested, the devil is a defeated enemy of God and His people. God will fulfill His purpose of good for the world, which He has made and redeemed (Rev. 21:9-22:5).

The proper application of the Revelation will result in a motivation for holiness and purity (1 Jn 3:3), which is deduced from the conviction

INTRODUCTION AND HEAVENLY COMMISSION TO WRITE

that Jesus could come at any time, then everyone will face a judgment of our lives. A solemn warning is given to those who are unprepared for this climactic and sudden event. Our evaluation will be on the basis of how beneficial we were to the accomplishing of the Great Commission during our lifetime in the Church Age.

It must be noted that most intense opposition to the gospel and the evangelical church since the writing of the Book of Revelation has occurred in the last third of the 20th century to the present, there has been an estimated 1 million martyrs in the period 2000-2010, in contrast to an estimated 34,000 Christian martyrs in 1900 (*International Bulletin of Missionary Research*). The anti-Christian spirit is increasingly active in the world today.

There is a special benefit to those who take part in this study, "who hear it and take it to heart what is written in it, because the time is near" (Rev. 1:3). Taking "it to heart" means that one's life is lived in the light of these truths found in the Revelation. In this study each major thought is followed by an application or Reflection question for discussion or personal meditation.

A basic Outline to Revelation:

I. Introduction – "What you have seen" (ch. 1)

II. Letters to the Seven Churches – "What is now" (chap 2-3)

III. The Revelation of the Future – "What will take place later" (chaps. 4-22)

I. INTRODUCTION – "WHAT YOU HAVE SEEN" (REV. 1)

A. PROLOGUE (1:1-3)

1:1

The revelation of Jesus Christ, which God gave him to show his servants what must happen very soon. He made it clear by sending his angel to his servant John,

The purpose of the Book of Revelation is to "unveil or disclose" (*apokalupsis*, Eng. "apocalypse") Jesus Christ. Probably the greatest desire in God's heart is to reveal Himself to the world to erase all doubts and skepticisms, but He waits till the church's mission is first accomplished (Matt 24:14) and the timing is perfect (Rev. 14:15).

This revelation was given to John, simply referred to as "his servant" (*doulos*, "one who gives himself up to another's will, devoted to another without regard to one's own interest," STRONG). In other words, it was someone Jesus could trust to receive and transmit this revelation to others.

The urgency of the revelation is that it contains data that would happen quickly (*en tachen*, "sudden, without delay"- as in Acts 12:7; 22:18), thus refers to quickness in which these events will occur once they begin.

The term "immanent return" means "ready to take place or impending." The prophecies of this Book could begin at any time, but they will occur rapidly once they begin. The message was "made clear" (*semaino*, "make known by signs or symbols" to indicate it beyond a doubt; "intentionally produce an impression to signify something," FRIBERG). The book was not written to confuse, but to clarify the issue by using symbols and make them unforgettable.

The angel may refer to Gabriel, who brought messages to Daniel, Mary and Zechariah, but here is unnamed. A number of false religions claim angelic messengers gave their founder new truths, but when they contradict the true gospel of grace through faith these false angels are to be condemned and rejected (Gal 1:8).

John may have been the only living apostle at the end of the first century. John is referred to as a "servant." Some one said, "The true test of a servant's heart is whether or not he is willing to act like one, when he is treated like one."

Reflection: Why would the author put so much emphasis in the beginning of this Book on the quickness of the occurrences of these events?

USE OF SYMBOLS

Why did John use symbols? Weirsbe describes the reasons as (1) a "spiritual code" that would be known only by Christians, especially in the first century, thus leaving it a puzzle to outsiders; (2) the benefits of symbols is not weakened by time, but continue to have their effect; (3)

INTRODUCTION AND HEAVENLY COMMISSION TO WRITE

the symbols not only convey information, but also values and arouse emotions. He illustrates this by saying that John could have said, "A dictator will rule the world," but instead described a "beast."

The use of symbols is not to be "spiritualized" to mean anything that our imagination can invent, but rather some are explained in the text itself (Rev. 1:20; 4:5; 5:8); others are explained in the OT use of the same symbols (Rev 2:7, 17; 4:7) and a few are not explained at all (i.e., the "white stone" in Rev 2:17). With more than 300 references to the OT in the Book of Revelation, it is clear that any interpretation must fit in the entire scheme of what God has already revealed, or we can misinterpret this vital Book.

TRUTH

1:2

[John] who then testified to everything that he saw concerning the word of God and the testimony about Jesus Christ.

John remembered and recorded accurately what he had seen and had been taught. Jesus had promised His disciples that they would "remember what I told you of them" (John 16:4). The word "testified" is *martureo*, "to be a witness," which implies "attestation, verification and validation." One of the assurances of our Bible text is that the Holy Spirit enabled the apostles to remember all that Jesus taught so that we could have an accurate, infallible record of His teachings in the gospel.

In this case, as soon as he saw the vision John was writing almost immediately. The two phrases, "Word of God" and "testimony about Jesus Christ" give the importance of this Book. John saw how the Word of God fits together and how the end-time prophecies are all harmonized. The latter phrase could also be translated "testimony (from) Jesus Christ" (a subjective genitive), where Jesus gives the testimony or "validity and verification" of the message.

Reflection: How is the fact that we are studying an eyewitness inspired report of future events, an encouragement to believe precisely what is written?

THE ONLY PROMISED BLESSING TO READER

1:3a
"Blessed is the one who reads the words of this prophecy aloud,

This is the only book that is promised a special "blessing" (*makarios*, "fortunate, privileged, recipient of divine favor"). The condition for this "blessing" is for the one who "reads" the Book, which is translates the word *anaginosko*, "to know accurately, distinguish between" ideas, thus to be discerning and to give special attention to this divine revelation. This Book is called "this prophecy" (also the "Word of God and testimony of Jesus"), which is not only future events, but also moral and spiritual applications for exhortation and comfort. In the Bible it refers to truths received by direct revelation from God (1 Cor 14:30). Careful attention is to be given to these descriptions of these literal events and personages. There are seven "beatitudes" in the Book of Revelation (i.e. "Blessed are those..." as there are seven in Matthew 5) in Revelation: 1:3; 14:13; 16:15; 19:9; 20:6; 22:7. All total there are 49 uses of "blessed" in the NT.

Reflection: Describe the "blessings" in these verses:

Luke 12:43

John 13:17

Acts 20:35

Rom 4:7

James 1:12

1 Pet 4:14

1:3b

and blessed are those who hear and obey the things written in it, because the time is near!

1:3b At this time there were few copies of the NT so in the congregations one would read any manuscript available and the audience listened intently. In the Hebrew mind you cannot "hear" without obeying, thus the conditional blessing requires both. To "obey" (*threo*) means to

INTRODUCTION AND HEAVENLY COMMISSION TO WRITE

"guard, watch over, preserve" or "apply, practice." As the Word of God is read, the wise person is always looking for wisdom principles that he can apply personally. This is the objective of the Reflection questions at the end of each unit. The reason for this response is that the "time is near." The word for "time" is *kairos*, "a period of time" (i.e. "time of the end" – Dan 8:17; 11:35, 40; 12:4, 9), thus it is not a moment or instant of time, but a new age that is about to begin. The word "near" (*eggus*, "soon to come to pass" THAYER) refers to the opposite of being in the unrelated distance, but speaks to the next event in prophetic history.

Reflection: How does Mt 24:33 relate to this verse? How does God see time in 2 Pet 3:8-9?

B. JOHN'S SALUTATION TO HIS READERS (1:4-8)

1:4

From John, to the seven churches that are in the province of Asia: Grace and peace to you from "he who is," and who was, and who is still to come, and from the seven spirits who are before his throne,

1:4a The author, an Apostle, and the recipients are identified at the beginning of the letter, as the seven churches of the Roman province of Asia Minor (chaps. 2-3) that were associated with the Apostle Paul's ministry (Acts 19:10, 26). Proof of authorship being an apostle or someone closely associated with an apostle was necessary for the NT Books to be accepted in the "canon" of the NT. Though only two of these seven churches are mentioned in Acts, Paul's disciples likely founded them (like Epaphras in Colossians 1:7 and 4:12). The literal recipients imply that this was a meaningful and clear message to a real church in John's time, not just a mysterious symbolism. The Christian greeting of "grace and peace" refers to their standing before God (in grace) with their resulting personal experience (peace). Ignore the grace of God and one forfeits the peace of God (Heb 12:14)

Reflection: Is this an unusual type of greeting in the NT? The Trinity is invoked in the salutation. What is unusual about these descriptions?

1:4b Notice the repeated three-fold use of the preposition "from" revealing a three-fold ministry of the Trinity: grace and peace come from (1) the eternal One who is (present continuously being...), who "was" (imperfect tense which means He had no beginning or ending of His being) and is the "coming One;" (2) the grace and peace is from the seven spirits. Seven in the Bible is associated with perfection and the Spirit is seen in a seven-fold ministry in Isa 11:2, though the Spirit is one (Eph 4:4); and (3) grace and peace come from Jesus Christ, the Redeemer. The Holy Spirit is referred to as the "seven spirits" who are "before" the throne (*enopion*, "in the presence of, on behalf of," GINGRICH) as in Isa 11:2-3; Rev 3:1; 4:5; and 5:6. Christ is mentioned last. Thus the trinity is the source of grace and peace.

Reflection: How many descriptions of His person and character can you find in the following verses? (hint: at least 7).

THE REDEEMER

1:5

and from Jesus Christ– the faithful witness, the firstborn from among the dead, the ruler over the kings of the earth. To the one who loves us and has set us free from our sins at the cost of his own blood.

1:5a The three-fold description of Jesus reveals His ministries as Prophet ("faithful witness"), which implies a previous death, described as a substitutionary death for the sins of the world (Heb 5:1-10; 9:11-14; 10:14) and an acceptance of Christ's offering by the Father (Acts 2:23-24, 31-32; 4:25); Priest ("firstborn of the dead") and King: ("ruler of the kings of the earth"), which refers to a present rule (though they are unaware) that is leading toward the fulfillment of everything described in this Book. Reference to the resurrection states that He was the first with an everlasting resurrected body proving that His followers would likewise have a similar resurrection (mentioned in 40 verses in the NT).

Reflection: Why was the resurrection promise so important to Christians, especially in the first century?

John 11:25

Rom 6:5

1 Peter 1:3

INTRODUCTION AND HEAVENLY COMMISSION TO WRITE

1:5b Evangelical Christianity is the only religion that gives an absolute expression that sinful men can be totally freed from the consequences of their sins. Jesus is the one who "loves us" (present continuous action) and has "set us free" or "washed us" in a one-time act when we were saved (the sense of the aorist verb tense). Some versions have "washed" instead of "freed" (Greek difference is *lousanti* versus *lusanti*, only the letter "o", but if read, they sound similar). Whichever is correct, the enabling act of the liberation was the shedding of His blood in a substitutionary, sacrificial, bloody death as a just payment for the sins of mankind. Regardless which is correct, the results are the same: a one-time act of freeing us, once-and-for-all from all our sins (inherited, imputed and personal) and guilt and its punishment (physical, spiritual and eternal death). We are freed and cleansed forever!

Reflection: Can you write out the two-fold reasons for praising the Lord in this text?

THE ETERNAL PURPOSE FOR BELIEVERS

1:6

and has appointed us as a kingdom, as priests serving his God and Father– to him be the glory and the power for ever and ever! Amen.

1:6 He has made us all a singular "kingdom" (*basileia*), thus not calling us "kings" (*basileus*) as some translations. This text focuses on our unity and bond to each other, as servants of the same King and His will. Likewise we are all "priests" ministering to God and to people. The eternal prospect of knowing and serving Jesus in this age with eternal purposes should be high motivation to fulfill His plan of the ages. John is so excited that he launches into a doxology of praise. Notice the "power" or "dominion" (*kratos*), which means "mighty rule, sovereignty," which belongs only to Jesus forever.

Reflection: How is the believer's privilege described in these verses?

Rev 5:10

Rom 8:17-18

2 Tim 2:12

READERS SHOULD BE LOOKING FOR HIS COMING

1:7

"(Look! He is returning with the clouds, and every eye will see him, even those who pierced him, and all the tribes on the earth will mourn because of him. This will certainly come to pass! Amen.)"

1:7 The "blessed hope" (Tit 2:13) of the believer is when Jesus returns to earth, "the glorious appearing of the great God and our Savior, Jesus Christ." This passage in Titus is the clearest statement in the NT of the deity of Christ, "God and Savior." Rev 1:7 points to the Second Advent when Jesus returns "with the clouds" just as He departed and as was promised (Acts 1:9-11). Every "eye will see him," thus His Return to earth is quite visible and majestic, whereas His ascension was only witnessed by His disciples. The reference to "those who pierced him" technically refers to the Roman soldiers, but Israel assumed the guilt of crucifying the Savior in Matt 27:25, which refers to the "children" or descendents of the actual guilty. Zechariah 12:10 describes this moment of revelation when the surviving Israel understands that their ancestors had killed their Messiah. "All the tribes" (*phule*, "kindred, families, peoples") refers not just to Israel, but to all the nations.

Reflection: Why do you think there is such a contrast between the "blessed hope" of Titus and the "mourning" of Rev. 1:7 when picturing the Second Coming?

1:7b The literal phrase, "yes, Amen!" (1:7) is better translated, "This will certainly come to pass!" as the literal meaning or nuance of the expression.

THE AUTHOR OF THE REVELATION

1:8

I am the Alpha and the Omega," says the Lord God– the one who is, and who was, and who is still to come– the All-Powerful!

1:8 The salutation ends with a powerful expression of the subject of the Revelation in four clear titles: "the Alpha and the Omega" (why are the articles "the" important?). This is the first and last letter of the Greek alphabet: the A and Z. It is an expression of God's knowledge

INTRODUCTION AND HEAVENLY COMMISSION TO WRITE

and wisdom (Col 2:3), stressing Christ's omniscience and infinite knowledge and wisdom.

The expression "Lord God" is used by John eleven times in the Revelation as a reference to Jesus Christ. The title "One who is, and who was, and who is to come" is repeated again in 4:8 and 11:17, which refers to the living Christ who came once before, and is coming again.

He is the "Almighty" (*pantokrator*, "the all-powerful One"), which translates "God of hosts" in the Septuagint, the Koine Greek version of the Hebrew Bible translated between the third and second century BC and completed before 132 BC. This word stresses the omnipotence of God. It is used 10 times in the NT and 9 are in Revelation. The rest of the Book gives the details of these events. There is no better concise description of the Person and work of Jesus Christ.

Reflection: How did Daniel see the same vision in Dan 7:13-14?

C. THE VISION OF CHRIST WHILE EXILED ON PATMOS 1:9-18

Patmos was the scene of the reception of the visions of the Revelation. According to several Early Church fathers, John was sent to the penal island Patmos as a prisoner in exile following his pastorate in Ephesus. The first commentator on the Book of Revelation, Victorinus, wrote that John worked as a prisoner in the mines on this island. The supposed cave where John lived can be visited. When Emperor Domitian died in AD 96, John was permitted to return to Ephesus.

THE COMMISSION OF WRITING THE REVELATION (1:9-11)

1:9

I, John, your brother and the one who shares with you in the persecution, kingdom, and endurance that are in Jesus, was on the island called Patmos because of the word of God and the testimony about Jesus.

1:9 The author refers to himself two more times in the Book (21:2 and 22:8), to clarify that it was written by an apostle from beginning to end. John identify with his fellow-believers who were being persecuted as well under Domitians reign before AD 96. Three areas of shared identity or "fellow partakers" with the readers in (1) "persecution" (*thlipsis*, "pressing together, distress, oppression"), (2) "kingdom," that is, they were sharing in the membership of the spiritual kingdom of Christ before the manifestation of the physical kingdom at the Second Coming, and (3) "endurance" (*hupomone*, lit. "remain under," Lexicon: "steadfastness, constancy, patience" or loyal to the faith regardless of the persuasion to apostatize).

Reflection: Could you identify with John? How hard is it for you to give a testimony of your faith when you know you will be criticized or worse?

John was persecuted because of his faithful proclamation of and faith in the Word of God (most of the NT had by now been written) and the testimony "of" or "about" Jesus. Apparently the laws had made public proclamation of the Bible and message about Jesus a crime.

Reflection: Has what you have said about the Bible or Jesus ever caused you any conflicts with others? Write it down or share it in your own group.

COMMAND TO WRITE

1:10

I was in the Spirit on the Lord's Day when I heard behind me a loud voice like a trumpet,

1:10 John was "in the Spirit" which means, I believe, that he was enjoying a time of inward communion with God, not in a mystical ecstasy, but with his conscious mind and being. The expression is used twice of Jesus and 24 times of the apostles. It refers to the inner being of a person.

Here is a sampling: "pressed in the spirit" (Acts 18:5); "Paul purposed in the spirit" (Acts 19:21); "He is a Jew, who is one inwardly…in the Spirit" (Rom 2:29); "Walk in the Spirit" (Gal 5:16); "Be renewed in the spirit of your mind" (Eph 4:23); and "live according to God in the spirit" (1 Pet 4:6). Thus internally Paul was involved fully with his mind in a vision the Spirit was giving to him.

However, this text implies that the Spirit had unusual control of John's conscious mind through which He would clearly reveal the details of the end of the age.

INTRODUCTION AND HEAVENLY COMMISSION TO WRITE

Reflection: Do you walk with the Lord with your whole spirit, mind and soul or is it only emotional? What is the difference?

1:10b

The phrase "the Lord's Day" is only used here in the Bible. It could refer to the first day of the week, but more likely in this context, refers to being in the middle of the "day of the Lord," which refers to the climactic events of the Second Coming. See these verses for similar expressions: Isa 13:6, 9; Joel 1:15; 2:1, 11, 3:14; Amos 5:18; Zeph 1:7-8, 14; Mal 4:5; 1 Thes 5:2; and 2 Pet 3:10. Thus what follows is as John saw the events of the "day of the Lord" or the "Lord's day."

Note: this vision unlikely refers to one 24-hour-day communication, but rather is a record of a series of visions that John was given over a period of time. This view seems more likely since John was commanded 12 times in the Book to write what he saw (1:19; 2:1, 8, 12, 18; 3:1, 7, 14; 14:13; 19:9; 21:5). One vision he was told not to write down (10:4) because of its severity.

Maybe there is a principle here, that God wants the lessons He teaches us to be recorded for others as well. (Of course, ours are not inspired revelations, but lessons we learn can be valuable for our posterity). John heard a loud voice (*phonen megalen*, origin in English of "megaphone"), with which God communicated this revelation.

Reflection: Have you ever kept a journal of God's dealing with you?

1:11

saying: "Write in a book what you see and send it to the seven churches– to Ephesus, Smyrna, Pergamum, Thyatira, Sardis, Philadelphia, and Laodicea.

The seven churches, as pictured earlier, are listed in clockwise fashion beginning at Ephesus on the coastline of Asia Minor, going north to Smyrna, then East to Pergamum, then southeast until Laodicea. Were these churches independent or very much alike in their behavior, philosophy and church ministries?"

JOHN'S VISION OF THE CHRIST AMIDST THE CHURCHES (1:12-16)

1:12

I turned to see whose voice was speaking to me, and when I did so, I saw seven golden lampstands,

1:12 Hearing a voice, John turned to see seven golden lampstands surrounding the glorified Christ. The description is a little unusual because the lampstand of the Jewish Temple or the Menorah, was one lampstand with seven lamps made of solid gold. The picture to the right depicts the Menorah being taken from the Temple treasury by the Roman booty (AD 70) carved on the Arch of Titus in Rome. However, these lampstands seem to be seven individual lampstands. The significance of the golden "lampstands" will be explained later (1:20), where the lampstands are the seven churches receiving this Book.

Reflection: What significance can you see in this vision of the lampstands that Jesus wanted to communicate to John and the churches?

1:13-16 DESCRIPTION OF THE LORD

1:13-15

and in the midst of the lampstands was one like a son of man. He was dressed in a robe extending down to his feet and he wore a wide golden belt around his chest. 14 His head and hair were as white as wool, even as white as snow, and his eyes were like a fiery flame. 15 His feet were like polished bronze refined in a furnace, and his voice was like the roar of many waters.

1:13 A person was standing among the lampstands, "like a son of man," a phrase used in Daniel 7:13 as a clear reference to the Messiah, the "Ancient of Days," that is, God Himself. The vision depicts the characteristics of the person able to accomplish all the events to be revealed in the rest of the Book.

The description of the Man John saw was of a priest dressed in a long robe, with a golden belt or sash around his chest. His hair and head were white, probably in brilliance and purity (See Matt 17:2) and similar to the One whom Daniel saw in Dan 7:9. His eyes were like "a fiery flame," which is described again in Rev 2:18. They were searching and penetrating, missing nothing, suggesting the Bema seat judgment for believers (1 Cor 3:12; 4:5; 2 Cor 5:10-11).

Two more attributes are described: his feet and his voice. His feet like polished bronze "refined in a furnace," that is glowing red from a furnace heat. "Bronze" is another symbol of divine judgment in the OT. His voice was like the "sound of many waters," as the roar of a mighty waterfall, which speaks of overwhelming authority when He speaks. Is there a relation to the bronze altar in the temple where the sacrifice for sin occurred and divine judgment fell?

Reflection: How do you feel about relating to this majestic and intimidating Person?

1:16

He held seven stars in his right hand, and a sharp double-edged sword extended out of his mouth. His face shone like the sun shining at full strength.

This powerful Person held seven stars in his right hand. We are not left to our imagination since these seven stars will be explained in 1:20. The right hand signifies power and authority (Mark 14:62) as well as His strength and protection.

A "sharp two-edged sword" came out of His mouth, which is the expression used of the Word of God (Heb. 4:12). This text used the word, *makaira*, "a small penetrating sword" worn on one's side. However, our text (Rev 1:16) uses the word sword (*rhomphaia*, a long sword worn on the right shoulder), which implies a warrior or soldier status (Christ is no longer a babe in a manger, nor a Man of Sorrows crowned with thorns, but now is revealed as the King of glory, ready to come in sweeping judgment, war and destruction (John 12:48) on all who reject Him. This sword is mentioned 9 times in Revelation.

His face was as brilliant as the sun depicting His blinding glory that Paul saw in Acts 9:4. Everything is revealed in this light, before which it is impossible to hide. This view was more than awesome; it was frightening. This is Someone you do not want as your enemy.

Reflection: How should such an awe-inspiring person be treated?

We stand for presidents, kings and judges when they enter the room, but we fall to the floor when Christ appears.

THE WORSHIP OF HIM WITHOUT FEAR

1:17

When I saw him I fell down at his feet as though I were dead, but he placed his right hand on me and said: "Do not be afraid! I am the first and the last,

How did Paul respond when he saw the same image? (Acts 9:4). Notice that John would rest with his head on Jesus' chest at meals (Jn 13:25) as a close friend, but not now. His humanity hid His divinity, but once unveiled, trite familiarity, frivolous and shallow "best-friend" relationship is not the response He deserves. The evident sovereignty and holiness becomes a terror of judgment to the unbelieving world, but the basis of comfort and protection to the believer in Christ, because he knows from the Word that Christ saves, cleanses and purifies through the death-sacrifice of Christ on the cross for our benefit and His undeserved love-commitment to His followers.

Reflection: How did the disciples respond when Jesus unveiled Himself on the Mount of Transfiguration sixty years before (Matt 17:6)? How did Daniel respond when he saw Jesus for who He really is (Dan 10:8-9)? How did Isaiah respond (Isa 6:5) when he same the same Jesus (John 12:41)? Do some see Jesus as a "good guy," "best friend" or "grandfather" image who will do our beck and call? (see Heb 12:28-29).

1:17b However, Jesus tells John an expression written 12 times in the gospels, and Jesus twice told the same expression to Paul in Acts (18:9 and 27:24), "Do no be afraid." This time it is because of the fearfulness of His indescribable majesty, as though no human being could survive in His presence (Ex 33:20). Worship is not a pep rally, but a humbling submission to the King and a deep rejoicing that He could still love us.

Reflection: What astonished Moses when he saw the same thing (Deut 5:24)?

INTRODUCTION AND HEAVENLY COMMISSION TO WRITE

1:18

and the one who lives! I was dead, but look, now I am alive– forever and ever– and I hold the keys of death and of Hades!

1:18a Jesus says, "I am the first and the last." This expression is similar to 1:8 and is applied to Christ in 2:8; 21:6 and 22:13. This phrase declares that Jesus is the same Jehovah revealed in the OT in Isa 41:4, 12-13. He was before creation and will be long after creation is dissolved. He is the self-existent One who sees the beginning from the end and is in total control of it all.

"I am the one who lives!" the resurrected One, "I was dead, but look, now I am alive." Only as the eternal, self-exist God became a man could He die humanly, but He never ceased to live as God (1 Pet 3:18). His death as a perfect sacrifice without blemish for the sins of mankind that became the only acceptable payment the Father could accept in order to forgive any sinner willing to trust in Jesus' payment for his sins.

This infinite Person gave an infinite sacrifice for all sins and corruption of man and creation. His resurrection proves the Father can justly forgive the sins of all who hear, repent, and believe the truth of this amazing grace.

Jesus had said to Peter and John, that John would "remain until I come" (John 21:23). John is now told that he is looking on the One he had been waiting to see again. Jesus keeps His Word and does what He says He will do.

Reflection: What assurance does Rom 8:31 give us at this point?

1:18b Jesus declares that He holds the "keys of death and Hades," that is, Jesus has the authority to decide who dies and who lives. Satan lost any authority over death for the believer (Heb 2:14-15).

Jesus had promised "he who believes in Me will live even if he dies... because I live you will live also" (Jn 11:25; 14:19). Paul declared that "to be absent from the body and to be at home with the Lord" (2 Cor 5:8 and Phil 1:23). This declaration means that Jesus conquered Satan and took the keys of death from him, "through death he [Jesus] could destroy the one who holds the power of death (that is, the devil)" (Heb 2:14).

Furthermore, He "set free those who were held in slavery all their lives by their fear of death" (2:15). The knowledge that Christ "loves us and released us from our sins by His blood" (Rev 1:5) gives us an undeserved assurance to be balanced with a proper reverential fear of His glory.

Reflection: How would you explain the fear of his glory and holiness balanced with the assurances of His promises? Does one eliminate the other or does one magnify the other?

THE COMMANDMENT TO WRITE (1:19-20)

1:19

Therefore write what you saw, what is, and what will be after these things.

1:19 John is told to write three things: (1) what he had just seen, "what you saw" (written in 1:10-16); (2) then "what is," which refers to the next vision he will be given of the existing seven churches in chapter 2-3, which describe the present state of the churches in seven different views; (3) finally he is told to write the next series of visions, "what will be after these things," that will describe the events that will take place after these churches cease to exist (chapters 4-22).

This sequence becomes the outline of the book: the past or a heavenly glance, the present church status and the future global events of the end of time.

Reflection: How will this view or perspective help every Christian to do God's will?

THE EXPLANATIONS

1:20

The mystery of the seven stars that you saw in my right hand and the seven golden lampstands is this: The seven stars are the angels of the seven churches and the seven lampstands are the seven churches.

1:20 The "mysteries" of the "stars" and the "lampstands" mentioned earlier are explained. A mystery is a past-unrevealed truth that is now explained. This is not something mysterious or mystical, but is simply unknown truth, previously not revealed to men, but now is made clear. Symbolic language usually is explained in the context or in similar passages of the Bible. These are not spiritualized, or allegorized, but interpreted as the imagery of Scripture as God defines it. Always a good idea!

The "stars" are "angels" (*aggelos*, "angel, messenger, envoy, one who is sent") and the "lampstands" are symbols of the seven churches, which will be explained in the next chapter.

Who are the angels? Is this part of the angelic or spiritual warfare that goes on unaware by humans (Dan 10:13, 20, 21) that is far beyond our power or knowledge?

Are these messengers or pastors of the churches about to be described?

Although the letters are addressed to the angels of the churches it is obviously written for everyone in the churches. The lampstands are a precise symbol for the local churches to shine in the darkness of this world.

Reflection: How should a church shine as a lampstand?

Different views of the seven churches

1. The seven churches represent seven historical ages or epics of the history of the church. This is only evident in retrospect and hardly possible for the early churches to have understood; however, it is remarkable how it fits our history to the present time.

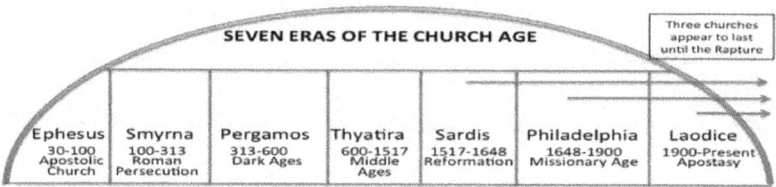

2. The seven churches represent seven typical churches of the first century as well as seven churches of all time.

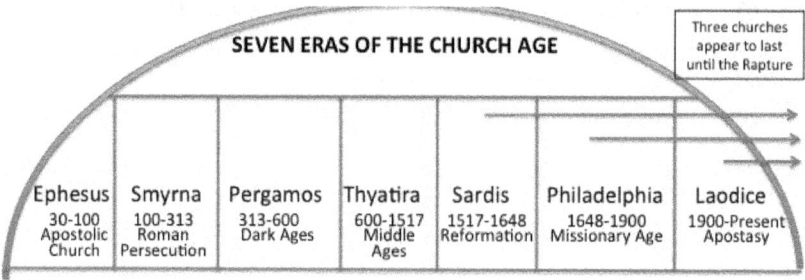

CHAPTER 2

LETTERS TO THE SEVEN CHURCHES OF ASIA
PART 1

"In spite of their failures, the message of the end times was delivered to the churches to live in the light of Christ's return."

As stated in 1:11 this Book was a letter to seven churches scattered clockwise in a semi-circle around Ephesus in the order that a messenger would take to deliver copies of this Book. It is likely that they were daughter churches from the believers discipled and trained through the ministry of the church at Ephesus, founded by Paul and later pastored by the Apostle John.

Luke wrote that as a result of the teaching at Ephesus "all who lived in Asia heard the word of the Lord" (Acts 19:10). The impact of the church at Ephesus stating, "this Paul has persuaded and turned away a large crowd, not only in Ephesus but in practically all of the province of Asia" from idol worship (Acts 19:26^{NET}) to the living God.

This expansion was accomplished through the disciples of Paul since the Apostle did not stray from Ephesus during this time (Paul was "reasoning daily in the school of Tyrannus. This went on for two years..." (Acts 19:9-10).

Paul's strategy was an early model of church multiplication through church-based leadership training. Paul reiterated in his exhortation to the leadership of the church at Ephesus to continue his model of ministry (Eph 4:11-12).

Though much of the NT was addressed to some of the early churches, these seven churches appear selected for a broader meaning than merely their common beginning and convenient distribution. There were many other churches, such as Colosse, Magnesia and Tralles, but the representative nature of these churches seemed to have been significant.

There are three views to the meanings of these churches in this book of prophecy:
1. They were merely seven historical churches described to give the readers a glimpse of the real condition of the early first century churches.
2. They were selected to reveal seven types or conditions of churches throughout the Church Age, since the exhortations appear to be addressed to a broader audience than merely these 1st century church members.
3. The church descriptions in the order given appear to reflect the various periods of church history from the first century until the present. This view could not have been understood until near the end of the 20th century to see in retrospect through historical comparisons. It would have had little to no meaning to the readers of the 1st century. Furthermore, the first three churches may seem to be consecutive, but the last four appear concurrent; at least all culminate in the Rapture of the Church.

Each of the churches is addressed in a similar outline: 1) a salutation to the recipients; 2) a representation of the Lord that is unique to each church; 3) an acknowledgement of the "works" of each church with words of commendation or approval (except Laodicea); 4) a special exhortation or rebuke to the churches (except to Smyrna and Philadelphia); and 5) a special promise to the overcomer.

Philips uses these titles to represent each church: Ephesus, the loveless church; Smyrna, the persecuted church; Pergamos, the over-tolerant church; Thyatira, the compromising church; Sardis, the sleeping church; Philadelphia, the church with opportunity; and Laodicea, the complacent church.

Whatever we may learn from these two chapters as Jesus describes His perspective of the Early Church at the end of the Apostolic age, it becomes evident that they were not perfect then nor have the churches ever been perfect since then. Rather than attempt to emulate a supposed "perfect" early church, that is often more imagination than reality, we should seek to know the whole Word of God now and apply it as accurately as we dare in our age.

A. THE CHURCH AT EPHESUS (2:1-7) –
THE SUPERFICIAL LOVELESS CHURCH

Ephesus at the end of the first century was a major seaport city of Asia Minor where the great temple to Artemis (or Diana), protectorate goddess of wild animals and virginity, one of the seven wonders of the world, is located. The temple was 425 feet long, 220 feet wide and 60 feet high with great folding doors and 127 marble pillars, some covered with gold. The worship of Diana was "'religious immorality' at is worst" (Warren W. Wiersby, *Wiersby's Expository Outlines on the New Testament*, Victory Books).

The immorality of Ephesus was related to the priests, prostitutes, musicians, dancers and frenzied, hysterical cult worshipers of Artemis. Paul first came to Ephesus in AD 53 (or 43 years before John wrote

Revelation) on his third missionary journey (Acts 19-20) and stayed there longer than in any other city, which eventually provoked a riot because his preaching had turned multitudes from their idol worship (Acts 19).

The population was between 250,000 and 500,000 with a large amphitheater seating 25,000 (see Acts 19:29), which remains to this day. Aquila, Priscilla and Apollos and Timothy labored in this city. After the fall of Jerusalem (AD 68-70) John ministered here about thirty years, before and after his exile in Patmos.

SALUTATION (2:1)

2:1

To the angel of the church in Ephesus, write the following: "This is the solemn pronouncement of the one who has a firm grasp on the seven stars in his right hand– the one who walks among the seven golden lampstands:

2:1a This part of the letter or Book of Revelation was written to the "angel" of the church (*angelos*, "messenger"- used 171 times in the NT of which 77 references are in the Revelation). Every reference in the NT refers to the angelic supernatural beings, except for seven references that refer to humans: Matt 11:10; Mk 1:2; Luke 7:24, 27; 9:52 and James 2:25. John the Baptist, his disciples, the apostles sent to Samaria and the two spies in Jericho. The preponderance of usage refers to angelic beings (165 out of 171). There is no clear interpretation as to who these angels are. There are other groups of seven angels as well (i.e., seven trumpet archangels; seven bowl angels). The word *angelos* can refer to human messengers or emissaries, as the Hebrew expression, "Haggai, the messenger of the Lord" (Hag. 1:13) in Greek (LXX) is translated *ángelos kuriou*. However, the text reads in the second person ("I know your works") as though it were addressed to the church as a whole, not to a single "angel."

Reflection: If there were an angel in every church, what do you think he would do (Heb 1:14)?

2:1b The command to John to "write the following" indicates that this content was not John's opinions, imaginations or ideas. This is the meaning of 2 Peter 1:20, "no prophecy of the scripture is of any private interpretation," which is better translated, "No prophecy of scripture ever comes about by the prophet's own imagination" NET.

Reflection: What we have recorded is authentically the words and mind of God alone. Why are we assured NT authors did not write independently from God's revelation ("not by private interpretation" or private understanding)?

2:1c The Author of this letter is the One who holds the "seven stars in his right hand" (i.e. the seven churches, 1:16) as one who is ever in control and who "walks among the seven golden lampstands" as ever present and active among the churches, always available for provision and fellowship.

The word "has a firm grip" (*krateo*, "hold firmly, not to discard or let go, keep carefully and faithfully," THAYER), indicates the inseparable bond between Christ and His churches.

This is the Savior who has all authority in heaven and earth (Matt 28:18). He will provide, protect, and enable them for whatever ministry they initiate for His glory. The picture is His availability to the church.

Reflection: What does it mean for Christ to have a "firm grip" on the churches through the "angels?"

THE COMMENDATION (2:2-3)

2:2

'I know your works as well as your labor and steadfast endurance, and that you cannot tolerate evil...

2:2a Christ states "I know your works" (*oida*, "full and complete knowledge"-used in each of the seven churches) to indicate that there are no secrets or reasons to appeal following His accusations since He is aware of all the affairs of human life on earth. Jesus begins with a commendation for what they are doing right.

Three words describe their accountability to Christ, who knows their "works" (*ergon*, "that in which any one is occupied, anything accomplished"- twelve times in Rev 2-3). He knew their achievements, accomplishments and businesses, likewise their "labor" (*kopos*, "exhaustion, intense labor united with trouble and toil," that is labor until weariness, and all out effort).

He knew their "patience" (*hupomone*, "endurance, perseverance" in trying circumstances – not patience with people, which is another word in Greek). This is called "staying power." The Ephesians were zealous and diligent in their service for the Lord, despite their difficulties.

Reflection: How are these three words linked in 1 Thess 1:3?

THEIR SPIRITUAL DISCERNMENT: TESTED FALSE APOSTLES

2:2b

...You have even put to the test those who refer to themselves as apostles (but are not), and have discovered that they are false.

2:2b Forty years before the Apostle Paul had warned that "savage wolves will come in among you, not sparing the flock; and from among your own selves men will arise, speaking perverse things, to draw away the disciples after them" (Acts 20:28-31).

Ephesus would test those who claimed to be apostles, but they were proven false. False teachers were a constant problem to the early church. Jesus warned of "false prophets" (Matt 7:15). John warned of "many deceivers"(2 John 7).

Paul confronted "false apostles, deceitful workers, disguising themselves as apostles of Christ" (2 Cor 11:13-15). These false teachers had one thing in common: they all wanted authority for giving new or "fresh" revelation, instead of teaching, explaining and "devoting themselves to the [genuine] apostles' teachings" (Acts 2:42). Believers are to "try the spirits" (1 John 4:1-6; see also 1 Cor 14:29), not naively accepting everyone who says they have a "revelation."

Reflection: How does their attitude of not "tolerating" such "evil" (*kakos*, "wrong, troublesome, injurious"- divisive?), who claim to be "apostles, and are not," compare with the contemporary pluralistic attitude of acceptance? How do you think they "tested" or "tried" these charlatans?

2:2c Later (2:6) the Ephesians are commended again because of their "hatred" for the "Nicolaitan practices" (*nikolaites*, "destruction of people" – This was an uncertain sect compared with the error of Balaam (2:14-15) who practiced sexual immorality). Maintaining purity of doctrine and practice was a constant battle in the early churches.

Reflection: How are Christians today prepared to maintain their doctrinal and lifestyle purity?

THEIR ENDURANCE

2:3

I am also aware that you have persisted steadfastly, endured much for the sake of my name, and have not grown weary.

2:3 They endured persecution, criticism, loss, and remained faithful. Three verbs are used to describe those from Ephesus: they "persisted" (*bastazo*, "to take up with the hands, or carry on one's person"); they "endured much" (*hupomone*, "steadfast, constancy.

The term is used in the NT as a characteristic of a man who is not swerved from his deliberate purpose and loyalty to the faith); they did "not grown weary" (*kopiao*, "become tired, loose heart, exhausted"). They suffered terribly; however, one common characteristic of suffering Christians is a tendency toward legalism, judgmental spirit and isolation.

Reflection: What does it take to discourage you from being faithful to witness and serve the Lord?

THE REBUKE (2:4)

2:4

But I have this against you: You have departed from your first love!

2:4 The zeal of the Ephesians and their commitment to purity perhaps gave them a sense of pride of accomplishment, legalism and false spirituality that blinded them such that they "departed" (*aphiemi*, "send away, divorce, forsake, give up") their "first love." The verb stresses an act for which they are responsible.

At one time they were characterized by their love (Eph 1:15) thirty years earlier. Sadly, this is a typical fatal flaw of second-generation Christians.

Christ still had their hands (exhausting labor), their heads (pure doctrine), but not their hearts (devotion to Christ and selfless motivation to give of one's self for others). Like Martha (Luke 10:38-42) they were so busy working for Christ that they had not time or passion to love or worship Him. They were evidently serving for selfish motives or approval of men.

Reflection: Were they serving for personal benefit, reputation, fame or pride of being the best? Could this be a symptom of second or third generation Christians?

Reflection: Israel fell into the same trap with later generations. See Jer 2:2-13 and Ezek 16:8-15 for how their superficial religiosity hurt their God.

THE EXHORTATION (2:5-6)

2:5

Therefore, remember from what high state you have fallen and repent! Do the deeds you did at the first; if not, I will come to you and remove your lampstand from its place— that is, if you do not repent.

Three things would be needed:
2:5a Remember. The mind-games or thought-patterns that creep into our consciousness must constantly be challenged by the reality of the Word of God. It is too easy to deceive ourselves into believing we are much better or more spiritual than we really are.

The Ephesians were to "remember" (present imperative thus, "keep on remembering, reflecting, recalling the past"), when they, as a church and as individuals, were passionate about pleasing the Lord Jesus alone. The description, "have fallen," is a perfect tense meaning a completed action with continuing results, thus a state of being, not a process.

They were working in the energy of the flesh in all its frustration, empty motivation, trying to please others to gain their approval, but little focus on Jesus.

SEVEN CHURCHES PART 1

Reflection: Someone has said, "Can you remember a time when you walked closer to the Lord? Who moved?" Christ is not after a "have-to" service, but a desire-to-please-Jesus-alone ministry.

2:5b Repent, Greek: metanoeo, means "to change the mind or purpose, to change one's values, beliefs or priorities." It begin with a true picture of where one is wrong today, then a change of mind and heart to humbly be transformed in mind and body (Rom 12:1). The verb tense is aorist, which emphasizes an immediate, urgent, and once-and-forever action. If the Ephesians were already laboring, persevering, enduring and separating from evil, what "deeds" did they need to return to?

Reflection: Was it adoration and worship that they lost in their busy-ness? Is there an answer in 1 Thess 1:3?

2:5c Repeat: "Do the deeds you did at the first." This does not refer to more activity. The word "first," *protos*, means "first in time, place, or rank." This refers to their early Christian experience when they first sensed the joy of the forgiveness of their sins and the realization of what Jesus had done for them on the cross in order to be able to forgive them justly.

The love and motivation to be obedient to all He says that this generated towards Jesus was refreshing, undeserved and yet immensely appreciated. Their hearts were overflowing with gratitude toward Jesus and only sought to tell him "thank you" every way possible, especially by taking seriously all that He said (John 14:15).

Warning: if this command is not heeded, Jesus said, "I will come to you and remove your lampstand from its place." The word "remove" (*kineo*, "cause to go, to move from a place," THAYER) has the idea of the lampstand being moved to another location and the loss of impact in being used as a light to the world.

The Ephesian church became a leading church through the 5th century, then declined. Notice the use of "quickly," (*tachu*) again with the meaning that when it starts, it will occurs without delay.

Reflection: How would the removal of the lampstand be like "Icabod" in 1 Sam 4:21?

NICOLATIANS – THOSE WHO REFUSE SUBMISSION TO COMMANDS

2:6

But you do have this going for you: You hate what the Nicolaitans practice– practices I also hate.

2:6 The reiteration of the commendation of "hating" the "Nicolatians practice-practices I also hate," Jesus says (this is repeated in 2:16). The Nicolatians are thought to have been a sect (sometimes associated with Nicolaus, one of the seven original deacons in the church in Jerusalem according to Acts 6:5) who apparently taught that Christians could engage in immoral behavior with impunity.

The Nicolaitan heresy seems associated with the doctrine of Balaam in 2:14-15, which appears to be an antinomian sect that advocated license or immunity in Christian behavior, including free love. This is the belief that believers are under no obligation to obey the laws or commands of ethics or morality.

This view often has a strong view of predestination, which secures one's salvation regardless of one's action, and a rejection of any form of legalism (obedience to a code of religious law to merit salvation), which is often exaggerated to mean any inconvenient rules of conduct.

Somehow "hating" one thing while returning to their "first love" seems incongruent. The key is the last phrase, "I also hate." No one can truly love Jesus without being like Him, thus hating what He hates and loving what He loves. They are inseparable.

In Ephesus this was merely a matter of certain actions, but in Pergamum it was tolerated as the norm. If deviant doctrine is not corrected quickly it will lead to immorality eventually, and nullify the Word of God. Worse yet, immorality unchecked spreads like wildfire.

Reflection: Can you think of examples in today's world of things that Christians should hate?

THE PROMISE (2:7)

2:7a

The one who has an ear had better hear what the Spirit says to the

churches. To the one who conquers, I will permit him to eat from the tree of life that is in the paradise of God.'

2:7a The imperative "had better hear" (*akouw*, aorist imperative: implying urgently) means "to attend to, understand, learn, take seriously," "what the Spirit says to the churches" (not the angel?).

Notice the appeal begins with the individual, then is applied to all churches. The Spirit speaks to the churches through the written Word of God, not angels. This is not a suggestion, but a command.

Jesus is talking to John, but the text refers to what the "Spirit says," thus the reference is how the Spirit later uses the text that John is writing to give the will of God to the reader (1:3) in the churches who are open to learn ("hears and practice") God's will from the written Word.

Reflection: How would you answer: do I have an ear to hear the Word of God? What would that look like?

THE PROMISED SUBJECT

2:7b

To the one who conquers, I will permit him to eat from the tree of life that is in the paradise of God.

2:7b The phrase, "one who conquers" (*nikao*, "come off victorious" as in "winning a legal case," VGNT), is firstly, described by John as one in whom "the Word of God abides" (1 John 2:13); secondly, one in whom the Greater One abides (1 John 4:4); thirdly, it is one who is "born of God" (1 John 5:4); and finally, it is one who "believes that Jesus is the Son of God" (1 John 5:5).

Faith in Christ, not individual faithfulness, is the concept of this term. The conqueror has overcome the damning power of the sinful world system by trusting in the transforming grace of God. Five of the seven churches were beginning to exhibit a worldly spirit, but all seven had some who had become conquerors.

Reflection: How would you define "conquerors?"

THE PROMISED REWARD

2:7c

... I will permit him to eat from the tree of life that is in the paradise of God.'

2:7c To such a one is given the "right to eat of the tree of life." The phrase "give to eat" means the granting of the "right" to the tree. We are not told what this will mean to the partaker, but this is not the right to salvation, nor necessary for maintaining one's salvation, which are always by faith without merit.

This tree is in the midst of the "Paradise "of God (*paradeisus*, "pleasure park" from a Persian word, in the LXX (Greek OT) is used to translate the "Garden" of Eden –Gen 2:8). Because of this literal tree God drove Adam and Eve from the Garden so they could not eat of it (Gen 3:22).

Jesus met with the thief in Paradise after their crucifixion (Luke 23:43), and it is the site of the heavenly tree of life (Rev 22:2, 14, 19) that will last for eternity. One of the most beautiful expressions of God granting the "overcomer" status to people of faith is seen in Hosea 14:1-4.

Reflection: How many comparisons to the believer today can you see in the Hosea passage?

B. THE CHURCH AT SMYRNA (2:8-11) – THE SUFFERING CHURCH

Thirty-five miles north of Ephesus on the Aegean Sea was Smyrna, a city rebuilt by Alexander the Great that became a rival to Ephesus, especially in idolatry. Though not named in Acts or the Pauline epistles, it was probably founded by disciples out of Ephesus (Acts 19:10), as was the church at Colossae.

Though one of the loveliest cities in Asia ("the Ornament of Asia") the imperial decrees against Christianity were strictly enforced here.
Smyrna was a wealthy city since it controlled the trade of the rich Hermus valley. It was the first city in the world to erect a temple to the

goddess Roma and to the spirit of Rome. Polycarp, the last disciple of the Apostle John, was killed here in AD 168. Smyrna's fidelity to Rome made any other religion a sign of rebellion, so Christ said to this church, "be faithful unto death."

Suffering is not to be considered unusual in the Christian life. "Consider it nothing but joy when you fall into all sorts of trials, because you know that the testing of your faith produces endurance... so that you will be perfect and complete, not deficient in anything" (James 1:2-4).

Reflection: Why did Peter consider suffering so valuable for Christians in 1 Pet 5:10?

The Agora of Smyrna (columns of the western stoa)

Persecution tends to purify the believer; hypocrites do not stay around when they have to suffer to let their faith be known. It is no coincidence that the church at Smyrna and Philadelphia received no rebuke in their letter from the Lord Jesus.

THE DESTINATION

2:8

To the angel of the church in Smyrna write the following: "This is the solemn pronouncement of the one who is the first and the last, the one who was dead, but came to life:

2:8 Typically a letter writer identifies the author at the beginning of the letter (in our culture we wait until the end of the letter). Here the Author identifies Himself as the "First and the Last" (as in 1:17; 21:6; 22:13), thus the eternal God who became a man. He voluntarily gave His life to suffer what sinners would have to suffer for their sinfulness, and then rose from the dead to offer all men the benefits of His death and resurrection if they would trust in Him. A literal translation is, "He came to be dead and began to live or came to life again," referring to the cross and resurrection.

Thus the suffering Savior is reveal to the church of Smyrna, which means "myrrh," a gum resin substance from a shrub-like tree that when crushed gives out a powerful fragrance that is used in burials. No matter how painful the persecution in Smyrna, the Savior has suffered the worst that human life can bring, thus He understands our suffering and is an ever-present comfort (Heb 2:15-18; 4:15).

Reflection: How is Christ an example to this persecuted church in Hebrews 12:3-4?

CHARACTERISTICS OF THE CHURCH

2:9

'I know the distress you are suffering and your poverty (but you are rich). I also know the slander against you by those who call themselves Jews and really are not, but are a synagogue of Satan.

2:9a Again Jesus states, "I know" (*oida*, "come to knowledge through experience") your "distress" (*thlipsis*, "pressure, metaph., affliction," esp. from outside sources pressing inwardly) that is trying to destroy the church.

Jesus had warned that "tribulaton or persecution" would come as a reaction to proclaiming the "word" (Matt 13:21), which would test the reality of their conversion. Likewise, He knew their "poverty" (*ptocheia*, "condition of one destitute of riches, extremely poor, life of a beggar, or totally dependent on others") which perhaps refers to slaves or believers who had lost everything as the result persecution, and the "slander" (*blasphemia*, "blasphemy, injurious, reproachful speech"), which resulted in persecution.

Reflection: If you are made fun of, ridiculed, persecuted or rejected because of your faith can you sense comfort in knowing that Christ is with you and suffered similarly? What is feeling about sharing in the poverty of Christ?

2:9b Smyrna was the leading center for the cultic emperor worship and fanatical devotion to Rome. Christians were willing to submit to the emperor's civil authority (as Rom 13:1), but refused to sacrifice to him, for which they were considered traitors and rebels.

Furthermore, the Christians refused to recognize the pagan pantheon of idols (Zeus, Athena, Apollo, Aphrodite, Asklepios and Cybele)

SEVEN CHURCHES PART 1

preferring an invisible God, which brought the accusation of appearing to be atheistic. Their pagan religion was the center of their social life, thus making Christians appear anti-social, arousing more suspicion. Everything in a pagan life was related to their religion, as today in pagan countries.

Reflection: Should Christians have been more compliant and should they have shared in the pagan activities?

2:9c To make matters worse, the unbelieving Jews accused the Christians of cannibalism (misunderstanding the Lord's Supper), immorality (exaggerating the intimacy of the "holy kiss" greeting – eg. Rom 16:16; 1 Cor 16:20, etc), family disintegration (when one spouse became a Christian it created conflicts – Luke 12:51-53), and political disloyalty and rebellion (Christians refused to offer the required sacrifices to the emperor).

Jesus declared that these accusing Jews were really not Jews (racially Jews, but religiously pagans, as most Jews today), but were part of a "synagogue of Satan." This description implies that the Jews met together to join Satan in plotting the destruction of Christianity.

Reflection: Do evangelical Christians confront groups today who slander, misrepresent and are committed to destroying Christianity (at least in spirit, if not consciously)? If so, who are they?

Further Reflection: There is a vast difference between loosing everything or suffering due to economic collapse, accidents, foolish mistakes or sickness, as opposed to suffering because of one's testimony for Christ. What do you think Jesus meant when He declared that they were "rich"? Check out the following verses.

1 Cor 1:5

2 Cor 6:10

2 Cor 8:9

Rom 8:18

James 2:5

Rev 3:18

THE COMMAND (2:10)

2:10

"Do not be afraid of the things you are about to suffer. The devil is about to have some of you thrown into prison so you may be tested, and you will experience suffering for ten days. Remain faithful even to the point of death, and I will give you the crown that is life itself.

2:10 The imperative, "Do not be afraid" (*phobeo*, "to put to flight by terrifying, seized by fright" – the same word can also mean to "reverence or venerate" in a different context) is a present imperative, thus "continually or repeatedly" be fearless. More persecution was coming. Jesus had told John sixty years before, "In the world you have tribulation, but take courage; I have overcome the world" (John 16:33).

The persecution was only a "test" (*peirazo*, "test for the purpose of ascertaining his quality," or "to solicit to sin") instigated by Satan through local officials, but it would be of short duration, only "ten days."

Most of the Roman persecutions from AD 100 to 312 were localized, short and intense; only in the final persecution was it empire-wide and lasted ten years (AD 302-312). Could this be the "ten days?"

True believers were not to be frightened by the threat of death or pain, since Christ was with them and He went through worse suffering before them. The honor of suffering for Christ was the hallmark of the faithful in the early churches.

Reflection: How do these verses encourage the believer?
Psa 56:11
2 Cor 12:9-10

THE PROMISE (2:11)

2:11

The one who has an ear had better hear what the Spirit says to the churches. The one who conquers will in no way be harmed by the second death.

SEVEN CHURCHES PART 1

2:11 With no reprimand Jesus promises the faithful [overcomer] they "will in no way be harmed by the second death." Jesus had warned His disciples that there is nothing as fearful as the "second death," which will be explained in Rev. 20:6, 14; 21:8. No believer will ever face the second death (John 5:24; 11:25; Eph 2:1, 5). He had said, "Do not be afraid of those who kill the body but cannot kill the soul. Instead, fear the one who is able to destroy both soul and body in hell" (Matt 10:28), that is, Jesus Himself. But this will never be the fate of the followers of Jesus.

James had written that by remaining faithful to the Lord until death a special "crown of life" would be their portion (1:12).

Model of the acropolis at Pergamum

Reflection: How would you respond if you had a knife to your throat and a camera recording your last words, and you are demanded to recant your faith in Jesus or die? Write your answer.

C. THE CHURCH OF PERGAMUM (2:12-18) – THE COMPROMISING CHURCH OR THE OVER-TOLERANT CHURCH

Pergamum was located about 20 miles inland from the coast and 45 miles north of Smyrna. It had been the capital of the Roman province of Asia for 250 years and its greatest city. It was a huge city with an acropolis on a thousand foot ridge and a lower city. A temple was dedicated to the cult of the emperor Augustus (29 BC), which became a major stumbling block to the early Christian church. The reference to the "throne of Satan" (2:13) is often interpreted as the emperor worship in

Temple of Trajan at Pergamum

the Temple of Trajan, along with a plethora of deities (temples to Zeus, Athena, Dionysus, Asclepius, Serapis, Demeter, etc. have been found).

The inhabitants were know as the chief temple keepers of Asia. When the Babylonian cult of the Magians was driven out of Babylon, they found a haven in Pergamum.

The title of the Magian High Pries was "Chief Bridge Builder," that is, one who bridges the gap between mankind and Satan and his hosts. The Latin title was written, "Pontifex Maximus," the title later transferred to the emperor Julius Caesar, then to the Roman Pope. This title goes back to Babylon and the beginning of the mother-child cult under Nimrod of Genesis 10 and his wife Sumerimus.

The city housed the 2nd largest library in the empire with 200,000 volumes, which was a gift from Anthony to Cleopatra, and considered itself the defender of Greek culture. There is no mention in the Book of Acts of the founding of the church at Pergamum. Paul passed through this region in Acts 16:7-8, but likely the church was founded by disciples of Paul from Ephesus (Acts 19:10). The intense pagan culture made living a different lifestyle very risky.

THE DESTINATION (2:12)

2:12

To the angel of the church in Pergamum write the following: "This is the solemn pronouncement of the one who has the sharp double-edged sword:

2:12 The challenge of being the first to proclaim the gospel and plant a church in any of these early cities cannot be overestimated, especially Pergamum. The only hope was a message that incorporated the power of God (Rom 1:16) to work in the hearts of pagan fanatical idolaters. The reiteration of the imagery of the sword (*romfaia*, "a long heavy, broad sword used by Thracians and other barbarian nations) from 1:16 and 19:15 refers to the concept of irresistible authority and devastating force of the Lord's judgment.

The sword is a symbol of the Word of God in Heb 4:12, which states, "the word of God is living and active and sharper than any two-edged sword, and piercing as far as the division of soul and spirit, of both joints and marrow, and able to judge the thoughts and intents of the heart." Paul also used this metaphor to describe the Word of God in Eph 6:17. Christ's judgment will be fulfilled precisely as described in the revealed Word.

Reflection: How is the imagery of the "sword" used in Rev 19:15? Is it positive or negative?

THE COMMENDATION (2:13)

2:13

'I know where you live– where Satan's throne is. Yet you continue to cling to my name and you have not denied your faith in me, even in the days of Antipas, my faithful witness, who was killed in your city where Satan lives.

2:13a Jesus again declares that He "knows" all about them, in particular, He knows where they "live" (*katoikeo*, present tense, "are continually dwelling"—*kata*, "down" and *oikew*, "to dwell" mean to settle down). Note: this was not a reference to a transient ministry, but a residential commitment to proclaim the truth of the gospel in a hostile environment.

The environment is described as "Satan's throne," which describes the extreme idolatry and demonic religious activity connected with the worship of the serpent god of Esculapius and the worship of the emperor of Rome.

Satan "blinds the minds of men" chiefly through false religions satisfying their need for mystical contact with the spiritual world, but it is demonic in nature. Their commendation was their courage: "You have not denied your faith," the central truths of the Christian faith.

Reflection: Is it easy today for you to live or work in a hostile, anti-Christian environment? Discuss what it is like and how to have courage.

2:13b To survive at the end of the 1st century must have required a considerable commitment to truth with the myriad of idolatrous activities everywhere in the city, especially the cult of emperor worship, which required an annual sacrifice to the emperor as a sign of loyalty.

This spiritual warfare (described in Eph 6:10-18) requires the knowledge of truth and righteousness (v. 14), clear understanding of the gospel (v. 15), a confident faith (v. 16), a personal salvation, how to use the Word of God (v. 17) and to constantly be praying, watching, persevering and supplicating for all saints (v. 18). Notice how this is more practical than mystical. It was likely that Antipas (means "against all") was executed because he refused to offer the sacrifice to the emperor.

Reflection: How can Christians be true and faithful in one area of their lives and compromise their testimony in other ways? Does this happen today?

THE REBUKE (2:14-15)

2:14a

But I have a few things against you: You have some people there who follow the teaching of Balaam, who instructed Balak to put a stumbling block before the people of Israel so they would eat food sacrificed to idols and commit sexual immorality.

2:14a Strange as it may sound, Christians will die for the truth, but compromise with morality. Jesus declared that there were some in the church who followed "the teaching of Balaam." To those who minimize the importance of doctrinal correctness and conformity to the revealed Word of God came this warning against three false teachings, which had crept into the church provoking the rebuke of the Lord Jesus. The teaching of Balaam was a distortion of the Christian doctrine of liberty as presented in 1 Cor 8-10 and Rom 14:1 – 15:3. When Balaam realized that he could not curse Israel, he attempted to corrupt them by enticing them to marry the beautiful women of Moab, which would defile their uniqueness and dissolve their separation from the world. Pagan corrupt practices would invade the morality of Israel.

Reflection: What did God do to stop the spread of Balaam's immoral teaching in Israel (Num 25:4-5, 9)?

Reflection: How did Peter interpret the doctrine of Balaam around AD 60 in 2 Peter 2:15-16?

2:14b

… who instructed Balak to put a stumbling block before the people of Israel so they would eat food sacrificed to idols and commit sexual immorality…

2:14b The church at Pergamum ignored the teachings of the apostle Peter, choosing to follow Balaam's teachings and philosophy. They evidently attended pagan feasts, engaged in their drinking and sexual immorality, while continuing to worship Jesus in their church meetings. Today the comparison would be the dangerous influence of pornography and common belief among some Christians that they can practice secret immorality and easily get forgiveness. The moral foundation of the believer is thus destroyed, apathy and superficial religiosity dominated the Christian life.

Reflection: Was this activity permitted to not offend their pagan neighbors? Was this an exaggerated friendship evangelism? How do the following verses apply to the lifestyles of the Pergamum church (and believers today)?

James 4:4

1 Pet 1:18 and 2:11

2:15

...In the same way, there are also some among you who follow the teaching of the Nicolaitans.

2:14c -15 The final error of some of the members was the doctrine of the "Nicolaitans." The introduction, "in the same way," indicates that the doctrine of Balaam and Nicolaitans resulted in the same immorality and secret sexual behavior. By exaggerating God's forgiveness and grace, they taught that Christians could participate in pagan orgies, i.e. ancient pornographic behavior. Perhaps the majority of the church at Pergamum did not participate in this error, but by tolerating this behavior as they continued to worship together, the church shared the guilt, which would soon bring the Lord's judgment.

The end result of these false teachers is to annul the authority of God's Word (esp. the commands) creating a compromise with the world (its viewpoint, worldview, values, priorities, and practices) which neutralized its witness to the lost.

Many go through a superficial worship on Sunday, but carry on secret lusts and immorality in their private lives. Some avoid all forms of immorality or worldliness, but have a heart full of jealousy, bitterness, criticism, envy or consumed with selfishly accumulating "stuff," fame or fortune for their own pleasure or indulgence.

Reflection: Were these false teachings of not being critical of immorality common in the early churches? (see 2 Cor 12:21)

Historical review: After emperor Constantine declared Christianity to be legal and tolerated (A.D. 313), then it was declared to be the state religion (A.D. 380) with civil authority to enforce its dogma and force the empire to unite around the sign of the cross and the Nicean Creed. Therefore, the church became complicit in the immorality of the state, finding it difficult to stop abuses, since it quickly grew accustomed to the power and finances that joined with the "spiritual" purposes of the church. In A.D. 392 Emperor Theodosius I passed legislation prohibiting all pagan cultic worship in public or private. The law thereafter only permitted Roman Christianity, punishable by torture and death. This act would then become legal justification for the Inquisition in the 12th thru 16th centuries against Muslims, Protestants and other dissident Christians.

Reflection: Why did some of the believers (Anabaptist), centuries later, insist on the "separation of church and state?"

THE COMMAND (2:16)

2:16a

Therefore, repent! If not, I will come against you quickly and make war against those people with the sword of my mouth.

2:16a Thirty-two times the word "repent" is used in the NT, to reflect a change of belief and values to conform to the Word of God in thought and deed. "Repent" (*metanoeo*, aorist imperative: "decide immediately...", to "change your mind"). Any refusal to conform to the Word of God will result in Jesus coming to "make war against" such persons. This is not a good thing! The same word is used in the Second Advent: "with justice he judges and goes to war" (19:11). In that end-time passage "out of His mouth comes a sharp sword" (19:15) which compares to the warning against Pergamum of Christ's coming to them "with the sword of my mouth." This suggests that the judgment is based on the truth of His Word. If one learns what the Word of God declares, and refuses to change or conform one's beliefs, values and behavior to its mandates, then the consequences can be painful. To Fear the Lord means to seriously believe that He will do exactly what He says.

1 Cor 5:6-7

2 Tim 2:24-26

2:16b

…. I will come against you quickly and make war against those people with the sword of my mouth

2:16b The warning of to "come against you quickly" (*tacheos*, "speedy, swiftly"), i.e., when Christ's response begins it will be unavoidable and inescapable. It is the same word used in Rev 22:12, "I am coming quickly"KJV. Either the believer repents of his worldliness and commits to obeying biblical principles and commands, or he will face divine discipline or chastisement and the loss of the light shining capacity of the church's ministry. The true Christian should live in the Word and by the Word, allowing it to transform his mind to be like Christ's (Rom 12:1-2; 1 Cor 2:16).

Reflection: What should the warning of chastisement "quickly" provoke in our lifestyle? (See 1 Jn 3:3)

THE PROMISE (2:17)

2:17a

The one who has an ear had better hear what the Spirit says to the churches. To the one who conquers, I will give him some of the hidden manna, and I will give him a white stone, and on that stone will be written a new name that no one can understand except the one who receives it.

2:17a The repeated phrase, "one who has an ear had better hear…" To walk with God there must be a willingness to understand, change and obey everything written in the Word of God. This is evidenced by our commitment to read, study and meditate on how to apply all that is said in the Word to our lives. Obviously this is a lifetime quest.

Reflection: The best way to do this is to constantly ask yourself the question: what does this verse mean that I should obey today?

2:17b

... the one who conquers, I will give him some of the hidden manna,

2:17b. To the faithful "overcomers" or "conquerers" (1 John 5:4-5) Christ promises three things will be given:
First, He promises to give them "hidden manna." The fact that it is "hidden" (*krupto*, perfect passive participle: "having been concealed, unknown, or keep secret") suggests a metaphorical meaning.

"Manna" was a honey-flavored bread that miraculously appeared daily during forty years for Israel's survival in the dessert (Ex 16). The "unseen" nourishment that the church is promised refers to the "bread of life…the bread that has come down from heaven, so that a person may eat from it and not die…If anyone eats from this bread he will live forever…" (John 6:48-51). This is a metaphor for the blessing of knowing Christ (Eph 1:3).

A portion of the manna was placed and hidden in the Ark of the Covenant (Ex 16:32-34; Heb 9:4), to always remind Israel that God was faithful to provide and sustain them in the worst of circumstances.

Reflection: How is this bread appropriated daily (Heb 3:7)?

2:17c

… I will give him a white stone, and on that stone will be written a new name that no one can understand except the one who receives it.

2:17c Secondly, He promised to give them "a white stone," (*pshfos*, "precious stone" like a diamond), which is only referred to here in Scripture. "White" (*leuke*) means "splendid, or shining." Thus, the understanding must be a 1st century cultural concept.

There was a Roman custom of awarding a white stone with the champion's names inscribed for the athletes, gladiators or warriors as they return from battle. If this pertains to our entrance into glory, look at how the "overcomers" are treated in 2 Pet 1:10-11. Whatever it represents, it means a special privilege for the faithful believer.

Reflection: Do you think it is worth the effort? (See also 1 Cor 15:58)

2:17d

... and on that stone will be written a new name that no one can understand except the one who receives it.

2:17d Thirdly, He promised a "new name" (*kainos*, "new kind, unprecedented, or novel") that is qualitatively different. If all things will be made "new" then we will be known by our new name, rather than our old name and reputation. It could show a special reward, or a new significant responsibility or privilege in Christ's kingdom. Whatever these may mean, they are meant to be motivational and worthwhile. There was every reason to repent, motivated by both the threat of judgment and the benefit of obedience; however, it always depends on the heart of the believers.

Reflection: Are you willing to repent of your besetting sin, selfishness or any contrary belief to the Word of God?

C. THE CHURCH AT THYATIRA (2:18-29) – THE WORLDLY CHURCH

The city (est. pop. 17,000) is located about 42 miles inland, SE of Pergamum, between Pergamum and Sardis. A city block in the center of the city called Archaeological Park (seen below) has yielded information on the guilds (labor unions) of bakers, bronze smiths, wool workers, potters, linen weavers and tanners that were active in the city. Such guilds often held banquets, which included eating food offered to idols and immoral sexual acts. These guilds made it difficult for believers to have a professions which required membership in these immoral unions.

One of Paul's converts in Philippi was named Lydia, a "seller of purple fabrics," from Thyatira (Acts 16:13-15), thus the Thyatira market extended to Macedonia.

THE RECIPIENTS (2:18)

2:18

To the angel of the church in Thyatira write the following: "This is the solemn pronouncement of the Son of God, the one who has

eyes like a fiery flame and whose feet are like polished bronze:

2:18 Christ reveals Himself in ways that are the most relevant to each church from 1:12-17. Now He is seen as divine judge. The tutelary or patron, guardian sun god of Thyatira, Tyrimnaios, is represented as flaming rays and feet of burnished brass as Apollo incarnate (as the emperor was considered), in contrast to the representation of Jesus in v. 18.

Jesus is presented as the "Son of God," which stresses His essence with the Father (John 5:18, "...he was also calling God his own Father, thus making himself equal with God"). This is the only use of the "Son of God" title in the Revelation.

Here the emphasis is on the judgment for this adulterous assembly. His "eyes like a fiery flame," which sees all, uncovers everything (similar in 19:12 and Dan 10:6), and consumes its object. This hypocritical church is soon to be uncovered.

The feet of "polished bronze" (like 19:15), for when He "treads the wine press of the fierce wrath of God, the Almighty," as He tramples out all impurities. This is not Someone we can deceive, nor Someone who ignores disobedience.

Reflection: How does 1 Pet 4:17 relate to this image of Christ?

THE COMMENDATION (2:19)

2:19

I know your deeds: your love, faith, service, and steadfast endurance. In fact, your more recent deeds are greater than your earlier ones.

2:19 This is the only church commended for improvements in spiritual matters, yet they tolerated "Jezebel" (2:20). Typically, Jesus looks for the positive before expressing His concerns.

Their deeds fall into 4 categories:
(1) "love" (where Ephesus was weak, Thyatira was strong), which seeks to benefit others without necessarily a concern for their own needs;
(2) "faith" (*pistis*, "fidelity or faithfulness"). True believers here were dependable, reliable, and consistent (v. 25). There is an interrelationship between love and faith in Gal 5:6; Eph 1:15; 3:17; and Col 1:4;
(3) "Service" (*diakonia*, "ministering to the needs of others"- 32 times in

the NT) is motivated by love, which seeks to benefit others regardless of how one may feel about them;

(4) perseverance (*hupomone*, Lit. "remain under," thus "constancy, endurance"). They learned how to stay under pressure to finish a task. As a result the Lord Jesus praised them.

Reflection: Why does Jesus seek to examine His children in 1 Cor 4:5?

THE REBUKES (2:20-23)

2:20a

But I have this against you: You tolerate that woman Jezebel, who calls herself a prophetess, and by her teaching deceives my servants to commit sexual immorality and to eat food sacrificed to idols.

2:20a Jesus holds sin against the believer, even though it might be forgiven. He will not let sin go without being confronted and punished. Believers are the reputation of Jesus in the world, so He is very protective of His name.

Reflection: What is the characteristic of a relationships with Jesus in Heb 12:6?

2:20b

… You tolerate that woman Jezebel…

2:20b The church "tolerated" (*eao*, "allow, permit, give up") the woman "Jezebel."

A woman named Jezebel had been the wife of Ahab, king of Israel (BC 869-850) who influenced Ahab to worship Canaanite gods (1 Kings 16:31). Her story is covered in 1 Kgs 18-21 and 2 Kgs 9. She framed Naboth who was stoned to death (in the picture above), and was accused of leading Israel to abandon the worship of Yahweh and practice "harlotries and sorceries" (2 Kgs 9:22).

Reflection: Which is easier: to not create a controversy over an issue of immorality or always confront persons acting immorally?

2:20c

... that woman Jezebel, who calls herself a prophetess, and by her teaching deceives my servants to commit sexual immorality and to eat food sacrificed to idols.

2:20c This "Jezebel" was influential in corrupting the "servants" (*doulos*, "bondman") in the Christian community in Thyatira. The leadership of the church allowed her as "prophetess" to teach error and lead the church into sinful practices. She may have taught a dualism where the spirit is good and the flesh is evil, but God is only interested in the spirit, so it doesn't matter what is done with the body.

Or she may have taught a antinomian view of God's grace that it really does not matter whether Christians sin or not, since God graciously forgives them completely.

She may have taught the Christians to experience or encounter the deep things of Satan either to combat him or to understand better how to witness to demon-possessed pagans.

These false teachings resulted in sexual immorality and idolatry and no one in the church did anything about it! Whenever one deviates from the teachings of Scriptures behavioral deviations are likewise inevitable.

Reflection: According to the Jerusalem Council, what were the Gentile churches to avoid (Acts 15:29)?

2:20d

... calls herself a prophetess, and by her teaching deceives my servants to commit sexual immorality and to eat food sacrificed to idols.

2:20d The errors are many in this church: allowing a woman to teach (1 Tim 2:12); allowing "prophets" to teach without "testing the spirits to see whether they are from God" (1 Jn 4:1); ignoring or refusing to be submissive to the inspired commandments of the Apostle Paul (1 Cor 14:37) demonstrated they were not God's prophets at all; additional warnings of false prophets in the local churches are seen in Mat 7:15; 24:11; and 2 Pet 2:1.

Reflection: Do churches today know and practices these verses?

SEXUAL AND SPIRITUAL IMMORALITY

2:21

I have given her time to repent, but she is not willing to repent of her sexual immorality. .

2:21 Another characteristic of God is evident in the statement: "I gave her time to repent" – how much time is not revealed. Thus, Jezebel is an unsaved woman pretending to be a prophetess who could manipulate the congregation through her power of persuasion and supposed prophecies.

The addiction to their sexual immorality trumped their loyalty to Christ and became a higher value than remaining above reproach and a pure vessel that Christ could use.

Note the change in person: "unless they repent of her deeds." Her teaching is responsible for motivating and condoning their immoral behavior. This indicates the special responsibility of teachers and pastors.

Reflection: Why is there a warning about not being too hasty to want to be a teacher? (James 3:1)

2:22

Look! I am throwing her onto a bed of violent illness, and those who commit adultery with her into terrible suffering, unless they repent of her deeds.

2:22 "I will cast her onto a bed of violent illness..." The phrase, "of violent illness," is not in the original, but is implied from what follows. The "bed" could refer to horrible sickness or death or hell – the ultimate end of those who refuse to repent.

This could refer to venereal diseases or plagues. If someone is not afraid that Jesus will do exactly as He says, then such a person will ignore the threat and become a fool. The fear that God will do what He says, is the beginning of wisdom. As with Jezebel of old, this prophetess was hardened beyond hope of repentance.

Reflection: How should such hardened people be treated in Prov. 14:3, 7; 17:10; and 23:9?

CHASTISEMENT FOR SIN

2:20

Furthermore, I will strike her followers with a deadly disease, and then all the churches will know that I am the one who searches minds and hearts. I will repay each one of you what your deeds deserve.

2:23 The consequences to the children, which probably refer to her philosophical children, the ones she has brought up in her error. As God did with Ananias and Sapphira He is capable of letting people reap what they have sowed. Mercifully He warns them to repent. Whatever happened to this "Jezebel" would be made known to all the churches (not kept secret) so that everyone would know that Christ is the One who "searches the minds and hearts."

Reflection: What do these verses teach about God's examination of our inner man today?

1 Chron 28:9

Ps 7:9

Prov 24:12

Jer 17:10

We do not know how many, if any, responded to this message. We do know that the Thyatira church a few decades later fell prey to the Montanist heresy (that believed in continual revelation from God apart from the Scripture) and went out of existence by the end of the 2nd century. By allowing this prophetess in the church, they were open to prophetic false teachings that followed later.

THE COMMANDS (2:24-25)

2:24

But to the rest of you in Thyatira, all who do not hold to this teaching (who have not learned the so-called "deep secrets of

Satan"), to you I say: I do not put any additional burden on you. 25 However, hold on to what you have until I come.

2:24 The church was divided between the prophetic and the scriptural believers, that is, "those who have not known the deep things of Satan" (*bathos*, "extreme, profound" – possibly referring to the mystical and imaginary encounters with invisible beings).

Evidently this sect within the church was dealing profoundly with satanic and demonic interactions, pretending to be from the Spirit. These prophets had gained spiritual pride for such encounters, supposedly making them invincible to the effects of immorality.

Moses revealed that anyone who had anything to do with "divination," or "familiar spirits" (Deut 18:10-12) was not to be permitted among the Israelites. They taught that it was necessary to experience the depth of immorality to appreciate the forgiveness of grace.

Reflection: What does these verses teach about how we are to respond to demonic influence: 1 John 4:1 and James 4:7?

2:25

However, hold on to what you have until I come.

2:25 Evidently the atmosphere was so overwhelming in the church and the blatant false teaching and immoral living was such that the faithful were given only one challenge: Those who kept with the Scriptures were commanded to "hold on" to what you have (*krateo*, "be powerful, become master of, keep carefully").

The nature of the command implies that it will not be easy. Jesus understands the difficult circumstances of His children and gives grace to be obedient to His Word.

Reflection: How is this comparable to Acts 15:28?

THE PROMISES (2:26-29)

2:26

And to the one who conquers and who continues in my deeds until the end, I will give him authority over the nations—

2:26 The "conqueror" is the one who believes that Jesus is the Son of God (1 John 5:5). The one who continues in His "deeds until the end" (in this context it refers to "holding on to what you have") by following Christ's life and character. "Let this mind be in you..." (Phil 2:5).

We can be "conquerors" and have victory over sin (Phil 4:13, "I can do all things through Him who strengthens me"). Such a person will receive two things: (1) Christ will give them "authority over the nations" – this promise comes from Ps 2:7-9 as the faithful participate in the millennial kingdom with the King of Kings. The "rod of iron" will destroy the individuals and nations that rebel against Christ. The second is in the next verse.

Reflection: The faithful prove themselves trustworthy now for responsibility in His kingdom later. Can Christ do give his followers such authority? How do these verses indicate that He has authority now?

Matt 28:19

John 5:22, 27

ROD OF IRON

2:27

he will rule them with an iron rod and like clay jars he will break them to pieces,

2:27 Likewise, (2) this shared reign with Christ will mean absolute authority over the nations. We have see how Christ gives time to reconsider the consequences of disobedience and repent, but there is a limit to His waiting. Whatever this means it implies He is not One to rebel against.

Reflection: How is the "iron rod" rule suggested in these passages?

Ps 2:9

Rev 12:5

Rev 12:10

SEVEN CHURCHES
Rev 19:15

RIGHT TO RULE

2:28

just as I have received the right to rule from my Father– and I will give him the morning star.

2:28 This amazing promise of incomparable privilege and authority to reign side-by-side with the King of kings seems beyond our imagination. Does He mean what He says? In addition He gives the faithful "the morning star." Far greater than any privilege, prestige or authority is personally knowing, having, and being close to the "morning star."

Reflection: Who is this "morning star" in these verses?

Rev 22:16
2 Pet 1:19

THE CONCLUDING CHALLENGE (2:29)

2:29

The one who has an ear had better hear what the Spirit says to the churches.'

2:29 Is the reader paying attention? Is he/she going to do anything about what was read? Three truths should be evident:
(1) it is very serious to practice or tolerate sin in those around you; God will judge for certain unrepentant sins in the church; (
2) a pattern of obedience to God's Word marks the true believer. If wrong, and corrected, he repents and grows stronger in righteousness and obedience.
(3) God's gracious promise of shared blessings with Christ is relative to the struggles with sin and error in churches. Those who heed this letter can share in unbelievable privileges.

Reflection: How is the benefits of faithfulness reiterated in these verses?

2 Tim 2:12

Rev 5:10

Rev 20:6

CHAPTER 3

SEVEN CHURCHES OF ASIA, PART 2

"This clear promise is how the Philadelphia church will not go through the coming Tribulation described in chapter 4-19"

The church at Sardis (3:1-6) – The Feeble Church

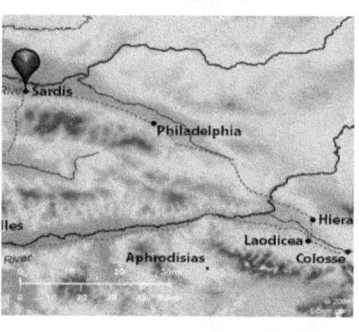

Sardis was one of the oldest and most important cities in Asia, located on the main trade route running east and west through the Hermus River valley in the Anatolian kingdom of Lydia. The acropolis of Sardis was on a peak about 1,500 feet above the valley road. Though not discovered until 1958, it was the site of another temple of Artemis (similar to Diana in Ephesus and Rome) and the goddess Cybele, which have been excavated along with a large theater, and bath/gymnasium complex. Ruins of an ancient Christian church exist next to the pagan temple. Some of the first coins were minted in Sardis due to the discovery of gold in the sand of the river Pactolus. It was also famous for its woolen garments, as reflected in Christ's message to the church.

Artemis at Sardis

THE RECIPIENTS (3:1)

3:1

And to the angel of the church in Sardis write, `These things says He who has the seven Spirits of God and the seven stars: "I know your works, that you have a name that you are alive, but you are dead.

3:1a As the city had long since passed its glory days, so the church was more form than genuine substance, more show than reality. Like the city itself, the church gloried in its past splendor, importance and leaders who gave them "a name." Now they ignored their present internal deterioration. Fafme, success and importance can breed corruption. Nothing escapes the All-seeing God who "has the seven Spirits of God," or the Holy Spirit, in all His manifestations and the seven "stars" or churches in His control.

THE COMMENDATION

.. I know your works, that you have a name that you are alive…

3:1b. They had a reputation of being alive; apparently an opinion shared by their neighboring churches. Other than their appearance, there were no words of commendation to the believers. There were no doctrinal problems to correct. Neither was there any mention of opposition or persecution. Could it be that they had correct doctrine and form, but no obedience to the commands?

Reflection: How do churches get a reputation for being "alive?" How could you have such a reputation yet be "dead?"

THE REBUKE

...but you are dead.

3:1c Christ cut their self-pride short by declaring that they were actually "dead." They had a façade of being alive, but nothing was genuine. Like the Pharisees (Matt 23:27-28) they were more interested in appearances than reality or like the surprised "Christians" in Mat 7:21-22 who supposedly could do miracles, healings and other marvels, but never even knew Christ personally. The unsaved in Sardis evidently saw the church as a respectable group of people who caused few problems, but they were neither dangerous to the *status quo* nor desirable as a unique religion.

Reflection: How could people come into the church and not be saved? Are people who think they have to be good to get into heaven genuinely saved?

THE EXHORTATION

Be watchful, and strengthen the things which remain, that are ready to die, for I have not found your works perfect before God. 3 "Remember therefore how you have received and heard; hold fast and repent...

3:2a As a group or church they were exhorted to "wake up" and to "strengthen" what little of a genuine spiritual life that they shared, but even that was about to die. Sounds like the same problem in Rome as Paul wrote earlier in Romans 13:11, "Knowing the time, that now is high time to awake out of sleep...".

Historically, twice in its history, Sardis had been captured, and each time it was because the sentries had failed to warn the city of impending attacks. A similar expression is seen in churches that grow accustomed to their blessings, complacent about their individual personal ministries, proud of their formalism, or suffer gradual shifts in doctrine as the enemy infiltrates in the ranks of church members creating apathy.

The first step to renovate a dying church is when to recognize something is wrong. When an organism is alive, there is growth, reproduction, individual cellular action and power. Many churches are dying and do not know it.

Reflection: : How would you define these four characteristics in today's churches?

3:2-3 All together they were given five commands to understand and obey:
1. "**Wake up**" – *gregoreuo*, Present tense, "continually be waking up," metaph. "give strict attention to, "take heed lest through remission and indolence some destructive calamity suddenly overtake one," STRONG).
2. "**Strengthen**" –*steizo*, aorist imperative, occurs in 13 verses, "fix, or establish." It is a Hebraistical phrase to men "set" in a certain direction, as when Jesus "fixed his face to go to Jerusalem." The idea is wholeheartedly and consciously to commit to the commands and principles of Scripture. Strengthening follows commitment.
3. "**Remember**" – *mnemoneuo*, 21 times this command is repeated in the NT. Here it is a present tense imperative, thus "continually and habitually be bringing to mind, or thinking of, or keeping in mind." Reviewing and systematically recalling the principles of these passages and Scripture, in order to stay wise in viewing life. Anyone who marginalizes or minimizes the importance of learning and reviewing biblical truths (though 2,000 or 3,000 years old) should be held suspect. As in politics, it is not new law that we need, but the application of what we already have.
4. "**Obey or hold fast**" – *tereo*, used 75 times in the NT, here it is the present imperative, thus "continually and habitually be attending to carefully, preserving for a purpose, or maintaining." A person begins to grow spiritually when he/she learns truths from Scripture, then consciously decides to practice the commands, principles, and examples given in Scripture. As he chooses to take commands and principles from God's Word as correct and true over what he feels or culturally thinks, then the transformation of the mind (or thinking)

begins, which in turn transforms one's life. They were forgetting or not learning the Word and thus becoming apathetic. They were content with their form of worship, even though it had no meaning to obey or truths to live by.

5. **"Repent"** – *metannoeo*, 32 times this command is given. It is an aorist imperative, meaning to "immediately change and commit to change one's mind, feeling remorse, regret" for one's disobedience. This response results in being transformed "by the renewing of your mind" (Rom 12:1-2). This transformation takes learning new truths in God's Word, trusting them and committing to obey them in practical life.

Reflection: What is your plan to practice these commands and others that you find in Revelation? Remember the promise in Chapter 1. Have you begun to make a list of all commands and principles to review?

THE WARNING

Therefore if you will not watch, I will come upon you as a thief, and you will not know what hour I will come upon you.

3:3b If this exhortation was ignored, they could expect God to chasten them suddenly and unexpectedly ("never know at what hour"). There will be no time to repent or change once this judgment begins. The consequences are unavoidable. If you read Numbers 14 you will discover an excellent history of this kind of threat that God makes good. He does what He says.

Reflection: Does the thought of Jesus' sudden return at anytime play a part in your temptations and life plans?

THE PROMISE (3:4-6)

3:4

You have a few names even in Sardis who have not defiled their garments; and they shall walk with Me in white, for they are worthy.

3:4 The church as a whole was dying or already dead, but Christ recognized a godly remnant (a "few names" or individuala) that had not "stained their clothes." Clothing is a representation of the righteousness of God and then the righteousness of the believer.

This remnant of true believers had not compromised with the pagan society around them, nor had they become complacent and apathetic to the ministry.

This remnant was part of a revival within a dying church who sought an obedient godly life to honor their Lord. The majority of the church had allowed sin to destroy their zeal and formalism to cover their emptiness allowing them to pretend to be Christians.

Reflection: What does 1 Cor 4:5 teach one way that God seeks to honor those who live godly, useful lives?

OVERCOMER'S BENEFITS

He who overcomes shall be clothed in white garments, and I will not blot out his name from the Book of Life; but I will confess his name before My Father and before His angels.

3:5a The overcomer is dressed in "white" (defined in 3:18 as a righteous covering) and his name will be acknowledged before the Father and the angels. The verb "will never erase" (*ou me,* is the strongest form of negation in the Koine Greek) or be eliminated from the Book of Life. This is a categorical statement, with no implied threat that some could be erased. Six times John refers to the Book of Life (13:8; 17:8; 20:12, 15; 21:27), which reiterates its existence.

The unsaved are those who have never been written in the Book (Rom 13:8; 17:8), not those who were erased. Moses wrote how God had said some had "sinned against Me, I will blot him out of My book" (Ex 32:33). The Book of Life is not referred to by Moses, rather he spoke of the book or "scroll of the living" (Ps 69:28). The "foreknowledge" of God (1 Pet 1:2) knew from eternity past all those who would respond to Christ by faith and wrote their names in the Book before time began. Amazing!

Reflection: How are we made ready for eternity in Heb 12:23?

3:5b If God makes us "perfect" (1 Cor 5:21) that must be good enough. The confession before the Father is a major event. Jesus had promised "Everyone who confesses Me before men, I will also confess him before my Father who is in heaven" (Matt 10:32). For the true Christian, salvation is eternally secure in the promises of Scripture.

Reflection: How does this compare to Rom 8:31-39?

3:5b However, some will hear the words, "I never knew you," though apparently they had been nominal "Christians" doing good works (Matt 7:21). This church is like other great churches that were past their peak of blessing, having a few who were true believers, but being full of nominal Christians who come to feel good about themselves.

Vance Havner used to teach that ministries go through four stages: as a man, a movement, a machine, and then a monument. Sardis was at the "monument" stage, but there was a glimmer of hope.

Reflection: How important is knowing and following the true principles and commands of Scripture?

THE LISTENER

3:6

He who has an ear, let him hear what the Spirit says to the churches.

3:6 The final exhortation, as to all the churches, was to listen to what the Spirit is saying to the churches. The spiritually dead "zombies" need to heed the words of Jesus. The five commands were their only hope: "wake up, strengthen, remember," "repent," and "obey."

Reflection: How is "hearing" and "obeying" the same act?

F. THE PHILIDELPHIA CHURCH (3:7-13) -- THE FAITHFUL CHURCH

PHILADELPHIA

The city of Philadelphia is located in the same valley as Sardis and Smyrna. The city was founded to be a center of Greek culture and language, a outreach for spreading Hellenism to the interior of Asia Minor, especially Lydia and Phrygia. By A.D. 19 the Lydian language had been completely replaced by Greek. Along with the Greek language came the Greek religious

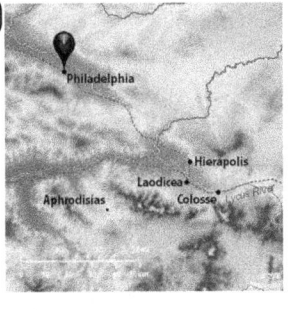

cults as well. It was located on a seismic fault, which erupted in A.D. 17 destroying the city (and ten other cities). It was also located on a major trade route to the interior of the country, thus citizens had a sense of broad outreach from their business enterprises. .

1. THE RECIPIENTS (3:7)

3:7a
And to the angel of the church in Philadelphia write,

3:7a Philadelphia was 28 miles beyond Sardis, built on a terrace 650 ft. ASL. The land around the city was extremely fertile, which produced a wine referred to by the Roman poet Virgil. The city was named after the king of Pergamum, Attalus Philadelphus, which is similar to the word meaning "brotherly love." The city was also known as the "little Athens" because of its magnificent temples and other public buildings, thus became a successful trade center.

"Philadelphia," the etymology of the word means "brotherly love." This concept occurs 7 times in the Bible (Rom 12:10; 1 Thes 4:9; Heb 13:1; 1 Pet 1:22; 2 Pet 1:7 (twice); here). In the text of Rev 3 alone it is used as the name of a city. Of interest is the fact that a Christian testimony continues in this city to the present day. The contemporary city is called Allen-Sheba, 20,000 population with many Christians.

3:7b
These things says He who is holy, He who is true, "He who has the key of David, He who opens and no one shuts, and shuts and no one opens.

3:7b The four-fold description of Christ has direct reference to this church:
(1) He is holy, a reverential and practical character of Christ ("the One who calls us is holy, so we should be holy in behavior according to "1 Pet 1:15). Jesus was addressed by a terrified demon, "I know Who You are: the Holy One of God" in Mark 1:24. Peter affirmed his belief by saying, "We have believed and have come to know that you are the Holy One of God!" (John 6:69);

(2) He likewise is True (*alethinos*, "genuine, authentic and real"), to remind us that His "Word is true from the beginning, And every one of Your righteous judgments endures forever" (Psa 119:160 NKJ),

which is to say, He is trustworthy. Truth and holiness are used together in Rev 6:10; 15:3; 16:7; 19:2,11;

(3) He "holds the key of David," which refers to the ascent of Eliakim to become the steward or prime minister to the throne of David as a metaphor of the Messiah. Eliakim was called "a nail in a sure place" and "all the glory of his father's house hangs upon him," a perfect description of the Messiah as well. As the prime minister had the authority to open the city and all its wealth, so the King of kings has the authority to open the doors to His (heavenly) treasury.

(4) Finally He can open or shut the doors to the kingdom as special opportunities to expand the kingdom. Isaiah records God's word as saying, "I act and who can reverse it?" (Isa 43:13; see also Isa 46:9-11; Jer 18:6). This same Messiah holds the "keys of death and Hades" (Rev 1:18).

Reflection: What does it mean for Christ to open and shut doors? Is this a one-time description or a general characteristic that continues?

2. COMMENDATION (3:8-9)

3:8

I know your works. See, I have set before you an open door, and no one can shut it...

3:8a The Author begins, "I know your deeds," which implies nothing escapes His attention, a thought that we can never lose awareness of, yet in this case, He found nothing to rebuke in the Philadelphia church. As the holder of the "key of David," He declares, "I have set before you an open door and no one can shut it," which refers to opportunities to take advantage of.

Christ is aware of our circumstances and potentials. Paul described "a wide door for effective service has opened to me, and there are many adversaries" (1 Cor 16:8-9). When he wrote 2 Corinthians Paul described "a door was opened for me in the Lord" (2 Cor 2:12). He wrote the Colossians to pray for his ministry "that God will open up to us a door for the word" (Col 4:2-3). Philadelphia was strategically located to spread the gospel.

Reflection: Is it our goal to never miss a providential opportunity to serve our Lord in our daily circumstances? How often does this cross our minds? Do we pray for wisdom to recognize these "divine encounters" or opportunities? Do we dare? Or do we care? Can God trust you with an open door of witness or service? Think back over the opportunities of today that were taken or missed. Analyze them to see what could have been done for the kingdom had we dared or cared.

3:8b for you have a little strength, have kept My word, and have not denied My name.

With nothing to criticize them for Christ begins a four-fold description of the characteristics of the Christians at Philadelphia:
(1) He knows their "strength." Philadelphia had "little strength" (*dunamis*, "power or ability"), probably means they were small in number. They had learned, as Paul did, that a believer together with Christ is a majority. As in Corinth, not many were well-off economically or educationally (see 1 Cor 1:26, "not many noble…") and "I am well content with weaknesses, with insults, with distresses, with persecutions, with difficulties, for Christ's sake; for when I am weak, then I am strong (2 Cor 12:10);
(2) He knew their obedience, "you have obeyed my word."

Job said it this way, "I have not departed from the command of His lips; I have treasured the words of His mouth more than my necessary food" (Job 23:12). Jesus had said, "If anyone loves me, he will keep My word" (Jn 14:23) (3) He knew their faithfulness and courage, "have not denied My name" (*arneomai*, "to renounce, disown, repudiate, disregard"), implying that it was costly to them to be identified as followers of Christ. Jesus taught that if we deny Him before men, He will deny us before the Father (Matt 10:33; Luke 12:9);

Paul taught that this was a requirement to "reign with Him; if we deny Him, He also will deny us" (2 Tim 2:12). The Tribulation saints will demonstrate this quality as well in refusing to take the mark of the beast, "Here is the perseverance of the saints who keep the commandments of God and their faith in Jesus" (Rev 14:12); (4) He knew that they had persevered, that is they kept the word "of My perseverance." (*hupomon*, "remain under, patient enduring"). True believers show themselves "steadfast" (2 Thess 3:5).

Reflection: Have you ever felt ashamed to be identified as a Christ follower? How does the use of this word in Luke 9:23 fit in this context?

SEVEN CHURCHES

Indeed I will make those of the synagogue of Satan, who say they are Jews and are not, but lie-- indeed I will make them come and worship before your feet, and to know that I have loved you.

3:9 Part of their limitations was the opposition from the "synagogue of Satan" (as in Smyrna in 2:9). At this time the most frequent opposition to Christianity was the Jewish religion. If it is not Jewish, the opposition will usually come from another false religion; however, the thought here is of encouragement: every false religious person/leader one day will fall at the feet of Jesus as they recognize Him for who He is. This verse points to a time when these very hostile Jews will be converted and humbled before these Gentile believers. There is coming a day when "all Israel will be saved" (Rom 11:26).

Reflection: How are these verses meant to be an encouragement?

Isa 45:23

Rom 14:11

Phil 2:10-11

3. THE PROMISE (3:10-12)

Because you have kept My command to persevere, I also will keep you from the hour of trial which shall come upon the whole world, to test those who dwell on the earth.

3:10 Normally a rebuke preceded the Promise, but there is no rebuke here. The first promise was due to their willingness to "persevere" (*hupomone*, "endurance, constancy, remain under" –"not swerved from his deliberate purpose his loyalty to faith and piety," STRONG), brought the responding promise, "I will keep you from the hour of trial that is going to come upon the whole world to test those who live on the earth."

The phrase, "those who live on the earth," is a technical term that refers to people who make this earth their home, "men of the world who have their portion in this life" (as Ps 17:14b).

This clear promise is how the Philadelphia church will not go through the coming Tribulation to be described in chapters 4-19. Christ declares, "I will keep you ..." (*tereo*, "to attend to carefully, take care of, guard"), "from the hour" (*ek*, "out of, out from, or away from"). The term for this event is called by the theological term the "rapture," which is a term is not found in Scripture. This is not a promise to keep them "through the hour," which is a different preposition (*dia*). Rather, they are to be carefully taken out of (*ek*) the coming "hour of testing" for the world, which refers to a distinct time of horrific persecution. Was this written just for this little, weak church in Asia Minor in the 1st century?

This phrase "taken out of" is debated since some believe that the church will go through the Tribulation Period (post-tribulationists). They take it to mean that God will preserve the church through the midst of the Tribulation judgments, emerging save till the end, that is, "taking them out" the other end of the Tribulation, preserving the church through it all. However, the only other time the phrase *tereso ek* ("taken out of") occurs in Scripture is in John 17:15, where Jesus prays, "I do not ask You to **take them out of the world**, but to keep them from the evil one." This does not refer to preserve them within Satan's power, because all believers have been "rescued...from the domain of darkness" and "transferred ... to the kingdom of His beloved Son" (Col 1:13). Christians "turn from darkness to light and from the dominion of Satan to God" (Acts 26:18). The unregenerate remain in the power of Satan (John 5:19), but believers are freed.

Several aspects of this "test" should be noted: (1) the test is yet future since the church has yet to be taken "out of" the earth; (2) this test is for a definite time, though limited, "the hour of testing"; (3) it is a test designed to expose the true believers; (4) the scope of this test is worldwide; (5) the term "those that dwell on the earth" is used to describe unbelievers in the Book of Revelation (6:10; 8:13; 11:10; 13:8, 12, 14; 14:6; 17:2, 8), thus this period is not designed for the church; (6) this "hour of testing" is Daniel's Seventieth Week (Dan 9:25-27), the time of Jacob's trouble (Jer 30:7), the seven-year tribulation period. "The Lord promises to keep His church out of the future time of testing that will come on unbelievers." As with Noah and the flood, so the Church will be miraculously taken away from the scene of unprecedented disasters coming on earth.

Reflection: As the world sets up for the coming events descirbed in chapters 4-19, how should this effect how we live or what should be our values in this life?

3:11

I am coming soon. Hold on to what you have so that no one can take away your crown.

3:11 The second promise Christ made, "I am coming quickly." This "coming" is distinct from the promised "coming" to the other churches (2:5, 16; 3:3), which were warnings of chastisement on rebellious congregations (as Acts 1:11; 1 Cor 11:28-30).

This "coming" precedes the hour of testing that ends with the Lord's Second Coming or Advent. It is Christ's coming to "gather together" His Church (2 Thess 2:1), not to bring judgment to it. The term "quickly" (*tachu*, "fast") is not a reference to proximate time, but to quickness or shortness of time, which carried with it an implied "threat," (especially to the unbeliever, 2:16).

The believer's future status of reigning with Christ will be determined by our present faithfulness to finish the Great Commission (2 Tim 2:12), but it will be curtailed in an instant at the Rapture. "That no one may take your crown" refers to a wreath worn as a symbol of honor, victory or a badge of a high office. Paul referred to "crowns" 4 times (1 Cor 9:25; Phil 4:1; 1 Thes 2:19; 2 Tim 4:8). James mentioned it once (1:12) and also did Peter (1 Pet 5:4). God's delight for eternity will be to honor those who were faithful to Him during their lifetime. Whatever this means the rewards were a significant motivation for faithfulness.

Reflection: What do these verses imply about this reward?

2 John 8

2 Tim 4:8

3:12

He who overcomes, I will make him a pillar in the temple of My God, and he shall go out no more. And I will write on him the name of My God and the name of the city of My God, the New Jerusalem, which comes down out of heaven from My God. ...

3:12a The third promise to the overcomers was that they will be "pillar in the temple of...God." This could be a possible analogy to the OT Temple construction (1 Ki 7:21) when the pillars of the Temple had a person's name written on it (Boaz and Jachin), which traditionally symbolized Mercy and Severity. This could refer to some memorial God has in mind for the faithful throughout the ages. The security of Christ's promise that the faithful "shall go out no more" (*ou me*, the most emphatic negation in Greek, "not at all, certainly not, by no means"). They will become an inseparable part of the heavenly temple of God.

Reflection: Do you think it would be worth it to go through persecution now because you are not ashamed of Christ in the public arena?

3:12b ... And I will write on him My new name.

The fourth promise was that Christ will "write on him the name of [his] God". This signifies an intimate relationship that we have with Him forever. Likewise, Christ promises to write on believers the name of the city of his God, which signifies our new and eternal citizenship in heaven's city, the New Jerusalem, which is described in Rev. 21.. And finally, He promises to write Christ's new name as well, which will signify a privilege to call Christ his eternal name, yet to be revealed. Three names that declare ownership. Because believers have identified themselves with Christ unashamedly, so He will identify Himself with us. The 144,000 will have a similar experience in 14:1.

Reflection: How can we allow these descriptions to motivate us to faithful and purposeful living?

4. THE EXHORTATION (3:13)

3:13

He who has an ear, let him hear what the Spirit says to the churches.

3:13 If the values of this Book are important to all believers, then hearing these exhortations at the close of each letter to the churches should result in a sense of recommitment to faithfulness and boldness for the ancient readers as well as for us today. It becomes obvious that God anoints the churches that are loyal to Him and His Word with His power, presence and with open doors for evangelism now and eternal blessings, especially of being delivered from the horrible time of testing to come on the global scene (beginning in Rev 4).

Reflection: When you hear or understand a truth, how easy is it to change and how does a person change?

G. THE LAODICEAN CHURCH (3:14-22) -- THE LUKEWARM APOSTATE CHURCH

Laodicea was located on the road 20 miles before Colosse, about 40 miles from Philadelphia. It had been destroyed by an earthquake about AD 60, but had been rebuilt thanks to the wealth from its strategic banking center and the capability of the city to support itself without any aid from Rome. Its main industry was wool cloth that was used for black wool clothing and rugs. Laodicea was also a center for ancient medicine, especially a famous eye salve.

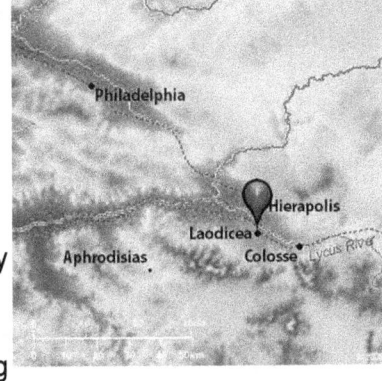

Paul inevitably went through Laodicea but there is no evidence of Paul's ministry here nor in six of the seven churches. Timothy, Mark, and Epaphras (Col 1:7) appear to be the first to introduce Christianity in Laodicea. However, Paul's students from Ephesus spread the Word throughout Asia, likely including Laodicea (Acts 19:10). Even when he wrote Colossians he had not visited Laodicea (Col 2:1). Epaphras founded the church at Colossae, which was nearby (Col 1:6-7), so he may have had a hand in founding this church as well. It may be that Archippus, Philemon's son (Philemon 2), was the pastor (Col 4:17), since the 4th century Apostolic Constitutions or emperial decree named Archippus as the bishop of Laodicea (vii, 46). Ancient Laodicea had a large surrounding wall, three marble theatres and was built on seven hills.

Laodicea colonnaded street

The Laodicean church represents the apostate churches throughout history that is made up of unregenerate followers of an empty religion. It is the only church that Christ had nothing positive to commend. As a result this is the most threatening of the seven letters.

1. THE WRITER (3:14)

3:14

And to the angel of the church of the Laodiceans write, `These things says the Amen, the Faithful and True Witness, the Beginning of the creation of God:

Acqueduct system in Laodicea

3:14a The Author identifies Himself with three divine titles that are distinct from any of the phrases from the vision in 1:12-17:
(1) the Amen (*amen*, "truth, certainty, may it be fulfilled" or metaph. "the True One"). The word means that which is firm, fixed and unchangeable. He is the One who guarantees and fulfills the promises of God. Whatever He says is true.
(2) The Faithful and True Witness, thus whatever He says will never fail, but surely come to pass. He is "the way, and the truth and the life" (Jn 14:6); Christ's assessment of Laodicea is flawless;
(3) The Beginning of the creation of God (*arche*, "ruler, authority"); this One is the Creator, Sustainer and architect of creation. However, He Himself was not a part of the creation as in John 1:2-4 where the Logos "was" (imperfect tense) at the beginning of time, that is He was already being or there when the beginning of everything took place. In vs. 3 it declares that "all things were made through him." A better title may be that He is the "Originator" of all creation (BDAG 138 s.v.3), or the "First Cause" of all that was created. Those who wish to distort the deity of Christ must put a spin on the words of the text usually from a translation rather than the usage of the original language.

Reflection: How does this title fit in the description of Christ in Col 1:16-18?

3:14b From the use of the titles of Christ it can be deduced that the Laodicean church had bought into some of the heresies of a neighboring church in Colosse, that of early Gnosticism. This may be why the Colossian letter was commanded to be read in the church of Laodicea as well (Col 4:16).

This false teaching made Christ to be a created being, one of a series of emanations from God. They supposedly had a secret, higher spiritual knowledge beyond the simple words of Scripture. The false teaching about Christ and the mystical insights and knowledge mark the cultic false teaching of Laodicean and Colossian churches.

Reflection: What do you think these titles meant to this early church?

2. THE REBUKE (3:15-17)

3:15

I know your works, that you are neither cold nor hot. I could wish you were cold or hot.

3:15 A note from the NET Bible is helpful here:

> Laodicea was near two other towns, each of which had a unique water source. To the north was Hierapolis which had a natural hot spring, often used for medicinal purposes. The east was Colossae which had cold, pure waters. Laodicea had no permanent supply of good water. Efforts to pipe water to the city from nearby springs were successful, but it would arrive lukewarm. The metaphor in the text is not meant to relate spiritual fervor to temperature. This would mean that Laodicea would be commended for being spiritually cold, but it is unlikely that Jesus would commend this. Instead, the metaphor condemns Laodicea for not providing spiritual healing (being hot) or spiritual refreshment (being cold) to those around them. It is a condemnation of their lack of works and lack of witness. (*NET Bible* note on Rev 3:15).

It was not the church itself, which probably looked fine from the outside, but the people in the church that made the Lord sick, because it was useless; neither healing nor refreshing.

Reflection: How do you think these verses apply to this kind of person?

Matt 7:22-23

Rom 10:2

2 Tim 3:5

3:16

So then, because you are lukewarm, and neither cold nor hot, I will vomit you out of My mouth.

3:16 Again the reiteration that no church (or person) can escape the all-knowing, ever present God ("I know your works…") who is aware of every attitude, action, thought or deed. The expression "I could wish" (*ophelon*, "a wish" that has not happened or that a thing be done which probably will not be done," THAYER).

The disgusting taste of the lukewarm water made a person nauseating, rather than refreshed. Just because there is a church organization that purportedly worships the Lord Jesus, this does not mean that He is pleased with it. The attitude and effective ministry of each of the member and of the church as a whole determines Christ's desire for the church.

Reflection: Imagine Christ being nauseated over a lukewarm Christian Church? Explain.

John R. W. Stott wrote:
> "Perhaps none of the seven letters is more appropriate to the twentieth-century church than this. It describes vividly the respectable, sentimental, nominal, skin-deep religiosity, which is so widespread among us today. Our Christianity is flabby and anemic. We appear to have taken a lukewarm bath of religion."

THE ANALYSIS FINAL:

3:17

Because you say,'I am rich, have become wealthy, and have need of nothing'-- and do not know that you are wretched, miserable, poor, blind, and naked—

3:17 The Laodecean church was characterized by pride, ignorance, apathy, self-sufficiency, self-deception and complacency. Prosperity or success blinds a person to his spiritual reality. Our ego and self-centeredness always leads us to think we are much better than Christ's opinion of us. We deceive ourselves.

With no "need" the tendency is to rely on personal resources or abilities and thus God is left out of one's life (consciously or unconsciously, the end result is the same). The evolutionist consciously wants a world where there is no need of a sustaining God or Creator.

The lukewarm Christian dreams of being independently wealthy, staying healthy and all one's desires fulfilled. God only is as useful as the hope that He will bring this about: the American dream. Few dare to be so generous in kingdom investments that there is barely enough to subsist personally, when they need God's involvement to make it. Few Christians enjoy living a life of real dependency on God's provision. They would rather resolve their needs themselves.

Reflection: How does the end description of v. 17 compare to 1 Cor 3:13-15?

Reflection: Can you imagine a person who is "wretched, miserable, poor, blind and naked" but thinks that he/she is "happy, enthusiastic, rich, has the proper perspective on life and looks good"? He is totally self-deceived like the person of 1 John 1:8, "If we claim we have no sin, we are only fooling ourselves and not living in the truth." Only by knowing the truth from God's Word about sin can you see yourself as God does. Do you have a mature Christian friend who can help you with a reality check?

3. THE EXHORTATION (3:18-19)

3:18

I counsel you to buy from Me gold refined in the fire, that you may be rich; and white garments, that you may be clothed, that the shame of your nakedness may not be revealed; and anoint your eyes with eye salve, that you may see.

3:18 The Lord "counsels" (*sumbouleuo*, present active, "I am continually or habitually advising...") the Laodiceans to do three things: (1) to "buy from Me [the Lord]"; (2) to buy "white garments that you may be clothed", and (3) to "anoint your eyes with eye salve."

(1) Obviously these are metaphors that refer to heavenly consequences from earthly actions. The gold refined in the fire may be a reference to Peter's use of the same metaphor: "Such trials show the proven character of your faith, which is much more valuable than gold—gold that is tested by fire, even though it is passing away – and will bring praise and glory and honor when Jesus Christ is revealed" (1 Pet 1:7). That is, the trials of persecution make evident the genuine faith of the believer, thus the priceless riches of a true salvation becomes "rich in good works" and lays up a "treasure of a good foundation for the future" (1 Tim 6:18-19). Christ wanted them to have true riches, which is a true faith tested by trials resulting in eternal riches beyond comparison to earthly goods.

(2) They were told to buy… "white garments," which appear to be angelic (Mark 16:5) or heavenly clothing (Rev 3:4), which is described as practical righteousness in our daily lives (Rev 19:8). It is the righteousness that always accompanies genuine saving faith.

(3) The anointing of the eyes refers to understanding the practical application of God's principles. Only then can we see our lives in the light of eternity and the holiness of God rather than in comparison to each other or our own self-aggrandized view of ourselves. Proverbs 23:23 states, "Buy the truth, and do not sell it, get wisdom, discipline and understanding." The NET Bible gives a helpful historical note with this verse:

> The city of Laodicea had a famous medical school and exported a powder (called a "Phrygian powder") that was widely used as an eye salve. It was applied to the eyes in the form of a paste the consistency of dough (the Greek term for the salve here, *kollourion*, [Latin collyrium] is a diminutive form of the word for a long roll of bread).

Christ is urging the church to "open their eyes so that they [might] turn from darkness to light and from the dominion of Satan to God, that they may receive forgiveness of sins and an inheritance among those who have been sanctified by faith in [Him]" (Acts 26:18).

Reflection: If they don't "see" the truth, can they be saved?

LOVED ONES ARE ALWAYS CORRECTED

3:19a

As many as I love, I rebuke and chasten. Therefore be zealous and repent.

3:19a The Lord manifested His love for the church, in spite of its unbelief, by rebuking them and chastening them. If He did not care, He would let them do whatever they wanted and reap whatever the consequences. By adding the nuances of the verbs we see here a free translation of what Jesus says, "All those I am continually loving, I am continually rebuking and continually chastening. So begin immediately to burn with zeal [for eternity's values] and immediately repent [or change your thoughts of your sinful reality]."

To "reprove" (*elegcho*, "to convict, by conviction to bring to the light, expose") is the first work of the Holy Spirit in an unsaved person (Jn 16:8) showing them their need of a Savior. One should be able to determine if he is loved by Christ if he is being "disciplined" (*paideia*, "rearing of a child, training, or chastisement").

Reflection: If a person can sin, and continually get away with it without correction or sense of guilt, he might seriously need to check his salvation reality. Christ expects us to take seriously His admonitions. What are Christ's chastisements like for you? Have you ever recognized them?

3:19b

...Therefore be zealous and repent.

3:19b In order for the Laodiceans to be saved they would have to "be zealous and repent." The word for "zealous" (*zeloo*, aorist imperative means to "immediately begin to burn with zeal, desire earnestly, pursue, strive after") refers to being open to and desirous of knowing the truth with all your heart, no matter how convicting. Finally, the command to "repent" (*metaoeo*, aorist imperative means to "immediately or urgently change one's mind." It is used 32 times in the NT). Until they could see themselves in the light of the Scriptural understanding as sinful and unacceptable before God, then change their minds or personal perspective of how good they thought they were, tso they could understand their need for the Savior (Gal 3:24).

Reflection: Do you think someone could be saved if he still thinks he is good enough, or has to be good to be acceptable to God? Explain.

4. THE PROMISE (3:20-22)

3:20

Behold, I stand at the door and knock. If anyone hears My voice and opens the door, I will come in to him and dine with him, and he with Me.

3:20 Christ follows His call to repentance with a gracious invitation to anyone inside the church who is listening for His voice and opens the door, Christ is willing to come into him and dine with him forever. In the meantime, Christ is now outside the church, asking for anyone who will open the door to him. It is either Christ asking people to come outside the apostate church to Him, or He is waiting for some inside the church to be willing to invite Him in. From all appearances, this is a totally unsaved "church" that is pictured here. The verb tense nuances are interesting: Christ is continually "knocking" (present tense), for anyone who at one time hears (aorist tense) and at one time opens (aorist tense) the door, Christ will certainly come in (future tense). The verb "sup" or "dine" (*deipneo*) refers to the last meal of the day before night falls, symbolical of the coming judgments to be announced.

Reflection: Is this a good verse for explaining how to be saved? Explain

3:21

To him who overcomes I will grant to sit with Me on My throne, as I also overcame and sat down with My Father on His throne.

3:21 The overcomer is promised a share in the glory of Christ's throne and a joint-reign with Christ in the millennium reign (Rev 20). This privilege is beyond comprehension or description. Paul wrote, "For I consider that the sufferings of this present time are not worthy to be compared with the glory which shall be revealed in us" (Rom 8:18 NKJ). Those who follow Christ in His humility, rejection and suffering will likewise share with Him in His glory. What privileges for the true believer! They make any suffering now as inconsequential and any embarrassment we might feel as absurd.

Reflection: Can you see how this promise would motivate a true believer to be bold, faithful and courageous in extending the kingdom? How does it affect you?

5. CONCLUSION 3:22

3:22

He who has an ear, let him hear what the Spirit says to the churches.

3:22 For the last time, Jesus advises the listeners to listen or take seriously the voice of the Spirit, that is, the revealed written Word of God, which is the clear voice of the Spirit. The church of Laodicea was so content with herself that it would have been difficult to see any wrong in herself, or be interested in serving others with the gospel message, much less be involved in a sacrificial ministry. This church had lost its sense of spiritual renewal and burden for the lost. The people wasted their energies and lives in the pursuit of success, pleasures and stuff, trying to maintain themselves "good enough," but not "fanatical" or overdoing it with their religion. They had to be entertained as in the Roman theater or see some personal benefit for coming to church. They were lukewarm, not very useful for anything and quite tasteless.

Reflection: No wonder it made Jesus sick. Is anyone listening to what Jesus is saying? Do you know any churches or individuals like this? Do you ever feel "lukewarm?"

Jesus had told John to write what he saw (chapter 1), then the "things that are" (chapters 2-3), and now "what will take place after this" (chapters 4-22), i.e., after the churches. Chapters 4-18 are described as taking place within a 7-year period called "The Great Tribulation" (Rev. 7:14), which culminates with the Second Coming of Christ (Rev 19) and initiates the millennial kingdom (Rev 20), after which all time as we know it ends and eternity begins with the description of the New Jerusalem and the new heavens and new earth (Rev 21-22).

CHAPTER 4

THE HEAVENLY SCENE

"Whatever these events mean, they are to take place after the period of the seven churches, that is, the Church Age, and are still future from our perspective."

With the conclusion of the descriptions of local churches John is exposed to the incredible experience of viewing the throne of heaven and the beginning of the most amazing revelation ever given to mortal man, the events of the end of time. Then John was commanded to write everything he had seen. We have the privilege of studying the record exactly as John wrote it down.

Part III. The Revelation of the Future:
"What will take place later" (chapters 4-22)

A. VISION OF THE THRONE IN HEAVEN

1. THE INVITATION TO COME UP (4:1)

Whatever these events mean, they are to take place after the period of the seven churches, that is, the Church age, and thus are still future from our perspective today. The activities build in a crescendo of global events that destroy the majority of humanity before Jesus comes again to set up His kingdom. This is the "revelation" of Jesus Christ.

Everyone will finally see Him for who He is and what He can do. Nothing could be more important to the readers who would soon be faced with the loss of everything in this life, but what will happen to the readers in the next life will be incomparable to any suffering in this life. Our experience, as John's, will begin after being called up to partake of the end time events from the arena of heaven.

4:1a
After these things I looked, and behold, a door standing open in heaven. And the first voice which I heard was like a trumpet speaking with me, saying, "Come up here, and I will show you things which must take place after this.

4:1a Following the vision of the seven churches, John is given another vision of the heavenly scene. He has the same experience that the believers at the Rapture will have. The "open door" was a view into the third heaven (2 Cor 12:2). This is where Christ is seated at the right hand of God. Stephen saw this same scene that John will describe (Acts 7:55-56); likewise, Paul was "caught up to the third heaven" (2 Cor 12:2), probably after being stoned in Lystra (Acts 14:19-20). From this vantage point John writes what he witnessed that was about to

THE HEAVENLY SCENE

begin.

Reflection: Can you imagine seeing the reality of heavenly life and then returning to earth? How would it affect your life?

4:1b

John heard a voice as "the sound of a trumpet," commanding and authoritative, inviting him, "Come up here, and I will show you things which must take place after this." The pretribulational view is that John's experience was similar to, or a "type" of, the Rapture of the believing Church before the events of Rev. 4-19 begin. As John saw these events taking place from heaven, so will the church be witnesses of the same. Jesus had told Peter, "If I will that he remain till I come, what is that to you? You follow me" (John 21:22). John had waited sixty years to experience the coming of the Lord, and now he was to experience it and record it so that all the churches could know what will happen. If John's experience depicts the Rapture, we can see more of the Rapture described in 1 Thess 4:13-18 and 1 Cor 15:51-53.

Reflection: Can you find at least 15 things that will happen at the Rapture in these two passages? Write out the aspects of the Rapture described in these verses.

(1) 1 Thess 4:14:

(2) 1 Thess 4:15

(3) 1 Thess 4:16

(4) 1 Thess 4:17

(5)

(6)

(7) 1 Cor 15:51

(8)

(9) 1 Cor 15:52

(10)

(11)

(12)

(13) 1 Cor 15:53

(14)

(15)

4:1c

"Come up here, and I will show you things which must take place after this."

4:1c The timing of the events that John saw is declared to be sequential ("after these things," i.e. after the churches or after churches cease to be), these events will occur, though the exact timing is not described (it could have been a longer or shorter time between these revelations. However, they refer to future events as evident from 1:19, "... will take place later."

This future aspect is again reiterated in 4:1, when John uses a Greek construction with *dei*, "something that must take place AFTER these things." These events are not optional or conditional, but certain, and they are sequential following the events of the churches in chapters 2-3. The emphasis indicates that the following events have nothing to do with the churches; indeed, no churches are referred to from chapter 4 through 19. The church believers are conspicuously absent even though many will be converted in the Tribulation period. In John's vision he was gone from the earth during the time of the Tribulation, so believers will be in the Throne Room with Christ awaiting the events to unfold.

Reflection: As John suddenly heard a trumpet calling him up to heaven to witness the events of the Tribulation; How does this compare to the Rapture of the church believers?

2. THE THRONE ITSELF (4:2-3)

4:2

Immediately I was in the Spirit; and behold, a throne set in heaven, and One sat on the throne.

4:2 John was "in the Spirit" (aorist tense) seeing the throne of God and the One who sat on it in all His majesty and honor. The idea is that the spirit of John was taken to heaven, but his body remained on Patmos. The breath-taking scene that suddenly appeared before John was the same scene that Isaiah saw in Isaiah 6:1-4, which provoked the conviction of utter unworthiness from Isaiah and total commitment to His purpose (6:6).

Reflection: Why would Isaiah's reaction be an instinctive response to this scene?

THE HEAVENLY SCENE

4:2b The OT prophet Micaiah saw the Lord on His throne in 1 Kings 22:19, "I saw the Lord sitting on His throne, and all the host of heaven standing by Him on His right and on His left." Daniel likewise saw this throne in Dan. 7:9-10, "...the Ancient of Days took His seat; His vesture was like white snow and the hair of His head like pure wool. His throne was ablaze with flames, its wheels were burning fire. A river of fire was flowing and coming out from before Him; thousands upon thousands were attending Him, and myriads upon myriads were standing before Him." Ezekiel gives one of the most detailed descriptions of the heavenly throne in Ezek 1:26-28.

Reflection: Do you feel comfortable about standing before such a throne?

4:3

And He who sat there was like a jasper and a sardius stone in appearance; and there was a rainbow around the throne, in appearance like an emerald.

4:3 The splendor of the throne and He who sat upon it appeared as precious stones, jasper and sardis. A jasper may have resembled an emerald in its green or red color and the sardius or carnelian was usually red in color appearing as a ruby. This stone is the most reflective of the semi-precious stones. In the high priest's breastplate, these stones appear representing Reuben and Benjamin, respectively as the first and last stones on the breastplate. The throne was encircled by a rainbow or glowed in multiple colors. "Spectacular" is hardly adequate to describe it. Someday we will see it.

Reflection: What do you think Col 3:1-3 mean in the light of these verses? How does this scene represent a life-value for the believer?

3. THE 24 ELDERS (4:4)

4:4a

Around the throne were twenty-four thrones, and on the thrones I saw twenty-four elders sitting, clothed in white robes; and they had crowns of gold on their heads.

4:4a As John's view moved beyond the throne itself, he saw an emerald-like rainbow around the throne and then a series of 24 thrones with people sitting on them. The Twenty-four elders are probably OT and NT honored representatives of the saints from both eras, because the New Jerusalem will have twelve Patriarchs or tribes of Israel from the OT (Rev.21:12) and twelve apostles from the NT (Rev 21:14). They are clothed in white garments, which symbolize Christ's righteousness, and appear to have been evaluated and rewarded since they are on thrones and have "crowns" (*stephanos*, a wreath or garland given as a prize to victors in public games").

Reflection: What were the apostles to judge from these thrones? Is this the same as the 24 elders?

Reflection: Believers are told that they will have unprecedented authority. According to 1 Cor 6:3, who are believers going to judge?

Reflection: This was the ambition of the twelve disciples. According to Mark 10:35-40, James and John felt self-confident enough to think that they were qualified for the highest responsibility in Christ's earthly kingdom. It was apparent that they coveted this power. Why do you think all the other disciples got mad when they heard what James and John had privately requested a position of authority (10:41)?

Reflection: What are the two kinds of authority according to Jesus and which is prohibited (Mark 10:42-43?

4:4b

and they had crowns of gold on their heads.

4:4b There is a different word for the crown of a sovereign ruler, which is called a "diadem" (*diadema*). Such crowns had been promised to loyal believers at Smyrna, "Be faithful until death, and I will give you the crown of life" (2:10). This group of elders is referred to 12 times in the Book of Revelation. In the Law of Moses there were 24 orders of the priesthood. The apostles were promised 12 thrones in Matt 19:28.

In Mark 10:40 Jesus stated that there were seats (thrones?) at His sides and that they were prepared for someone. Whoever these elders were, they passed this test to be there. They could not be Jews or other believers out of the Tribulation, since these elders are already enthroned at the beginning of this period. There is no biblical

THE HEAVENLY SCENE

reason to divide the group into two groups of twelve (one group from the OT – patriarchs; and one from the NT – apostles). The apostles were promised thrones and specific responsibilities that pertain to Israel (Matt 19:28). Is this a separate group? The vision of the 24 elders appears to be much broader. They, more than likely, represent the raptured, glorified, rewarded church and are now living in the place prepared for them as Jesus promised (John 14:1-4). This may mean that the seat among the 24 elders is still an open issue!

Reflection: What did Jesus' question to the two disciples indicate what the qualifications would be for serving this close to Jesus' side in the kingdom according to Mark10:38?

4. THE SEVEN SPIRITS OF GOD (4:5)

4:5a

And from the throne proceeded lightnings, thunderings, and voices...

4:5a What an awesome view of the throne of God! Terrifying "lightnings, thundering and voices," must have been frightening and awsome at the same time. This was a powerful throne, and appeared to be a judgment scene as never seen on earth. There was no question in John's mind that this One Who sat on the throne had power over all nature, heaven, angelic beings, and everything that lived.

The same "flashes of lightning and sounds and peals of thunder" (16:18) will occur later in the Tribulation period at some of the most devastating earth-moving events since creation. In a continual display of power desiring to be unleashed, lightning and thunder, such as Moses (Ex 19:16) and Ezekiel (1:13) saw when God threatened His judgment will be manifested around the globe in Rev 8:5. John saw a glimpse of the wrath to come.

Reflection: How would you respond to such a scene?

4:5b

Seven lamps of fire were burning before the throne, which are the seven Spirits of God.

4:5b Furthermore, the scene shifts to the seven Spirit manifestations. What are the seven descriptions of the Spirit in Isa 11:2? Isaiah described the manifestation or traits of the Spirit as wisdom, understanding, counsel, strength, knowledge, reverence, and deity. In Zech 4:1-10, power is added; in Rev 1:4, grace and peace are emphasized.

Reflection: What else can we learn about the Spirit's ministries in John 16:8?

With the Father on the throne and the manifested Spirit surrounding the throne, the stage is set for the revelation of the Son, Christ Jesus Himself as the slain Lamb of God.

5. THE FOUR LIVING CREATURES (4:6-8)

4:6

Before the throne there was a sea of glass, like crystal. And in the midst of the throne, and around the throne, were four living creatures full of eyes in front and in back.

4:6 The imagery of brilliance and reflected colors on a crystalline sea must have been breathe-taking. The "sea of glass" is not a sea, as there is no sea in heaven (21:1). In Rev 15:2, this is the same scene of the appearance of the martyred saints of the Tribulation Period in worship and admiration for the Lamb of God who sits upon the throne. Evidently it is a crystal glass that is as vast as a sea, giving it this appearance. The scene describes a transparent glass-like surface with dazzling lights refracting through jewels and crystals in astounding manners beyond our description (See Rev 21:10-11, 18 for more descriptions).

Reflection: What does such brilliance and beauty say about the nature of our God?

4:6b The four living creatures are magnificent, powerful beings are referred to by name in 54 verses (once in the NT) and described at length by Ezekiel (1:4-25) in an almost incomprehensible perspective as he attempted to analyze the amazing scene that he saw, but it was evident that both Ezekiel and John saw powerful and supernatural beings that could be unleashed to carry out any command given to them. Ezekiel 10:15 identifies these four living beings when he wrote, "Then the cherubim rose up. They are the living beings that I saw by the river Chebar." The four living creatures are cherubim, a higher order of angels associated in Scripture with God's holy power (1 Sam

THE HEAVENLY SCENE

4:4; 2 Sam 6:2; 22:11; Ps 80:1; 99:1; Isa 37:16).

The first mention of these cherubim was when they drove Adam and Eve out of the Garden of Eden (Gen 3:24). Symbols of two cherubim were placed in the Holy of Holies in the Temple, to cover the ark, symbolically guarding the holiness of God (1 Kings 6:23-28). Satan, before his fall was the "anointed cherub who covers," whose duty had been to "cover" God's throne (Ezek 28:14, 16). These beings accomplish tasks that God delegates to them, rather than God just declaring a thing done by fiat. These creatures are extremely powerful, though not omnipotent, as will be seen.

4:6c John and Ezekiel attempted to describe the amazing scene before them: (1) they were "full of eyes in front and in back" (v. 8; Ezek 1:18; 10:12), which describes their awareness of everything around them, though they are not omniscient. The eyes will be described as part of the representation of the every watching, always alert angelic being overseeing the creation and mankind.

Reflection: How does it make you feel to know that such powerful creatures are ministering spirits to the believers? (Heb 1:8)

THE FOUR CREATURES

The first living creature was like a lion, the second living creature like a calf, the third living creature had a face like a man, and the fourth living creature was like a flying eagle.

4:7 The features of these cherubs were characterized by a lion, a calf, a man and a flying eagle. It should be noted that the twelve tribes of Israel were divided into four groups as they camped around the tabernacle. Each group had a banner: the tribes with Reuben (a banner of a man), others with Dan (a banner of an eagle), others with Ephraim (a banner of a calf or ox) and the rest with Judah (a banner of a lion).

The four living creatures, each having six wings, were full of eyes around and within.

4:8 The importance of these powerful angelic beings at the beginning of the Revelation is to clarify that these beings are fully capable of unleashing the devastation that is to come. The six wings are described in Isaiah 6: "with two [they] covered [their faces], and with two [they] covered [their] feet, and with two [they] flew" (Isa 6:2).

Four of their six wings had something to do with worship (with 2 wings they covered their face – even exalted angels cannot look on the magnificence of the glory of God without being consumed as Moses was protected by the hand of God from the radiance of His glory (Ex 33:22-23) and with 2 wings they covered their feet because they were on holy ground in God's presence). Worship is their perpetual function day and night.

Reflection: As we proceed through the Book of Revelation the preeminence and priority of worship in the presence of the Lord will become increasingly apparent? If you could describe your practice and priority of worship at this time on a scale of 1 to 10, what would it be? Can you share your present perspective of worship?

MacArthur gives a clear definition of what is being witnessed in heaven:

> Fittingly, the scene in heaven culminates in worship directed toward God on His throne. In this passage and in chapter 5 are five great hymns of praise, during the singing of which the size of the choir gradually increases. The hymns of praise begin in verse 8 with a quartet—the four living creatures. In verse 10, the twenty-four elders join in, and in 5:8, harps are added to the vocal praise. The rest of the angels add their voices in 5:11. Finally, in 5:13, all created beings in the universe join in the mighty chorus of praise to God. Worship is reserved for God alone, since there is no one in the universe like Him. In 1 Chronicles 17:20 David prayed, "O Lord, there is none like You, nor is there any God besides You" (cf. Pss. 86:8–10; 89:6–8).

This mighty oratorio of praise and worship may be divided into two movements: the hymn of creation (chap. 4), and the hymn of redemption (chap. 5) (MacArthur, John: *Revelation 1-11*. Chicago : Moody Press, 1999, S. 155)

Reflection: How comfortable you will be in such a scene of praise and worship? How should this effect our view of corporate worship in our churches?

THE HEAVENLY SCENE

4:8b

... And they do not rest day or night, saying: "Holy, holy, holy, Lord God Almighty, Who was and is and is to come!

4:8b Worship begins with the focus on the holiness of God. The triple repetition is found in Isaiah 6:3 and shows perpetual amazement of God's attributes in heaven. Holiness describes God's distinctness and separation from any form of evil, error, injustice or wrongdoing—a trait that not even the angels can claim (some of them sinned) or humans (all of whom have sinned). Habakkuk best describes the amazement: "[His] eyes are too pure to approve evil, and [He] can not look on wickedness with favor" (1:13). When Isaiah saw this scene he cried out, "Woe is me, for I am undone! Because I am a man of unclean lips, And I dwell in the midst of a people of unclean lips…"(Isa 6:5). Only because of His grace and mercy does God withhold His just wrath against all sinners, whose sin He detests.

Reflection: Why was a glimpse of God's holiness a frightful thing to Isaiah? What kind of response should singing of His "holiness" bring within our spirits?

HE IS COMING

4:8c The day is soon coming, in our text, when Christ will return and the day of mercy and grace will end. God's just wrath against sin will be unleashed. Unrepentant sinners will cry out "to the mountains and to the rocks, 'Fall on us and hide us from the presence of Him who sits on the throne, and from the wrath of the Lamb; for the great day of their wrath has come, and who is able to stand?'" (Rev 6:16-17). Unbelievers are fearful of the One we love.

Reflection: What characteristic of our loving God will He reveal at this time?

HE IS MIGHTY

4:8d The four beings refer to God as the "Almighty" or the "All-Powerful," the title that describes His limitless power that none can oppose. The Psalmist wrote, "Our God is in heaven! He does whatever He pleases!" (Ps 115:3). This is especially evident in creation: "He spoke, and it was done; He commanded, and it stood fast" (Ps 33:9).

This same power is able to aid the believer. Paul praised the Lord because He is "able to do [far more] abundantly beyond all that we ask or think, according to the power that works within us" (2 Cor 9:8) and this same power assures the believer that "He is able also to save forever those who draw near to God through Him, since He always lives to make intercession for them" (Heb 7:25).

The Almighty is on the believer's defense, but He is on the offense against the rebellious evil of the lost world. This power will be hurled against sinful mankind in terrible, inescapable judgments during the Tribulation before the Lord's return for His earthly reign.

The wrath of God is hard for humans to understand because we do not think sin is so bad. It is just a slip or mistake to us, but to God it is a "deal-breaker."

Reflection: How do you fit these verses into your worldview and God concept?

Mal 3:2

Ps 90:11

HE IS ETERNAL
Who was and is and is to come!

4:8e The final title phrase of the Almighty is the one "who was and who is, and who is to come!" refers to His eternal existence "Who was" is the imperfect tense meaning that He always was being, it never began, just was always there. "Who is," in the present tense refers to continual being, ever existing in the present.

"Who is to come," is the present tense to referring to His future manifestation, which is both a "blessed hope" (Tit 2:13) for the believer and the dreaded fear of the unrepentant. He is eternal and has created us to live eternally.

Reflection: How does the contrast of these two eternal destinies compare:

2 Cor 4:17

Rev 14:11

THE HEAVENLY SCENE

6. WORSHIP IN HEAVEN (4:9-11)

4:9

Whenever the living creatures give glory and honor and thanks to Him who sits on the throne, who lives forever and ever,

4:9 The "whenever" ("at the time that") indicates an occasional eruption of praise by the four living creatures, as they give glory (*doxa*, "opinion"), honor (*time*, "valuing by which the price is fixed, reverence"), and thanks (*eucharistia*, "gratitude" from which we get the word Eucharist) to the One on the throne, provokes a spontaneous act of worship from all the 24 elders and then in 5:11 all the saints around them join in the worship along with the rest of the angelic beings. In 5:13 all the created beings in the universe join in the chorus of a crescendo of worship.

There is only one Being in the universe worthy of worship and it is reserved for God alone (see 1 Chron 17:20). David wrote, "None can compare to you... For you are great and do amazing things. You alone are God...Who is like the Lord among the heavenly beings?... a God who is honored in the great angelic assembly, and more awesome than all who surround him?" (Psa 86:8-10; 89:6-8).

Reflection: How do you practice giving glory, honor and thanks to the Lord? How are these three related?

TWENTY-FOUR ELDERS

4:10

the twenty-four elders fall down before Him who sits on the throne and worship Him who lives forever and ever, and cast their crowns before the throne, saying

4:10a The 24 elders who fall prostate (*pipto*, "throw oneself to the ground" as a sign of devotion or humility) before the throne in worship follow the worship of the four living creatures. This is the first of six times the elders fall down before God (5:8, 14; 7:11; 11:16; 19:4).

Such a posture communicates reverence and submission. After prostrating before the Lord the 24 elders "cast their crowns before the throne." They were not preoccupied with their own importance or holiness, which is incomparable to the glory of God.

Reflection: What postures do you practice in devotion/prayer? How significant is posture?

4:10b The fact that these 24 elders possess "crowns" may indicate that they have already been rewarded, since being honored with a throne and a crown are the results of the Judgment Seat of Christ (2 Cor 5:10; Mark 10:40).

If the saints are rewarded at the beginning of the Tribulation Period, then the rapture must have already occurred. Time for this to have occurred is relative since time is only relevant inside the universe. In the presence of God we are not bound by the limits of our universe. The Judgment Seat of all believers could occur in a few moments by earth-time, yet be experienced over a lengthy time in God's presence. .

Reflection: We cannot imagine the significance of how living sacrificially for the kingdom now will be honored then. Where is your treasure (Matt 6:21)?

HE IS CREATOR

4:11a

You are worthy, O Lord, To receive glory and honor and power ...

4:11a Their cry to the Lord is, "You are worthy, O Lord..." (*axios*, "having weight, befitting honor" – used of a Roman emperor when he marched in a triumphal procession). The emphasis in this praise is the glory of God in creation, Who has the right and power to redeem and to judge His creation. The Creator aspect of God is throughout Scripture (Gen 1:1; Ex 20:11; Isa 40:26, 28; Jer 10:10-12; 32:17; Col 1:16).

The audacity of men who refuse to recognize the revelation of God in creation preferring a supposed chance/luck random sequence of developments that fortunately turned out perfectly in in billions of circumstances from micro-biology to astro-physics is worse than naïveté. It is a hardened refusal to give honor to the awesome Creator-Designer. Science should live in amazement, instead of surprise at how lucky and meaningless we are.

Creation is the first chorus of this song of praise before the Creator. Existence only makes sense when we see the purpose and design of time and creation. Redemption is senseless without a Creator and a

THE HEAVENLY SCENE

purposeful creation beginning.

Reflection: Why is creation so important a concept in worship?

4:11b
For You created all things,

4:11b It is because of His "will" (*thelema*, "what one wishes, desires or determines to be done;" a derivative of thelo, "to desire") "…they exist (*eimi*, "to be" imperfect tense, thus at the time of observation they "were being, existing") and were created" (*ktizo*, aorist passive, a one-time act – not a progressive incomplete action, which would be another tense, "make something that did not previously exist before") seems out of sequence, but the author is beginning with what he saw ("… they were existing"), then gives the reason for how and why they exist ("… [they] were instantly created"), thus augmenting the reason for their worship. The NLT translates this phrase, "they exist because you created what you pleased."

Reflection: Have you told the Lord how grateful you are that He was pleased to create you in your circumstances for such a time as this? How does Psalm 139:13-17 describe our planned, personal and purposeful creation?

4:11b
And by Your will they exist and were created.

4:11c Their praise contemplates the lost creation being redeemed to become the new creation, thanks not just to the Creator, but the Creator-Redeemer. God has waited thousands of years since creation to judge Satan, the demons, sinners and to put an end to sin and its influence in His creation once and for all time. This final act is about to begin. The drama and sense of expectation among those around the throne must be extreme. This is the climax of all creation: the Revelation of the Son of God in all His glory, power and majesty. The process is about to begin to bring about this revelation.

Reflection: What does the phrase in the Lord's Prayer, "The kingdom come," mean to you now?

CHAPTER 5

THE SEVEN-SEALED SCROLL

"This scroll was written to describe the events that will occur on earth at the beginning of the end of time just before Jesus returns."

The events of chapter 4 appear to be pointing towards a climactic event, which was the appearance of a conclusive end-time description that would come to pass exactly as written, a pre-written history of future events. Not even the "god of this world" (2 Cor 4:4) has the power to write history before it occurs. This history is the story of how Jesus has decided to reveal Himself to mankind in a public, indisputable manner.

1. THE SEVEN-SEALED SCROLL INTRODUCED (5:1)

5:1

And I saw in the right hand of Him who sat on the throne a scroll written inside and on the back, sealed with seven seals.

5:1a John was witnessing the pre-recorded epic of future events. In addition to this scroll there was another scroll written that described every individual's make-up (Psa 139:13-17), which came to pass precisely as it was written before creation began. What a phenomena that every individual is distinct as every snowflake down to the fingerprints and DNA. This scroll, likewise, was written to describe the precise events that will occur on earth at the beginning of the end of time just before Jesus returns.

Reflection: If every part of our physical being was designed by God to make us unique vessels for His purpose, what does this imply concerning His ability to describe these future events that were penned on this scroll likewise before creation began?

5:1b As John witnessed the resounding worship scene of angelic beings, the twenty-four elders (representing the church after the rapture and Judgment Seat of Christ in heaven-5:9) in chapter 4, he now begins to notice a "scroll" (*biblion*, "book, roll") that was written on both sides, but sealed seven times as the scroll was unrolled. Scrolls of either papyrus material or animal skin, were used until the invention of the codex or modern type square page book bound together to be opened one page at a time. However, this type of scroll was often used as a title-deed to a piece of property, thus this scroll becomes the procedure Jesus will follow to inherit what is properly His. It was not uncommon for a scroll to be written on both sides. The inside would

THE SEVEN-SEALED SCROLL

be the primary text, and on the outside would be a brief outline of the contents of the inside of the scroll. Ezekiel saw this same scroll and described it as "written on the front and back, and written on it were lamentations, mourning and woe" (Ezek 2:9-10). The contents of this scroll are the events of Rev 6-22.

Reflection: How would you describe the importance of this document as evidence in this chapter?

5:1c The book is sealed seven times to reveal its content sequentially and only at an appointed timetable. But more importantly, the seal could not be broken except by the appropriate person for whom the document was written. Zechariah saw a "flying roll" or scroll that "the length thereof was twenty cubits [30 feet], and the breadth thereof was ten cubits[15 feet]" (Zech 5:1-3). The revelation of God is recorded forever and is treated in heaven with the most profound respect. We have the privilege of studying the same text. The challenge in heaven was who could break the seals, and launch the content into reality.

Reflection: How does such a written document in heaven affect your view of the written document we can open freely and discover God's truth?

2. THE QUESTION: "WHO IS WORTHY?" (5:2-5)

5:2

Then I saw a strong angel proclaiming with a loud voice, "Who is worthy to open the scroll and to loose its seals? 3 And no one in heaven or on the earth or under the earth was able to open the scroll, or to look at it.

5:2-3 The Dilemma: The unnamed "strong" angel (also in 10:1 and 18:21) asks in a loud voice: "Who is worthy…?" Who has the virtues, power and authority to begin the end of all creation? Who, but the Creator Himself. It has to be Someone who could "loose" the contents of the seals. The verb "loose" is luo, "to discharge from prison, release from bonds," which means initiating the countdown to the Second Coming and all the events described. It was not just the opening of a scroll to read it as we do the Bible. Who has the divine right to open the seals? Who has the power to unleash its contents? Who could control the Satanic and demonic assault on creation that will ensue? Who could bring to a conclusion the effects of sin and reverse the curse on all creation? The search through the whole of creation revealed no one. The only solution is Someone outside of all creation.

Reflection: Can you imagine looking for a Savior among mortal, sinful, and limited men? How fruitless and foolish, yet billions search in vain. What if there were no One who was All-Powerful who could control what was about to happen?

THE SEARCH

So I wept much, because no one was found worthy to open and read the scroll, or to look at it. .

5:4 The Agony: The pause in the revelation of the Person of Jesus must have been primarily for John, because the elders knew what was coming. Was this a dramatic pause? John still had not seen Jesus. Was there no solution? John wept in heaven. This is the same word that is used when Jesus wept over Jerusalem (Luke 19:41) and when Peter wept after his denial of knowing Jesus (Luke 22:62), and refers to a deep and unrestrained emotion.

John had witnessed his Savior crucified, had seen the early believers martyred, had seen Jerusalem destroyed and the inhabitants massacred, and John had seen the churches barely surviving as they struggled against enormous odds and internal weakness . Would there be no end? No hope? John could not help himself. Where is Jesus?

Reflection: Have you ever felt despair or desperation when all hope was dissolved?

5:5

But one of the elders said to me, "Do not weep. Behold, the Lion of the tribe of Judah, the Root of David, has prevailed to open the scroll and to loose its seven seals.

5:5 The Appearance: John must have been standing among the 24 elders, because one turned to him and told him to stop crying. Then he proceeds to present the Savior. This dramatic introduction of the revelation of Jesus Christ in power and authority amplified the uniqueness, majesty and supremacy of Jesus.

THE SEVEN-SEALED SCROLL

All of heaven was about to erupt in exuberant praise and worship. John was told, "Do not weep," that is "stop weeping." John sees Jesus now for the first time.

Reflection: How do you think John felt when he saw Jesus for the first time in heaven? Had He changed?

3. THE LAMB (5:6-7)

And I looked, and behold, in the midst of the throne and of the four living creatures, and in the midst of the elders, stood a Lamb as though it had been slain, having seven horns and seven eyes, which are the seven Spirits of God sent out into all the earth.

5:6a The "Lion" (5:5) referring to His Second coming (only called the "Lion" here in Revelation), and the Lamb (used 27 times in Revelation), which refers to His first coming, are the same Person, the Lord Jesus Christ. The "seven horns" are symbols of strength (1 Kings 22:11) and refer to the strength of a ruler as in Dan 7:24 and Rev. 13:1.

5:6b The "seven eyes" are interpreted as "seven Spirits of God," and refer back to 1:4 and 4:5 as descriptions of the seven-fold manifestation of the Holy Spirit as revealed in Isa 11:2. The symbolic meaning refers to the fullness of the Spirit evident in His person. Notice what the Spirit does: "sent out into all the earth."

Reflection: How is this omnipresence described Zech 4:10?

Reflection: What is the purpose of the universal searching presence of the eyes of the Lord in 2 Chron 16:9?

SCROLL IS OPENED

Then He came and took the scroll out of the right hand of Him who sat on the throne.

5:7 The only One who is worthy in the entire universe, the Lamb of God, takes the scroll, as if to say, "Now is the time. Let the end begin." We cannot imagine the drama of the scene, but the response was overwhelming. The time that all of history since creation and the fall of sinners has waited for the Revelation that was about to begin.

Reflection: How is this anticipation described in Rom 8:20-23?

4. THE WORSHIP OF THE LAMB (5:8-14)

5:8

Now when He had taken the scroll, the four living creatures and the twenty-four elders fell down before the Lamb, each having a harp, and golden bowls full of incense, which are the prayers of the saints.

5:8a Before great men, people rise to their feet, but before deity, people fall on their face in honor, fear, humility and worship. Though only the four living creatures and the twenty-four elders are mentioned here, later the entire multitude of heaven is joined with them (5:11).

Each elder has a harp (Gk., *kithara*) used for worship in song and a bowl of incense (symbolic of the "prayers of the saints" (See Psa 141:2 where prayer and incense are compared). Singing, praying and worshipping are part of the heavenly activity.

Reflection: What comparison between incense and prayers can you see? Is there any?

A NEW SONG

5:9

And they sang a new song, saying: "You are worthy to take the scroll, And to open its seals; For You were slain, And have redeemed us to God by Your blood Out of every tribe and tongue and people and nation, 10 And have made us kings and priests to our God; And we shall reign on the earth.

5:9-10 The roots of this new song go back to Calvary. The depth of the praise comes from the gratitude and appreciation for three primary facts: First, the grandest, most majestic, and highest Being in the universe had voluntarily been slain for others; secondly, He redeemed the saints that John saw around the throne; thirdly, they were promised to co-reign with Christ. This One who is incomparable in the entire universe was "slain" (*spiazo*, aorist tense, thus "once and for all…" +

THE SEVEN-SEALED SCROLL

"slaughtered, violently put to death"). Incomprehensible, except that His death was on purpose and all planned to "redeem" (*agorazo*, aorist tense, thus "once and for all…" + "bought, paid for in a market place") all who would believe.

Reflection: How did Paul describe this act of "being bought" and what did it imply in these verses?

Acts 20:28

1 Cor 6:20

1 Cor 7:23

2 Pet 2:11

TOTAL GRATITUDE

5:9b No one is there because of any personal merit or goodness. Everything is owed to this amazing Person Who paid their debt, which they could never have paid, just because they accepted his death as the just price for their sins. This vast group of grateful believers included some from "every tribe and tongue and people and nation."

How this will be accomplished is through God's present followers as they are willing to let their lives become the instruments through which God's Spirit can work empowering their preaching of the gospel in every language and people group on earth. All those new believers will appear on this future day before the throne.

Reflection: What had Jesus said would be necessary before He would begin His Second coming in Matt 24:14? What does this mean for our priorities?

MISSION ACCOMPLISHED

5:9c Secondly, The prime motive for world evangelism is the command of Jesus to tell everyone the Good News, and the promise that "the gates of hell will not prevail against [the church]" (Matt 16:18). Here is the end view of the Great Commission: someone made it to the last people group, tribe, and language group with the gospel message and some believed in every group. This is a task that has a guaranteed successful end. Believers who see this and value this moment in time more than life itself, will pour out their lives to participate with Christ in bringing some (not all) from every tongue, tribe, and people group on earth.

Reflection: If we know that this is His strong desire, how big a priority should it be in our individual lives?

A NEW ROLE

5:10

And have made us kings and priests to our God; And we shall reign on the earth

5:10 Thirdly, He promised to make them "kings and priests to our God" to "reign on earth." The privilege of just being there at this moment would be enough, but to be promised the responsibility of becoming a king and priest in a future kingdom where Christ will reign "on earth" is overwhelming. Life now has the chief objective of qualifying us for a future responsibility with Christ in His earthly reign following His Second Coming.

Reflection: How did Paul express this concept in these verses?

Rom 8:18

2 Tim 2:12

This group appears to be the complete Church that has been raptured, evaluated, and rewarded, now awaiting the consummation of the Return of Christ to earth. There will be another group that will come out of the Tribulation Period, but this group is already in heaven before the Tribulation begins. It is the culmination of the church.

THE HEAVENLY CHOIR

5:11

Then I looked, and I heard the voice of many angels around the throne, the living creatures, and the elders; and the number of them was ten thousand times ten thousand, and thousands of thousands,

5:11 John's sight is now drawn to this vast multitude of millions [lit. "myriads and myriads"] of believers who came out of the Church Age awaiting the beginning of the seven-year Tribulation Period (Rev.

THE SEVEN-SEALED SCROLL 111

6-19) before the beginning of the millennial reign with Christ (Rev. 20). These are not specific numbers, but descriptive terms of a vast army of believers. Their lives had been transformed as they heard and believed the gospel message during their lifetime.

Reflection: What is the biggest choir you have seen? What is the biggest auditorium or stadium you have seen? Can you imagine the sound of millions singing this praise? What is the reason for the praise?

5:12

saying with a loud voice: "Worthy is the Lamb who was slain To receive power and riches and wisdom, And strength and honor and glory and blessing!"

5:12 This vast choir with a "loud voice" (not necessarily singing) or shout, "Sing to him a new song! Play skillfully as you shout out your praises to him! "(Psa 33:3 ᴺᴱᵀ). In this case it is a seven-fold praise: "worthy is the Lord Jesus to receive power, riches, wisdom, strength, honor, glory and blessing."

It was not that Jesus will receive these attributes, but a recognition that this was His character since before creation. The Savior has all these attributes, thus is praiseworthy. It was on the basis of the death of the Lamb that praise erupts. Heaven's worship always exalts the cross and the redemption won on that day.

Reflection: How often is the cross or the death of Christ mentioned in your worship time? It is the theme of eternity.

UNIVERSAL PRAISE (5:13-14)

5:13

"And every creature which is in heaven and on the earth and under the earth and such as are in the sea, and all that are in them, I heard saying: "Blessing and honor and glory and power Be to Him who sits on the throne, And to the Lamb, forever and ever!"

5:13 This universal worship scene is to reiterate the fact that everyone is there only by the grace of God, especially in sending the Savior (the "Lamb"). The universal praise is because there was a universal offer. "Every creature" sings praise to the Father and the Son. The unity of the Father and Son is a strong emphasis in the Revelation.

Reflection: Do you enjoy worshipping the Lord Jesus? This is what heaven is all about. Because people understand the greatness of the cross, they grasp the significance of what it cost the Savior to redeem us to Himself and therefore, they can do no less than express their gratitude and thanks with worship and praise.

5:14

Then the four living creatures said, "Amen!" And the twenty-four elders fell down and worshiped Him who lives forever and ever.

5:14 Like a wave, it begins next to the throne with the 4 creatures who shout "Amen!," then the twenty-four elders follow suit and fall on their faces in worship, presumably followed by the vast multitude who owe everything to the One who lives forever and ever...thus we will likewise, with him, live forever. Meditate on His grace in accepting you as His own, not because there is any goodness or merit in you, but because He cleansed you through His blood to make you acceptable to His holiness. What grace!

Reflection: Do you have to be singing to praise Him? How often are you thankful for His grace, forgiveness, acceptance, and presence in your life? Or do you merely thank Him for health or things or when you are happy?

Where does the 7 years of the Tribulation come from?

There was a strange prophecy revealed to Daniel that has a direct bearing on these numbers. Due to Israel's apostasy Babylon had taken her into captivity. Daniel had gain the respect of the king of Babylon and ramained in that position when overtrown by Persia. God gave a vision of His purpose for Israel in Daniel 9:24:

> "Seventy weeks ["sevens"] have been determined concerning your people and your holy city to put an end to rebellion, to bring sin to completion, to atone for iniquity,   to bring in perpetual righteousness, to seal up the prophetic vision, and to anoint a most holy place."

Seventy "sevens" equals 490. In the Jewish calendar seven "sevens" was the Year of Jubilee (Lev 25:8-12), that is, 49 years. If the measure were days it would mean 1 1/3 years, which would not be enough time for the prophecies of 9:24-27. There had been 70 sabbatical years [one every 49 years] that Israel had ignored, now God was to collect, thus 490 years would be required.

The first three objectives of 9:24 would be accomplished at Calvary, and the latter three in the millennium. The prophecy is broken up into three periods that would begin with the "issuing of the decree to restore and rebuild Jerusalem" (9:25). The only decree given by a Persian monarch to rebuild the city was by Artaxerxes Longimanus on March 5, 444 B.C. (Neh 2:1-8). Oddly, there would be two periods, one of 7 "sevens" (49 years) and 62 "sevens" (434 years) "until an anointed one, a prince arrives" (9:25). However, "after the sixty-two weeks, an *anointed one* [Heb., "Messiah"] will be cut off ..." The first period was the time to rebuild the city of Jerusalem (444-395 BC). The second period (62 "sevens" (434 years) was the period until the "anointed one will be cut off" (9:26). The exact day was fulfilled on Jesus' Triumphal Entry into Jerusalem on the eve of His crucifixion. This fulfilled 69 of the 70 weeks of the prophecy. The seventiety "seven" is yet unfulfilled.

The final "seven" year period begins when "the coming prince" [Antichrist] confirms a "covenant with many for one week" (9:27) or seven years. In the middle of this period [3 1/2 years] this prince "will bring sacrifices and offerings to a halt," implying that the temple and sacrifices will be reinstituted in Israel, but this false peacemaker prince [Antichrist] will end the Jewish sacrifices and demand the Jews and the world to worship him (2 Thes 2:4; Rev 13:8).

The Book of Revelation will explain "the decreed end [that] is poured out on the one who destriovs" [the Antichrist] at the end of the 70th week of Daniel (Dan 9:27). If the first 69 "sevens" of years (434) were fulfilled literally, the final "seven" will be as well.

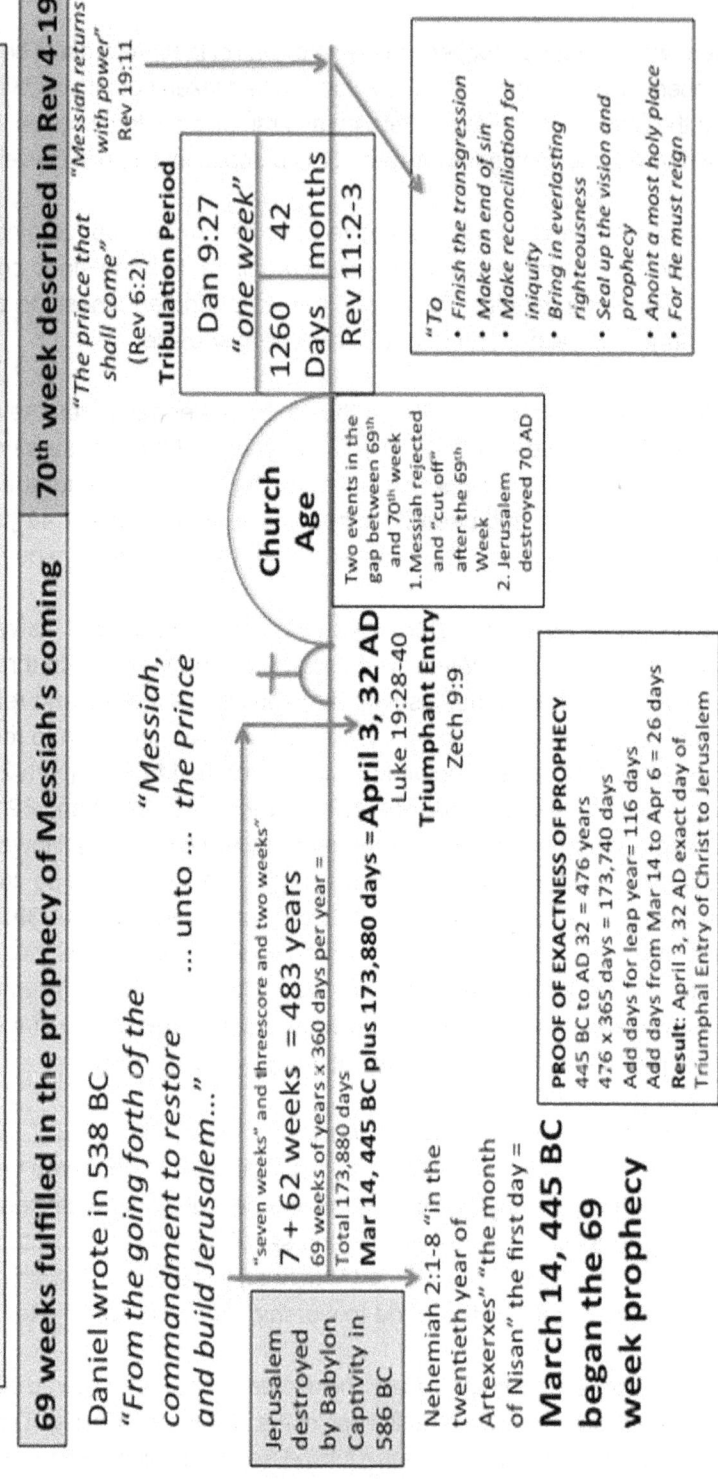

THE SEVEN-SEALED SCROLL

The Seven Year Great Tribulation Events

Judgment Seat of Christ → Marriage Supper of Lamb → 2nd Advent with saints → Armageddon

Church is raptured

7 Seals (Rev. 6)
1. White horseman
2. Red horseman
3. Black horseman
4. Pale horseman
5. Persecuted saints
6. Great earthquake
7. Seven Trumpets

7 Trumpets (Rev 8-9)
1. Hail, fire, w/blood
2. Asteroids poison 1/3 of sea
3. Asteroids poison 1/3 of water
4. A third of sky darkened
5. Locus from Abyss torment for 5 months
6. 1/3 of men die
7. Massive earthquake

7 Bowls (Rev. 16)
1. Loathsome sores
2. Sea turn blood- all sea life dies
3. Fresh water becomes as blood
4. Men scorched by sun
5. Darkness & pain
6. Euphrates river dries up as Eastern kingdoms invade
7. Earth is shaken again

Daniel's 70th Week

1,260 days – 42 months | 1,260 days – 42 months

Events at Beginning
1. Antichrist appears as the Little Horn, the man of sin, & White horseman
2. Antichrist makes a covenant with Israel

Events of first 3 ½ years
1. Antichrist rises to power over Roman Confederacy
2. Israel returns to land in unbelief.
3. Israel rebuilds under patronage of Antichrist
4. Temple rebuilt & sacrifices begin
5. World Church dominate all religions and Inquisition-like oppression returns.
6. War, famine, economic chaos (2-4th seals)
7. Worldwide evangelism and martyrdom (5th seal)
8. Natural disaster & worldwide fear of divine wrath (6th seal).

Events of Mid-Tribulation
1. Satan cast from heaven (Rev 12)
2. Russia and Egypt invade Israel (Ezek 38-39)
3. Russia is destroyed by God
4. Antichrist defeats Egypt, Libya and Ethiopia
5. Antichrist breaks covenant with Israel
6. Antichrist destroys World Church
7. Obligated worship of image of Antichrist
8. Two Witnesses begin their ministry
9. Israel flees persecution by the Beast
10. 144,000 chose Jews serve Messiah

Events of 2nd 3 ½ years
1. Great Tribulation judgments begins
2. Antichrist reigns with world leaders with support of Western Confederation
3. False Prophet promotes worship of Antichrist by everyone
4. Jerusalem overrun by Gentiles
5. 144,000 continue to preach but eventually martyred
6. Mark of Beast used for worship and commercial requirement
7. Multitudes converted and martyred
8. Israel specifically persecuted by Antichrist.
9. Trumpets and bowl Judgments poured out on empire of Antichrist.
10. Blasphemy increases as judgment intensifies.

Events of the end of the Tribulation
1. Commercial Babylon destroyed
2. Kings from East and North invade Israel
3. 2/3 of Jerusalem destroyed
4. Armies of world gather at Armageddon
5. Christ returns with His saints.
6. The Antichrist's army destroyed
7. The Antichrist and False Prophet cast into Lake of Fire
8. The Beast locked in Abyss for 1000 years.

CHAPTER 6

OPENING THE SEVEN SEALS

"The four horsemen of the Apocalypse are only the beginning of a horrible series of judgments against sinful mankind."

The seals will cover the entire seven-year period of the Tribulation. The first 4 seals will cover the first 3-½ years, and the last 3 seals, the remaining 3-½ years. The seventh seal contains the seven trumpet judgments (8:1-11:19) and the seventh trumpet (11:15) contains the seven bowl judgments (16:1-21). Thus the seven seals contain all the judgments until Jesus returns.

1. THE FIRST SEAL (6:1-2) –WHITE HORSE = FALSE PEACE

6:1

Now I saw when the Lamb opened one of the seals; and I heard one of the four living creatures saying with a voice like thunder, "Come and see."

6:1 The loud voice commanding John to "come and see" implies a different location from the heavenly scene. John returns to earth in his vision to witness a sequence of events that will take place within a 7-year period (Dan 9:26), which will begin with an attempt at global unification and peace, but will collapse into global chaos and massive disasters that will probably be blamed on the Jews and Christians, ultimately leading to a global attack on Israel called "Armageddon," which will climax at the Second Coming of Christ. Meanwhile, the Church is gone from the world scene, as we have seen in chapters 4-5.

Though there are different views on when the rapture occurs, in the following passage notice that a restraining force in the world is holding back the manifestation of the Antichrist, but at some point the Restrainer/Protector will be taken away, unleashing the rise of the Antichrist, the "ruler of the people" mentioned in Dan 9:26.

> 2 Thess 2:3-7 "Let no one deceive you by any means; for that Day will not come unless the falling away comes first [i.e., either a great apostasy or the Rapture] and the man of sin [i.e., the Antichrist] is revealed, the son of perdition, 4 who opposes and exalts

---

4 From the Greek (*anti-* "against" + *-nomos*, "law") belief that members of a special religious group are not obligated to obey the laws of ethics or morality to obtain their salvation. This is a common charge by Roman Catholics, false religions and Jews against Protestant and Evangelical Christianity who prefer to control followers by legalistic standards.

himself above all that is called God or that is worshiped, so that he sits as God in the temple of God,[yet to be built in Jerusalem] showing himself that he is God. ...2:6 And now you know what is restraining,[i.e., the Holy Spirit] that he may be revealed in his own time. 2:7 For the mystery of lawlessness is already at work; only He who now restrains [i.e. the Spirit] will do so until He is taken out of the way [i.e. at the Rapture]."

Reflection: If the Rapture brings the end of the "restraining" work of the Spirit, and initiates the events of the Great Tribulation, will the Church ever see or identify the Antichrist? Explain:

CONQUER FOR PEACE

6:2

And I looked, and behold, a white horse. He who sat on it had a bow; and a crown was given to him, and he went out conquering and to conquer.

6:2 Each of the seals is another outpouring of God's wrath. As soon as the Lamb opens the first seal a white horse and rider holding a bow (without arrows), wearing a victor's crown (*stephanos*) is revealed. Who is he? There is a similarity to Christ in 19:11 where it is clearly Christ riding on a white horse, which in the first century was a symbol of victory. Of course, Christ is opening the seals, so He cannot be in the seal. Other differences are: the armament is different (a bow instead of a sword), the situation is different (to conquer vs. retribution) and here three horsemen follow bringing catastrophes (instead of the millennium).

Though similar, this person is best identified as the appearance of the "man of sin," the Antichrist, the great world leader who comes to resolve a world in chaos. As each of the other three horses represent changing circumstances, so this horse is a global force at work. The white horse is the symbol of peace, so this charismatic leader will first rise on the scene as the key to unify the world under one global government promising world peace. He is successful in securing global covenants for peace, even with Israel.

Reflection: How did Daniel see this coming in Dan 9:27? How long will it last?

This rider will have an unusual persuasive power to deceive the nations. How did Paul describe this leader's capabilities in 2 Thes 2:9-11?

2. THE SECOND SEAL (6:3-4) – RED HORSE = WAR

6:3

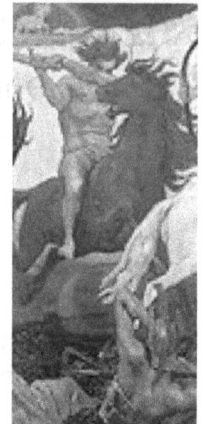

When He opened the second seal, I heard the second living creature saying, "Come and see."

6:3 The superficial, idealistic peace plan that was temporarily structured dissipates in local feuds, vendettas, and global aspirations. Idealism never contemplates the true human selfish, greedy, self-centered apathy, egotistical nature as revealed in Scripture, so failure is inevitable. This rider has the ability to instigate multiple wars all over the globe. He carries a great sword, *machaira*, a short, stabbing sword used by Roman soldiers and used by assassins. Genocides, slanders, riots, massacres, revolutions will be commonplace in the daily news as rebellion breaks out around the globe.

Reflection: How did Jesus describe these days in Mark 13:7-8?

DESOLUTION OF PEACE

6:4

Another horse, fiery red, went out. And it was granted to the one who sat on it to take peace from the earth, and that people should kill one another; and there was given to him a great sword.

6:4 Possible explanations could be that the Antichrist will need to enforce his peace plan with military threat, but his desire for world dominance will now provokes global rebellions that will continue until Jesus returns. As head of the Western confederacy he will do what no leader had been able to do, though many have tried, that is, to bring peace in the Middle East. This may include the negotiation for the rebuilding of the Temple, which by the mid-Tribulation is already constructed when the Antichrist commits the "abomination of desolation" (Dan 11:31; 12:11; Matt 24:15).

For more description of the "abomination of desolation" see Dan 11:36-45, which will occur at the mid-tribulation point.

Reflection: Have you ever been tempted to compromise to gain what you really want? One can only wonder what was given up or compromised to secure the temple grounds. Could it have provoked retaliation and wars?

3. THE THIRD SEAL (6:5-6) – BLACK HORSE = FAMINE

6:5-6

When He opened the third seal, I heard the third living creature say, "Come and see." So I looked, and behold, a black horse, and he who sat on it had a pair of scales in his hand. 6 And I heard a voice in the midst of the four living creatures saying, "A quart of wheat for a denarius, and three quarts of barley for a denarius; and do not harm the oil and the wine.

6:5-6 As a result of worldwide cost of wars the food supply is either confiscated or destroyed by the armies involved. The world banks can no longer control the resulting global economic collapse of all paper-debt monetary systems returning to a barter and silver/gold economy. A "quart of wheat" and "three quarts of barley," both for a day's wage. A denarius was a Roman silver coin, worth about fifteen cents, the daily wage for a common laborer. Either the wheat would make one meal or the barley would make 3 meals per day, but there would be none left to buy either wine or oil. The laborer could not earn enough to feed his family.

Even the barley has such low nutritional value that it is used to feed the livestock on these starvation wages. The scales in the rider's hand will be used for rationing the limited food supply as a result of the wars (see Matt 24:7). Olive oil and wine were used to cook with and purify the water, so they needed to be carefully protected. Global chaos is beginning to escalate, but it will get much worse. Riots, looting and mayhem break loose destroying the food chain and civilized governments. The beginning of this condition is increasingly evident. As people loose hope of recovery, desperation takes over, especially as people by the hundreds of thousand die of starvation.

Reflection: Have you ever been hungry for a day because of lack of food? Have you seen misery, poverty, and hopelessness? ... this is only the beginning. What would you do if there were no food in the grocery stores?

4. THE FOURTH SEAL (6:7-8) – PALE (GREEN) HORSE = DEATH

6:7

When He opened the fourth seal, I heard the voice of the fourth living creature saying, "Come and see."

6:7 The fourth horse is "pale" (*chloros*, "ashen" from which we get the English word "chlorophyll" and "chlorine"), thus a pale, yellow-green color of a corpse in decomposition. The rider's name is "Death." The inevitable consequence of war and famine is widespread disease and death.

The extent of this devastation results in the death of 25% of the world's population (6:8). At the current population of nearly 7 billion will result in 1.75 billion deaths in a few months. This level of devastation has never been witnessed in human history, but this is barely the beginning of God's judgment.

Reflection: How does this perspective modify your view of God's nature?

FAMINES AND PLAGUES

6:8

So I looked, and behold, a pale horse. And the name of him who sat on it was Death, and Hades followed with him. And power was given to them over a fourth of the earth, to kill with sword, with hunger, with death, and by the beasts of the earth.

6:8 As devastation mounts people get desperate demanding stringent government control and execution for violators. Ethnic groups are blamed for catastrophes and genocides become the solution, especially against Jews and anyone who becomes a Christian.

This rider was given power "to kill with the sword, with hunger, with death, and by the beasts of the earth." The unleashing of the 4th horseman of Death will use the "sword" (2nd horseman of war), "hunger" (3rd horseman of famine) and "death" (*thanatos*, "death" but may also refer to disease as the cause of death as in 2:23 and 18:8), as well as "beasts of the earth."

The most deadly animal that every lived is the rat, which become infected with fleas that carry multiple diseases such as the Black Plague. In the seventh and fourteenth centuries this plagued wiped out 50% of the population from China to Europe in a few years. These creatures thrive in populated urban areas where soon 60% of the world population will live.

Reflection: How many funerals have you attended? What if everyone in your family were killed by a plague, would it motivate people to turn to God?

By the fourth seal we are approximately at the mid-point of the Tribulation period. Now the situation begins to worsen in an accelerated manner. Yet God is still leaving the door open for anyone to repent and be saved, but they will not escape the life-threatening circumstances of the Tribulation.

Reflection: How do these authors describe this period of time?

Jer 30:7

Dan 12:1

Matt 24:21-22

5. THE FIFTH SEAL (6:9-11) – THE PRAYERS OF THE MARTYRS

When He opened the fifth seal, I saw under the altar the souls of those who had been slain for the word of God and for the testimony which they held.

6:9 John's vision now shifts back to the heavenly scene where he sees souls of those recently arriving in heaven ("a white robe was given to each of them") who had been saved in the Tribulation period, but had been "slain" (*sphazo*, violently killed, or murdered") for their faith in the "Word of God" and for the "testimony which they held." (See 7:14).

How they heard and understood the gospel after the rapture is not revealed. It perhaps can be surmised that they had heard the gospel before the Rapture by faithful witnesses, but postponed their commitment to Christ until it was too late.

Now they became the target of the antichrist's persecution (and probably most of the blame for the earth's calamities), which begins in the first half of the Tribulation, then escalates in the second half as intimated in 6:11. We see the inequity of criticism against Christians today ("spirit of antichrist;" 1 Jn 4:3), and even though more Christians have been martyred globally in the past two decades than in the previous 2,000 years, this is insignificant compared to the first 3-1/2 years of the Tribulation. The number martyred is enormous (7:9). But the second half of the Tribulation will even be worse for anyone who dares to believe.

Reflection: From the following verses see if you can put together the circumstances that would provoke the anger of the Antichrist against the Tribulation believers. Did they recognize who he was?

1 Thes 2:3-4 (What does he claim and where?)

1 Thes 2:9-10 (Why are so many deceived?)

Rev 13:3-4 (What if someone does not worship?)

Rev 13:5 (How long is 42 months?)

Because these believers know the Word of God, and testify to what is happening in the light of Scriptures, they are not tolerated. What a price to pay to know the truth. What do these verses reveal about this group?

Rev 12:17

Rev. 19:10

Rev 20:4

MARTYR'S PRAYER

6:10

And they cried with a loud voice, saying, "How long, O Lord, holy and true, until You judge and avenge our blood on those who dwell on the earth?"

6:10 The souls under the altar who were cruelly killed by the ruling authorities are begging the Lord to avenge their deaths. As horrible as these plagues (4th horse) become, they do not compare to how Jews and believers are treated everywhere in the Tribulation.

How different these prayers are compared to Stephen's prayer of forgiveness (Acts 7:60). This is like the imprecatory prayers in Psalms.

Such prayers are not seeking vengeance, but justice and intervention against all that is against God and dishonoring to Him. It is not directed against individual vendettas, but rather against the whole anti-God global system.

God's response is for them to "rest" (*anapauo*, "keep quiet in patient expectation"). Evil must become so evil that it cannot be worse, thus meriting the horrendous wrath that is pending against the evil world system. Then sin will once and for all be done away with. Their prayers are answered in 16:5-7 and 19:2.

Patience is one of the most difficult traits of God to learn (mentioned in 33 verses in the NT). No one wants retribution more than Jesus, but He is patient (Rev 1:9) and asks His followers to be likewise, hoping more will repent regardless of the cost.

Reflection: In what circumstances does one learn patience in Rom 5:3? Do you find it easy to be patient? Is there a relationship between patience and trust in God?

"Under the altar" describes the location of this special group, distinct from the myriads of saints around the throne in Rev. 4-5. The "altar" refers to a part of the heavenly Temple (of which the earthly tabernacle was modeled- Heb 8:5) of special honor, but distinct from the location of the Church to indicate a different group of believers coming out of the Tribulation Period.

Number of martyrs

6:11

Then a white robe was given to each of them; and it was said to them that they should rest a little while longer, until both the number of their fellow servants and their brethren, who would be killed as they were, was completed.

6:11a "Each of them was given a long white robe..." These martyred spirits are not ghosts, but substantive bodies of dead saints, that are capable of wearing a robe. It is evident that departed believers have a temporary body in heaven that is awaiting their resurrected bodies (20:4)

The patience would wait "until the full number is reached..."[NET] This statement implies that there is a certain number of martyrs that will be murdered before God begins to pour out His wrath. Until now the chaos is the result of the rise of the AntiChrist and the economic collapse.

This is not an arbitrary number, but a knowledgeable number. He knows who they are, when they believe, and when they will be killed. Jesus spoke of a great number of Jews that will perish in this period (Matt 24:9, 16-22) and Rev 7:9-17 describes a host of Gentiles who will be killed out of all nations, tribes, peoples, and tongues. These are horrible days for believers. If we care about people now, we must give them the gospel message before it is too late. Even if they are saved after the rapture it will be horrible for them.

Reflection: Discuss whether the fact that there will be believers in the Tribulation is a motivation to witness now, or an excuse to believe that they will be saved anyway in the Tribulation Period.

until both the number of their fellow servants and their brethren, who would be killed as they were, was completed.

6:11b The prayers of the martyrs give some good principles. It is evident that the saints in heaven do not know "when" God will judge sinful mankind. They are still echoing the prayer "Thy kingdom come!" God made it clear that their martyrdom was not accidental, or unnoticed, but rather was part of His plan, so they should not fear nor fret. He makes no mistake. The Lord asks for patience and trust by the answer given "…a little while longer." It would happen, but in His timetable. Justice in the world system is in God's hand; it is seldom immediate; and we are to "rest for a little longer" as well.

Reflection: Can you see any other principles of prayer in this dialogue?

What about the promise of protection from God's wrath in Rev 3:10? Does this promise only apply to the Church and not to the Tribulation Period? The wholesale martyrdom of saints during the Tribulation Period, both the first half and second half, demands that the promise to the Philadelphian church be seen as "keeping [the Church] out of the hour of testing" that will come on all mankind. The fifth seal is a description of this testing that the Church will be kept from by a previous Rapture.

6. THE SIXTH SEAL (6:12-17) — EARTHQUAKES AND METEORITES

The beginning of divine acts of judgment

6:12-13

I looked when He opened the sixth seal, and behold, there was a great earthquake; and the sun became black as sackcloth of hair, and the moon became like blood. 13 And the stars of heaven fell to the earth, as a fig tree drops its late figs when it is shaken by a mighty wind.

6:12-13 The horrible sixth seal opens with a "…great earthquake… sun became black as sackcloth… moon became like blood" then "the stars" fall "to the earth"… "the sky receded as a scroll" (6:14a) from the ash covering from the massive volcanic explosions. This all resulted in "every mountain and island being moved from its place" (6:14b) This is an unparalleled changes to the geological earth surface, since the time of the flood.

The sixth seal introduces the heavenly signs as mentioned in Matt 24:29 and Joel 2:31. These six frightening natural disasters occur in the latter part of the second half of the Tribulation, just before the Second Advent. Cosmic disturbances are mentioned just before the first trumpet (8:5), in connection with the fourth trumpet (8:12), fifth trumpet (9:1) and seventh bowl (16:17-21). Jesus spoke of great disturbances in the atmosphere in Matt 24:29 and Joel 2:30-31 refer to the events at the close of Day of the Lord. If we look at these descriptions one at a time we begin to see their terrible destruction to the planet earth.

The **first disaster** is a "great earthquake" (*megas seismos,* "great or abundant shaking") is used in the LXX in Joel 2:10 to describe the heavens trembling. He shook the earth at Mt. Sinai (Ex 19:18) and at the death of His son (Mat 27:51, 65) and locally when he released Paul and Silas from jail at Philippi (Acts 16;25). Because of an earthquake that resulted in the jailor experiencing the fear of the Lord, which brought him to Christ. There have been many localized earthquakes in history, and there will be many more during the first half of the Tribulation, but this global earthquake is incomparable. It is the "dream earthquake" that seismologist fear and know can occur. People will be afraid to go into buildings so seek protection from falling debris in shelters. These are the survivors of world wars, devastating famines, and global epidemics of deadly contagious diseases, and now the worse catastrophes imaginable begin.

The **second disaster** is the darkening of the sun, which is the perception from earth as the volcanic ash from multiple mega-eruptions blankets the atmosphere, bringing a darkened earth, creating the **third sign disaster** of the reddish moon appearance as its reflection filters through the ash covering. Every aspect of life that depends on the sun and the moon will be affected. Life on earth is threatened. The volcanic rifts are only waiting a slight shift in the crust to begin to erupt. Every seismologist knows how viable such eruptions are today. Only a few strategic eruptions could blacken the sun for the whole earth, causing major catastrophes and major climate changes.

The **fourth disaster** describes the falling stars, as seen from earth when huge asteroids or meteors bombard the earth. Many computer models of this possibility have been developed and movies made of a few asteroids striking earth, but multiple major asteroids and meteor showers penetrating through the volcanic ash covering in the ionosphere would be terrifying to witness. John likens these multiple asteroid impacts to a fig tree in the wind loosing all its figs. These were designed to be astrological signs or omens that should cause reflection or repentance.

Reflection: Why would the people on earth not repent at these celestial signs?

MORE 6TH SEAL

6:14

Then the sky receded as a scroll when it is rolled up, and every mountain and island was moved out of its place.

6:14 Then suddenly and inexplicably the fifth disaster occurs when the sky splits apart like a scroll from the earthly perspective revealing the disaster of what's left of life on earth. Just when men think the worst is over, the sixth disaster strikes. The whole crust of the earth begins to move and shift. The "continental drift" theory becomes reality and in perceived motion not gradually imperceptible. The damage to civilized urban structures will be unimaginable. There has never been a doomsday scenario that can compare to this destructive event, while man is totally helpless to stop any of its destruction. And the worse is still yet to come.

Reflection: If you have friends or family members who have not heard the gospel, do you want them to go through these judgments? This is the main thought that this Book should provoke.

The seven trumpets and bowls appear to end in a similar terrifying climax, perhaps overlapping and accelerating, each one lasting a shorter time, thus building toward an overwhelming conclusion. There are seven elements of creation (earth, sun, moon, stars, sky, mountains and islands), which are all shaken from their normal existence.

Reflection: Only a fool sees merely coincidences [not evidences] in these universal upheavals, especially of this global magnitude, and yet refuses to see the Designer-Judge-Savior trying to get men's attention.

Reflection: How can fear help people make good decisions? Why do we have to learn to fear God?

Luke 12:5

Heb 10:30-31

RESPONSES OF THE POPULATION

6:15

And the kings of the earth, the great men, the rich men, the commanders, the mighty men, every slave and every free man, hid themselves in the caves and in the rocks of the mountains.

6:15 From leaders to slaves (seven classes of people are listed) the fear is universal, but there is no mention of repentance. The elite of society include the "kings" (*basileus*, "leader, lord, or commander"), "great men" (*megistos*, "princes, nobles, or magistrates"), "rich" (*plousios*, "wealthy, abounding in things, or self-satisfied"), "commanders" (*chiliarchhos*, " commanders of a thousand soldiers"), "mighty" (*dunatos*, "powerful, strong, influential, or authority" who usually scoff at fear), as well as the common people of the lower classes made up of "slave" (*doulos*, "one who gives himself up to another's will, or servant," or employee?), and "free man" (*eleutheros*, "unrestrained, or not bound") will equally be gripped with fear. They are hiding from the cataclysmic upheavals of the earth and sky. This is the warning before the storm. In the midst of plagues, pestilences, wars, cruel injustices, and massive convulsions of nature yet still human depravity refuses to recognize and seek God.

Reflection: The global simultaneous nature of these eruptions and calamities can only be attributed to God yet notice how John describes the reaction of the majority:

Rev 9:21

Rev 16:11

GETTING MAD INSTEAD OF SAD

6:16

and said to the mountains and rocks, "Fall on us and hide us from the face of Him who sits on the throne and from the wrath of the Lamb!

6:16 Notice that this "prayer" is to the Earth or Nature, not to God. All insurance policies have a phrase, "Act of God," to blame the unexpected and unexplainable on God, as though He is the cause of all disasters.

In this day, there will be a general acknowledgement of God's wrath and the notion that final Judgment Day has come, but like the demons who are seducing the world population (1 Tim 4:1), they believe God is there and they are fearful of Him, but they refuse to repent (James 2:19). They just get madder and madder at Him. When people are led by demonic influences they reap the consequences.

Reflection: How did Paul describe these consequences in 2 Thes 2:11-12?

6:17

For the great day of His wrath has come, and who is able to stand?

6:17 By refusing to repent and trust in Christ, their hearts become hardened, and God that hardens their hearts further such that they are unable to repent and believe, but face the just consequences of their heart's decision to reject God in their lives. This is the same process that Pharoah experienced when responding to the ten plagues of Exodus. Everytime he hardened his heart, God hardened it more.

Reflection: How did Jesus describe these days?

Matt 24:29

Luke 21:11

Luke 21:25-26

Nahum wrote, "Who can stand before His indignation? Who can endure the burning of His anger? (Nah 1:6) and the author of Hebrew wrote, "It is a fearful thing to fall into the hands of the living God" (Heb 10:31 NKJ). The one thing in life you do not want to do is to get God angry with you.

Reflection: How does God's chastisement, judgment or wrath strike the unrepentant in 1 Thess 5:3?

Students of prophecy see Revelation 7-19 as the second half of the Tribulation Period. The devastation and persecution have been bad up to this point, but after the "abomination of desolation" when the Antichrist declares himself to be God incarnate, giving serious persecution to any dissonant who will not worship him takes on global proportions and God's wrath becomes unimaginable.

Yet in spite of horrendous conditions great multitudes of people will be saved from both Gentiles (7:9) and Jews (Rom 11:26). When people know the truth, but continue to prefer to enjoy their sins and the convenience of unbelief, then "there no longer remains a sacrifice for sins [Christ is the only acceptable sacrifice – if rejected, there is none other], but a terrifying expectation of judgment and the fury of a fire which will consume the adversaries" (Heb 10:26-27).

The Seventh Seal will unleash the seven trumpet judgments (Rev 8). Now it begins to get worse in an accelerating manner. But first, John sees the survivors of the earlier plagues and catastrophes, one on earth and one in heaven.

CHAPTER 7

THE SAVED OUT OF THE TRIBULATION

"The amazing event of the Tribulation Period ... will be the conversion of Israel."

After the horrendous events of the first six seals, John writes a parenthetical section, before presenting the seventh seal (8:1). Two groups will survive the global holocaust of God's wrath in the trumpet and bowl judgment, as well as the life threatening strategy of the Antichrist to eliminate all believers in the true God. The first group will escape the wars, famines, diseases, plagues, unrestrained sinfulness and vicious persecution of the Tribulation; they will enter into the millennial kingdom alive.

The second group will be martyred almost as soon as it became evident that they have believed in Jesus, and then they are immediately taken into the presence of the Lord and preserved there until Jesus' kingdom begins. Some of those who are saved during this period will survive the Antichrist's holocaust (13:7-10; 14:12-13; 17:6; 20:4), and the trumpet/bowl judgments of natural disasters, famines, etc., and enter alive into the millennium.

Jesus taught that many believers will survive to populate the initiation of the millennial kingdom. He described it as the Judgment of Nations or the sheep and goat judgment in Matt 25:31-46. The "goats" (the unsaved) will be cast into hell (25:41-46) and the "sheep" (the saved) will hear Jesus say, "Come, you who are blessed of My Father, inherit the kingdom prepared for you from the foundation of the world" (25:34). These believers survive the Tribulation period describe in Matthew 24 and Rev 6-19. These people of the nations are Gentile nations that many of the prophets foresaw coming to salvation (Isa 2:2-4; Mic 4:1-5; Zech 8:20-23).

The amazing event of the Tribulation Period, however, will be the conversion of Israel. Initially she makes a pact with the Antichrist unbeknown. Until the mid-tribulation take-over of the Temple and his self-proclaim deification (the "abomination of desolation" Matt 25:15ff), Israel is part of the peace treaty that results in the rebuilding of the Temple in Jerusalem (2 Thes 2:4), which by the mid-tribulation point will exist.

Israel is told to flee the Antichrist's horrible persecution that will follow (Matt 24:16ff). Over the next 3 ½ years some of Israel will be saved (Rom 11:26). Zechariah 12:10 to13:1, and 13:8-9 describe the conversion of Israel to the Messiah in the midst of a horrible persecution that kills 2/3 of the nation, but 1/3 "I will bring the third part through the fire, refine them as sliver is refined, and test them as gold is tested. They will call on My name, and I will answer them; I will say, 'They are My people,' and they will say, 'The Lord is my God'" (Zech 13:9).

Revelation 7:1-8 describes the first group of the Tribulation Jews who come to trust in Jesus as their Messiah. Other Jewish survivors are described in Rev 12:16-17. Our text gives no indication of symbolism, but rather real and unexaggerated numbers from real tribes of Israel, all of which fits in the broader scope of a literal prophetic fulfillment (i.e., the "first fruits" of a redeemed Israel – Zech 12:10; Rom 11:25-27). Erroneous interpretations attempt to allegorize or spiritualize these numbers to mean something different from the simple reading of the text.

1. THE SEALING OF THE 144,000 OF ISRAEL (7:1-8)

A. THE BRIEF PAUSE FOR ISRAEL'S ENCOUNTER WITH HER MESSIAH (7:1-3)

7:1

After these things I saw four angels standing at the four corners of the earth, holding the four winds of the earth, that the wind should not blow on the earth, on the sea, or on any tree.

7:1 "After these things" introduces a new vision by John (4:1; 7:1; 15:5; 18:1; 19:1) and indicate a chronological sequence after the sixth seal. John sees four angels who are given power to control the environment. There is nothing "pre-scientific" about this description (Morris). They are standing in the primary points of the compass (north, south, east, and west) to control or "holding" (*krateo*, "restrain, hold in check, lay hands on one in order to get him into one's power") the winds on earth and bring them to a total stillness or the pausing of the "winds" by the angels may refer to a momentary halt in the judgments. It is like the calm of the eye of a storm, with the worse part coming.

Reflection: Why do you think God allows this pause in the midst of chaos?

SEALED AND PROTECTED (7:2-3)

7:2

Then I saw another angel ascending from the east, having the seal of the living God. And he cried with a loud voice to the four angels to whom it was granted to harm the earth and the sea,

7:2-3 The reason for the pause in God's judgments is a fifth angel's task of sealing the "servants of our God on their foreheads." Some want to identify this angel with Christ, but the word "another" (allos) means another of a similar kind in a sequence and the use of "we" in 7:3 identifies this angel with the other four.

This angel arose from the "east" (from the isle of Patmos this would point toward the eastern end of the Mediterranean or the land of Israel). His task was to "seal" (*sphragis*) the servants of our God." The verb means to "mark for security, to confirm authentication, to prove one's testimony to a person that he is what he professes to be" (Strong).

(Skeptics want the description of the "four corners" to imply a flat-earth belief, thus "pre-science." Yet these terms are common in modern expressions)

Reflection: God put His "seal of approval" on Jesus (Jn 6:27) and all believers are "sealed" by the Spirit (2 Cor 1:22; Eph 1:13; 4:30). How does a believer know he is sealed or not?

7:3

saying, "Do not harm the earth, the sea, or the trees till we have sealed the servants of our God on their foreheads."

7:3 The Antichrist will seal his followers on their right hand and forehead (Rev 13:16-17), but there are likewise eternal consequences of receiving his mark (Rev. 14:9-11 and 19:20). Anyone who rejects this mark of the Beast will lose his life during the second half of the Tribulation (Rev. 20:4).

Reflection: Put yourself in their shoes: would you give up your life by refusing the mark to be faithful to the Lord or would you compromise, take the mark of the Beast in order to survive?

"The servants of our God" are not only marked as belonging to the Lord, but, as the blood on the doorpost in Egypt signaled the death angel to pass over their houses in Egypt (Ex 22:22-23) so the seal on these Jewish "servants" will protect them from the effects of many of the judgments to come (9:4). Other Jews will not have this privilege.

This will be extremely dramatic in a world where plagues and disasters will be common. To have a large group of Jewish Christian young men who defy

THE SAVED OUT OF THE TRIBULATION

the Antichrist and are untouched by the global chaos will be a remarkable testimony to God's ability and purpose with His chosen People.

Reflection: Why would God do this?

(Some interpret the group of 144,000 in Rev 14 as a second group of 144,000. One group for the first part of the Tribulation and a second group for the second half of the Tribulation. This will be discusses in chapter 14)

(It should be noted that the highest number of Western missionaries has been about 42,000, but at least 1/3 of this number are wives with household responsibilities. If we include international missionaries from the Third World, the number rises to just over 100,000, with 30,000 wives included. Nothing has ever compared to a 144,000 army of single servants of their Messiah.)

These Jewish servants are described in Rev 14:1-5 as "...not defiled with women, for they are virgins. These are the ones who follow the Lamb wherever He goes. These were redeemed from among men, being firstfruits to God and to the Lamb. And in their mouth was found no deceit, for they are without fault before the throne of God."

These were the first ones who accepted Jesus as their Messiah at sometime in the first 3 ½ years of the Tribulation. During the catastrophes of the first half of the Tribulation these men are proven and found to be faithful. The mark on their forehead is to protect them from the judgments to follow the seventh seal.

The only indication of their objective is seen in their title as "servants of our God" (7:3) and the phrase they "follow the Lamb wherever He goes" (14:4), thus they become a "Christ follower" or disciple. Do these descriptions indicate that they are missionary evangelists who will preach the gospel to every people group? How were they saved? How did they gain their Bible knowledge especially the NT? How are they different from the early Jewish evangelists of the NT who took nearly 20 years before they were interested in evangelizing the Gentiles? (See Acts 11:19). How could they travel over the globe after the disasters of the 5th Seal? How could they learn the two to four thousand languages that are yet unreached in so short a time, under horrendous conditions of the second half of the Tribulation?

The author sees this group as a powerful ministry to the Jewish people in Israel or wherever they are located that may well result in the Jewish people understanding of the Messiah so that when they see Him come again the nation is born in a day! (Rom 11:26).

Reflection: Does this text indicate that these 144,000 are the key to world evangelism? If they are not, who will finish this task then?

B. THE 144,000 ISRAELITES IDENTIFIED

7:4-9

"And I heard the number of those who were sealed. One hundred and forty-four thousand of all the tribes of the children of Israel were sealed: 5 of the tribe of Judah twelve thousand were sealed; of the tribe of Reuben twelve thousand were sealed; of the tribe of Gad twelve thousand were sealed; 6 of the tribe of Asher twelve thousand were sealed; of the tribe of Naphtali twelve thousand were sealed; of the tribe of Manasseh twelve thousand were sealed; 7 of the tribe of Simeon twelve thousand were sealed; of the tribe of Levi twelve thousand were sealed; of the tribe of Issachar twelve thousand were sealed; 8 of the tribe of Zebulun twelve thousand were sealed; of the tribe of Joseph twelve thousand were sealed; of the tribe of Benjamin twelve thousand were sealed."

7:6-9 The sealing of the 144,000 are the "firstfruits" of the Israel's national conversion (Rom 11:26) that may have followed a dramatic and visible manifestation of Jesus as their Messiah: "the Lamb standing on Mount Zion, and with him were one hundred and forty-four thousand..." (14:1).

If this is the mid-tribulation revelation to the 144,000 of Israel it partially fulfills the Zachariah passage, "they will look to me, the one they have pierced. They will lament for him as one laments for an only son..." (Zech 12:10-13:1, 8-9). These 144,000 are given an Apostle-Paul-Damascus-Road encounter with Christ. How long the pause for this rendezvous with Jesus will last and what was communicated is unknown, but they heard sounds from heaven, songs and praise being given to the Lord (14:2-3) that convinced them that the One they had rejected and crucified as a people had been and always will be their Messiah. Only such a personal appearance of Jesus could explain the dramatic and virtual immediate conversion of this large group of single Jewish men, just as it did with the Apostle Paul.

It is assumed that these converted Jews had the task of converting the

THE SAVED OUT OF THE TRIBULATION

surviving Jewish remnant to their Messiah.

Reflection: Would your life be any different if you had had a personal visible encounter with Jesus?

(If the Jewish nation lost the same proportion of human race in the first half of the Tribulation (25%) then their 14 million would now be reduced to approximately 11 million. This would be a huge evangelistic task for 144,000 in 3 years or so.)

Tribal Identity, "...from the tribe of...": Though the carefully maintained tribal records of every family's genealogy back to Abraham was lost in the destruction of Jerusalem in AD 70, Jesus knows who pertains to which tribe.

Some question the possibility of reconstituting the tribal relations because the ten tribes of Israel were deported in BC 722 with the Assyrian Captivity, never to officially return. However, the faithful in each of the tribes in the north had long since migrated to Judah. In 2 Chron 30:1-11 representatives were summoned to partake in a Passover.

Another problem in the listing of the tribes is that there are at least nineteen different ways of listing them in the Old Testament, depending on the time and circumstances, and none of them fully agree with this list.

Reflection: how would you feel if you had met Jesus face-to-face? Would you have lived any differently?

Is the 144,000 to be taken literally or symbolically? The details of specific numbers of specific tribal participation and a further detail of each personal characteristic all point to a literal interpretation. Two tribes are left out of the list: Ephraim and Dan, both highly idolatrous tribes. The tribes of Joseph and Levi are included. Joseph substituted for his son, Ephraim.

(Sometimes they are listed by chronological birth order (Gen 29:32-35:18), sometimes by Jacob's blessing order (Gen 49:3-27); sometimes by order of encampment (Num 2:3-31); sometimes by the order of the census in Num 26:4-51; or the order of blessing and cursing (Deut 27:12-13); or the order of Moses' blessing (Deut 33:6-25); or the order of the gates of the city (Ezek 48:31-34) or other means of listing the tribal origins.)

Purpose of the 144,000

What is their ministry or purpose? Commentators tend to move into speculation at this point, because there is no clear description. They want to make the 144,000 global evangelists that will win the people from every tribe and nation to the Messiah. Some have excused the lack of interest in evangelism of unreached peoples because they are convinced the 144,000 will finish the task. Is this even possible in the chaotic, destructive world of the Tribulation Period?

Firstly, Travel would be extremely difficult.
Secondly, logistics seem impossible to finance all that would be necessary to reach the lost tribes in the jungles with economies destroyed in the sixth seal, much less reaching people groups in Muslim territories by Jewish evangelists.
Thirdly, the unlikely ability to learn new languages (4,000 language groups have never heard the gospel as of 2009) in an absurdly short time period (i.e., barely a few years when normally skilled linguistics require 5 years to learn any language sufficiently well to communicate the gospel clearly) make this a nearly impossible feat.
Fourthly, there does not appear to be any chronological sequence to the events in the chapter. There is no connection of the 144,000 with the vast Gentile people groups already in heaven when they are sealed.
Fifthly, the most difficult obstacle to this view is that the Jews tend to have little or no interest in Gentiles (at least in Bible times), much less remote, primitive, poor, pagan Gentiles. It took the first Jewish disciples, after spending 3 years with Jesus, almost 20 years before they even accepted Gentiles as Christians (Acts 15, AD 49), much less personally became involved in Gentile evangelism (we only know this by tradition).

Can we expect contemporary Jews to radically change their culture? Finally, the author cannot find any biblical link between the two groups in Rev. 7. The fact that they are in the same chapter does not mean that there is a cause and effect between the two groups, when the text makes no evangelistic link.

However these Gentiles in 7:9-17 came to Christ, the Bible does not insinuate that the 144,000 had anything to do with it. It is amazing how many pastors depend on the 144,000 to finish their task of reaching the last of the unreached people groups to fulfill the Great Commission.

Reflection: How then could the multitudes of Gentiles come to know the gospel in the Tribulation?

(The Matt 24:14 context is the issue. If Jesus is saying that the gospel must be preached to every ethnic group (*ethnos*) "then the end will come," to the Church as the objective of the Great Commission before the Rapture, then global people-group evangelism must be a priority for the church. The Rev. 5 passage declares that the Church was successful, because at the beginning of the Tribulation representatives of every "tribe, language, people and nation" (Rev 5:9) are present in heaven.

After the Rapture left-behind family members, and others of each of these groups who had heard the gospel from their acquaintances, but postponed accepting it, or assumed they were saved, will evidently be saved when suddenly the events they had heard about concerning the Rapture and the Tribulation begin to be fulfilled.

For this scenario to take place, the Church must be successful in reaching every people group with the gospel and leave a witness to the yet unsaved in these groups.

CONTRASTS OF TWO GROUPS IN REVELATION 7:

7:1-8	7:9-17
Jews	Gentiles from all nations
Numbered –144,000	Not numbered, nor could be
Sealed on earth for protection	Martyred, standing in heaven worshipping
Chosen at the middle of the Tribulation	During the first half of the Tribulation

2. THE MULTITUDE OF MARTYRS (7:9-17)

7:9

After these things I looked, and behold, a great multitude which no one could number, of all nations, tribes, peoples, and tongues, standing before the throne and before the Lamb, clothed with white robes, with palm branches in their hands,

7:9 "the great multitude" - John then shifts his attention back to the heavenly scene where he views a vast multitude of people (*ochlos*, "used for common people, as opposed to leaders and rulers; the ignorant multitude, the populace") who are the same group of martyrs under the altar in Rev 6:9 and now are "before the throne and before the Lamb." The group is made up of people from "all nations [*ethnos*, ethnic groups], tribes, peoples, and tongues." The constant repetition of this phrase (Matt 24:14; 28:19-20; Rev 5:9; 7:9; 14:6) indicates the fulfillment of the heart desire of God. His purpose is for all kinds of people to be with Him for eternity.

Reflection: What can we do to make Jesus' desire a reality until the Rapture?

standing before the throne and before the Lamb, clothed with white robes, with palm branches in their hands,
 7:9b They are standing with "palm branches in their hands." Where do the palms come from? The palm branch is a symbol of joy and triumph in the celebration of the Feast of Tabernacles (15th day of the seventh month), when they celebrated the ingathered fruits. Is this the heavenly celebration of the completed gathering of the harvest of the believers from earth? In Zech 14:16 it appears at the beginning of the millennium the Feast of Tabernacles will be renewed to celebrate the survival of Israel through the Tribulation as formerly they celebrated her preservation in the desert of the Negev. God seems to delight in the celebrations of His provision, protection and providential help.

Reflection: How should we celebrate His interventions in our lives?

MARTYR'S PRAYERS

7:10-12

and crying out with a loud voice, saying, "Salvation belongs to our God who sits on the throne, and to the Lamb!" 11 All the angels stood around the throne and the elders and the four living creatures, and fell on their faces before the throne and worshiped God, 12 saying: "Amen! Blessing and glory and wisdom, Thanksgiving and honor and power and might, Be to our God forever and ever. Amen.

7:10-12 Their "cry" (*krazo*, present tense: "continually or habitually," expresses a highly emotive passion) or praise, which provokes another period of worship by everyone around the throne. Their declaration of thankfulness, "Salvation belongs to our God who sits on the throne, and to the Lamb!" The angels can sing this, but only redeemed people who have accepted Christ's sacrifice for their personal sins can ever know the joy of forgiveness.

No one in heaven is proud about how good they were on earth. It is only by His grace that anyone will stand before the Lord accepted and welcomed.

"All" the angels (in 5:11 it was "many"), the four living creatures and the elders (presumably all the believers with them in heaven) fall down before the Lord in worship. They sing to Him seven words of praise: blessing, glory, wisdom, thanksgiving, honor, power, and might. Six of the same words are used previously (5:12-13) but in different order. Here the word, "thanksgiving," replaces "riches."

Evidently, by changing the word order and words, forces the worshipper to think about what he is saying. Jesus had said "there is joy in the presence of God's angels when even one sinner repents" (Luke 15:10).

Reflection: Can you imagine the immense joy of the angels when those they had heard about repenting and believing in real time, are now in their presence worshipping the Savior together?

INQUIRY INTO ORIGIN OF THIS MULTITUDE IN HEAVEN

7:13-14

Then one of the elders answered, saying to me, "Who are these arrayed in white robes, and where did they come from?" 14 And I said to him, "Sir, you know." So he said to me, "These are the ones who come out of the great tribulation, and washed their robes and made them white in the blood of the Lamb.

7:13-14 The elder explains that this multitude come out of "the Great Tribulation" during the first 3 ½ years. These believers were killed in the catastrophes of the sixth seal (as Mat 24:29,30, compare with Dan 12:1). This is the group in heaven before the terrible judgments on the Antichrist and those who have his seal on their foreheads.

How can robes washed in blood come out white? Though this is metaphorical language there are some interesting concepts. In Rev 19:8 the white linen is defined as the "righteousness" that covers the saints. This righteousness-covering is granted by faith and includes the remission of all sins (Rom 3:22), and is accredited or granted to the believer because of his faith in Christ (Rom 3:3, 5, 6, 11), and is described as the "gift of righteousness" (Rom 5:17). This is the reason for their rejoicing.

We can't imagine what this will mean to be totally accepted fully righteous in the awesome presence of the host of heaven and our holy God. All of this and much more awaits us because of the life's blood shed by "the Lamb," the Lord Jesus, was accepted as full payment for all our sins.

Reflection: Why are we repeatedly told to rejoice in the Lord? (See Phil 3:1, 3; 4:4; 1 Thes 5:16; 1 Pet 1:8)

(There is an optical phenomenon that occurs when a red object is seen through a red lens, all the redness in the object disappears. In the Scriptures sin is seen as the color "red," not the popular concept of black. See Isa 1:18, "red like crimson..." Thus when sinful red object (a sinner) is seen through the red lens of a blood covering, all the redness in the object disappears. God does not see our sins because He sees us through the blood covering!)

SERVING WITH CHRIST

7:15

Therefore they are before the throne of God, and serve Him day and night in His temple. And He who sits on the throne will dwell among them.

7:15 They are fully accepted before His presence and "serve (*latreuo*, present tense: "continually rendering sacred services, worshiping God") Him day and night." In the presence of the Lord there is no "day nor night" (Rev 22:5), so this concept means a perpetual service. What is this service? What were the souls under the altar told to do?

Reflection: Who else is doing the same thing? (See Heb 7:25 for answer) How should this affect our service now?

THE SAVED OUT OF THE TRIBULATION

RELEASE FROM TERROR

7:16

"They shall neither hunger anymore nor thirst anymore; the sun shall not strike them, nor any heat;"

7:16 The promise to these saints in heaven is the relief from "hunger...thirst... [scorching] sun...[intense] heat" that may indicate the means of their deaths or suffering during the first six seals of God's judgment.

This group is clearly not part of the Church, or the 144,000 that will appear in the second half of the Tribulation Period. The second half of the Tribulation brings another harvest of martyred believers who are terribly treated by the Antichrist for their belief in Jesus.

ETERNAL SHEPHERD

7:17

for the Lamb who is in the midst of the throne will shepherd them and lead them to living fountains of waters. And God will wipe away every tear from their eyes.

7:17a He will "shepherd them and lead them..." (*poimaino*, "to feed, tend a flock, keep sheep"). To shepherd means that God will keep them in His care, even through martyrdom. Can you explain this. He will also "lead them" (*hodegeo*, "guide, escort, instruct in learning"), which He will give them reasons to be faithful, to suffer faithfully, and persevere.

Reflection: If you were to go through persecution for being a follower of Jesus, what would you want Jesus to tell you that would keep you faithful?

7:17b "Springs of living water..." refer to the spiritual nourishment from the Lord's presence. In Rev 22:17, "...let the one who is thirsty come, let the one who wants to take the water of life free of charge..." (See also 21:6: 22:1).

Reflection: How would you explain the fulfillment of these promises? Did the hearers understand the idea of immediate thirst quenching?

7:17c "God will wipe away every tear from their eyes": God does not promise to alleviate or eliminate the suffering, now or later, but He does promise to be with them "always" (Matt 28:19-20) through their suffering, then when life is ended and the pain goes on, especially for those left behind as they continue in the same emotional mind-set into heaven. So God promises to wipe away all tears once they arrive in heaven. He promises this again in Rev 21:4.

Reflection: How do you think God will make crying a thing of the past?

Now the worse imaginable affliction to mankind is about to begin.

CHAPTER 8

THE SEVENTH SEAL AND THE SEVEN TRUMPETS

The six seals are not even comparable to the accelerating judgments to follow.

Revelation 8 begins after a brief pause to describe two of the main personalities in the final events of the Tribulation Period. First we saw the believing saints who will be killed in the first half of the Tribulation. After that came the choosing of the 144,000 Jewish men who become followers of Christ and will live through the last half of the Tribulation untouched by neither the horrible judgments to men nor by persecution from the Antichrist. Now the stage is set for the second series of seven judgments called the Trumpets. The sixth seal will be so devastating that a quarter of the earth's population will die, but this judgment is not as bad as the coming trumpet judgments.

The first six judgments (Seals) last for 3 ½ years, but the final 21 judgements cover the last 3 ½ years, so they begin to accelerate, each taking less and less time from beginning to end. The bowls and thunders may occur in the last year or six months of the Tribulation. The series of judgments are related since the 7th seal is the 7 trumpets (Rev 8:6-21)and the 7th trumpet is the 7 bowls (Rev 16:1-21). Between the 6th and 7th trumpet judgments, there will be the 7 thunder judgments, which are so bad they cannot be described by John. As bad as this is, probably the worse part is how the Antichrist leads men to treat each other.

I. THE OPENING OF THE 7TH SEAL (8:1)

8:1

When He opened the seventh seal, there was silence in heaven for about half an hour.

8:1 At the opening of the seventh seal, there was revealed seven more judgments followed by seven more and then seven more. The sixth seal was bad, but now three successive series of seven judgements each are indescribable. The text gives no explanation for the "silence in heaven for about half an hour." It was like the calm in the middle of a hurricane; the worse is to come. Was it a gasp of horror at the unprecedented destruction described? Was it a prayer that accompanied the presentation of incense with prayers (8:3-5), which initiated the seven trumpets? Was it the solum recognition of how terrible God feels about sin and His wrath against rebellion in His own creation? The Psalmist wrote, "The earth feared and was still when God arose to judgment" (Psa 76:8-9).

7 trumpets, 7 bowl judgements, three of which are so bad they are called "woes" (trumpets 5,6, & 7) and 7 thunders – which are so bad God told John not to describe them how horrible they are in 10:3-4.

II. THE SEVEN ANGELS ARE GIVEN SEVEN TRUMPETS (8:2)

8:2

And I saw the seven angels who stand before God, and to them were given seven trumpets.

8:2 The scene begins with seven angels who "stand" (*histemi*, perfect tense, "have been standing") on purpose as awaiting instructions. The use of the definite article, "the" seven angels, though the article is not translated, indicates this to be a unique and high-ranking group of angels. There are other angels as well, but these seven are given trumpets, which signal the unleashing of seven severe judgments. As Jesus taught, (Matt 13:39-41, 49-50; 16:27; 25:31) angels will play a key role in bringing about the judgments of God in the Tribulation. Each trumpet will signal judgments to begin on earth. The first four trumpets destroy the earth's ecology (8:6-12), the next two unleash demonic destruction of humanity (8:13; 9:1-11, 13-19), and the seventh trumpet introduces the seven bowl judgments to finalize God's wrath on mankind.

Reflection: Are we beginning to understand how much God hates sin? How will we think of disobedience knowing how God will judge it in the future?

III. THE GOLDEN CENSER (8:3-5)

8:3-4

Then another angel, having a golden censer, came and stood at the altar. He was given much incense, that he should offer it with the prayers of all the saints upon the golden altar, which was before the throne. 4 And the smoke of the incense, with the prayers of the saints, ascended before God from the angel's hand.

8:3-4 Before the seven angels could sound their trumpets, a solemn event needed to take place. Another angel appears. The word "another" (*allos*, "another of the same kind") means that this angel was another of the special angels around the throne. He stood (*histemi*, perfect tense, "stationed" as in NET) at the golden altar (vvs. 3, 5), which is a heavenly pattern as used in the temple. This may have been a regular function of this angel. Was this the angel that took the coal from the altar and gave it to Isaiah in Isa 6:6?

One of the services in the temple was to take hot coals from the brazen altar, site of burning sacrifices, twice a day and carry them to the Holy Place to the incense altar (Ex 30:7,8) just in front of the Holy of Holies, to ignite the incense, which arose in a fragrant smoke, symbolic of the prayers of the saints (Rev 5:8).

Reflection: What does incense tell you about God's perspective of our prayers?

THROWING HOT COALS TO EARTH

8:5

Then the angel took the censer, filled it with fire from the altar, and threw it to the earth. And there were noises, thunderings, lightnings, and an earthquake.

8:5 The momentary silence of half an hour was suddenly broken as the angel took hot coals from the altar and filled his censer, then in an aggressive, perhaps surprising act, he threw the hot coals toward earth. The results were dramatic. It must have appeared as fireballs or meteorites falling out of the sky as an ominous sign that the worst is about to begin.

The thunder, "rumblings" (phone, "sound, tone," probably like the sound of a tornado), lightnings and earthquake (probably as powerful as the earthquake of the 6th Seal) are only the introduction to the most terrifying judgments or catastrophes ever experienced by earthly men.

Reflection: What would make men continue to refuse to surrender to Christ in the face of such global manifestations?

Reflection: : Millions have been preaching the gospel they had heard before the rapture. In spite of millions coming to know Christ, many of whom would be killed, the majority continues to reject the obvious truth, even blaming God without surrendering to Him. How is this explained in these verses:

Rev 9:20-21

Rev 16:9, 11

John 3:19-20

Heb 10:26-27
(Written by same author in about the same time.)

IV. THE FIRST FOUR TRUMPETS: THE DESTRUCTION OF EARTH'S ECOLOGY (8: 6-13)

A. THE FIRST TRUMPET (8:6-7) – PLANT LIFE

8:6-7

So the seven angels who had the seven trumpets prepared themselves to sound. 7 The first angel sounded: And hail and fire followed, mingled with blood, and they were thrown to the earth. And a third of the trees were burned up, and all green grass was burned up.

8:6-7 The beginning of the end. The prelude of the angel with the censer was incomparable to this first Trumpet's judgment, which burns up a third of the earth's surface, its green vegetation consumed in a moment. Ecologists today virtually worship the earth's plant life, "Mother Earth," "Mother Nature," etc.

Eventually God will destroy all of the earth's vegetation and begin anew (2 Pet 3:10 with Rev 21:1). Joel 2:30 describes this as the "Day of the Lord": "I will show wonders in the heavens and in the earth: Blood and fire and pillars of smoke." This could be the result of the earthquake from the angel with the censer, or an eruption on the sun's surface sending a small fireball through space that could devastate the earth's surface in a matter of seconds.

Fire from the sky destroyed crops and vegetation in Egypt as one of the judgments on Egypt in the time of the Exodus (Ex 9:25).

B. THE SECOND TRUMPET (8:8-9) – SEA LIFE

8:8-9

Then the second angel sounded: And something like a great mountain burning with fire was thrown into the sea, and a third of the sea became blood. 9 And a third of the living creatures in the sea died, and a third of the ships were destroyed..

8:8-9 No sooner had the first Trumpet judgment occurred than suddenly there was a massive asteroid impact. Twenty-five percent of the earth's population had been killed in the first half of the Tribulation

(6:7), plus an innumerable amount in the 6th Seal (6:12-17).
Scientists are well aware of the impact of a massive asteroid anywhere on the earth's surface. The whole earth will see this coming, but no one knowing where it will strike or how to avoid it. The result will be a three-fold catastrophe:

(1) A third of the sea becomes blood, whether in appearance or literal from the death of the sea-life,
(2) A third of the sea-life died
(3) A third of all ships were destroyed.

Were such an asteroid to strike the Pacific or Indian Ocean where fleets from different countries often operate the shipping lanes and military fleet operations, such destruction will be very plausible. The resulting tsunamis would devastate any lowlands around the globe.

C. THE THIRD TRUMPET (8:10-11) – COMET OR METEORITE

8:10-11

Then the third angel sounded: And a great star fell from heaven, burning like a torch, and it fell on a third of the rivers and on the springs of water. 11 The name of the star is Wormwood. A third of the waters became wormwood, and many men died from the water, because it was made bitter.

8:10-11 The Third Trumpet quickly will follow the second and sound like what Jesus said in Luke 21:11, when He said there will "be terrifying sights and great signs from heaven" when a great star (*aster*, from which we get "asteroid") falls to earth. This sounds like a massive and fiery meteorite attack that will disintegrate and disburse over a vast territory falling into the waterways of the earth polluting the rivers and water systems.

The meteorite will be called "Wormwood" (*apsinthos*, only used in this verse in the NT, but 7 times in the Greek OT (LXX or Septuigent), connected with poisoned drinking water in Jer 9:15 and 23:15); it will poison a third of the earth's water supply. This is similar to what God did in Egypt in Exodus 7:20.

There are no data on the deaths that will occur as a result of the first two trumpets, but here John writes, "many men died" as a result of the poisonous waters. Most cities receive their water supply from rivers or lakes, which will be exposed to this ambient pollution.

There is a growing sense that life on earth is coming to an end, but still most refuse to repent. The deaths in the first three trumpets will be collateral damage, but the sixth trumpet will directly kill sinners that survive (9:15).

Reflection: Have you ever known a person to repent and accept Christ because of his experience going through catastrophe?

D. THE FOURTH TRUMPET (8:12-13) – ATMOSPHERIC

8:12

Then the fourth angel sounded: And a third of the sun was struck, a third of the moon, and a third of the stars, so that a third of them were darkened. A third of the day did not shine, and likewise the night.

8:12 The judgments shifted from the earth surface to the solar system in a dramatic fashion. One can only imagine the think tanks, conferences, and strategies that scientists will call to resolve these events, of course, without any possible reference to the source being God's promised judgment. Only in the movies will mankind escape this destruction.

The sun, moon and stars were "struck" (Gk *plesso*, Latin, *plango*, *plaga*, "smitten"), not as just a blow, but as a disease or "plague" (as the derivative of this word in Rev 11:6; 16:21). This partial eclipse may last a while, but it is temporary, since later God will increase the heat from the sun in 16:8-9.

As a result the temperatures will plunge to unheard-of lows, killing crops, causing exaggerated and strange tides, creating unpredictable storms and huge loss of animal and human life. This dramatic day has been prophesied for hundreds of years before Christ.

Reflection: How will the surviving Jews understand these events as they reflect on these verses?
Isa 13:9-10

Ezek 32:7-8

Joe 2:10, 31

Joel 3:15

Amos 8:9

THE FINAL WARNING

8:13

And I looked, and I heard an angel flying through the midst of heaven, saying with a loud voice, "Woe, woe, woe to the inhabitants of the earth, because of the remaining blasts of the trumpet of the three angels who are about to sound!

8:13 These trumpets will sound in quick succession but things are about to get worse, so God gives another warning, as He will several more times before the end. For the Jewish reader of the OT prophets, they must know they are facing the judgments of the end of time.

Reflection: Notice how God describes his coming judgments as "eagles:"

Deut 28:49;

Hos 8:9

Hab 1:8

"Woes" are the warning of God's horrendous judgment; in this case, each woe refers to one of the final three trumpets (9:1-21; 11:15). It is sad how sin blinds men's minds to reality. But even when they recognize the cause of their calamity as being God's judgment (6:15-17), they will not repent, in fact, will hate God all the more.

Reflection: In following verses describe the justice of God in these judgments:
Rev. 9:20-21

Rev 16:9, 11

Will the Jews be hearing these verses in their ears: Heb 3:7-8, which is a translation of Psa 95:8?

CHAPTER 9

TRUMPET JUDGMENTS #5-6 AND WOES #1-2

"Until now the disasters have been impersonal, environmental or geological. Now they become personal, affecting nearly every person alive."

he fact that these final trumpets are given considerably more explanation implies that the judgments are becoming more severe, as will become self-evident.

E. THE FIFTH TRUMPET (9:1-11) - OPENING THE ABYSS

OPENING THE BOTTOMLESS PIT. 9:1-2

9:1

Then the fifth angel sounded: And I saw a star fallen from heaven to the earth. To him was given the key to the bottomless pit.

9:1a The fifth trumpet (and first "Woe") is directed by Satan, which may explain why it is a "woe"-judgment. Satan is committed to destroying God's creation. The "star" that fell from heaven is a metaphor since "it" is referred to as "him" (v.1) and "he" (v. 2) and "king" (v. 11), thus the metaphor refers to a person that fell to earth (See Isa 14:12-17 and Luke 10:18).

The question surfaces: If this is a reference to Satan, what was he doing in heaven in the first place? The amazing patience of our God is nowhere more evident than in His treatment of the horrible creature Satan.

For millennia Satan has been granted access to God's presence, where he incessantly accused the believers of their unworthiness before God (Rev. 12:10; Job 1:6). Finally this wickedness will come to an end in heaven as he is cast from God's presence definitively (Rev 12:7-9 will describes this event).

Reflection: What is one of his characteristics found in Rev 12:9? Do Christians ever help him in his task by their accusing and criticizing attitudes and actions toward other believers?

Jesus saw this same event and described it during His ministry, "So he said to them, "I saw Satan fall like lightning from heaven" (Luke 10:18).

9:1b This "woe" is reiterated in 12:12, "Woe to the inhabiters of the earth, for the devil is come down." Up till now the disasters have been impersonal, environmental or geological. Now they become personal affecting nearly everyone personally.

Why anyone would trust Satan or believe his lies is inconceivable, because he is totally committed to our destruction. He is limited now in

TRUMPET JUDGMENTS #5-6 AND WOES #1-2

the Church Age, but then he will be unrestricted except to the 144,000 and the two witnesses.

Reflection: Have you ever prayed a prayer of thanksgiving for 2 Thess 2:7?

Reflection: When Satan was given freedom to persuade Job to curse God, what did he do to him? See Job 2:4-10. This is what Satan wants to be able to do to all mankind. He hates God's creation.

9:1c The cast-out Satan is given the key to the Abyss (*abussos*, "bottomless pit" KJV), which is the abode of some of the demons or the present imprisonment of certain fallen angels (demons). This location will be Satan's incarceration during the reign of Christ (Rev 20:1-3). Evidently he is given the key temporarily to release his demon horde of fallen angels to afflict the earth. Later the "Beast" will come forth from the Abyss (11:7 and 17:8).

Reflection: How did Peter and Jude describe this place?

2 Pet 2:4

Jude 6-7

The demons that possessed the man of Gerasenes pleaded with Jesus not to send them to the Abyss (Luke 8:31). They, instead, pleaded to be sent into swine!

Reflection: What can be deduced about demons from this encounter?

According to Rev. 1:18, how could Satan ever get the keys to open the Abyss to release his imprisoned cohorts or to hell itself?

9:2

And he opened the bottomless pit, and smoke arose out of the pit like the smoke of a great furnace. So the sun and the air were darkened because of the smoke of the pit.

9:2 At a command from the fallen Satan, an opening occurs evidently in the earth's crust releasing enormous amounts of smoke and gasses from the earth's interior with such explosive power to launch the smoke and fumes into the upper atmosphere where it catches the jet stream, quickly blanketing the earth with smoke and darkening the sun and sky.

Reflection: How many times has the atmosphere been polluted with fumes and gasses from volcanic activities already?

LOCUST WITH POWER AS SCORPIONS (9:3-5)

9:3

Then out of the smoke locusts came upon the earth. And to them was given power, as the scorpions of the earth have power.

9:3 Out of the smoke came unique locust-like creatures with stinging tails like a scorpion and they were given "power" (*exousia*, "authority, liberty to do as one pleases") of scorpions. These are a new species of huge insect-like animals described later (9:7-10). Their sting is very painful, but not lethal as some scorpions.

Swarms of locust can be enormous, covering thousands of miles. However, there has never been anything like either the massive swarms of these creatures or the locust-scorpion demon controlled creature committed to aggressively attacking every human being.

Imagine how they feel after being locked up in the Abyss since Satan's original heavenly rebellion before Creation, waiting to strike against everything God created with a vengeance. It should be noted that there are about two-dozen species of scorpions that are capable of killing a human.

Reflection: Have you been close to or bit by a scorpion? Will this demonic infestation cause many to repent? (See 9:20-21)

9:4

They were commanded not to harm the grass of the earth, or any green thing, or any tree, but only those men who do not have the seal of God on their foreheads.

9:4a Contrary to the previous Trumpets and the locust's nature, these creatures were prohibited from harming the physical creation or any green vegetation (only 2/3 left), but were to aggressively afflict "men" (*anthropos*, "generic term for mankind, men and women").

The fact that there even existed "green grass" indicates that a few months had passed since the first trumpet when "all the green grass" was scorched (8:7). The grass may have at least partially recovered in the interval.

9:4b In the darkened sky of the day and pitch black of night, strange flying scorpions that could only attack humans would sting everyone, except those with the "seal of God" (i.e., the 144,000 Jewish Christians). It appears that others who became Christians had to suffer along with the unbelievers through a number of the plagues, though some authors state that the "seal of God on their foreheads" (Rev 22:4) of any believer would protect him, but this is not very clear.

9:5

And they were not given authority to kill them, but to torment them for five months. Their torment was like the torment of a scorpion when it strikes a man."

9:5 They were likewise limited as to the time that they could afflict humans: only for five months, which happens to be the normal life-span of locusts (usually from May to September). Some authors suggest that each sting itself would last for 5 months.

Reflection: Have you ever had a bee sting or been bitten by a scorpion?

INABILITY TO SUICIDE

9:6

In those days men will seek death and will not find it; they will desire to die, and death will flee from them.

9:6 The incessant affliction of these demon-locusts would cause many to seek death, to no avail, even when they tried to suicide. All hope of surviving or things getting better were gone.

The land had been destroyed through innumerable earthquakes, volcanoes, sun-bursts scorching the earth, corpses everywhere, seas full of dead fish, water supplies poisoned, the atmosphere repeatedly filled with contaminants and finally the sulfur (?) stench of the smoke that blanketed the earth with its smell carrying with it this horde of demonic-locust-scorpions.

The demons had such control over the people that they prevented them from committing suicide, primarily in order to molest them even more.

Reflection: Have you ever gotten to a point of despair?

DESCRIPTION OF THE LOCUST (9:7-10)

9:7-9

The shape of the locusts was like horses prepared for battle. On their heads were crowns of something like gold, and their faces were like the faces of men. 8They had hair like women's hair, and their teeth were like lions' teeth. 9 And they had breastplates like breastplates of iron, and the sound of their wings was like the sound of chariots with many horses running into battle.

9:7-9 Now we will see how terrifying these supernatural demon-locusts appear when examined. Joel (2:4) described the locust plague of his day as horse-like, making similar sounds in their massive hordes. But there have never been insects or animals that will look like these beasts. Science fiction has invented comparable beasts, i.e., the "Species."

Can you imagine the terror on earth of having millions of such beasts unleashed against mankind? They have human faces indicating they are intelligent beings, long hair like a woman, and lion-like teeth (as vampires) just as Joel saw (1:6). They have armored plates making them invincible to weapons and impossible to resist. Their wings make a roaring noise as of chariots charging into battle (Joel 2:5, "the noise they make—like the rumbling of chariots… like a mighty army moving into battle"). This was the most fearsome sound of warfare in the ancient world.

Reflection: How would you like to live in terror? Can you imagine the terror in the eyes of everyone you meet?

LIMITED AFFLICTION

9:10

They had tails like scorpions, and there were stings in their tails. Their power was to hurt men five months.

9:10a These demoralizing and frightening beasts had stinging tails to inflict their venom, which indicates they had to be close to their victims to torture them. They could not kill men (9:4-5), but only torture them.

The fear and desperation of mankind gave a strong motivation for suicide, but even this was futile (9:6). God often used desperate situations to leave people no option but to call on Him; however, this generation refuses to turn to God except to curse Him.

Reflection: Have you ever known anyone this obstinate?

9:10b However, there are two limitations: they will not harm those with the seal of God and they will only do their evil for five months. Notice that their power will be "given" to them (they have no such power themselves), thus the same One who will give them this power could limit its use as well.

This indicates that God's sovereign power over demonic powers is always effective. At present, the demons are limited to willing listeners. If we consciously resist demonic influence and seduction (1 Peter 5:8-9), then the demon "will flee from you" (James 4:7). The believer, especially the 144,000, will have the authority to be free of this demonic terror.

THE KING OF THE DEMON-LOCUST

9:11

"And they had as king over them the angel of the bottomless pit, whose name in Hebrew is Abaddon, but in Greek he has the name Apollyon. ,"

9:11 Real locust do not have a leader (Prov 30:27), but these demon-beasts do. He is the "angel" of the Abyss. This is not Satan, who is the "prince of the power of the air" (Eph 2:2) and he does not go to the Abyss until after the Tribulation (20:1-3).

This is another high-ranking angel in Satan's hierarchy. His name is "Abaddon" (Heb) or "Apollyon" (Greek), which means in both languages, "Destroyer or Exterminator." At times Satan may appear as an "angel of light," but the name of this angel is more genuine to his character.

Reflection: How did Jesus describe this terrible period of time in Matt 24:21?

Note: These horrible tortures are not God's direct action. God will merely unleash these demonic hordes to do what they want to do to man. God only limits their destruction, but He is not the cause of it. Were it not for His limitations all humanity would be destroyed by these invincible demonic hordes.

God is teaching humanity that choosing to accept the Satanic lies and deceptions has dire consequences, that if not limited, can be devastating. He destroys his own followers. If man wants to believe Satan's lies, then He will give mankind the relationship with Satan they deserve.

WARNING OF MORE TO COME

9:12

One woe is past. Behold, still two more woes are coming after these things.

9:12 God is giving warnings with the purpose of encouraging people to repent and believe. If they persist in their unbelief and rebellion against God then they reap the consequences. God always will accept anyone who repents.

Likewise, this message will renew the hope of believers that survive to know that things are accelerating to a conclusion.

Reflection: By giving this warning of more to come, is this generating a fear in the hearts of men? Is this a good thing?

F. THE SIXTH TRUMPET (9:13-21)
ARMY OF 200 MILLION KILL 1/3 OF MANKIND

9:13

Then the sixth angel sounded: And I heard a voice from the four horns of the golden altar which is before God

9:13 The second Woe now begins with the sixth Trumpet judgment. The angel remains in the proximity of the Altar where the prayers of the Tribulation martyrs are requesting justice. The sixth Trumpet will unleash an even more severe demonic attacks on humanity; this one will be unrestrained and bring massive deaths to a third of the world's population. What a contrast with the scene of the sixth Trumpet judgment, which begins at the "four horns" of the altar (Ex 27:2) where sinners could cling to for mercy, but on earth no one is interested!

EXACT DAY OF EXECUTION

9:14-15

saying to the sixth angel who had the trumpet, "Release the four angels who are bound at the great river Euphrates." 15 So the four angels, who had been prepared for the hour and day and month and year, were released to kill a third of mankind.

9:14-15 Four angels have been bound at the River Euphrates, the most important river in the Middle East, which runs 1780 miles. It was related to the Garden of Eden (Gen 2:14) where sin began, the first murder was committed (Gen 4), the rebellious tower of Babel (origin of a complex of false religions that spread across the world) and the site of the captivity of Israel (Ps 137:1-4). This was the region of the first three major world powers that oppressed Israel (Assyria, Babylon and Medo-Persia). The River Euphrates in the north and the River of Egypt were the borders of the original Promise Land (Gen 15:18). Later it will be the launching point of the final siege against Israel at the battle of Armageddon (16:12-16).

Since demons are former angels, and the fact that they are "bound" (*deo*, "fasten with chains") would indicate that these are likely demons, being held back from attacking. The objective of this demonic army is to destroy a third of mankind.

At 7 billion by today's population, after 25% killed during the 4th seal (Rev 6:7-8), leaving 5.25 billion, then this judgment would mean the death of 1.732 billion people, leaving 3.5 billion (less those who died in other catastrophes). Thus, less than 50% of the population remains alive after the 6th Trumpet judgment!

Reflection: In the foreknowledge of God this date has been precisely set from eternity past. Only the Father knows when this moment will be (Matt 24:36). Global events are marching to an unseen clock that is never late.

Does this mean that the timing of all events in history is marching to a precise clock that foreknows events to the moment of their occurrences? How does this make you feel?

DESCRIPTION OF THE HORSEMEN

9:16-17

Now the number of the army of the horsemen was two hundred million; I heard the number of them. 17 And thus I saw the horses in the vision: those who sat on them had breastplates of fiery red, hyacinth blue, and sulfur yellow; and the heads of the horses were like the heads of lions; and out of their mouths came fire, smoke, and brimstone.

9:16 A standing Army of 200 million has seemed impossible until recent history. In 1965 the Chinese Red Army claimed to have an army of 200 million! (Time, May 21, 1965). John was told this figure at the time when the entire Roman Empire was about 40 million and the global population was estimated at 300 million. Is this description of these creatures in figurative language, or is it a first century attempt to describe modern warfare?

Since the description of the horses shows them having a lion-like head, whatever it referred to was unknown in John's contemporary warfare. Many feel that this is a demonic army using elements of hell: fire, smoke and brimstone.

John noted that it was the "horse"-vehicle that killed the people by incineration, not the rider. Whatever this army is, it is coming from the East and North from Israel or the Mediterranean, just as predicted in Daniel 11:44.

The dragon-like horses are either a historically unprecedented demonic invention never seen before, or an attempt by a first century witness to describe modern warfare, aircraft and weaponry.

THREE PLAGUES

9:18-19

By these three plagues a third of mankind was killed-- by the fire and the smoke and the brimstone which came out of their mouths. 19 For their power is in their mouth and in their tails; for their tails are like serpents, having heads; and with them they do harm.

9:18-19 Whatever spews out of these "mouths" will kill a third of the population of the world. In the chaos of these days this army could come from any number of sources humanly speaking. The motives of this war led by these four "angels" can only be speculated. Is this a political move to take over the chaotic world? Who is killed, likewise is not described.

The elements are similar to the destruction of Sodom and Gomorrah (Gen 19:24-28) and the common elements of hell itself (Rev. 14:10; 19:20; 20:10; 21:8). The victims are incinerated by fire, asphyxiated by smoke and brimstone (sulfur): a horrible way to die. The certainty of the passage is that God is pouring out His wrath on mankind who refuses to repent. Mercy is now history.

Not only does the weaponry spew out of the "mouth" or front, but likewise, extends out of its tail area. The "tails" have "heads" and "with them do harm." Modern helicopters can fire weapons in both directions.

There are a number of unanswered questions in this narrative, but explanations in future chapters should fill in some of the gaps. This is only one source of affliction in the Tribulation. While these judgments are occurring, the Antichrist is crating his own destruction, while attempting to bring mankind under his dominion.

UNREPENTANT MANKIND LIVES EVER MORE PERVERTED LIVES

9:20
But the rest of mankind, who were not killed by these plagues, did not repent of the works of their hands, that they should not worship demons, and idols of gold, silver, brass, stone, and wood, which can neither see nor hear nor walk.

9:20 After the deaths of over half of the population of the world in barely 4 years men are hardened in their self-destruction lifestyle. The world sees the worst catastrophe since the Flood, yet there is no brokenness or repentance. On the contrary, there is a deep dedication to idolatry, and trust in the Antichrist. The fire, smoke and sulfur ("brimstone") are called "plagues" because they are fatal.

Reflection: No one in this day will be able to plead ignorance of the knowledge of the gospel. The message of the 144,000 Jewish evangelists (7:1-8) as well as the multitude of Gentile evangelists who will lead multitudes to Christ (Matt 24:14); also the ministry of the two witnesses (11:1-14) and a special angel messenger in the sky (14:6-7). Why do men prefer to trust in idols, especially of the Antichrist?

RAMPANT PERVERSIONS

9:21

And they did not repent of their murders or their sorceries or their sexual immorality or their thefts.

9:21a The world's survivors are amazingly defiant refusing to believe in the Lamb of God. They prefer their sin and the Antichrist (13:4-8), ever hardening their own hearts (16:9, 11). So God complied with their wishes when He "blinded their eyes and He hardened their heart, so that they would not see with their eyes and perceive with their heart, and be converted…" (John 12:38-40).

Every vestige of civilization has been destroyed. To survive people must take what they can from the ruins, fighting off marauders, gangs and thugs. Drugs, when available are the only escape for many. Rape and pillage have become the norm.

Reflection: Is this fair of God to let this happen?

9:21b *First* of all, they would not repent of their idolatry (9:20). A turning from false belief in one's own goodness, or a belief in a false religion or god, to the Truth of the gospel message, always manifests genuine salvation.

The Septuagint (Greek translation of the OT) translates Psa 96:5 as, "All the gods of the peoples are demons." Paul stated the same message that "the things which the Gentiles sacrifice, they sacrifice to demons" (1 Cor 10:20).

There are no false gods, because none exists; however, there are supernatural demons that manifest themselves in dreams, visions, mystical encounters and even miracles to deceive the people (1 Tim 4:1).

Secondly, as a consequence, there will be uninhibited murders and violence (2 Tim 3:1-5, 13). People will follow the demon's lust for blood, cruelty and perversions.

Thirdly, John refers to the people's "sorceries" (*pharmakeia*, "the use of or the administering of drugs, poisoning" or the use of drugs to induce visions, hallucinations).

Fourthly, we see their "immorality" (*porneia*, "illicit sexual intercourse, adultery, fornication, homosexuality, lesbianism, bestiality, incest," etc.). This is the root English word for "pornography." Sexual perversions will become totally unchecked as in Sodom and Gomorrah.

Fifthly, people will refuse to repent of the "thefts" (*klemma*). Honesty and integrity will be gone from society as people fight for the basic necessities of life in a deteriorating world.

Reflection: Which situation is easier to live under: anti-Christian or moral perversion?

The Seventh Trumpet is delayed until 11:15-18. The author will fill in the other parallel events that are occurring to further demonstrate the justice of God in all His judgments.

CHAPTER 10

THE LITTLE BOOK

The message of the angel is:
"THERE SHOULD BE DELAY NO LONGER..."

This chapter describes a pause between the sixth and seventh trumpets, as there was between the sixth and seventh seal judgments. During this pause John will introduce seven "thunder" judgments that he will be prohibited to describe. There will be a similar pause between the sixth and seventh bowl judgment. These pauses are God's demonstration that He is in total control and that He has not forgotten His people because they will survive and be the ultimate victors over the destruction of the world system.

A. INTRODUCTION TO THE ANGEL (10:1-2)

10:1

I saw still another mighty angel coming down from heaven, clothed with a cloud. And a rainbow was on his head, his face was like the sun, and his feet like pillars of fire.

10:1-2 Another parenthetical section (10:1 thru 11:14) breaks the sequence of events to catch the reader up with other simultaneous events taking place on earth. Some want to see this angel as Jesus, who appeared as the Angel of Jehovah in the OT (Gen 16:13; 24:7; 31:11, 13), but there is no indication this angel is anything but an angel, however a "mighty" angel (*ischuros*, "strong of soul to sustain the attacks of Satan" – as 1 Jn 2:14).

The use of "other" (*allos*, "another of the same kind") indicates this angel is similar to the trumpet angels. Others speculate that it was Michael the archangel. He certainly was unusual with a rainbow around his head.

Seeing this splendor we are tempted to see him as more than angelic, but the description of the angelic splendor of Lucifer before his fall, typical among these "mighty" angels, compares to this image: "You had the seal of perfection.. perfect in beauty...

Every precious stone was your covering: the ruby, the topaz and the diamond; the beryl, the onyx and the jasper, the lapis azuli, the turquoise and the emerald; and the gold, the workmanship of your settings and sockets, was in you" (Ezek 28:11-13). Such covering would reflect all the colors of the rainbow.

The significance of a "rainbow" symbol to God's people in a day of

THE LITTLE BOOK

horrific destruction would have to remind them of the promise never to destroy the world by water (Gen 9:12-16). God is merciful and everything has a purpose. One of the greatest assurances God gives His people was written at the close of the OT in Malachi 3:16-4:2.

Reflection: How many promises can you find in this passage that will comfort those in the Tribulation?

(If the author wanted to describe an "angel" of a different category or kind, he would use the word *heteros*, "another of a different kind.")

LITTLE BOOK

10:2

He had a little book open in his hand. And he set his right foot on the sea and his left foot on the land.

10:2 The "little book" (*biblaridion*, "diminutive of 'book or scroll'") is distinguished from the scroll of chapter 5 and it is "open" (*anoigo*, perfect passive tense, "having been opened") to reveal the terrorizing judgments to come. Ezekiel saw a scroll and described it as "both sides were covered with funeral songs, other words of sorrow, and pronouncements of doom (Ezek 2:9-10 NLT).

This massive angel, like the Colossus of Rhodes, is standing with one foot in the sea and one on land to symbolize the authority of God over all realms of earthly life as was seen in 7:2.

A statue of Apollo, the sun god, built in Rhodes, an island between Crete and Turkey. This was one of the 7 wonders of the ancient world standing 105 feet tall. It was the greatest statue built in the ancient world. Ships would sail between its legs, but it was destroyed by earthquake in 227 BC.

Reflection: Would you like to see a book that described what was going to happen over the next few months? What if it were mostly terrible news? How would you react? Would you have believed then?

II. THE MESSAGE OF THE ANGEL (10:3-4) – SEVEN THUNDERS

10:3

and cried with a loud voice, as when a lion roars. When he cried out, seven thunders uttered their voices.

10:3 The angel makes a "loud voice" (*mega phone*, the two words combine in English to "megaphone") commensurate with his enormous size. The sound is similar to a "lion's roar," frightening, deep, and loud. Immediately seven Thunders responded. In Exodus 19:19 God spoke to Moses in thunders, "Moses spoke, and God thundered his reply for all to hear" (Ex 19:19 NLT).

When Paul met Jesus on the road to Damascus, the men with him "hearing a voice" (*phone*) uses the same word. The nature of the voice is evident on other occasions when God spoke as in 1 Sam 7:10, "The Lord thundered with a great thunder on that day against the Philistines and confused them, so that they were routed before Israel." Isaiah warned, "From the Lord of hosts you will be punished with thunder and earthquake and loud noise" (Isa 29:6). Amos also predicted a loud judgment cry (Amos 1:2; 3:8).

Reflection: What is the typical meaning of these loud announcements from God Himself?

SEVEN THUNDERS KEPT SECRET

10:4

Now when the seven thunders uttered their voices, I was about to write; but I heard a voice from heaven saying to me, "Seal up the things which the seven thunders uttered, and do not write them.

10:4a John heard "a voice (*phone*) from heaven, like the sound of many waters and like the sound of loud thunder, ..." (Rev 14:2). As Paul and the men with him heard this loud "voice," (Acts 9:5-7), so John understood the seven thunders and began to write them down, but John was told to "seal up" (*sphragizo*, "keep secret", Strong adds, "for security from Satan") what the seven thunders said. Daniel was also told to seal up part of the vision he saw (Dan 12:4).

Reflection: Why would God not tell us?

10:4b The purpose of the "revelation" is to reveal what is going to happen, not to conceal it, but some things people are not ready to know or understand.

Reflection: How should we understand things not revealed in these passages?

Deut 29:29

Daniel 12:9

John 16:12

2 Cor 12:4

III. ANNOUNCEMENT OF THE END IN IMMINENT (10:5-7)

10:5-6

The angel whom I saw standing on the sea and on the land raised up his hand to heaven 6 and swore by Him who lives forever and ever, who created heaven and the things that are in it, the earth and the things that are in it, and the sea and the things that are in it, that there should be delay no longer,

10:5-6 This magnificent angel raises his hand to make an oath (as in Deut 32:40) to emphasize the uttermost importance of what he was about to say. The prohibition of making oaths (Matt 5:34-35) was intended to prevent the use of swearing about something in order to deceive (typical of the Pharisees – Matt 23:16-22).

The angel stakes his statement on the eternal nature (as in 1:18; 4:9, 10; 15:7) and creative power (as in 4:11; 14:7) of the eternal God as evidenced by everything in the universe that what he is about to say is true.

The message is: THERE SHOULD BE DELAY NO LONGER. This specifically answers the prayer of the saints under the altar (6:10), though it is not immediate: there are still the Seven Bowl judgments (16:1-21), which would imply weeks or perhaps months to unfold, but once the seventh angel sounds the trumpet there will be an accelerated end to the Tribulation.

Finally the prayers of the saints for millennium will be answered, "thy kingdom come!" Indeed, this is the very shout of heaven when the seventh angel sounds the trumpet, "The kingdom of the world [will] become the kingdom of our Lord..." (11:15).

Reflection: With this announcement what characteristic of God has reached its end from 2 Pet 3:9?

10:7

but in the days of the sounding of the seventh angel, when he is about to sound, the mystery of God would be finished, as He declared to His servants the prophets.

10:7 The "mystery of God" refers to truths or realities that had previously been hidden from mankind by the wisdom of God. This mystery of God will "be finished" (*teleo*, Aorist tense, "immediate close of a process, fulfill, so that the thing done corresponds to what has been said," STRONG).

"Mystery" refers to previously unknown details that will only be revealed from this point to the end of the Revelation, with the new heavens and new earth being created. Many of the end-time prophets spoke of these times in generic terms like Daniel, Ezekiel, Isaiah, Jeremiah, Joel, Amos, and Zechariah.

In the midst of the chaos of the Tribulation, the end-time believers who read this will understand that God is in control of these horrendous events and the end is near, when He will return to earth to establish His earthly kingdom for a millennium.

Reflection: Why do you think it has been wise to keep these end-time events a "mystery" unrevealed?
Here are some other mysteries in the NT:

Eph 3:6 and Rom 11:25; 16:25 – Jews and Gentiles will become one body

Eph 1:9-10 – Will be revealed with this 7th Trumpet – the climax of history

Reflection: Do you really want the Second Coming of Christ?

Do you want Christ and His people vindicated? Do you believe justice

THE LITTLE BOOK

must be done?

Do you have friends who you could help avoid this terrible time by sharing the gospel now?

IV. EATING THE SCROLL (10:8-10)

10:8-9

Then the voice which I heard from heaven spoke to me again and said, "Go, take the little book which is open in the hand of the angel who stands on the sea and on the earth." 9 So I went to the angel and said to him, "Give me the little book." And he said to me, "Take and eat it; and it will make your stomach bitter, but it will be as sweet as honey in your mouth.

10:8-9 What is on the scroll? John was told to eat the scroll rather than keep it. Could it be that the 7 thunders are written on the scroll, which John had been restricted from describing.

The lesson could also be illustrating the receiving of divine revelation, which seems sweet to receive, but then one must proclaim it no matter how horrible the effects of evil and judgments on people. The eating symbolized the incorporating the Word of God into our being, our values, our purpose in life, etc. (Ps 19:10; J34 15:16; Ezek 3:1-3).

God's kingdom cannot be established without the destruction of Satan and all who willfully follow his deceit and lies.

Reflection: What are some sweet promises in God's Word for us today that have some bitter consequences?

10:10

Then I took the little book out of the angel's hand and ate it, and it was as sweet as honey in my mouth. But when I had eaten it, my stomach became bitter.

10:10 John's bitter taste reflects the "sorrow and anguish" similar to what Paul felt concerning the lost of Israel (Rom 9:1-3).

Reflection: Why did Jesus weep over Jerusalem? (Mat 26:76)

V. SECOND COMMISSION OF JOHN TO WARN THE NATIONS (10:11)

10:11

And he said to me, "You must prophesy again about many peoples, nations, tongues, and kings.

10:11 This second commissioning (first in 1:19) concerned the message of these final revelations to be given. What he was about to be told was yet more disastrous than anything previous. Once he knew the truth, it was his responsibility to declare the truth to "many" (*polus*, "much, large") or as large a number of people as possible.

His target audience was not one people, one nation, one tongue and one king, but many people groups, a lot of ethnic groups, as many languages as possible and many kings, until every people group had heard the gospel message (Matt 24:14; 28:19-20).

The result of this commission has been the Second-Coming motivation for world missions, which will result in the multitude (the "many") that will be raptured and appear in heaven at the beginning of the Tribulation period (See Rev. 5:9-10).

Reflection: How has your study of the Revelation and the Second Coming events affected your motivation and vision for world missions so far in this Book?

Reflection: Is this commission to John to tell the world of these end-time prophecies still important to us to fulfill?

Although after the sixth trumpet we are chronologically well into the last half of the Tribulation period some of these descriptions go back to the beginning of the second half of the Tribulation period when the seven trumpets were beginning, according to the time element in vs. 2, forty-two months or three and one-half years.

The best way to understand this chapter will be to take each description literally, unless obviously a figure of speech is used (i.e. the two olive trees). However, the discussion of the "temple of God" and the "holy city" [i.e., Jerusalem] has all the elements of being literal, since Paul spoke of the temple and the Antichrist in 2 Thes 2:4.

The seven thousand killed by the earthquake and the two witnesses all appear to be understood as accurate numbers of real people.

What is evident again and again, even in the midst of horrendous judgments against mankind, is the forgiving and seeking nature of our God. In the first half of the Tribulation one has to suppose the chief witnesses were the results of previous evangelism of the Church age who had postponed accepting Christ until the truth was obvious.

Most of this group was killed in the first half of the tribulation (7:9). In the second half of the tribulation the chief witnesses would be the remnant of the earlier believers, the 144,000 who would not be affected by the plagues and judgments against mankind (7:1-8), the "angel flying in midheaven" (14:6) and the two witnesses (chapter 11). Israel in the OT was a stereotype of the world in how they treated the messengers of God.

Reflection: Look up these verses and briefly write how prophets were received:

2 Kings 17:13-15

2 Chron 36:15-16

Jer 44:4-6

CHAPTER 11

THE TWO WITNESSES AND 7TH TRUMPET

"One of the final opportunities God gives the world are Two Witnesses ... These will be dangerous men who will generate a lot of animosity" n the midst of terrible rebellion and persecution there will be a remnant in Israel who will believe (Rom 9:27, "… it is the remnant that will be saved"). All through history God has raised up faithful witnesses to proclaim the truth without wavering, often in the face of horrible persecution . Now two amazing and bold witnesses to the truth rise to the forefront of the evangelistic proclamation in the midst of the tribulation and will continue in Jerusalem for 42 months before being killed just after the sounding of the Seventh Trumpet near the end of the tribulation period.

I. THE MEASUREMENT OF THE TEMPLE (11:1-2)

11:1

Then I was given a reed like a measuring rod. And the angel stood, saying, "Rise and measure the temple of God, the altar, and those who worship there.

Solomon's Temple

11:1 John is taken to Jerusalem and given the unusual task of measuring "the temple of God, the altar and those who worship there." The "reed" (*kalamos*, a plant that grows in the Jordan Valley) sometimes could reach fifteen or twenty feet in height. The stalk had a number of functions, but especially it was an ideal measuring stick. Ezekiel used such a rod to measure the millennial temple (Ezek 40:3-43:17).

What John saw gave him great encouragement, because, when he wrote the Revelation (95 AD), the Temple had been destroyed by the Romans 25 years previous in 70 AD, at which time Rome slaughtered over one million Jews and destroyed Jerusalem.

John had to measure the "temple" (*naos*, "sacred edifice or sanctuary, that is, the Holy Place and the Holy of Holies"), not the whole temple grounds, and specifically not the outer courts. Only priests could enter these two temple rooms. Worshipers could only gather around the brazen altar of sacrifice. Somehow the temple will be rebuilt in Jerusalem during the first half of the Tribulation period and orthodox Jews will again offer sacrifices according to Mosaic Law.

After a brief period of time the temple will be desecrated ("abomination of desolation" – Dan 9:27; 12:11; Matt 24:15) by the Antichrist (2 Thes 2:4) and the Jews will lose control of Jerusalem at the mid-point through the Tribulation.

The Antichrist will seek to rule the world and be worshipped (Rev 13:15) by all people. In our text, John was to count the worshipers who came to the temple.

Reflection: We don't know the results of this measuring, so one has to ask: who was the beneficiary of this measurement? How many will survive according to Zechariah 13:8-9?

GENTILES TREADING JERUSALEM

11:2

But leave out the court which is outside the temple, and do not measure it, for it has been given to the Gentiles. And they will tread the holy city underfoot for forty-two months.

11:2 The outer courtyard was not to be measured, because it was given over to the Gentiles. Today the temple grounds are under the control of Muslim Gentiles (non-Jews). Somehow they will relinquish control of the temple grounds to permit the building of the Jewish temple: an impossibility today.

However, the genius Antichrist will negotiate this as part of the covenant Israel will make with him (Dan 9:27) at the beginning of the 7-year Tribulation period. The "holy city" (Jerusalem) later will be ("trampled") under Gentile rule for 42 months of the Tribulation period.

Since the temple will be built during the first half of the 7 years and sacrifices reinstituted, this 42 month period must apply to the second half, when massive opposition and holocausts are instituted against the Jewish people and Christians.

Reflection: Which Christians ever see the reconstruction of the temple according to the pre-tribulation rapture view?

The Bible refers to five temples that followed the model of the Tabernacle (Ex 25ff): (1) Solomon's temple completed in 960 BC (1 Kgs 7-8) which was destroyed in 586 BC, (2) Zerubabel's rebuilt temple after the exile (516 BC), (3) Herod's renovated temple (at the time of Christ) was finished by 20 BC and destroyed in 70 AD by the Romans, (4) Tribulation temple (described in our text with the restoration of sacrificing, Matt 24:15; 2 Thes 2:4; Dan 9:27; 12:11), (5) Millennial temple will be built by the Lord himself (Isa 66:20-23; Ezek 40-48; Hag 2:9; Zech 6:12-13). In the New Jerusalem there will be no temple (Rev 21:22).

II. THE MINISTRY OF THE TWO WITNESSES (11:3-6)

A. THE PRINCIPLE OF THEIR MINISTRY

11:3

And I will give power to my two witnesses, and they will prophesy one thousand two hundred and sixty days, clothed in sackcloth.

11:3a One of the final opportunities that God gives the world are these "two witnesses" (*martus*, "witness in a legal sense, or one who is a spectator of anything," from which we get the English word "martyr"), so He specially empowers them to incinerate their enemies (11:5), stop the rain at will or turn water into blood and to strike the world with plagues at will (11:6). These will be dangerous men and will generate a lot of animosity.

These two witnesses will be dressed in "sackcloth", which depicts mourning and contrition (Jer 4:8; Matt 11:21), because of the compromise Israel made with the Antichrist and the devastation in Jerusalem caused by the Antichrist.

11:3b They are called to be witnesses and their ministry is called "prophecy" (11:6). The witnesses proclaim all that they have seen (witness) and what they will have been told by revelation (prophecy). They will be warning all who will hear or through broadcasting of the disasters of the last half of the Tribulation before Christ returns, while calling people to repent and have faith in Jesus Christ.

Their ministry will last 1,260 days (i.e. 3 ½ years), which coincides with the terrible oppression of the Antichrist in Jerusalem when many Jews flee for their lives (Rev 12:6). Sometimes referred to as 3 and one-half years, or 42 months (divided by 12 = 3 ½), or 1260 days (divided by 30 days, which are the days in a Jewish calendar month) = 42 months = 3 ½ years. These are synonyms.

The Bible requires that two people's testimony is necessary to confirm a fact or a truth (Deut 17:6; 19:15; Matt 18:16; John 8:17; 2 Cor 13:1; 1 Tim 5:19; Heb 10:28).

A. THE POWERS OF THE WITNESSES (11:4-6)

11:4

These are the two olive trees and the two lampstands standing before the God of the earth.

11:4a The "two olive trees and two lampstands" remind the reader of the vision of Zechariah (4:3, 12), who likewise saw the same vision. When he asked the angel who the two olive trees were, he was told, "These are the two who are anointed to serve the Lord of all the earth" (4:14), that is, they are prophets or special witnesses of God.

The two lampstands may refer to the Gentile believers and the believing Jewish remnant, as in Zechariah the single lampstand referred to Israel. These witnesses will not have an easy assignment, in fact, it will be probably the most difficult ever given to mortal man.

Reflection: Do you shrink back from what God is challenging you to do?

11:5

And if anyone wants to harm them, fire proceeds from their mouth and devours their enemies. And if anyone wants to harm them, he must be killed in this manner.

11:5 The two types of actions of each of these two witnesses are remarkably similar to Moses and Elijah who witnessed against Pharaoh and Ahab (both similar or types of the Antichrist): fire consuming enemies and the power to stop any rain from falling (as Elijah); and the power to turn bodies of water into blood and cause all sorts of plagues (as Moses). Malachi gave a prophecy that Elijah would come again "before that great and terrible day of the Lord" (Mal 4:5,6), which is reiterated in Matt 17:11 (Acts 3:21).

The death and burial of Moses is shrouded in mystery (Deut 34:5,6) and later Michael contended with Satan over the body of Moses (Jude 9). The Jews expected a Moses-like prophet to come at some point in the future (John 6:14, which was a misunderstanding from Deut 18:18 – Moses referred to the Messiah).

Then came the remarkable scene of the Transfiguration, when Jesus demonstrated His heavenly glory. He appeared with Moses and Elijah at his side (Matt 17:2-3), which anticipated the Second Coming.

Reflection: Do you see any reason in this text that would require an allegorical interpretation, instead of a literal one?

11:6

These have power to shut heaven, so that no rain falls in the days of their prophecy; and they have power over waters to turn them to blood, and to strike the earth with all plagues, as often as they desire.

11:6 Whether these two witnesses are actually Moses (or Enoch?) and Elijah, they will have similar powers. If God gave one such powers, he could give it to another. Anyone seeking to do them harm will be incinerated with "fire which proceeds out of their mouths" (v. 5) as in the OT.

The miracles were to protect and authenticate these messengers as true prophets. In a world of chaos and collapse, false religions, agnostics and every perversion imaginable, and rampant crimes, all people will be able to do to these prophets is listen to them.

Reflection: Is God just in allowing this destruction to occur?

With already poisoned water supplies from the third trumpet judgment (8:10-11), now this 3 ½ year drought during their preaching will only add to their torment and the devastation to crops and the loss of human and animal life through thirst.

To make matters worse, they will have the power to change into blood what water might be left . Then they will strike the earth with plagues as often as they desire. They will be identified with the wrath of God and thus will be hated as equally as they hate God.

Reflection: How do you incorporate the concept that God will send such witnesses to the world into your view of God's nature?

(This is not unprecedented in Scriptures: Fire proceeded from the presence of the Lord in Lev 10:2; Num 11:1; 16:35; and Psa 106:17-18.)

(Exactly the time that Elijah stopped the rain in Israel (James 5:17, also Luke 4:25).)

B. THE DEATH OF THE WITNESSES (11:7-10)

11:7

When they finish their testimony, the beast that ascends out of the bottomless pit will make war against them, overcome them, and kill them.

11:7 God's protection will prevail until they have accomplished their mission. The word "finish" (teleo, "bring a process to a close, complete") is used of by the Apostle Paul, "I have finished my course" (2 Tim 4:2). This passage is the first mention of the "beast" (of 36 references in Revelation, mostly in chapters 13 and 17) that has come out of the abyss (as the demonic locust in 9:1-12) who will overcome and kill the two witnesses.

There have been many "antichrists" in history (i.e. Caigula, Nero, Stalin and Hitler), as John declared in 1 Jn 2:18 (see also 2 Thess 2:7), but none like this future leader. One has to wonder what is meant by the phrase that he "will make war against them."

Two lonely prophets the object of a war! Once successful here he makes war on all the saints or believers (12:17). Daniel saw the same vision where the "little horn" prevailed against the saints. The Antichrist will only prevail here because the purpose of the two prophets will have been fulfilled ("they... finish[ed] their testimony"].

Reflection: Likewise, our God will preserve us in the midst of hazardous duty until our mission is complete. Can you rest in this and not be afraid to take on challenging tasks for His glory?

(The "beast" is not Satan, who is referred to as a "dragon" (12:3, 9), but rather the Antichrist, who is the Satan inspired world leader who imitates Christ, demands to be worshiped (13:1-8). Though a mortal man, the Antichrist is empowered by demons coming from the abyss.)

THE GREAT CITY

11:8

And their dead bodies will lie in the street of the great city, which spiritually is called Sodom and Egypt, where also our Lord was crucified.

11:8 Meanwhile, the corpses of the two witnesses are left in the street in Jerusalem for all to see where they were killed . This may be to further desecrate their bodies and dishonor them or perhaps because of fear of getting close to the dreaded prophets. In the law, such bodies were to be buried the same day (Deut 21:22-23).

The "great city," which is identified as Jerusalem, is called "Sodom and Egypt," to demonstrate that the Jewish capital has become corrupt, perverted and the enemy to all that is called God.

Furthermore, with cunning, deceit and charisma the Antichrist will make Jerusalem the seat of his reign over the world (2 Thess 2:3-4). Jerusalem becomes the center of global idolatrous apostasy as Babylon originally was and then Rome has been through Church History.

Reflection:: Can you handle being disgraced by this world if you honor the Lord in your life? Can you handle the thought of being a martyr?

DEATH OF THE TWO WITNESSES

11:9-10

Then those from the peoples, tribes, tongues, and nations will see their dead bodies three-and-a-half days, and not allow their dead bodies to be put into graves. 10 And those who dwell on the earth will rejoice over them, make merry, and send gifts to one another, because these two prophets tormented those who dwell on the earth.

11:9-10 His victory over the two witnesses will again catapult the Antichrist into world renown. He will soon dominate all people groups (13:7). These groups of "people, tribes, tongues, and nations" will be committed to the Antichrist and will celebrate the death of the witnesses.

These survivors will now reject whatever witness to the gospel they have heard from earlier Christians, thus they will become easily deceived by the Antichrist. Believers in these groups will have been raptured (Rev 5) or killed for their testimony (Rev 7). Now all "those who dwell on earth..." (v. 10) will witness the martyrdom thanks to a technological capability that has only been possible since the late 1980's with the advent of television and Internet connections.

This passage is the only reference to the word "rejoice" in the Revelation and it refers to celebrating the death of these two prophets. Finally their tormenting ministry will be over. The description of the celebration that will follow sounds like Christmas or the Jewish Feast of Purim (Esther 9:19-22), but this celebration is motivated by finally being able to terminate the two witnesses.

This "spirit of antichrist" is evident when worldly criticism or rejoicing is expressed at the death of godly leaders. Anyone who calls the people to repent of their sins will face the same opposition. If one seeks to please everyone or to make others happy or to be appreciated by everyone, it will be very difficult to accomplish what the Lord wants him to do.

Reflection: Can you see why these witnesses could never worry about what other people thought of them or approved of their ministry?

C. THE RESURRECTION OF THE WITNESSES (11:11-13)

11:11-12

Now after the three-and-a-half days the breath of life from God entered them, and they stood on their feet, and great fear fell on those who saw them. 12 And they heard a loud voice from heaven saying to them, "Come up here." And they ascended to heaven in a cloud, and their enemies saw them.

11:11-12 After 3 ½ days of disgrace and scorn lying an the open street, giving plenty of time for the whole world to see them, suddenly the "breath of life from God entered them" and the stood to their feet, with everyone looking.

The terror came from their amazement at their resuscitation and/or the return of their power to torment the world with a vengeance. Almost as suddenly there was a loud voice , evidently to be heard by observers in Jerusalem, saying "Come up here." These were the same words spoken to John when he was called up to heaven in Rev 4:1.

The two witnesses suddenly begin to ascend towards the sky entering into a cloud as they disappear. This description compares to the departure of Jesus (Acts 1:9) and those who will be raptured before the Tribulation Period (1 Thess 4:16-17). The point is: the living God of heaven (not the Antichrist) has the authority over the "breath of life" in mankind, and only those who believe in Christ will live with Him forever.

Mid-tribulationists make this the moment of the Rapture of the Church, that is, the Church has passed through all the disasters of the Seals and Trumpets. They consider that the real Tribulation does not begin until the 7th Trumpet, which occurs in 11:15. They consider the "saints" in Dan 7:25 to be the Church (not Israel) and the division of the period (Dan 9:27) to mean that the Church must suffer through the first half of the Tribulation.

11:13

In the same hour there was a great earthquake, and a tenth of the city fell. In the earthquake seven thousand people were killed, and the rest were afraid and gave glory to the God of heaven.

11:13 The ascension of the two witnesses was marked by a dramatic earthquake, which will occur within the same hour, making the connection indisputable. This quake will destroy a tenth of the city of Jerusalem, which sits near a geological fault line. This time 7,000 residents of Jerusalem will be killed as a judgment from God. The survivors will be "afraid and give glory to the God of heaven." Ezekiel prophesized of an earthquake that would precede the end of time (Ezekiel 38:19-20). It could be that this means the survivors will recognize the fallacy of their anti-God beliefs and will be converted or that they will recognize the obvious hand of God in what transpires (that is in itself giving Him glory), but will not submit to Him personally and unconditionally. This may be the key to the Jewish revival in the Tribulation (Rom 11:4-5, 26). One day everyone, willingly or not, will bow the knee to Jesus (Phil 2:10) and declare Him as the only God.

Reflection: If forced to bow the knee to Jesus before the throne of God, will they be saved?

It is interesting that there was an earthquake at the death of Jesus on the cross (Matt 27:64) and at the resurrection of Jesus (Matt 28:2).

THE TWO WITNESSES AND 7TH TRUMPET

III. THE SEVENTH TRUMPET (11:14-19)

11:14
The second woe is past. Behold, the third woe is coming quickly

11:14 The flying eagle had warned of three "woes" of terror (8:13), but only two had passed (the first in 9:1-12; the second in 9:13-21, and 11:1-13). This woe will come "quickly" (*tachu*, "speedily, suddenly"), that is, there will be no holding it back once it starts. Most of the uses of this word refers to the second coming, but here it is the last judgment.

This will be the final count-down to the battle of Armageddon (11:18) with no way to avoid the coming catastrophe.

Reflection: When you are warned of coming consequences, how to you respond? Is it natural to you to be rebellious, unbelieving that the threat is real, or rather to be broken and take the warning and change?

A. PRAISE FOR HIS COMING REIGN (11:15-17)

11:15
Then the seventh angel sounded: And there were loud voices in heaven, saying, "The kingdoms of this world have become the kingdoms of our Lord and of His Christ, and He shall reign forever and ever!

11:15a Following the interlude since 9:21 (as there was an interlude between the 6th and 7th seal (6:1—8:5), the scene shifts from Jerusalem to the heavenly throne. The actual events will be described in Rev 16. The chapters 12-14 walk through the Tribulation period again from man's perspective. This is the beginning of the end..

This Trumpet may cover the last 6 months or less of the seven years of Tribulation. However, the heavenly multitudes know where it is all going: "the kingdoms of this world have become the kingdoms of our Lord and of His Christ..."

These final judgments are no longer partial, but complete destruction of the old world system in preparation for a new beginning to humanity. This is so certain to happen that the angels are singing as though it had already happened. Daniel had seen this moment when he wrote, "During the reign of those kings, the God of heaven will set up a kingdom that will never be destroyed; no one will ever conquer it. It will shatter all the kingdoms into nothingness, but it will stand forever" (Dan 2:44).

This is the apex of all human and redemptive history; what all of time has waited to experience.

Reflection: This is the object of the "groaning" in Rom 8:22-25 that believers even now "with perseverance we wait eagerly for it." The waiting is over.

..."The kingdoms of this world have become the kingdoms of our Lord and of His Christ, and He shall reign forever and ever!

11:15b The translations miss an important truth. The word "kingdoms" (*basileia*, singular, "kingship, dominion") is not plural, but singular. All the different nations, cultures, language groups and politics are actually only one kingdom under one king.

This person is known in the Bible by different names, but basically he is the devil (Matt 4:1), or Satan (1 Tim 5:15). Three times in John's gospel Jesus called Satan "the ruler of this world" (John 12:31; 14:30;16:11).

During the Tribulation all mankind will unite under one visible kingdom under the Antichrist/Beast in Rev 13:1-4. Satan will not give up without a struggle. He has dominated the world scene for thousands of years and now will lose it in a few months.

The verb "has become" (*ginomai*, aorist tense) is considered a proleptic aorist. This is a future event that is so certain to happen that it is spoken of as though it already had occurred.

(Name such as the accuser (Rev 12:1), the adversary (1 Pet 5:8), Beelzebul (John 17:15), the god of this world (2 Cor 4:4), the prince of the power of the air (Eph 2:2), the roaring lion (1 Pet 5:8), the ruler of the demons (Mark 3:22), the ruler of this world (John 12:31), the serpent of old (Rev 12:9; 20:2), and the tempter (1 Thess 3:5).)

11:15c In the timeless heavenly scene that day is as though it had arrived, though time must lapse before it is an earthly reality. Often there is no distinguishing between the early millennial kingdom and the eternal kingdom. At the end of the millennium there will be a relatively smooth transition into the eternal kingdom.

Reflection: If He is going to reign forever how does it make sense to let Him reign or rule over our lives now?

WORSHIPPING IN HEAVEN

11:16

And the twenty-four elders who sat before God on their thrones fell on their faces and worshiped God.

11:16 The twenty-four elders, as an expression of all the believers behind them, are ecstatic. It is finally happening.

The announcement that the final trumpet is about to sound and it is done, sends a rippling effect through the throngs of heaven as they will fall on their face before the throne (Repeated praise in 5:8, 14; 7:11; 19:4) to worship the King.

11:17

saying: "We give You thanks, O Lord God Almighty, The One who is and who was and who is to come, Because You have taken Your great power and reigned"

11:17 Their praise begins with thanksgiving (*eucharisteo*, present tense, "continually being grateful") to the Lord God Almighty (*pantokrator*, "he who holds sway over all things"). Nine out of ten uses of this word are found in the Book of Revelation (1:8; 4:8; 15:3; 16:7, 14; 19:6, 14; 21:22).

There are no mistakes or resistance to His unchangeable will. The eternal nature of Christ is expressed in the phrase "who is and who was and who is to come" means the ever present God at any point in history.

But the key reason for praise is that Christ has "taken" (*lambano*, perfect tense, "have taken with the hand, has lay hold of" as a completed action, without fail) your great power (*dunamis*, "inherent power, power residing in a thing by virtue of its nature") and "reigned" (*basileuo*, inceptive aorist tense, "begun to reign").

Reflection:: Everyone who knows Him, wants Him to reign over them now and forever in His kingdom. How does one make this happen today in our personal lives?

B. RAGE FOR HIS JUDGMENTS (11:18)

11:18

The nations were angry, and Your wrath has come, And those who fear Your name, small and great...

11:18a Not everyone trusts Him so they do not want Him to reign in any way. This verse alludes to Psa 99:1. They cannot stand the idea of Christ reigning over the whole earth (Psa 2:1-2, 4-5). Today a theocracy is held as the worse thing that could happen to mankind.

Christians in politics will be persecuted to avoid this happening. People are so hardened that the most painful judgment is taken as more reason to hate God (This rage will be described in chapters 12-19). The author's grandfather went to his grave hating God because he suffered a 3-year drought on a Kansas farm that broke him.

This hatred will fester into rage, motivating them to gather to fight against Him on the plain of Megiddo at the battle of *"Har-Magedon"* (Armagaddon) to stop Him from reigning over them. In spite of repeated opportunities to repent, they will harden their hearts against Christ, justifying their bitterness and rejection only to be punished forever in hell.

Reflection: How do you feel about Christ reigning over every aspect of your life now?

11:18b ... And the time of the dead, that they should be judged,
The "time" for judging (*kairos*, "a season, right time, limited period of time, decisive epoch"). There are a number of judgments in the Scripture. This is a reference to the "season" when the judgments will occur; it is not a reference to any one of the future judgments.

Each of the verbs in this passage is in the aorist tense which usually describes a past action, but it is so certain that it is spoken of as already having happened.

The fact that God will judge unbelievers is a reiterated truth of Scripture

(Isa 30:27-33). Eventually all wrong will be made right. That is justice. Christ brings judgment to His foes and rewards to His servants. The nature of both judgment and reward reflect the omnipotence of God; therefore, are beyond imagination.

Reflection: How does one live in the light of the inevitability of being judged for our whole life?

11:18c... And that You should reward Your servants the prophets and the saints,
Notice that it is the "dead" who are judged. It is not over until it is over! No failure is final. It is not the accumulation of good or bad that matters for the believer. Our sins are forgiven and never to be judged again.

Christ will forever reward our works that are useful for His kingdom. The ones rewarded in this passage are His "servants the prophets... saints and those who "reverence" (*phobeo*, "fear, terrify") your name, both small and great." There is nothing God prizes more than those committed to His purpose in this world.

Reflection: What are the implications of these verses?
Psa 19:11

Matt 5:11-12

Rom 8:18

Col 3:23-24

Rev 22:12

11:18d And should destroy those who destroy the earth.
The second aspect of the judgment is to "destroy those who destroy the earth" (*diaphtheiro*, "to change for the worse, to corrupt, of minds and morals; to consume").

This is not an ecological, but a moral judgment. It refers to those who pollute the world with their false beliefs, rebellion, anti-God attitude and followers of the "mystery of lawlessness" (2 Thess 2:7). When the corruption of sin reaches its peak, God will destroy the earth and create a new one.

Reflection: How is this described in these verses?

Rev 21:1

Isa 65:17

Isa 66:22

2 Pet 3:12-13

C. REVELATION OF HIS HEAVENLY TEMPLE (11:19)

11:19

Then the temple of God was opened in heaven, and the ark of His covenant was seen in His temple. And there were lightnings, noises, thunderings, an earthquake, and great hail.

11:19 Before the 7th trumpet there is an insight into the heavenly scene that depicts the Temple being fully opened in heaven. This would have been unimaginable in the OT. At the moment of Christ's death (Matt 27:50) the vial of the "temple" (*naos*, "the Holy Place") was torn from top to bottom (Matt 27:51).

This was an enormous and heavy curtain that hung from the top of the Temple to the ground, from side to side, making it impossible to see into the Holy of Holies. Only the High Priest entered here once a year (Heb 9:7). The Ark of the Covenant that never was seen by the Jewish people suddenly now is laid open for all to view.

This exposure declares openly God faithfulness to His covenant in saving His people and in punishing His enemies. The opening of the heavenly Temple releases the angels with the seven bowls.

Reflection: What comes out of the open temple?
Rev 14:15, 17

Rev 15:15

Rev 16:17

Reflection: In the light of these astonishing events that will surely take place, what conclusions does Peter draw about how we should live in 2 Peter 3:11?

CHAPTER 12

THE WOMAN AND THE MAN CHILD

"The conflict of the ages... Satan's frantic effort to thwart God's plan."

The chapters 12-15 describe the seven great persons of the end times.

Even though the Seventh Trumpet had sounded (11:15), the details of this final Trumpet Judgment will not be recorded until chapter 16. This parenthesis describes a number of concurrent events and relationships going on during the second half of the Great Tribulation period. All of these persons are introduced in Chapters 12-13:

(1) the woman clothed with the sun, who represents Israel (12:1-2);
(2) the red dragon with seven heads and ten horns, represents Satan (12:3-4);
(3) the male Child, represents Jesus (12:5-6);
(4) the archangel Michael, who casts Satan out of heaven (12:7-12);
(5) the offspring of the woman, persecuted by the dragon (12:13-17)
(6) the beast who came out of the sea, represents the future world dictator (13:2-10)
(7) the beast out of the earth, the false prophet (13:11-18).

The chronological sequence begins again in chapter 16. Meanwhile, John is told of the cause of the rebellion and persecution against God's people. The signs and symbols that John will use depict different aspects of these demonic inspired earthly trends.

This portion will describe the conflict of the ages. Revelation 6-11 describes the events leading up to the 7th Trumpet from the human perspective, and chapters 12-14 review this same time period giving the heavenly and demonic perspective. This portion will reveal Satan's frantic effort to thwart God's plan.

A. FIRST PERSON: THE PREGNANT WOMAN (12:1-2)

12:1

Now a great sign appeared in heaven: a woman clothed with the sun, with the moon under her feet, and on her head a garland of twelve stars.

12:1 The "great sign" (*mega semeion*, "huge symbol that point to a reality") is the give-away for symbolic language. This is the first of seven signs in the last half of Revelation (12:3; 13:13, 14; 15:1; 16:14; 19:20). The literal

THE WOMAN AND THE MAN CHILD

approach to interpreting Scripture allows for the use of symbolic language, but it always alludes to a literal reality. As a symbol this imagery is not of a literal woman, as with another symbolic woman, the harlot of 17:1-7.

There are several other symbolic women in Revelation: Jezebel (2:20) was false teacher who symbolizes paganism; the bride of Christ (2 Cor 11:2), which represents the Church, but the church is pictured as the virgin bride (2 Cor 11:2, the Lamb's wife in Rev. 19:7).

The context indicates that this woman represents Israel (v. 5), which is also depicted as a woman in the OT, i.e., the adulterous wife of *Yahweh* (Hos 2:2-13; Isa 50:1). The "sun...moon...eleven stars" (Joseph was the 12th star) are additional imagery that is associated with Israel in Joseph's dream in Gen 37:9-11.

This woman is "clothed with the sun" (*periballo*, perfect passive, "has been arrayed, put around") as the splendor of her status as a chosen nation ("For you are a people holy to the LORD your God. The LORD your God has chosen you to be a people for Himself, a special treasure above all the peoples on the face of the earth"- Deut 7:6). In spite of the way Israel has treated God, He is always giving her the best and considers her His chosen people.

Reflection: Does this illustrate the grace of God or the merit of Israel?

BIRTH OF MAN-CHILD

12:2

Then being with child, she cried out in labor and in pain to give birth.

12:2 The woman is "with child" (who will become the Messiah man-child), which further identifies her as Israel, since the Church did not exist yet. Being in labor, she "cried out" (*krazo*, present tense, "continually crying out or praying for vengeance") in "labor pains" (*odino*, use figuratively, "suffer greatly" for a good purpose as Gal 4:19), and "pain to give birth" (*basanizo*, present tense, "continually to test by the touchstone" used to test the purity of gold or silver, "to torture, vex with grievous pain, struggle against the wind").

These three verbs describe the status of Israel (Mic 4:9, 10), especially in the Tribulation period, as she waits for the Messiah to reveal

Himself. The nation will be in pain of oppression by Rome when the Messiah first comes and later she will be even more severely oppressed by the Antichrist. No nation in history has suffered as much and as long as Israel. Because she is favored and precious to God, she is hated and despised by Satan.

Reflection: Why is it that followers of Christ are so persecuted according to John 15:20?

Seven-headed Beast as Satan

B. SECOND PERSON: THE RED DRAGON WITH 7 HEADS AND 10 HORNS (12:3-4)

12:3

And another sign appeared in heaven: behold, a great, fiery red dragon having seven heads and ten horns, and seven diadems on his heads.

12:3 The Sign of the Red Dragon is clearly identified in the context (v. 9) as Satan, the archenemy of God and all that is His; thus, the color red for bloodshed. The 10 horns refer to 10 kings (Dan 7:24) who will reign simultaneously with the coming world ruler.

The multi-headed monster crowned with diadems or kingly crowns, depict the sequence of leaders led by the "god of this age" (2 Cor 4:4) whom God will allow to create havoc with willing naive power mongers. The seven heads of the Dragon have the crown during the period of this symbol, that is, during the ages before the Tribulation.

There is a similar vision in Rev 13:1 of the Beast where the crowns are now removed from the seven heads and placed on the ten horns, which represent the coalition of leaders ruling with the Antichrist in the Tribulation Period (17:12; Dan 7:23-25).

It should be noted again that this is a "sign," or a symbol of the Dragon's character, but his actual appearance is as a beautiful "angel of light" (2 Cor 11:14). Only in Revelation is he called a "Dragon" or "Serpent" as when he appeared in Gen 3.

Reflection: How does Satan instigate his will as described in 1 Tim 4:1-2?

THE WOMAN AND THE MAN CHILD

12:4

His tail drew a third of the stars of heaven and threw them to the earth. And the dragon stood before the woman who was ready to give birth, to devour her Child as soon as it was born.

12:4a The Dragon is called a "star falling from heaven to the earth" with the key to the bottomless pit. With the Satanic star came "a third of the stars in heaven." Satan's seductive powers deceived 1/3 of the angelic beings to join his revolt against God (verses 7 and 9 indicate these stars are angels).

The number of angels in his rebellion this group include (1) 1/3 of the heavenly angels, which are described as "myriads of myriads, and thousands of thousands." The word "myriad" is the highest number that the Greek language can express. (2) The locust-scorpion demons released from the pit in the fifth trumpet (9:1-3) number uncounted millions. (3) The demonic army of 200 million (9:16) that will be released from the pit then cross the Euphrates River and slaughter millions.

There is no suggestion of re-confining these demons to the pit, so they remain free to roam. In addition to these newly released fallen demon angels from the pit, there are millions of other demons that have roamed the earth for millennia deceiving and destroying God's human image-bearers (Eph 6:12; Col 2:15). This increased number of demons means there will be unprecedented demonic influence to destroy God's creation.

Reflection: Can angels be everywhere now? Can they know what you are thinking? Can they be resisted? (1 Peter 5:8-9)

12:4b The Dragon-Satan was present at the birth of the man-child to kill the woman's child. Typical tactic is to kill the godly. Cain was prompted to kill Abel (1 Jn 3:12 with Gen 4:7).

Satan was a "murderer from the beginning" (Jn 8:44), so when Christ was born he moved Herod to slaughter all the new born children in Bethlehem to hopefully destroy the Messiah (Matt 2:13, 16). His efforts to kill Jesus always failed (Luke 4:28-30), "because His [Jesus'] hour had not yet come" (Jn 7:30; 8:20).

When Satan moved the crowd from praising Him one day to shouting "Crucify Him" a day later, the change can only be attributed to demonic influence. What Satan sought to do by crucifying Jesus ends up becoming his own destruction.

Reflection: How is that explained in these verses?
Col 2:15

Heb 2:14

C. THIRD PERSON: THE MAN CHILD (12:5-6)

12:5

She bore a male Child who was to rule all nations with a rod of iron. And her Child was caught up to God and His throne.

12:5 The male Child is identified as the One who will "rule all nations," explains why Satan continually attempted to destroy anyone in the Messiah's ancestry to prevent His planned birth. Jesus Christ "was born of a descendant of David according to the flesh" (Rom 1:3; 9:5), thus humanly speaking Jesus came from Israel (the "woman" symbol).

When He accomplished redemption's plan so that God could be just in forgiving sinful men, He was taken up to heaven and exalted on His throne. This same One will rule with a "rod of iron" in the future millennial kingdom (12:10; 2:26-27; 11:15; 19:15).

In the meantime, though he succeeded at deceiving created man to reject and rebel against his Creator (Gen 3:15), he failed at stopping the completion of redemption's plan (Heb 1:3). Satan does not give up, but continues to destroy what he knows God wants, especially regarding Israel who will be at the center of the millennium (Zech 12:10-31:1; Rom 11:25-27).

Thus Israel has become Satan's special target. He is constantly seeking her destruction by seducing the world into the spirit of anti-Semitism, genocides and holocausts. His efforts at destroying the Church of Christ have likewise failed overall, though millions have been martyred. Now, in the midst of the Tribulation the intensity to destroy Israel and all believers becomes exponential (see vss. 13-17). This great conflict now will begin.

Reflection: Why is there such hatred for the Jews in many nations, often without cause?

12:6

Then the woman fled into the wilderness, where she has a place prepared by God, that they should feed her there one thousand two hundred and sixty days.

12:6a At the beginning of the seven-year period Israel had made a covenant with the Antichrist (to possibly secure the right for rebuilding the Temple?), not knowing the evil intent or nature of this world leader (see Dan 9:27).

In the middle of the seven year period, this wicked leader will cease the sacrifices in the new Temple, then will declare himself as God incarnate (2 Thes 2:4) demanding global worship. When Israel refuses the Antichrist, he declares war on Israel for 3 ½ years (1,260 days).

This is when Jesus said, "then those in Judea must flee to the mountains…then there will be great suffering unlike anything that has happened from the beginning of the world until now, or ever will happen" (Matt 24:16, 21).

Reflection: When does one stand and resist, and when does one flee for protection?

12:6b The provision for Israel for 1,260 days (42 months) was foretold by Hosea, "in the future I will allure her; I will lead her back into the wilderness, and speak tenderly to her…" (2:14). As God miraculously fed Israel in the wilderness for 40 years, now He will give provision and protection for the woman in the wilderness. The time span is more specific in 12:14, "a time and times and half a time," that is, 3 ½ years.

Reflection: What is meant by a "remnant"?

D. FOURTH PERSON: MICHAEL CAST SATAN OUT OF HEAVEN (12:7-12)

12:7

And war broke out in heaven: Michael and his angels fought with the dragon; and the dragon and his angels fought.

12:7 Not only is there war on earth, but war in the heavens. One of the mythical images of Satan is with pitchfork in hand tending to his followers in hell. But Satan is not in hell (yet), nor will be until the end of the millennium (20:7-10). Since there are degrees of punishment in hell according to your knowledge of reality (Mat 11:23-24), Satan knows the consequences of his rebellion at the beginning of creation, will merit him the worse punishment for eternity. His fervor to destroy God and all that is His, he thinks, is his only way out.

C. S. Lewis in *The Screwtape Letters*, (New York: Macmillan, 1961), p. 9, wrote, "There are two equal and opposite errors into which our race can fall about the devils. One is to disbelieve in their existence. The other is to believe, and to feel and excessive and unhealthy interest in them. They themselves are equally pleased by both errors and hail a materialist or a magician with the same delight."

Meanwhile, Satan, who cannot be in two places at once, must travel between heaven and earth "seeking someone to devour" (1 Peter 5:8) and to "deceive the whole world" (12:9), and while in heaven he attempts to discredit all that believe in Jesus (12:10) and create more rebellion among the angels.

The war with Satan and his fallen angels has been unending since the creation of man (Isa 14:12-14; Ezek 28:11-18). He is declared both "the god of this world" (2 Cor 4:4) and the leader of "spiritual forces of wickedness in the heavenly places" (Eph 6:12), until now. This war will reach a crescendo in the Tribulation.

Present activities include (1) seeking people to "devour" or destroy (1 Pet 5:8); (2) oppose the gospel (Matt 13:19, 37-39; Acts 13:10); (3) oppress individuals (Luke 13:10-16; Acts 10:38); (4) incites or entices sin to disrupt, discredit and pollute the church (Acts 5:1-11); (5) seduces humans to believe false teachings and lies about reality (1 Tim 4:1).

As successful as he is in the present time to deceive and destroy he is limited and restricted. In this future period he will be almost unlimited in his ability to deceive and destroy mankind. Only with the two witnesses and the 144,000 will he be temporarily limited.

Reflection: What would you say to these believers to encourage them?

EJECTION OF SATAN

12:8

but they did not prevail, nor was a place found for them in heaven any longer.

12:8 Something triggers the necessity for Michael to eject Satan and his hordes from his liberties in the heavenly scene. How this battle is fought is not revealed. These creatures operate in realms that are unknown to mortal man. They can travel at speeds beyond our imagination, can move mountains and utilize enormous "physico-spiritual energies" (Morris, *The Revelation Record*).

One glimpse of this on-going battle in heavenly realms is seen in Daniel 10, when an angel was sent to answer Daniel's prayer (Dan 10:12), but was delayed 3 weeks by a powerful demon who was in control of the Persian Empire (Dan 10:13). Michael had to come to this angel's defense to accomplish the mission.

In Daniel 12:1 the prophet is told, "at that time [the Tribulation Period] Michael, the great prince who stands guard over the sons of your people, will arise. And there will be a time of distress such as has never occurred since there was a nation until that time; and at that time your people, everyone who is found written in the book, will be rescued." This great battle in heavenly realm will surely be vicious and beyond anything humans could imagine.

The TV series "Heroes" of mutated super people perhaps is a glimpse into the last effort of Satan to retain his foothold before the throne. But in the end he will fail and be cast forever from the presence of God, losing his ability to accuse the believers (v.7). What will benefit heaven, will now totally pollute the earth (12:12).

When this event takes place is debated: the two options are either at the rapture or at the latest is mid-tribulation of the 3 ½ year mark. With and even greater vengeance, Satan attacks all that belongs to God, especially Israel.

Reflection: If the most powerful being in all creation focuses on your destruction, what would you do, especially if you lived in Israel?

WHAT IS GREAT IN HEAVEN IS TERRIBLE ON EARTH

12:9

So the great dragon was cast out, that serpent of old, called the Devil and Satan, who deceives the whole world; he was cast to the earth, and his angels were cast out with him.

12:9 Michael and the angelic armies are successful in cleansing heaven once and for all of satanic influence. Whenever this occurs in the 7 years, the increasing viciousness of the Antichrist creates unparalleled fear and panic throughout the world. Now Satan knows he only has a "short time" (v. 12). This is his second expulsion from heaven; the first was at the end of the first week of Creation (Isa 14:12; Luke 10:18).

This four-fold identity leaves no doubt as to who the Dragon is: (1) "serpent of old" (20:2) identifies him as the serpent in the Garden of Eden (Gen 3:1ff). Paul feared that this beguiling serpent had twisted the minds of the Corinthians into believing false concepts (2 Cor 11:3). (2) The Dragon is called the "Devil" (*diabolos*, "slander, defamer or false accuser;" See v. 10).

His perpetual task has been to discredit and slander as unworthy any follower of Christ before the angels and the throne of God. This is the world's greatest gossip. Thank God, "we have an Advocate [*parakletos*, "one who pleads another's cause before a judge, counsel for defense"] with the Father, Jesus Christ the righteous [One]" (1 Jn 2:1).

The promise that "God is for us, who can be against us?" means nothing to Satan. Then Paul questions "who will bring a charge against God's elect? God is the one who justifies; who is the one who condemns?" (Rom 8:31-33).

Whoever this person is (the devil) he has always been insignificant, but he never gives up to accomplish his evil intent. (3) The Dragon is "Satan" (*satanas*, "adversary, opposer"), who the most glorious created being of all creation, the "star of the morning" (Isa 14:12), but tragically his pride demanded that he be "like the Most High" (Isa 14:14). His rejection turned him into a bitter, vengeful enemy of his Creator and all creation.

Satan is determined to take the whole creation to hell with him. Though severely limited by God, he is free to persuade God's free creatures made in the image of God through his lies, deceit ("deceives," *planao*, "cause to stray, lead astray, or mislead"), manipulation and temptation. All who will not trust God's Word to be true will become open to joining Satan's way of thinking that God is not necessary and his lies are better than the truths of God.

Satan's chief earthly cohorts are identified by their hatred for Israel and the Church. Often these haters may not even know why they hate biblical Christianity so much. It is an emotional response.

The demons of Satan's army can perform "signs" or miracles to persuade the merchants and tycoons of the world to join his global financial kingdom (18:23) and the rest of the world to join him in his ultimate rebellion against God at Armageddon (16:14; 19:19).

There Satan and those deceived by him will be defeated in the bloody battle of Armageddon (16:14; 19:19), following which, he will be thrown into the abyss (bottomless pit) for 1,000 years. At the end of the millennium Satan will be released one final time to "come out to deceive the nations, which are in the four corners of the earth" (20:8).

Finally, his vain and foolish attempts to usurp God's throne utterly and finally fail when Satan, "the Beast and the false prophet," along with the demons and all the deceived, will be cast "into the lake of fire and brimstone[sulfur]" where they will be "tormented day and night forever and ever" (20:10).

(His famous deception is to convince the sinner that sin is harmless; no one will ever know; it does not harm anyone; you can get away with it this once; you deserve it or need it, etc.; then, once you have committed the sin, his accusing is endless; now you are worthless, everyone will know about it; you are destroyed; give up; you'll never be good enough to be a Christian, etc.)

Note: this place called the "lake of fire" was not prepared for humans, but for "the devil and his angels" (Matt 25:41). Only fools join in this absurd rebellion.

Now the full force of the Satanic powers for the first time in history is unleashed from three sources:
(1) the demons (fallen angels) that are operating on the earthly scene throughout world and Church history;
(2) the fallen angels that had been captive and reserved in the abyss

now suddenly released in form of the locust/scorpion creatures (9:1-3) and the 200 million who possessed the destructive army (9:13-16) when they are released in middle of the Tribulation; and

(3) now the myriads of angels that were in heaven with Satan and will fall to earth with him in the Tribulation period. This unparalleled and vast demonic horde is no longer restricted (except for the 144,000 and the 2 witnesses) from destroying God's creation.

Reflection: How does this concept give you motivation to witness today?

THE AMAZING PATIENCE OF OUR GOD – THE VICTORY IN HEAVEN

12:10

Then I heard a loud voice saying in heaven, "Now salvation, and strength, and the kingdom of our God, and the power of His Christ have come, for the accuser of our brethren, who accused them before our God day and night, has been cast down.

12:10a Such outbursts of praise are not unusual (i.e., chapters 4, 5, 7, 11, 15, 19), but this time the praise refers to the kingdom that is finally about to begin. The "salvation" here implies the broader sense of the word, which encompasses the salvation of individuals through the cross, but also the salvation of all creation, which groans within itself till this "deliverance" (Rom 8:19-22).

The "strength" (*dunamis*, "inherent power, residing in a thing by virtue of its nature") alludes to God's omnipotence, which assures that all things will work for the good of the establishing His kingdom (11:15). The "power (*exousia*, "ability or power of authority") of His Christ "have come" (*ginomai*, aorist tense of a future event, "absolutely will come to pass"). The celebration heralds fact that the purpose of history is about to take place in time and space. The anticipation must be electrifying in heaven.

Reflection: Do you live now to be of value for the fulfillment of His purpose now, so He can trust you for His purposes when He returns? Do you really want the kingdom of Christ to come quickly?

12:10b At long last the "accuser" (*kategoreo*, present tense, "continually makes accusation before a judge") of the believers is "cast down" (*kataballo*, "throw to the ground or earth"). The "accusations" go on day and night before the throne.

Notice that the only apparent accuser is Satan. God does not accuse; rather, He resolves the conflict by taking our punishment on the cross. Many are fearful of standing before Christ, believing that He will criticize us for all our sins.

However, He promised that our "sins and their iniquities will I remember no more" (Heb 8:12). The believer should never fear standing before the Lord. He paid for our sins on the cross so we will never be convicted of being unacceptable before the court of our holy God. Christ's shed blood-payment and the gift of His righteousness makes us perfectly righteous in His sight (2 Cor 5:21). Can you imagine the end of Satan's relentless slanderous accusation? Illustrations of his accusations are seen in Job 1:11 and 2:5.

Reflection: What would be his perpetual motivation to continually accusing believers?

THE VICTORY ON EARTH

12:11

And they overcame him by the blood of the Lamb and by the word of their testimony, and they did not love their lives to the death.

12:11 They "overcame" him (*nikao*, "conquer or came off victorious"), which seems to imply that the accusations were not just before the throne, but also will instigate accusations that will be faced by believers on earth during their lifetime. MacArthur states, "They did not defeat him by means of incantations, exorcisms, ritual formulas, or by 'binding' or rebuking him. Satan, being far more powerful than any human, is impervious to such fleshly tricks and gimmicks" (Revelation 12-22, p. 21). The three factors that will give these saints the victory will be:

(1) "by the blood of the Lamb" (1 Peter 1:18-19) as the basis of their confidence in death and eventual standing before the Lord. This is the "helmet of salvation" (Eph 6:17; 1 Thes 5:8). They knew they will never be rejected because they will trust in the blood of Christ as payment for their sins as well as for their whole being. They will know that they belong to Jesus (1 Cor 6:20; 7:23);

(2) by the "word of their testimony," which they will give under the severest tortures, always proclaiming the truth of Christ's death and coming again;

(3) by the fact that they "did not love their lives to the death." Another translation reads: "They did not love their lives so much as to shrink from death."[NIV] They will break away from attractions and loyalties that will make this commitment to Christ more difficult. Nothing here will compare to what awaits them in heaven (Rom 8:18; Phil 1:21, 23), and they will have "presented themselves," or given themselves, to God as an offering of thanksgiving for His mercy and grace (Rom 12:1-2), so their lives will no longer belong to them, but to the One who bought them with His blood (1 Cor 6:20). Thus death will hold no fear for them, so Satan will lose his power over them.

Reflection: Have you given your life totally over to the Lord? If He totally owns you, can He do with you whatever He wants, and you are fine with whatever that might be?

SATAN BEGINS PERSONAL ATTACKS ON EARTH

12:12

Therefore rejoice, O heavens, and you who dwell in them! Woe to the inhabitants of the earth and the sea! For the devil has come down to you, having great wrath, because he knows that he has a short time.

12:12 The heavens rejoice, but woe to the earth's inhabitants. Satan is coming in full force with "great wrath" (*thumos*, "violent outburst of rage, anger, boiling over"). His anger, resentment, bitterness and rage against all that belongs to God, on land and sea, will become an ongoing "woe" in addition to the three trumpet-woes (8:13; 9:12; 11:14). He will be furious over his new limitations (the earth will become his prison) and the scene of his impending doom. However, he does not believe it. Satan is determined to thwart God's plan for the future, but his time is short, that is, probably only the final 3 ½ years of the Tribulation.

He has been manipulating the Antichrist into absolute authority over the earth, and now he will turn his primary focus on using the Antichrist to destroy the Jews and Christians, whom he blames for all the calamities on earth. He will destroy their credibility, reputation, value to society, then convince the world that they must be eliminated from society and the world.

Reflection: What does John mean when he writes, "even now many antichrists have come" in 1 Jn 2:18? (See also 1 Jn 2:22; 4:3 and 2 Jn 7). Who would these people be today?

E. THE FIFTH PERSON: THE MAN CHILD (12:13-14)

12:13

Now when the dragon saw that he had been cast to the earth, he persecuted the woman who gave birth to the male Child.

12:13a The discourse returns to the subject of 12:6, which had been interrupted by the 12:7-12 episode, which described the war on earth. Satan will be furious. He will lose the war in heaven (12:8), lose access to God, and will no longer be able to accuse the Christians (12:10-11). He could not attack the Child, because He was taken to heaven (12:5). And now his time is short (12:12).

This historical attitude is racheted up to the maximum. If Satan can stop any promise from being fulfilled then God becomes a liar. If he can destroy Israel, then she cannot fulfill the prophecies in the millennium, thus God's Word fails.

The "spirit of antichrist" has permeated history in an unrelenting anti-Semitism. God has allowed the world to persecute Israel as a chastisement for their unbelief (Deut 28:15-68) to bring them back to Him. Satan's purpose in afflicting the Jews is to destroy them completely.

During the Church Age, the first major persecution of the Jews occurred during the First Crusades (1095-1099) as they marched across Europe and later in the Holy Lands. The Muslim and Jewish communities were annihilated.

England was the first country to expel all the Jews in 1290, followed by France in 1306 and Spain in 1492. The hatred against the Jews was augmented when they were blamed for the Black Plague (1348-1350).

The Russian Tsar killed tens of thousands of Jews and drove hundreds of thousands from the Russian Empire at the end of the 20th century. During Stalin's reign more than three million Jews were killed by 1920 and the Nazi party in Germany begin in the 1930's to systematically capture and kill more than 6 million Jews – more than half the Jewish population of Europe – were massacred in the holocaust.

Today the Muslim fundamentalist radicals are committed to eradicating the Jews and the Jewish nation, as well as the Christian nations – exactly the same commitment that the Antichrist will make universal.

Reflection: Have you ever met anyone with a strong anti-Semitic views?

12:13b The word "persecute" is *dioko*, "to make to run or flee, to pursue (in a hostile manner" as a result, during the Tribulation period, two-thirds of the Jews will be killed (Zech 13:8-9), but the remaining third will survive. In spite of the global anti-Semitism of the Tribulation Period a remnant will survive and be saved (Rom 11:25-29; Matt 24:13) and will help populate the coming kingdom of Christ on earth. The woman had "fled into the wilderness" (12:6), but God will care for her there (12:14).

Some hold that the remnant will flee to the Nabatean fortress of Petra in Edom, South of the Dead Sea. The Scripture is not specific as to where Israel will flee.

The Antichrist will rise in power as a protector of the Jewish people (Dan 9:27) and as a populists leader who can resolve the global crisis. Once his power is secure, he will break the pact with Israel and Satan will use him for his strategy to persecute and eradicate the Jewish people (Dan 11:31; 12:11; Matt 24:15-16; 2 Thes 2:3-4).

Reflection: What is the world's perspective of Israel today? Do some political leaders change their views once they are securely in their official position?

THE SURVIVOR'S ESCAPE THE FIRST WAVE OF ATTACKS

12:14

But the woman was given two wings of a great eagle, that she might fly into the wilderness to her place, where she is nourished for a time and times and half a time, from the presence of the serpent.

12:14 By a miraculous means, many in Israel will escape to the wilderness. The imagery of "two wings of a great eagle" (the largest bird in

Palestine) comes from the Exodus description of Israel's escape from Egypt, "You yourselves have seen what I did to the Egyptians, and how I bore you on eagles' wings, and brought you to Myself" (Ex 19:4), as well as the promised return from captivity in Isa 40:31, they will be "mounting up with wings as eagles" (See also Deut 32:10-11; Psa 91:4).

This metaphor could refer to the quickness of escape, the ease of escape or the means of escape to a place where she would be cared for. It is doubtful if this has any reference to aviation. There will be no alternative.

Whatever the process of evacuation and the duration of evading the Antichrist, it will be arduous, since the warning is given that pregnant women will be at risk (Matt 24:22) and the time must be shortened or no one will survive. It appears that part of the evasion tactic will be the aid that Gentiles offer as they intervene on behalf of the persecuted Jews (much as Corrie Ten Boom did in WWII).

After Jesus taught of the terrible time of Great Tribulation (Matt 24:15-51), He immediately taught about the Judgment of Nations (Sheep and Goats) at the end of the Tribulation Period. In the context, this judgment refers to the nations where the Jews will flee during the Tribulation.

The Gentiles that take care of Israel will be especially rewarded. In a providential way, God will allow many to escape the grasp of the Antichrist and the persecution occurring in the land of Israel, that will begin to spread worldwide.

The duration of this persecution is defined as "a time and times and half a time," or the second half of the 7 years of Tribulation. John, a Jewish author, uses a Hebraism for emphasis. Hebrew words have a singular, dual and a plural form (plural meaning is three or more). The phrase "time and times" means "one time plus two times" or a total of three.

This time frame coincides with the ministry of the two witnesses and the 144,000 whom the Antichrist could not harm. His frustrated attempts against these two groups may allow many of the other Jews to escape his dragnets. Robert Mounce wrote, "The antagonism directed against the church has its origin in the hatred of Satan for Christ."

Reflection: Can you give examples of people's reaction of hatred because of Christianity?

12:15

So the serpent spewed water out of his mouth like a flood after the woman, that he might cause her to be carried away by the flood.

12:15-The imagery of the flood like a river from the mouth of the Antichrist that overwhelms and drowns Israel like a tsunami and the escape like a bird (v14) is similar to Psalms 124.

The flood metaphor is common in the OT, referring to an overwhelming evil (Psa 18:4; 32:6; 69:1-2; 124:2-5; Nahum 1:8). The "flood" of lies and defamation to convince the world of anti-Semitism will become contagious among the earth's populations who, in turn, will seek out to destroy the Jewish nation and all Christians.

This satanically possessed Antichrist will perform miracles, call down fire from heaven (Rev 13:13; Matt 24:24), present persuasive arguments and "powerful delusion so that they will believe the lie" (2 Thess 2:9-11). What a contrast to the pure river of life that flows out from God's throne (Rev 22:1)!

Reflection: What deceit and lies are people believing today?

THE DIVINE PROTECTION IN THE SECOND ATTACK

12:16

But the earth helped the woman, and the earth opened its mouth and swallowed up the flood, which the dragon had spewed out of his mouth.

12:16 The earth opening up to swallow the flood is like the time in the rebellion of Korah when the earth opened up and destroyed Korah and his followers (Num 16:30-33). If this is a literal flood it is likely that Israel will concentrate in a low-lying sector, but more than likely it is a metaphor. God will use the earth to deliver Israel, as He did from Pharaoh by parting the Red Sea. God will intervene miraculously on behalf of His people (Ex 14:21-22; Isa 43:2).

Reflection: Why do His people not count on God's intervention? (See Isa 50:2).

THE BROADENING OF THE ATTACKS
AGAINST ALL BIBLICAL FAITH

12:17

Rather, if your enemy is hungry, feed him; if he is thirsty, give him a drink; for in doing this you will be heaping burning coals on his head.

12:17 "And" (*kai*) connects the escape of Israel with the rage of the Antichrist, who "was enraged" (*orgizo*, "provoke to anger"). Frustrated and unable to successfully wage war against the 144,000 or Israel in general, the Antichrist begins to pursue the "offspring" of Israel, i.e. the Gentile believers ("sons of Abraham by faith," Gal 3:7, 29). He pursues every expression of biblical faith in God (evident in 7:9-14, martyrs "from every nation, tribe, people and nation").

This group is identified by two characteristics: (1) they "keep the commandments of God" (*entole*, "an order, command, charge"). Submission and obedience to the Word of God is the mark of believers (Rev 14:12). Jesus had taught that one demonstrates his love to Jesus if he would "keep my commandments" (Jn 14:15, 21).

This is what makes Christians different: they take seriously and personally the 370 commandments for believers in the NT; (2) "have the testimony of Jesus Christ." This does not refer to the truths about Christ, but is talking about the truths that He gave the world when He was on earth as revealed in the NT.

As dark as these days may seem Satan's aggression against the Church and the Jewish nation will ultimately fail. At the sound of the Seventh trumpet the shout of heaven is "The kingdom of the world has become the kingdom of our Lord and of His Christ; and He will reign forever and ever" (11:15). Satan's attempts to stop the coming reign of Christ on earth will all fail.

The believers (Jews and Gentiles) who survive through the Tribulation will become the initial inhabitants of Christ's earthly kingdom for a thousand years. "But he who endures to the end shall be saved" (Matt 24:13).

There is already a vast spiritual battle against Israel and the Church in our present day, but soon it will escalate beyond the atrocities of the Inquisition and the Holocaust. The darkest time is yet to come, but there is a bright new day coming when Christ returns to reign.

CHAPTER 13

THE BEAST

Why is there a growing hatred for the Jews around the world?

As the world's economy, political infrastructure, health and physical structures collapse, the demand for a strong global leader to bring order to the world scene becomes universal. When, in a chaotic situation, such a person with amazing ability, knowledge, power, charisma and leadership arises, the world will fall at his feet.

F. THE SIXTH PERSON: THE BEAST OUT OF THE SEA

They will gladly grant him total dictatorial powers to solver their insurmountable problems. This king of the end times, Satan (the Dragon), presents himself in an unholy trinity of persons: the Dragon, the Beast of the sea (the Antichrist – 13:1-10) and the Beast of the earth (the false prophet – 13:11-18). Though many false Messiahs have claimed to be the One, just as Jesus predicted (Mark 13:6, 21-23), none compare to this monster.

The fourth beast of Daniel also had ten horns (Dan 7:7-8). In Rev 12 the Dragon was introduced as one who is in conflict with the woman (Israel) and her offspring (Christ and His followers). In Revelation 13 and 17 the beast has become the ruler of the world, but in Daniel 7 the little horn on the beast possessed the world ruler. Paul wrote of this demonic person, "Do you not remember that while I was still with you, I was telling you these things?" (2 Thes 2:5).

The Antichrist was well known in NT times, probably from Daniel 7. According to Daniel 7:24 there will be a ten-horn (ten-leader) confederation, then another horn (the Antichrist) will arise and destroy three of the other rulers and subjugate the remaining seven leaders in his rise to power, thus leaving a 7-leader confederation under the Antichrist. This chapter will give more details of the rage and strategy of the Dragon and his Beasts in this final conflict against God.

1. INTRODUCTION TO THE ANTICHRIST

13:1a

Then I stood on the sand of the sea. And I saw a beast rising up out of the sea, having seven heads and ten horns, and on his horns ten crowns...

13:1a John saw a beast coming up out of the sea. If we let the Scriptures

THE BEAST

interpret the symbols, we can be assured of a clear understanding. In Rev 17:15 the sea is explained as a symbol of humanity, so this beast will arise out of the Gentiles as a world leader. He is seen as having seven heads and ten horns with crowns (*diadema*, "kingly ornament," not won in athletics or battlefield). In Daniel 7:24 it is explained that the "ten horns are ten kings."

Beast of the sea, the Antichrist

This description sounds similar to the dragon in 12:3, except that the crowns are on the heads of the dragon and on the horns of the beast of the sea. Rev 17:9 reiterates Daniel's vision that the horns are kings. Their crowns symbolize their leadership or authority, but these horns are part of the Beast, so they follow him, and he, in turn, belongs to the Dragon, Satan.

Then in 17:10, John saw that by his time (100 AD) five of the seven world kings of Daniel had already fallen, and one still existed. The kingdom of John's day was the Roman Empire. Going backward then, the earlier four kings were of Greece, Babylon-Persia, Assyria, and Egypt. Since the fall of Rome there has been no global kingdom, though many have attempted to unify the nations of the world. None have or will succeed until the seventh head of Daniel is successful in the Tribulation. However, the stage is set in contemporary politics for such a global unification.

The ten horns represent the final form of Gentile world power. The Dragon has control over the seventh head with his crown, the Beast of the sea, has dominion over the ten horns with crowns, which are the Antichrist's global federation of nations.

These heads and horns are further described in 17:9-14. This invincible leader will have brought a temporary peace on earth, then will lead the world through horrible times, ultimately blaming the catastrophes on Israel which he will need to destroy for the sake of the survival of humanity.

Reflection: What are some of the reasons given for the hatred of the Jews today?

13:1b

... and on his heads a blasphemous name.

13:1b On each head is a "blasphemous" name (*blasphemias*, "slander, speech injurious to divine majesty"). As the naming of the first century emperors with a divine name was a common practice in John's day so it will be in the future. This blasphemous leader attributes his success to his divinity, claiming to be God (2 Thes 2:4).

2. DESCRIPTION OF THE ANTICHRIST

13:2

Now the beast which I saw was like a leopard, his feet were like the feet of a bear, and his mouth like the mouth of a lion. The dragon gave him his power, his throne, and great authority.

13:2a The three animals mentioned here are similar to those described by Daniel in chapter 7:4-8, which were identified as: a leopard (Greece—Dan 7:6); a bear (Media-Persia—Dan 7:5), a lion (Babylon—Dan 7:4); and a "terrible beast" (the Antichrist). John saw them in reverse chronological order, since he was looking backward in history, while Daniel was looking to the future. It seems as if the final world empire will be the composite of all the evil and power of the former empires.

13:2b This beast is the presentation of Satan's great imitation or counterfeit of Christ to the world. He is not Satan, though the Antichrist has many characteristics of Satan. He will be an extraordinary man, but he will be totally without morals ("lawless one"—2 Thes 2:3, 8,9) doing whatever he pleases (Dan 11:36), but also he can do "miracles, perform signs and false wonders and every kind of evil deception" (2 Thes 2:9-10). His power is so great that no one can oppose him; in fact, God has lifted all restraints from limiting his evil powers (2 Thes 2:7). People that are impressed with feelings and phenomena will be duped. He will be granted the authority that Satan promised Jesus in the wilderness (Matt 4:8-9), but Jesus refused to accept the proposition. It appears that this man accepts the offer.

Reflection: How is the literary Faust similar to the Antichrist?

3. MIRACULOUS DECEPTION AND MANIPULATED WORSHIP (13:3-5)

13:3

And I saw one of his heads as if it had been mortally wounded, and his deadly wound was healed. And all the world marveled and followed the beast.

13:3 Evidently not everyone will want to follow his leadership as the Antichrist resulting in an assassination attempt. Someone will deliver a wound "as if it had been mortally wounded" from a sword (13:14), yet he will survive, astonishing the entire world. This is referred to four more times in Revelation (13:12, 14; 17:8, 11), so it will be significant to his future power.

This healing will gain the sympathy even of possible enemies, and may be made to appear as a resurrection, which is beyond Satan's power, but it could be a supernatural healing of a near fatal wound. More than likely this refers to one of the "lying wonders" or a counterfeit resurrection made to appear supernatural, or it could possibly be a claim to be the reincarnation of Christ in the body of the Antichrist, which would be believable in today's worldview.

The fabricated lies will change from age to age. "All the world marveled" (*taumazo*, "be astonished, amazed" with the result of "honor, admire, worship") and "followed the beast". The world will follow anyone it admires, but here it implies venerates or worships.

Reflection: Can people today fake special healings to gain approval or popularity?

WORSHIP TO THE BEAST

13:4

So they worshiped the dragon who gave authority to the beast; and they worshiped the beast, saying, "Who is like the beast? Who is able to make war with him?"

13:4 At last Satan's goal is reached: he is worshipped, even though under false pretences. Isaiah 14:14 reveals that Lucifer had said, "I will make myself like the Most High." He fools the world into believing that he is Christ.

Paul described this group as those who "did not receive the love of the truth so as to be saved" (2 Thes 2:10), thus they are deceived easily and fall into worshipping the Antichrist.

This deception will be augmented and perpetuated by the False Prophet who will obligate or " makes the world and those who dwell in it to worship the first beast [Antichrist]" (Rev 13:12). By worshipping the Antichrist, the people are actually worshipping the Dragon or Satan. Paul wrote, "The things which the Gentiles sacrifice, they sacrifice to demons, and not to God" (1 Cor 10:20). When the unsaved think they are worshipping the god of their religion, they are actually worshipping the demon that was impersonating that god.

There is no hope here for such people. Their astonishment is expressed in two rhetorical questions: "Who is like the beast?" and "Who is able to make war with him?" Great leaders are unique or out of the ordinary in some facet of their lives and are admired for that quality. Surviving an assassination attempt for the cause of humanity gains great empathy from the world population. These questions may refer to the attempt on his life that failed.

Reflection: What if this person who attacked the Antichrist were to be a Jew? How do you think the Antichrist and the rest of the world would react?

LIMITED AUTHORITY TO BEAST

13:5

And he was given a mouth speaking great things and blasphemies, and he was given authority to continue for forty-two months.

13:5 Great leaders are acclaimed for their speaking ability, because they need someone to inspire and motivate the masses to cooperate and work together. This amazing leader "was given a mouth speaking great things." Some translations read, "speaking proud words" ([NET, NIV]) or "arrogant words" ([NAS]). Inspired by his possessing spirit, Satan, he will persuade, create false hopes, deceive and slander all that belongs to God (*blaspheme*).

The passive mode of the verb, "was given a mouth" points back to the God who is in control, not making things happen, but allowing free expression of the sinful nature unrestrained. His arrogance and self-exaltation peak when he "takes his seat in the temple of God, displaying himself as being God" (2 Thes 2:4).

Daniel described this person as having "a mouth uttering great boasts" (Dan 7:8) and "...arrogant things" (7:20). The Antichrist "will speak out against the Most High ... and will speak monstrous [presumptuous] things against the God of gods" (7:25 and 11:36).

THE BEAST

His followers are so hardened that God's judgments do not bring any repentance, but rather, they join the Antichrist in his tirades against God. In 16:9, the world follows their example after another catastrophe when "men were scorched with fierce heat; and they blasphemed the name of God who has the power over these plagues, and they did not repent…"

The Antichrist is given this power to persuade willing hearers for 42 months or the last half of the Tribulation period. His reign of terror will temporarily control the world.

Reflection: Do people ever blame God today when they are devastated or overwhelmed by losses? Why?

BLASPHEMY OF THE BEAST

13:6

Then he opened his mouth in blasphemy against God, to blaspheme His name, His tabernacle, and those who dwell in heaven.

13:6 The extreme of blasphemies only provokes more loyal followers to his rage against God. It is interesting to note on some campuses and in other social circles that the more outrageous or slanderous a claim or theory that discredits God and Christians, the more enthusiastic the followers become.

The target of the Antichrist's blasphemies is the "name" of God and all that it represents of God's nature and attributes. The blasphemies or slanders against the "tabernacle" in heaven and those who dwell in heaven" are to convince the living that heaven is a detestable place where no intelligent person would ever want to go. He continues his slanderous accusations against the believers in heaven as he had previously been allowed to do before the throne (12:10).

Reflection: When people are hurt how do they often instinctively respond to the source of their pain or rejection?

THE POWER OF THE BEAST

13:7

It was granted to him to make war with the saints and to overcome them. And authority was given him over every tribe, tongue, and nation.

13:7a Verses 5-7 describe a series of passive verbs that show how all of the abilities and authority were given to the Antichrist. They were not innate in his person. Here he "was granted" the ability to make war with the saints.

God gives the opportunity, but it is his sinful nature that manifests its fullness by attempting to destroy all that pertains to God. In this environment of blaspheming God, anyone who professes Christ as Savior stands out immediately and is eliminated (6:9-11; 7:9-17; 11:7; 17:6; Dan 7:25). One consolation is that for every believer who is killed, it brings the end of the Tribulation that much closer (6:10-11).

Jesus taught, "Do not fear those who kill the body but cannot kill the soul. But rather fear Him who is able to destroy both soul and body in hell" (Matt 10:28). In his paranoia the Antichrist will perceive the Jews and believers as threats to his authority. His power is only to make war and to physically kill, but he has no authority over their faith, which cannot be destroyed.

Paul wrote in similar times, "neither death, nor life, nor angels, nor principalities, nor things present, nor things to come, nor powers, nor height, nor depth, nor any other created thing, will be able to separate us from the love of God, which is in Christ Jesus our Lord" (Rom 8:38-39). Their faithfulness till death will be a repetition of Job's experience, "Even if he slays me, I will hope in him..." (Job 13:15).

Reflection: Can you see how God could permit your difficult circumstances?

And authority was given him over every tribe, tongue, and nation.

13:7b The Beast's authority will extend to "every tribe, tongue and nation" to demonstrate that there is no escape for any one on earth. His ambition to be dominate over the world will drive him to control "every tribe, tongue and nation." It is interesting that selfish ambition

THE BEAST

will motivate him to accomplish in a few months what the Church did not accomplished in 2,000 years!

Reflection: Why was it more important to the Antichrist to reach every people than it was for the church to do so?

THE DEVOTED OF THE ANTICHRIST

13:8

All who dwell on the earth will worship him, whose names have not been written in the Book of Life of the Lamb slain from the foundation of the world.

13:8 The phrase "all who dwell on the earth" refers to non-believers, since the term is defined by those "whose names have not been written in the Book of Life of the Lamb…" Seven times in the NT believers are described as those whose names are written in the book of life (3:5; 17:8; 20:12, 15; 21:27; Phil 4:3).

True believers are promised that their names would not be erased from the book of life (Rev 3:5), but are eternally saved through faith in Christ (John 3:15; 5:24; Acts 13:39; 16:31; Rom 3:22-30; 4:5; 10:9010; Gal 3:22-26; Eph 2:8-9).

On the other hand, unbelievers are not recorded in the book of life will all "perish, because they did not receive the love of the truth so as to be saved" (2 Thes 2:10). Furthermore, they rejected the truth because they "took pleasure in wickedness" (2 Thess 2:12).

Reflection: How are religious unbelievers so easily deceived to believe a lie?

PLEA TO UNDERSTAND THE REVELATION

13:9

If anyone has an ear, let him hear.

13:9 As John wrote to the seven churches, now he exhorts the inhabitants of the earth. Finally the dream of religious man: a universal world church will finally be realized – however, it is satanic and blasphemous. The appeal is for anyone in this future apostate world to turn from the Antichrist to God, but this was not the message to those in the churches (as in Rev 2-3), which could indicate that the Church has been raptured. This was a frequent challenge in the gospels (Matt 11:15; 13:9, 43; Mark 4:9, 23; Luke 8:8; 14:35) and fifteen times in the NT.

Three beasts: Satan, Antichrist and False prophet

It should be noted that the "hearing" does not refer to a mystical or audible sound from heaven, but rather to the written Word of God that man is accountable to know and obey.

There is a Hebraism behind this expression: in Hebrew the word for "hear" and "obey" are the same word, the context determining the meaning. Thus, to have an ear, means to have a predisposition to obey any applicable command. The "ear" and "heart" are practically synonymous.

Reflection: Do you really want to "hear" what God is saying in His Word? How can a person be predisposed to okay anything discovered in His Word?

A PROVERB OF DESTINY

13:10

He who leads into captivity shall go into captivity; he who kills with the sword must be killed with the sword. Here is the patience and the faith of the saints.

13:10 There is justice in the providence of God, but often it is not immediate. These slogans are designed to encourage the believers in the midst of this Tribulation. The horrible treatment they are receiving eventually will be just as bad for the ones who are causing the affliction on God's people.

Likewise it was a warning not to take matters into their own hands by attacking the enemies of God's people. The believer is to maintain his "steadfast endurance" (14:12). God's plan is set. Those who will suffer in prison will go to prison; those who will be killed, will be killed.

THE BEAST

These exact numbers are known and set. They are to let the beast do his worse and take it (1 Pet 4:14). No matter what happens, they will be victorious (Rom 8:37).

Reflection: How many principles for suffering can you derive from 1 Peter 2:19-24)?

Reflection: What is the "patience and faith" of believers? Is this passivism?

(Principles of 1 Pet 2:19-24:
(1) Suffering finds favor with God if done rightly;
(2) Suffering should be unjust;
(3) Keep doing good regardless;
(4) Enduring suffering is favor with God;
(5) We are called to suffer, that is, it is part of His plan for us;
(6) Following Christ means to suffer;
(7) Do not retaliate or answer back or justify yourself;
(8) Commit yourself to God and trust in His care;
(9) Cease from sin; (
10) Live righteously in obedience.

G. THE SEVENTH PERSON: THE BEAST OUT OF THE EARTH (13:11-18)

13:11

Then I saw another beast coming up out of the earth, and he had two horns like a lamb and spoke like a dragon.

13:11 This beast comes "out of the earth" (as opposed the first beast who came "out of the sea" or the Dragon who came out of the "abyss"). "Another" (*allos*, "another of the same kind") speaks of the close bond between the beasts. This second beast is referred to as the "false prophet" in 16:13, 19:20 and 20:10.

This beast only has two horns like a harmless lamb, but he speaks like the Dragon (or Satan). His speaking ability comes from Satan's ability to be "a liar and the father of lies" (John 8:44), as he demonstrated in the Garden of Eden (Gen 3:2-6) where he deceived the best and sharpest of God's creation.

Furthermore, Satan's pawns can "disguise themselves as servants of righteousness" (2 Cor 11:15), as they spread lies, deceits, and "doctrines of demons" (1 Tim 4:1), evidently as religious leaders. False prophets have proliferated throughout Scripture and easily deceive God's people through their lies.

Reflection: How are Christians suppose to avoid being deceived today? (See 1 Jn 4:1)

THE GREATEST WORSHIP LEADER

13:12

And he exercises all the authority of the first beast in his presence, and causes the earth and those who dwell in it to worship the first beast, whose deadly wound was healed.

13:12 This beast's speaking, (singing?) and miracle-working power focuses on worship experiences indicating that he is a religious leader who supports the political beast, the Antichrist, or the first beast. His "authority" is derived by demonic possession from the abyss and is focused on getting the world to "worship" the first beast. His influence becomes global in a short time span.

Religion is the key to any kingdom. Humans are worshippers of themselves, false gods or the true God. This person is distinct from the Antichrist, since he exercises his authority (for signs) in the presence of the Antichrist (stated three times – 13:12, 14 and 19:20).

Because of this religious propensity, man is easily deceived into thinking that anything that "feels" good or spiritual is genuine. He is able to "cause" (*poieo*, present tense, "continually to make, prepare, be the cause of") the earth to "worship" (*proskuneo*, "kiss the hand, fall on the knees and touch the ground with the forehead, make obeisance") the Antichrist (first beast).

His message is likely that if everyone unites in total submission, the Antichrist can bring an end to the calamities around the world. Those who fall for this deception will face a terrible judgment (14:9-11; 16:2). However, the convincing element is the supposed miraculous healing of the Antichrist.

Reflection: How popular are miracle workers today?

THE BEAST
HIS SIGNS

13:13

He performs great signs, so that he even makes fire come down from heaven on the earth in the sight of men.

13:13 Not only will the false prophet be involved in the healing (perhaps the faked fatal wound as well), but the power to perform "great" (*megas*) signs will include "making fire come down from heaven in front of people."

These Satanic signs will be viewed by the world in live action. They, however, will be deceived by "the deception of wickedness" especially "for those who perish, because they will not receive the love of the truth so as to be saved" (2 Thes 2:9-10). Those who reject the true gospel will readily accept this false prophet who "makes fire come down from heaven" (*poieo*, present tense, "continually or repeatedly... is making...") as Elijah (1 Kings 18:36-38) or one of the two witnesses? (11:5).

Satan is the master magician, able to imitate supernatural signs in clear view of the public as in Pharaoh's court (2 Tim 3:8-9; Ex 7:11-12, 22). In a similar fashion, the false prophet imitates the Two Witness's ability to bring fire from heaven on their enemies (11:5). "Miracles" are super-natural events, that is, actions that are beyond human ability to do or explain.

Angels, or demons, can perform feats that are beyond human power to accomplish. These appear as "miracles," but they do not include creative powers (to make something out of nothing), nor life-giving powers. In Acts 8:9-11 Simon the magician was "called, 'the Great Power of God.' And they were giving him attention because he had for a long time astonished them with his magic arts."

Reflection: Is there danger in over emphasizing "miracles" today?

HIS RESURRECTION (RESUSCITATION)

13:14

And he deceives those who dwell on the earth by those signs which he was granted to do in the sight of the beast, telling those who dwell on the earth to make an image to the beast who was wounded by the sword and lived.

13:14 The false prophet "deceives" (*planao*, present tense, "continually or repeatedly... cause to stray, wander, roam about, lead from the right way") the desperate population who want someone to control their disastrous conditions. Since people had already rejected the gospel and joined the demonic spirits in blaspheming God (16:9, 11), the masses were easily deceived by lies and false notions and false hopes.

False prophets always turn people away from truth and from the Word of God. They want people dependent on new revelations and dreams, making the inspired revelation of God's Word antiquated and inferior.

God had warned of such experiences in Deut 13:1-3: "If a prophet arises among you, or a dreamer of dreams, and gives you a sign or a wonder, and the sign or wonder which he tells you comes to pass, and if he says, 'Let us go after other gods,' which you have not known, 'and let us serve them,' you shall not listen to the words of that prophet or to that dreamer of dreams; for the Lord your God is testing you."

The dependency on signs and wonders for proof of truth will lead to the acceptance of the proposal to build a massive statue of the Antichrist in the Temple in Jerusalem (2 Thes 2:4). The phrase "was wounded by the sword and yet lived" is given as proof that he is the Messiah and thus will save the world. As a result, the false prophet will be "telling" ("to tell" verb + infinitive has the nuance of "to order") the world to worship the image.

For those who have decided to reject God's Word, God grants them their desire when He will "send upon them a deluding influence so that they will believe what is false, in order that they all may be judged, who did not believe the truth, but took pleasure in wickedness" (2 Thes 2:11-12). Never since Nebuchadnezzar (Dan 3:1-11) has there been such idolatry, and now, on a global scale.

Once again, a state-religion will have authority to threaten with capital punishment those who do not conform. Only those who know the truth and trust it, will not be deceived in spite of the apparent miracle to follow.

Reflection: How does someone determine truth from falsehood?

THE BEAST
GLOBAL WORSHIP DEMANDED

13:15

He was granted power to give breath to the image of the beast that the image of the beast should both speak and cause as many as would not worship the image of the beast to be killed.

13:15 The second beast or false prophet was granted power to make this unique image appear to come alive. The Bible mocks idols as being unable to speak (Psa 115:5; 135:15-17; Isa 46:7; Jer 10:5). This image was given "breath" (*pneuma*, "spirit" not *zoe* or *bios*, which mean "life").

This will be an animation, which appears to be alive. The world wants so bad to believe in anything except the living God, they will prefer to trust in a statue that talks. The god-like character of the Antichrist becomes demonic when rebels appear and his paranoia demands elimination of all threats.

Sentences of death are passed upon all who are godly and refuse to worship the beast, as in the first century. According to Zechariah, two-thirds of the Jews will be killed (Zech 13:8-9), likely because of their refusal to worship the Antichrist.

Reflection: Would you yield to the pressure to compromise your religion or be willing to be killed for your faith?

13:16

He causes all, both small and great, rich and poor, free and slave, to receive a mark on their right hand or on their foreheads.

13:16 All people will be categorized or registered by "small and great, rich and poor, free and slave" probably as a means of controlling the population. The intent of the registry is to give a permanent mark on everyone. In stead of a registry card which can be lost, it will be decided to permanently mark everyone as a citizen of the new world order.

The "mark" (*charagma*, "to engrave") was often a tattoo or brand given to slaves, soldiers and devotees of religious cults. As Christ marked the 144,000 to protect them from God's wrath (7:2-3), so the false prophet marks his devotees to protect them from the wrath of the Antichrist against God's people. Without the mark anyone is subject to instant execution.

13:17 and that no one may buy or sell except one who has the mark or the name of the beast, or the number of his name.

13:17 As an added incentive to receive the mark, it will become necessary in order to make any purchase or sale. Standard negotiation of goods would be impossible without a mark. This will be easily enforced and applied in this digital, bar code era.

In most countries a national registration card (plus passport if one travels internationally) is necessary for any major purchase or sale and credit card application. In a world that is increasingly cashless, all finances are computer transactions and easily monitored and controlled. In some communist regimes this system has already been practiced as a means of population control.

Whatever the means of marking and monitoring this mark, today's technology makes this procedure easily applicable to a global political system.

Reflection: How would you avoid taking the mark?

THE NUMBER OF THE BEAST

13:18 Here is wisdom. Let him who has understanding calculate the number of the beast, for it is the number of a man: His number is 666.

13:18 There is much speculation for the meaning of 666 or the identification of whose name is equivalent to 666 by attributing a numerical value to each of the letters of a name. In alphabets of Greek, Hebrew and Latin each letter has been given a numerical value. A multitude of ways to combine the letters of certain names have been proposed, which thus arrive at a numerical value that has a predetermined meaning.

The letters of the names of leaders such as Nero, Caligula, Domitian, Napoleon, Hitler, Mussolini, Stalin and many others can be manipulated to arrive at the sum of 666.

However, the number's true meaning cannot be applied to any historical person. It will only apply to this mystery beast who will appear following

THE BEAST

the rapture of the Church. At sometime in the future the number will have a special meaning to the generation to which it is applied.

Obviously the number 6 is less than the number 7, which reflects perfection, thus "the number of a man" is less than perfection. Repeated three times, emphasizes the best of man is the beast of the Antichrist.

Reflection: What does the Scripture warn concerning those who try to save their lives by taking the mark and worshipping the beast in Rev 14:9-11?

Comparison chart of the Antichrist and False Prophet

The Antichrist

- He will be a man (13:18)
- He will rise out of the sea of humanity (13: 1; Dan 7:24, 9:27; 11:36-45)
- He will become ruler of the territory of the 7 kingdoms symbolized by the 7 heads (13:1; 17:8-17)
- He will become ruler of the 10 kingdoms that are formed inside the old Roman Empire territory (13:1; 17:8-017; Dan 7:23-24)
- He will be a blasphemer (13:1, 15; 17:3)
- He will revive the old Grecian Empire, the leopard (13:3; 17:8-17; Dan 7:6; 8:20-23)
- He will have characteristics of the Medo/Persian empire, the bear (13:3; Dan 7:5) and Babylon, the lion (13:3; Dan 7:4)
- He will receive his power, throne and great authority from Satan: (13:2; 16:13-16; 2 Thes 2:8-12; Dan 8:24-25; 11:38-39)
- He will not be assassinated and resurrected from the dead
- He will have all the world wondering after him (13:2-4, 8-18)
- He will be an object of worship (13:4, 14-18; 14:9-11; 15:2; 16:2; 20:4-6)
- He will be a supernaturally gifted orator (13:5-6; Dan 7:8, 11, 20, 25; 8:23, 11:36)
- He will be given power and success for 42 months (13:4; 11:1-3; 12:6, 14; Dan 7:25; 12:7)
- He will defy God and claim to be God himself (13:6; 2 Thes 2:3-4; Dan 7:25; 8:25; 11:36-39)
- He will make war on the Jews and Christians and multitudes will be killed by him (13:7, 15; 7:9-17,14,13; 15:2-4; 20:4-6; Dan 7:21; 8:23-25
- He will be given power over all nations inside the 10 kingdoms of the old Roman Empire territory (13:7; Dan 7:23, 24; 8:23-25; 11:36-45)
- He will be worshipped as God (13:8, 14-10; 14:9-11; 20:4-6)
- He will have a religious leader in the false prophet (Rev 13:11-17; 16:113-16; 19:20; 20:10)
- He will permit image worship of himself (13:14-17; 14:9; 15:2; 20:4-6)
- He will cause the mark of his kingdom, or name, or number to be branded on the right hand or forehead of his followers (13:16-18; 14:9-11; 15:2; 16:2; 20:4-6)

The False Prophet

- He will also be a man (*allos*, "of the same kind") (13:18, 11; 16:13; 19:20; 20:10) – Personal pronouns are used to indicate they are persons.
- He will come out of the earth (13:11)
- Both Beasts will die at Armageddon (19:20; Dan 7:11; Isa 11:4; 2 Thes 2:8)
- He will come after the first Beast and will be his Prophet (13:12; 16:13; 19:20; 20:10)
- He will come with a lamb-like appearance to deceive, but will speak like the dragon (13:12)
- He will exercise all the power of the first Beast or Antichrist before him (13:2, 12; 19:20; 2 Thes 2:8-12)
- He will cause men on earth to worship the first beast (13:12; 17:8-11)
- He will do great miracles, even to calling fire from heaven before men, counterfeiting God and His works (13:13; 19:20; compare Num 11:1-3; 26:10)
- He will deceive men by the miracles he will do in the sight of the first beast (13:14; 19:20)
- He will cause men to make an image of the first beast to be worshipped (13:14; 14:9-11; 15:2; 16:2; 20:4-6)
- He will have power to give life to the image causing it to speak and do personal acts (13:15; Compare Ex 7:10-12)
- He will cause the image to demand the death penalty to all who will not worship the Antichrist (13:15; 7:9-17; 15:2; 20:4-6)
- He will cause men in the kingdom of Antichrist to take a mark on their hands or forehead (13:16; 14:9-11; 15:2; 16:2: 10:4-6)
- He will make a law that no one can buy or sell if he does not have this mark (13:17)
- He will be equal to the first beast in sending demons spirits, working through ambassadors, to gather all nations to Armageddon (16:13-16; 19:19-21)
- He will be taken with the Antichrist at Armageddon and be cast alive in the lake of fire (19:20)
- He will still be in the lake of fire in conscious torment 1,000 years later (20:10)

CHAPTER 14

THE 144,000 AND GROUPS OF 3 ANGELS

Three visions of what God is doing in preparation for the final judgment to come.

God is now in the final stages of destroying evil and taking back His creation, which had abandoned Him. The Seal and Trumpet judgments of chapters 6-11 begin to show the authority of the Creator in the earthly realm. In Chapter 11 the 7th Trumpet sounded, but the judgments were held in abeyance until chapter 15. Chapters 12 and 13 give a review of the Tribulation including Satan's direct intervention to destroy Israel (ch. 12) and the demon-possessed leadership of the Antichrist and the False Prophet (ch. 13). In the meantime, chapter 14 describes through three visions what God is doing in preparation for the final judgments to come.

FIRST VISION

I. THE 144,000 ON MT. ZION (14:1-5)

14:1

Then I looked, and behold, a Lamb standing on Mount Zion, and with Him one hundred and forty-four thousand, having His Father's name written on their foreheads.

14:1 This vision begins with the fulfillment of the prophets when they wrote, "But for Me, I have installed My King upon Zion, My holy mountain" (Psa 2:6; see also Isa 24:23). This is the "end game" of the Tribulation, when the victory is won. The 144,000 were selected and sealed with the mark of God in 7:4-8 (also 9:4) to go through the last half of the Tribulation unharmed by the trumpet/bowl judgments and the Antichrist's attempts to destroy them.

The Antichrist is granted the power to kill the two witnesses, but not the 144,000. Now the scene is surrounded with harps playing in heaven, the battle on earth is raging and thousands have been martyred for not receiving the mark of the beast (13:15-17).

God always has His faithful people, even in the most corrupt and dangerous circumstances. Is this "Mount Zion" the heavenly scene at the end of the Tribulation (Heb 12:22-24) or the earthly Mt. Zion in Jerusalem, which will precede the coronation of Christ as He establishes His earthly kingdom (Zech 14:4ff).

The fact that a voice comes out of heaven (v. 2) indicates that this scene

THE 144,000 AND GROUPS OF 3 ANGELS

is on the earth in Jerusalem when Christ returns to Mt. Zion to establish His kingdom on earth. As a form of encouragement, John is shown the end of the terrible Tribulation and the chosen 144,000 that will survive unharmed. They have the Father's name written on their foreheads as all believers will have according to 3:12 and 22:4, instead of the mark of the beast (13:16; 14:11).

Reflection: How are all believers sealed today, and how can it be known for certain?

2 Cor 1:22

Eph 1:13

Eph 4:30

2 Tim 2:19

14:2

And I heard a voice from heaven, like the voice of many waters, and like the voice of loud thunder. And I heard the sound of harpists playing their harps.

14:2 John heard a "voice" (*phone*, "sound, a tone, as musical instruments") from heaven that sounded like the "voice of many waters" as in 1:15 and 19:6.

The next phrase is literally, "the sound of harpers harping with their harps," which emphasizes their instrumental music. The sound of many harpists playing together is beautiful music. The word for "harp" is *kithara* (root word for "guitar").

The multiplicity of harps playing in heaven suggests several things:
(1) Since few learn to play harps now, there will be numerous opportunities to learn new things, especially how to play an instrument of praise;
(2) The motivation for learning to play instruments is sparked by any and all new understandings of God as they are revealed, that will erupt in manifold praise by every means of expression.

Reflection: What is your chief motivation for praise and worship?

THE 144,000 JOIN THE HEAVENLY CHORUS WITH A NEW SONG (14:3-5)

14:3

They sang as it were a new song before the throne, before the four living creatures, and the elders; and no one could learn that song except the hundred and forty-four thousand who were redeemed from the earth.

14:3 The 144,000 (7:4) will never be killed by the Antichrist, but in the end of the second 3 ½ year period in the Tribulation they will stand on Mt Zion in Jerusalem when Christ appears. At that time they will appear before the Messiah to sing a new song before heavenly observers. The heavenly praise for redemption overflows to earthly participants at the return of Christ. The number is important, because not one is missing. Everyone who was sealed at the mid-Tribulation point is present in the end. As the number who will be killed in the Tribulation is specific (6:11), so the number of the 144,000 who survive the Tribulation is precise.

Other voices that John heard from heaven included Christ (1:10-15; 4:1; 10:7-8; 1112), the living creatures (6:1-7), and angel (5:2; 7:2), many angels (5:11-12), all of creation (5:13), the souls under the altar (6:10), and the eagle (8:13).

This group, like all believers, are all accounted for, never overlooked, and included in everything to come. This reveals the character of our God and Savior. The 144,000 had been saved after the Rapture and endured the worse persecution imaginable as well as the horrendous waves of God's judgments on humanity.

There are certain experiences, usually painful and frightening, that build a special fraternity of understanding. Foxhole soldiers are bonded for life, as are those that go through the horrors of the Tribulation. Those without this experience cannot genuinely understand these emotions. This group will live an amazing miracle for 3 ½ years. And then it will be over.

In addition, they are "redeemed" (*agorazo*, perfect passive, "have been... purchased in the market place or purchased with a price"), that is, "purchased" by the blood of Christ (Rev 5:9), just as the Savior must "pay for" the sins of all who repent and are saved at any time. Ample provision is made for any and all who will repent and believe. There is no other way to pay for our sins.

Reflection: How does Peter describe "redeemed" people in 1 Pet 1:18? How thorough is this redemption in Titus 2:14? Can you see why they would want to sing a song of praise to their Savior?

DESCRIPTION OF THE 144,000

14:4

These are the ones who were not defiled with women, for they are virgins. These are the ones who follow the Lamb wherever He goes. These were redeemed from among men, being firstfruits to God and to the Lamb.

14:4a Because of the turbulent times the 144,000 will not marry, nor will they lead a normal life (few will in these days). They will keep themselves from the mandatory perverse idolatry and pervasive immorality of this time. There is no indication that they will be evangelists, preachers, prophets or missionaries; rather, they will be virgin Jewish men who constantly face the persecution of the Antichrist, who will not be able to kill them.

As the Antichrist twisting the minds of men in every perverted manner, the we see their purity as opposed to the universal sexual immorality in the Tribulation. With no divine restraints or consciousness of public censorship limiting Satan's activity (2 Thes 2:6-7) morality will be whatever a person wants it to be.

Meanwhile the population, that is in rebellion, God will abandon to a reprobate mind (Rom 1:24, 26, 28) allowing sin to become as wicked as Sodom and Gomorra (Gen 19) or worse. Sexual purity is essential in any service for the Savior (1 Thes 4:3); therefore, the dramatic moral difference of the 144,000 in this deviant period will be remarkable.

Timothy was commanded to "flee youthful lusts" (2 Tim 2:22), and the Corinthian church to "flee immorality" (1 Cor 6:13, 18). Meanwhile, their task appears to be the preparation of Israel to recognize their Messiah when He comes again (Zech 12:10; Rom 11:15, 26-27).

Reflection: Why is moral character essential to communicate the gospel?

14:4b The 144,000 "followed" (*akoloutheo*, present tense, "continually joining the one who precedes as his attendant, join one as a disciple") the Lamb wherever He "goes" (*hupage*, present subjunctive, "continually would withdraw oneself, depart, sending one somewhere to do something," THAYER).

This group will become disciples of Jesus, learning from His Word, and will be committed to Christ's purpose for them whatever that might be. "If any of you wants to be my follower...you must put aside your selfish ambition, shoulder your cross, and follow me. If you try to keep your life for yourself, you will lose it. But if you give up your life for my sake and for the sake of the Good News, you will find true life" (Mark 8:34-35NLT). John had written, "My sheep hear my voice [especially in the Word] and I know them, and they follow Me" (John 10:27). Though we are not told of their mission, it was strategic and led many to Christ.

Reflection: Who are you following? Have you thought about, or told the Lord, what you will NOT do for His purpose in the world today? Is there anything you would not be willing to give up for His will? What have you learned to follow recently in your study of His Word?

14:4c The Lord has "redeemed," or purchased with the price of His blood and life, the 144,000 who will become the "firstfruits" (*aparche*, "first part of the production as an offering to God"). These are the first ones to be saved that will enter into the new millennium.

The household of Stephanas was called the "first fruits of Achaia" (1 Cor 16:15). These are the first of Israel to be saved in the coming revival among Israel when "they will look on Me whom they have pierced; and they will mourn for Him, as on mourns for an only son..." (Zech 12:10). Paul wrote of this coming revival: "a partial hardening has happened to Israel until the fullness of the Gentiles has come in; and so all Israel will be saved" (Rom 11:25-26).

All believers have been purchased by God (Acts 20:28; 1 Cor 6:20; 7:23; 1 Pet 1:18-19), though the 144,000 were unique because of their special purpose.

Reflection: How appealing is it to you to consider becoming a living sacrifice offering to Jesus? (see Rom 12:1-2).

144,000 WITHOUT DECEIT OR FAULT

14:5

And in their mouth was found no deceit, for they are without fault before the throne of God

14:5 Not only were these men pure externally, but internally their hearts will be pure as is evident in how they speak with "no deceit" (*dulos*, "craft, guile, lie" – from a verb "to decoy") and publically from other's perspective, they were "blameless" (*amomos*, "without blemish," or morally, "without accusation" as a sacrifice lamb had to be without blemish). The evil one and his unsaved all love to "live a lie" or love to "practice falsehoods" (Rev 22:15). True believers are always transparent and honest so they can be seen as unique (not absolutely perfect). They are willingly to be different so their message is seen as unique and life-changing.

Reflection: What does it mean to be a "peculiar people" in Tit 2:14?

II. THE MESSAGE OF THE FIRST GROUP OF THREE ANGELS (14:6-12)

SECOND VISION: GOOD NEWS OF GRACE

A. THE ANNOUNCEMENT TO TURN TO GOD

14:6

Then I saw another angel flying in the midst of heaven, having the everlasting gospel to preach to those who dwell on the earth-- to every nation, tribe, tongue, and people

14:6 The second vision of John is of three angels delivering God's final message to humanity concerning the end of human history. Angels are in every chapter from 4 through 12, thus are instrumental in bringing about God's objectives in this period. In the midst of the great wrath of God on earth, the first of the three angels is sent in mid-air to announce to the world the "everlasting gospel" to all the living on the earth among "every nation, tribe, tongue and people."

The term "midst of heaven" translates *mesouranema*, "the highest point in the heaven, which the sun occupies at noon." From this elevated position the angel would be most visible and also would be outside the reach of the Antichrist and demonic influences, which are at this time restricted to the earth (12:7-9). Earlier an eagle had announced the coming three Trumpet-Woes (8:13). How this will take place is not described.

Whatever the specifics, one thing is certain, the Lord is always "patient toward [mankind], because he does not wish for anyone to perish, but for all to come to repentance" (2 Pet 3:9). Despite God's gracious attempts to get the attention of the world through the two witnesses and the 144,000 untouchable Jews, and countless martyrs to the faith, the population in general rejects the gospel (9:20-21; 16:9, 11).

The description of the "eternal gospel" certainly implies that it is the unchanging Good News of salvation from sins for those who repent from the lies of the world and the Antichrist, to trust by faith in Jesus Christ.

This preaching to "every nation, tongue, tribe and people" is not the first time the gospel has reached to the ends of the earth. It is evident that someone got there before the rapture since the first group scene in heaven at the beginning of the Tribulation includes the redeemed "out of every tribe and language and people and nation" (5:9).

Reflection: Can you see the heart of God up to the very end? Can you describe what your church or an acquaintance or you are doing to reach the last tribe or people group or your neighbors with the gospel before the rapture?

MESSAGE OF THE ANGEL

14:7

saying with a loud voice, "Fear God and give glory to Him, for the hour of His judgment has come; and worship Him who made heaven and earth, the sea and springs of water.

14:7 The announcement is to "fear God and give Him glory, because the hour of His judgment is come." Jesus had given a similar warning, "Fear not those who kill the body but cannot kill the soul. Rather, be afraid of the One who can destroy both soul and body in hell" (Matt 10:28). The message is to "fear God" (not the Antichrist) "and give Him glory" (not the Antichrist or one's self). This will require a conscious change of loyalty and trust, which defines "repentance." One obeys the person he most fears.

The fear element primarily deals with the revealed Word, that is, one must be "fearful" that God is going to do exactly what He says He will do. If a person is not afraid of what God says, then he will make his own rules of life.

If God says all sinners who do not repent and trust Christ will spend eternity in hell with Satan and the Antichrist, then we'd best fear that He will do what He says, committing ourselves to get the gospel to as many as possible. If we are not afraid of what He says, then we will act as if He does not mean it.

The message in the text appears to be more of a warning than a means of how to be saved. Even in this detestable degradation of society God continues to warn people to repent from the worship of the beast and accept the good news of a forgiving Savior Who is soon coming as King. It is never too late until it is too late. No one will be able to say "I never knew" (Rom 1:20).

Only the fool denies the evidence God has provided in creation and "said in his heart, 'There is no God'" (Ps 14:1). If a person goes to hell it is because he did not want to know the evidence that leads to the only true God, or that no one intervened to show him the truth. Ironically, the more gracious God is to man, the more obstinate he becomes in his selfish, self-centered mind-set.

Even if man never heard the message, he should worship God because there is obviously a Designer-Creator who made the entire expanse of heaven, every form of life on land and sea and the earth itself. The amazing creation is a glimpse into the majesty, power, creativeness and intelligence of an awesome God worthy of all to worship.

For a study of who will be in hell review the following verses: Matt 25:41-46; Rom 6:23; 1 Cor 6:9-11; 2 Pet 2:4; Rev 20:10, 15; 21:8, 27).

Reflection: How do these verses declare this reasoning?

Psa 19:1-4

Isa 40:21-26

Rev 4:11

SECOND ANGEL: BAD NEWS OF JUDGMENT

14:8

And another angel followed, saying, "Babylon is fallen, is fallen, that great city, because she has made all nations drink of the wine of the wrath of her fornication.

14:8 The second angel warned that Babylon the Great City is fallen, a reference to an earthly institution with a global following, which is described as "fornication." The repetition of the judgment emphasizes the certainty of its doom.

"Babylon" refers to the mighty World Empire of the Antichrist. Everyone will think thought he and his Empire are invincible (13:4). From the beginning, "Babylon" has symbolized all that is evil, rebellious, false religion and demonic in the world, but, in the Tribulation, all these divergent focuses will be concentrated in the cult of the Antichrist.

The global religion, identified as the Harlot of Babylon, will be explained in chapter 17. With no more explanation, the reader must wait for 3-4 chapters for the explanation.

John is giving the end-view in these visions to show the futility of trusting in the Antichrist's power and authority. The immorality or "fornication" spoken of in this verse refers to the vast commercial/religious conglomerate, which will be described in Rev 17-18.

The most vivid description of the spiritual immorality or religious apostasy of ancient Israel is given in Ezek 16:17-37, which is a picture of the apostasy of the world. The Antichrist's Empire is doomed before it begins.

Only a fool would doubt the announcement of the angel then, and the Word of God for 2,000 years. All nations will trust their riches and their souls to this Empire, only to lose them both.

Reflection: Do people today immediately take God at His Word? Do Christians have to learn this quality or is it natural?

THE 144,000 AND GROUPS OF 3 ANGELS
THIRD VISION

ETERNAL DAMNATION TO ANYONE WHO WORSHIPS THE ANTICHRIST (14:9-11)

14:9

Then a third angel followed them, saying with a loud voice, "If anyone worships the beast and his image, and receives his mark on his forehead or on his hand.

14:9 The third angel brings another judgment warning for those who yielded to the beast accepting his mark and joining in his mandatory worship that they will become the chief object of God's wrath, both in the remaining time of the Tribulation and for all eternity (See Rev 13:16-17).

Since they will have chosen to bond themselves to the Antichrist and the Dragon, then along with them they will spend eternity in an unending torment for participating in their demonic attempt to destroy God's creation, people and plan. However, once again, God's grace extends a final offer to repent even in this final hour. No one goes to hell arbitrarily, or without personal consent to trust in the devil's lie.

Reflection: Can you describe how difficult it would be to oppose the pressure to receive the mark of the beast?

ETERNAL PUNISHMENT

14:10-11

he himself shall also drink of the wine of the wrath of God, which is poured out full strength into the cup of His indignation. He shall be tormented with fire and brimstone in the presence of the holy angels and in the presence of the Lamb. 11 "And the smoke of their torment ascends forever and ever; and they have no rest day or night, who worship the beast and his image, and whoever receives the mark of his name.

14:10-11 The doctrine of eternal punishment is clear and undeniable. Jesus and John spoke more on the subject of hell than all the rest of the Bible. This verse begins with an individual application, "that person," (lit. "himself, he...") will drink of the wine of the wrath of God," that is, the full fury of God's wrath. This is not a passing reaction, but a definite, deliberate, merciless, unchanging and unending wrath of a righteous God separating Himself and all those that belong to Him from unrepentant sinners forever and ever. The concept of "God's anger" being "mixed undiluted in the cup of His wrath" refers to the practice of condensing wine into a syrup, then diluting it with water when needing to drink.

This wrath is undiluted, maximum strength wrath without compassion on every individual who will not repent. No one escapes. It is politically incorrect to speak of "torture" today (*basanizo*, "to vex with grievous pains (of body or mind), to torment"). There is no annihilation, no ending of this torment forever. If a person chooses to be independent of God in this life, then God will grant that desire for eternity.

Nothing tells us how much God hates sin as much as the description of the punishment for sin. No wonder Jesus went to the cross! Fire and "brimstone" or "sulfur" were used to destroy Sodom and Gomorrah (Gen 19:24-25) and the lake of fire "burns with brinstone" (19:20; 20:10; 21:8). To make it worse is the phrase "...in front of the Lamb" (14:10).

The extent of this suffering is clear: the "smoke of their torment will go up forever and ever." If this is merely symbolical language, then the reality is worse, but there is no indication of symbolism here. Only a humanistic delusion of God makes this concept difficult to accept. The horror of the Antichrist pales in comparison to the horror of God's wrath.

Reflection: As we understand this aspect of the wrath of God, we begin to understand why Jesus did not want to suffer God's wrath for sin... but He did, so we could be free of it.

Eternal torment found in 20:10; Isa 66:24, Dan 12:2; Matt 3:12; Luke 3:17; 2 Thes 1:9. Jesus spoke of hell as "eternal fire" (Matt 18:18; 25:41), "unquenchable fire" (Mark 9:43) and where "the fire is not quenched" (Mark 9:48).
Jesus used the Greek word *gehenna* to describe hell. The word refers to the valley of Ben Hinnom, were in the OT Israelites would sacrifice their children to Moloch (2 Chron 28:3) and later they burnt their garbage and refuse (Jer 7:31). Jesus warned that this was far worse than physical death.

III. THE REWARD OF THE FAITHFUL (14:12-13)

14:12

Here is the patience of the saints; here are those who keep the commandments of God and the faith of Jesus.

14:12 Under these horrible Tribulation circumstances, the believers will need extreme patience or endurance (13:10) to "keep the commandments of God and the faith of Jesus." The "patience" (*hupomone*, "steadfastness, endurance." "The characteristic of a man who has not swerved from his deliberate purpose and his loyalty to faith and piety by even the greatest trials and sufferings," STRONG).

This is evidently a large group (7:9), which will be unmercifully persecuted. They will come to salvation through the ministry of other believers, the two witnesses (11:3-13) and perhaps the 144,000 (14:1-5). Jesus described this unprecedented persecution as a time of "great tribulation, such as has not occurred since the beginning of the world until now, nor ever will" (Matt 24:21). Their lives are characterized by their obedience to the commands of God and to their faith in Jesus (or faithfulness to Jesus).

Some Christians think that living by commandments is legalism and prefer to live without commands (antinomianism). The blessing of the Revelation is promised to those who obey the commandments in this Book (Rev 1:3). The will of God is always found by obeying all the commandments in the NT (1 Thes 4:3; 5:18; 1 Pet 2:15).

Most Christians do not even know the 10 Commandments, much less the 370 NT commands for believers. One of the major quests of Bible study should be to find and understand the commands, guiding principles and examples that are applicable to us today. This is not legalism, which seeks to become more righteous or acceptable before God by man-made cultural accommodations or supposed righteous superficial requirements.

We already have the righteousness of God by faith. The quest for obedience is not to be more spiritual or acceptable; rather, it is to demonstrate one's love for the Savior and to think like He thinks about life and relationships.

In spite of the slaughtering of innocent believers and global disasters, these believers will become a beacon in the dark world of the

Tribulation. Even at this time, the assurance that "all things ... work together for good to those who love God, to those who are called according to His purpose" (Rom 8:28). The true believer is able to rest in this truth. The assurance that at least some will endure through these horrible times will be an encouragement to those who suffer persecution now and those who will read this in the Tribulation to come.

Reflection: How are these verses likewise an encouragement to those in persecution?

Luke 21:19

2 Tim 4:5

Heb 3:6

THOSE WHO DIE IN THE END OF THE TRIBULATION

14:13

Then I heard a voice from heaven saying to me, "Write: `Blessed are the dead who die in the Lord from now on.'" "Yes," says the Spirit, "that they may rest from their labors, and their works follow them.

14:13 A voice from heaven tells John to write. There is a special blessing in being killed for one's faith, especially in the latter part of the Tribulation period, and may refer to the final year of the 7 years. "Precious in the sight of the Lord is the death of His godly ones" (Psa 116:15). They will have shortest wait until the launching of the new millennium of a new world order.

The deliverance from their affliction, torture and trial is immediate and permanent. "They will rest from their labor" (*kopos*, "beating of the breast with grief, difficult, exhausting toil"). This does not refer to the "labor" as of a job, where one works for a living, but to the labor "abounding in the work of the Lord, because you know your labor in the Lord is not in vain" (1 Cor 15:58). Not having received the mark of the beast will make their life difficult and dangerous.

Death to them is a welcomed reprieve, but unbelievers will never know a moment's rest throughout all eternity (14:11). The exciting aspect of the Lord's work is that the major results of a life are what happens after one is gone: "their deeds will follow them."

THE 144,000 AND GROUPS OF 3 ANGELS

Reflection: What do these verses teach about the coming rewards?

Heb 6:10

1 Cor 3:12-14

1 Cor 4:5

All men face the two options: a Christless eternity in torment or a blissful eternity with Christ. There are no other options.

This is the sixth time John heard a voice from heaven (10:4, 8; 11:12; 12:10; 14:2) and he will hear it three more times (18:4; 19:5; 21:3).

IV. THE MESSAGE OF THE SECOND GROUP OF THREE ANGELS (14:14-20)

The theme of the final judgment (14:6-11) is followed by a brief encouragement for the persevering saints (14:12-13). Now John returns to the announcement of the final judgments that will destroy the final semblance of human civilization (Matt 24:21-22).

As long as there remains a sliver of hope that things will get better, man will persist in his rebellion and independence. Man will keep thinking that it cannot get worse, but it does. Once man makes his choice of a false belief, then he is committed to justifying his error, until it is too late.

14:14

Then I looked, and behold, a white cloud, and on the cloud sat One like the Son of Man, having on His head a golden crown, and in His hand a sharp sickle.

14:14 "Then I looked, and behold..." introduces a new theme in Revelation (4:1; 6:2, 5, 8; 7:9; 14:1). The One like the "Son of Man" is probably Christ Himself who is called the "Son of Man" (1:13) wearing a golden crown. In His first coming Jesus came as a Servant, Sower, and the Savior (Luke 19:10); however, when He returns it will be to become the Ruler, Reaper and Rewarder to "judge the living and the dead" (2 Tim 4:1).

In the Gospel of Matthew the term "Son of Man" is used 25 times; this is the last time He is called the "son of man." The "crown" on his head is a *stephanos* worn by victors in war and athletics, not a *diadema*, a crown worn by a king. This is the crown of conquest and victory (Mat 24:30).

The Reaper is sitting, thus waiting for the right moment to reap the harvest. The sickle in His hand suggests the harvest time action of the final judgments. When the sickle is used as a weapon its razor sharp edge is designed to cut down everything in its path.

FIRST ANGEL: ANNOUNCEMENT TO BEGIN THE END PROCESS

14:15

And another angel came out of the temple, crying with a loud voice to Him who sat on the cloud, "Thrust in Your sickle and reap, for the time has come for You to reap, for the harvest of the earth is ripe.

14:15 The first angel of the second group calls to Christ to begin the harvest because the "earth is ripe" (*exeranthe*, "withered, overripe or rotten"). The fruit is no longer eatable; it is useless and needs to be "gathered up and burned with fire" (Matt 13:40).

The first group of angels have proclaimed that judgment is coming; now the declaration of the time is right. The "time has come for you to reap." The angel from God the Father is not commanding the Son of Man as much as he is giving the most exciting and climatic pronouncement of the history of mankind, "the time to reap has come" to begin the final judgments and to launch the millennium.

This was the time-question that sparked the curiosity of the disciples: "Lord, will you at this time restore the kingdom to Israel?" To which Jesus responded, "It is not for you to know times or seasons which the Father has put in His own authority"(Acts 1:6-7). Now the answer to that question from the Father is finally given. "Now is the time." The picture is of an over ripe field of rotting fruit (Joel 3:13) that has to be pruned off before beginning a new growth.

Reflection: Why has the Father waited so long?

THE 144,000 AND GROUPS OF 3 ANGELS

THE REAPING BEGINS

14:16

So He who sat on the cloud thrust in His sickle on the earth, and the earth was reaped.

14:16 The Son of Man will suddenly arise and sweet His sickle and the earth will be reaped. This is what time has been waiting for.

As a harvester swings his sickle to clear a field, so the launching of the rapid sequence of bowl judgment events launch the beginning of the end of the horrible process of the Tribulation that is described in chapter 16: malignant sores on the worshipers of the Antichrist (16:2), death of all life in the oceans and seas (16:3), the world's rivers and springs turn to blood (16:4), sun bursts that scorches humanity (16:8), painful darkness over the global realm of the Antichrist (16:10), massive invasion by the king of the east (16:12), a massive earthquake (16:18). This will bring us to the final stage of the end.

SECOND ANGEL: THE ANGEL OF DEATH

14:17

Then another angel came out of the temple which is in heaven, he also having a sharp sickle.

4:17 The second angel in this second vision has a sickle like that of the Son of Man to help in the harvest. This angel also comes out of the temple, implying that he is on a mission having been commissions by the Father.

Angels are the key instruments that God uses in bringing about the judgments of Revelation: they call forth the four horsemen, blow the seven trumpets, battle with Satan and his demonic army ejecting them from the heavenly scene, and now they will pour out the Seven Bowls in the next chapter.

This angel is the "grim reaper." The first harvest is described as a grain harvest where the grain is gathered for the final burning. This angel will assist the Son of Man in bringing about this final judgment. We are not told until the next angel's announcement what this second angel's mission will be.

Reflection: What light do these verses give regarding the involvement of angels in these end-time events?

Matt 13:39

Matt 13:49

2 Thes 1:7

THIRD ANGEL: THE ANGEL OF FIRE

14:18

And another angel came out from the altar, who had power over fire, and he cried with a loud cry to him who had the sharp sickle, saying, "Thrust in your sharp sickle and gather the clusters of the vine of the earth, for her grapes are fully ripe."

THE SECOND ANGEL CALLED INTO ACTION

14:18 The third angel comes forth with the power to use fire to destroy the remains. This angel is described as one who "came out from the altar." This altar in heaven is where the "souls of those who had been slain because of the word of God" will be praying (Rev 5:8; 6:9-11). It was the custom to gather at the altar and pray (Luke 1:10).

This place in heaven, however, will be full of martyred saints asking God to take vengeance on their assassins and pour out His wrath that was promised.

This Temple activity was describe in 8:3-5. Each morning the priest would take the hot coals from the brazen altar where the sacrifices were offered each day. He would carry these coals to the altar of incense to ignite the incense (Ex 30:7-8) producing a rising smoke and fragrant aroma, which was to symbolize the prayers of God's people (Rev 5:8), meanwhile all the people outside the temple were praying (Luke 1:10).

This angel will have the power over the fire of the altar. Likewise, this angel does not come from the throne of God like the angel in v. 17, but from the altar, which is associated with the prayers of the martyrs. God uses these angels to answer the prayers of the Tribulation saints.

The third angel commands the second angel to "Thrust in your sharp sickle and gather the clusters of the vine of the earth," i.e. the peoples of the earth.

The "grapes" or people are "fully ripe" (*ekmasan*, "to be fully grown, in prime condition"), a different word than was used in v. 15. That is, they are full of liquid, bursting at their capacity and ready to harvest.

The image is the fullness of wickedness that cannot get any worse. It is time for its elimination. When sin is left unchecked, the social, emotional, relational, and intellectual functions of man turn animal-like (take, kill and be killed), instead of God-like, in whose image we were made.

Reflection: Can you understand why God would decide again to destroy this corrupt humanity, and begin again?

THE THIRD ANGEL BEGIN THE REAPING

14:19

So the angel thrust his sickle into the earth and gathered the vine of the earth, and threw it into the great winepress of the wrath of God.

14:19 Continuing the analogy, the grapes are gathered, or will gather of their own accord, and are thrown into the "winepress" of the wrath of God. This sounds so organized and effortless, but when the angel swings the sickle, the results are catastrophic.

The survivors of the seven bowl judgments will be gathered together like grape clusters at harvest time, in a massive effort to eliminate anything related to God or the Jewish people.

In biblical times a wine press was made of two basins that were connected by a trough or canal. In the upper basin the grapes were stomped or crushed to release its juices, which flowed down the trough to the lower basin, which contained only the juices. It was a messy process, but the grapes had to be crushed. The splashing of the grape juice pictures the splattering of the blood of the armies of the Antichrist in the great and final battle of Armageddon.

Reflection:: Can you explain the nature of God in using this analogy in Isa 63:3 and Joel 3:13? What does it tell you about God as He really is?

DEPTH OF THE WINEPRESS

14:20

And the winepress was trampled outside the city, and blood came out of the winepress, up to the horses' bridles, for one thousand six hundred furlongs.

14:20 In the analogy, the wine press is outside the city. The reference to the "city" probably refers to Jerusalem (the "great city" in 11:18). The Lord graciously protects Jerusalem from the horrible carnage that is coming in the Battle of Armageddon (11:2; Dan 11:45). "Outside the city" does not mean immediately outside the gates, but to the north about 60 miles, on the Plain of Esdraelon or Meggido, one of the most fertile valleys in the entire world.

The unconverted people of the world will gather from everywhere to help rid the world of the remnant of Israel and any trace of Christians. The carnage will be so devastating that the blood will reach to the horses' bridles, though not as a lake of blood, but as it splatters or in streambeds.

The breadth of the battle scene is 1,600 stadia or about 180 miles. This is approximately the north-south length of Israel today. Isaiah described this battle raging as far south as Bozrah in Edom (Isa 63:1), though Jerusalem will be spared.

The indication from the chronology of the text is that this massive slaughter is about to take place (as in Isa 63:1-3; Rev 16:14; Dan 11:40-45). Further description of the great battle is found in Rev 19:11-21. This will be a World War in a matter of days at the Second Coming of Christ.

Until we accept and understand the necessity of God's judgment on sin and sinners, we will never appreciate the meaning of mercy. A "grandfather" image of God will never motivate our repentance, obedience or sincere worship. Someone wrote, "Those who know God well enough to fear his wrath know God well enough to desire his grace." God's crushing wrath is coming quickly. "Blessed are those who have had their sins forgiven, and blessed are those who lead others to God's mercy" (Life Application Bible Commentary, p. 177).

Reflection: What does the expression, "Grapes of Wrath," refer to? Knowing that this is the end of the Antichrist, why would he persist and fight against what God says will happen? Do you know anyone like this?

CHAPTER 15

THE SEVEN LAST PLAGUES (BOWLS)

"God's wrath against sin was demonstrated against Christ so He would be just in forgiving sinners, but in the Tribulation God's wrath is demonstrated against sinners -- not sin -- and Satan."

The last seven angels are introduced as they proceed out of the heavenly Temple to begin their final judgment-plagues for the earth. This will be the complete and final punishment on the wickedness of mankind and the destruction of the reign of the Antichrist. These seven judgments appear to occur in rapid succession at the very end of the 7 years period. This rapidity only makes their impact that much worse.

The purpose of chapter 15 is to demonstrate how God is just and holy in delivering these judgments against His rebellious creation and yet all these events are part of His perfect plan. The interchangeable use of "plagues" and "bowls" is designed to show different aspects of these judgments. The series of bowl judgments, as a group, make up the third "woe" (11:14), thus the third woe involves seven plagues, which will complete the mystery of God (10:7). As soon as these bowl judgments are completed Jesus returns to earth (Matt 24:30-31; Rev 19:11).

I. THE INTRODUCTION OF THE SEVEN ANGELS (15:1)

15:1

Then I saw another sign in heaven, great and marvelous: seven angels having the seven last plagues, for in them the wrath of God is complete.

15:1 John saw a "another" (*allos*, "another of the same kind") "great" (*megas*, "loud, fierce, huge"- used 11 times in this chapter) "and marvelous" sign, but we are not told what will be so great and marvelous, unless it will be the appearance of the awfulness of the plagues upon the earth, or just the fact that these seven last judgments will be the end of God's judgment on the Antichrist's reign.

A "sign" refers to a symbol of a lesson or truth. If sinners could realize how serious God is about dealing with sin they would be scared about offending Him. Just one sin of eating a forbidden fruit revealed the prideful, self-centered, selfish and distrusting nature that would manifest itself in a myriad of evil ways for thousands of years.

God's wrath against sin was demonstrated against Christ on the cross so that He would be just in forgiving sinners, but in the Tribulation God's wrath will be displayed against sinners (not sin) and Satan, in order to demonstrate that justice on earth is God's doing: "'Vengeance

THE SEVEN LAST PLAGUES (BOWLS)

is Mine, I will repay" (Rom 12:19). This is the day of "repayment."

The seven "plagues," (*plhgh*, "a blow, stripe or wound" – not in the sense of diseases or epidemics) are the seven bowl judgments (16:1). These are more widespread, global and far worse than the trumpet judgments in 8:2—11:19.

These are the "last" judgments, indicating that the bowl judgments come after the seals and trumpet judgments in chronological sequence and, as a group, constitute the seventh trumpet.

These coming judgments are so horrible that the "wrath" of God (*thumos*, "passion, rage, anger, heat, boiling up," a strong word describing God's attitude against sin) is considered "complete" (*teleo*, cumulative aorist tense, "brings to an end a long process –so that the thing done corresponds to what has been said," STRONG), thus it will be exactly as John described it to be. These judgments will accomplish God's just purpose in the Tribulation Period and the end of time. Zephaniah 3:8 describes this time:

> "Therefore wait for Me," declares the Lord,"For the day when I rise up as a witness. Indeed, My decision is to gather nations,to assemble kingdoms,to pour out on them My indignation, all My burning anger; for all the earth will be devoured by the fire of My zeal."

The action is necessary because God is bringing justice for global wrongdoing. However, the ultimate consequence of God's eternal wrath will be the sentencing of all unrepentant sinners to join Satan in hell forever (Matt 25:41).

The seven seals will destroy 25% of the earth (chs. 6-8), then the seven trumpets will destroy in a third of the earth (chs. 9-11) leaving a little less that 50% of the world population alive for the 2nd half of the Tribulation period (this does not include the number killed in the other catastrophes).

These "seven last plagues" (bowl judgments), are the worst judgments, and are directed against the entire world, which will take a huge death toll. These actions will completely destroy the reign and the evil Empire of the Antichrist. No place on the globe will be spared of the plagues: the land, the sea, rivers and lakes; the sky and the beast's kingdom.

Reflection: Do you believe that justice is important to God?

Author J. H. Keathley gives five purposes for the Tribulation Period:
(1) God's discipline on the Jews for their willful rejection of Christ as their Messiah. Rebels will be purged and a remnant will turn to Christ (Ezek 20:33-44; Zech 14:9-10);
(2) God's judgment on the Gentiles for anti-Semitism;
(3) It will demonstrate the true character and program of Satan as the source of sin, misery, war and murder;
(4) It will demonstrate to mankind the true rebellion and spiritually corrupt nature of man and how horrible he can be when given the right circumstances without the restraint of the Holy Spirit;
(5) God will demonstrate His absolute holiness, grace, faithfulness to His promises, His just decisions against Satan and sinners and that God remains in absolute control through the Tribulation.

II. THE PRAISE FROM THE MARTYRS OF THE TRIBULATION (15:2-4)

15:2

And I saw something like a sea of glass mingled with fire, and those who have the victory over the beast, over his image and over his mark and over the number of his name, standing on the sea of glass, having harps of God,

15:2a The sea of glass appears like the crystal sea in 4:6 and those who secure victory over the beast are the same group, though perhaps expanded now, as in 7:9-17. Is the "glass mingled with fire" a symbol of righteous wrath and judgment, or is the glass a window where the fire below is observed? (See "tormented with fire and brimstone in the presence of the holy angels" in 14:10).

The ones present will have had "victory over the beast" (the Antichrist, 13:1), "over his image" (13:14-15) and "over his mark" (13:16-17) and the "number of his name" (13:18). This repetition emphasizes the sphere or circumstances of this victory. The pressure to yield will be tremendous.

These will have "victory" (*nikao*, "conquer or prevail") over the beast by refusing to be intimidated by the threat of death, they will not yield to the mandatory idolatry. Victory comes because their fearlessness. "Fear" is used 77 times in the NT, either warning us not to be fearful or

THE SEVEN LAST PLAGUES (BOWLS)

we are exhorted to selectively fear God's pronouncements more than man's threats.

Reflection: From this sampling of verses define some principles of the NT fear:

Matt 10:28 (Luke 12:5)

Matt 10:31 (Luke 12:7)

Luke 5:26

Luke 12:32

John 7:13

Acts 5:5

Acts 13:26 (Rom 3:18)

Rom 8:15

2 Cor 7:15

Eph 5:21 (6:5)

Phil 1:14

Phil 2:12

1 Tim 5:20

2 Tim 1:7

Heb 2:14-15

15:2b They will be "holding harps given to them by God," as in 5:8 and 14:2, 13. The repeated emphasis on worship, especially with instruments like the guitar or harp (Gk., *kithara*, "string instruments"), communicates how important musical instruments and worship are to the heavenly host.

God Himself is making sure everyone can participate in the worship experience. The rejoicing in part is because the prayers of the Tribulation saints (6:9-10) are about to be answered, as God's just vengeance is poured out on those who had mistreated His people. This is why Paul warned for us not to take our own vengeance (Rom 12:19).

Reflection: Can you see the reason for not avenging one's self in James 1:20?

15:3

They sing the song of Moses, the servant of God, and the song of the Lamb, saying: "Great and marvelous are Your works, Lord God Almighty! Just and true are Your ways, O King of the saints!"

15:3 The "song of Moses" and the "song of the Lamb," (*arnion*, diminutive form, "little lamb") celebrated deliverance from dreaded enemies. The song of Moses rejoiced over Israel's deliverance from Egypt and the destruction of Pharaoh's army at the Red Sea (Exodus 15:1-18; Deut 32). It was sung in the afternoon service each Sabbath as a reminder to the Jews of God's deliverance and sovereignty.

The song of the "little" Lamb refers to the ultimate deliverance of the Church over Satan's attacks and dominion. God's people will be delivered from the power of the Antichrist and they will be in heaven because the Lamb, the Lord Jesus, was the sacrifice-lamb for the sins of the world and they will believe in Him. In these songs of praise for God is praised for His great deeds, justice, truth (16:7), glory and holiness.

John Phillips (*Exploring Revelation*, rev. ed.,Chicago: Moody, 1987; reprint, Neptune, N.J.: Loizeaux, 1991, p. 187.) compares these two songs:

> "The song of Moses was sung at the Red Sea, the song of the Lamb is sung at the crystal sea; the song of Moses was a song of triumph over Egypt, the song of the Lamb is a song of triumph over Babylon; the song of Moses told how God brought His people out, the song of the Lamb tells how God brings His people in; the song of Moses commemorated the execution of the foe, the expectation of the saints, and the exaltation of the Lord; the song of the Lamb deals with the same three themes."

Reflection: If you were to write a song of praise to the Lord today, list four things you would want to sing to Him in praise for specific things He has done or means to you today.

Several songs in the OT: A song of praise when the Lord gave them water in the dessert wilderness (Num 21:17-18). Moses taught the children of Israel a song of remembrance just before he died (Deut 31:19-22; 32;1-44). Songs were meant to teach or remember specific truths about God, not just songs to God, but about God so as not to forget, and to tell God in song how great He is for doing such and such... The lesson of a worship song is that God is TRUSTWORTHY.

15:4

Who shall not fear You, O Lord, and glorify Your name? For You alone are holy. For all nations shall come and worship before You, For Your judgments have been manifested.

15:14a The statement, "You alone are holy" (Gk., "because alone holy"). The NET Bible footnotes on this phrase states that there are three inferences:

(1) By omitting the 2nd person singular verb form, "You," grammatically puts more stress on the attribute of God's holiness;
(2) the "juxtaposition of 'alone' with 'holy' stresses the unique nature of God's holiness and complete 'otherness' in relationship to His creation." The term "holy" is not just a reference to purity, but to His unique distinction from all Creation. He is outside of creation, not a part of it.
(3) John's use of the term holy (*hosios*) is contrasted with the more common NT word, *hagios*. This term is often used in messianic contexts when referring to Christ, thus implying His deity.

Some have difficulties in honestly declaring that God's ways are just, when having to face trials and heartaches. Beware of these pitfalls:
(1) Questioning God's timing. We must learn to rest in His choice of methods and sequences of events, even when they are not our first choices;
(2) Resenting the outcomes. We say we trust God then resent His decision to take a loved one or end a cherished relationship. Remember: we do not know the future, so resenting God's decisions is premature. If our life is genuinely in His hands, then all outcomes are His choice and we are okay with it.

(3) Quarreling over an issue where we would have done it differently. We say that God is good, and attempt to defend His treatment of an unsaved person, or an innocent child. Explaining satisfactorily all actions as from God's design can raise doubts and weaken our own trust in God's character. By faith we trust in God's purpose in time and space. He makes no mistakes. It may be years before some things make sense, if ever.

Reflection: Have you ever been tempted to question God's goodness to you?

15:4b Then John gave a prophecy adding it to the doxology: "All nations will come and worship before you for your righteous acts have been revealed." The end is revealed before the battle begins. This is a quotation from Psa 10:7 or 86:9.

Because He is God, He is omnipotent, sovereign, and righteous; thus, He is Creator and Ultimate Judge to bring justice to all things, if not immediately, then ultimately. If He ignored sin, He would not be just and righteous Himself, and therefore, He would contradict His own nature. If there is evil, it must be quenched, punished and destroyed, or God is a contradiction in Himself.

The surviving world will recognize these truths and come to worship the coming Savior in person. The Psalmist wrote, "All the earth will worship You and will sing praises to You; they will sing praises to Your name" (Psa 66:4).

The actions of the Tribulation will be considered "righteous acts," which the survivors will consider a powerful argument for honoring such a Victor. Zechariah wrote, "it will come about that any who are left of all the nations that went against Jerusalem will go up from year to year to worship the King, the Lord of hosts, and to celebrate the Feast of Booths" (Zech 14:16). Isaiah wrote, "'all mankind will come to bow down before Me,' says the Lord" (Isa 66:23).

Reflection: Do you agree with the statement that the goal of missions during the Church Age is worship?

III. THE OPENING OF THE TEMPLE (15:5)

15:5

After these things I looked, and behold, the temple of the tabernacle of the testimony in heaven was opened.

15:5 "After these things" implies an interval of time between these two sections. The first section showed the saints in heaven praising God with a full understanding of the cause of His wrath; the second section, will emphasize the cause of what is about to happen.

The introductory phrase once again introduces a striking new vision four times in Revelation (4:1; 7:1; here; 18:1). John "looked" (*oida*, "perceive, discern, understand") and grasped the significance of what this means. This new vision will reveal the bowl judgments (ch. 16), but first John sees the angelic messengers of the bowls.

John had seen the sacred temple before, "the temple of God which is in heaven was opened; and the ark of His covenant appeared in His temple and there were flashes of lightening and sounds and peals of thunder and an earthquake and a great hailstorm" (11:19). The "temple" (*naos*) refers to the Holy of Holies, the inner sanctuary where God dwells, from which the angels will emanate.

This heavenly tabernacle was the original model from which Moses copied the plan for the earthly tabernacle in the desert (Heb 9:23). This is why the tabernacle/temple construction was so sacred: it was constructed to reflect the heavenly tabernacle.

The phrase, "tabernacle of the testimony" is a Greek translation from the Hebrew "Tent of Meeting" (Num 17:7; 18:2). The "testimony" (*marturion*, "witness to what is true") is derived from the presence within the ark of the covenant of the tablets of stone, which contain the Ten Commandments. These give witness to the universal sinfulness of man who is unable to obey them.

The law proves man is guilty before God and unacceptable to Him. On the other hand, the top surface of the ark is annually covered with blood from a sacrifice innocent lamb to prove that God has provided full payment for man's sinfulness. This illustrated the work of Christ on the cross (Acts 7:44; Heb 9:1-5).

Both the tabernacle and the temple represented the dwelling place of God and the place where man could meet God because his sins were covered.

Normally the tabernacle was covered with a veil only open to the high priest once a year, but now it is open for all to see everything that happens before the throne (11:19) and the expansion of the holiness of God confronting sinful man.

Reflection: Today what is the "tabernacle" of God on earth in 2 Cor 5:1? How is this going to be similar in the future in Rev 21:3?

The lies of Satan that men tend to believe are: (1) If God is loving, He would never send His creatures to hell; (2) God would be unjust to send anyone to hell.

A. THE COMMISSIONING OF THE SEVEN ANGELS (15:6-7)

15:6

And out of the temple came the seven angels having the seven plagues, clothed in pure bright linen, and having their chests girded with golden bands.

15:6 As the temple opened, seven angels came forth dressed in clean, shinning linen (symbolic of purity and righteousness and truth (1 Jn 1:5) with a golden sash diagonally across their chest (symbolic of God's glory).

In an apparent solemn commissioning, one of the four living creatures (Cherubim or highest ranking of the angelic hosts) brought to each of the seven angels a bowl of "plagues" or the "wrath of God." The "bowls" (*phiale*, "a broad shallow bowl, saucer") were not for pouring, but for splattering or spilling the entire content at once. These were basins used in the temple for various purposes including catching the blood of the sacrifices (Ex 27:3; 1 Ki 7:50; 2 Kings 25:15).

There would be no holding back as the entire content of the bowl would flood the earth as a unit, affecting everyone. Perhaps before this begins, we should be motivated to pray for people groups, cities, and nations around the world that the gospel would reach their area soon.

Reflection: James said, "You do not have because you do not ask" (Jas 4:2). Who is asking for the nations, tribes and people today?

15:7

Then one of the four living creatures gave to the seven angels seven golden bowls full of the wrath of God who lives forever and ever.

15:7 The cherubim ("four living creatures") are committed to protecting the glory of God and His righteousness. They are the commissioning agent to these final seven angels, distributing to them the most horrible of all the judgments with full divine authority.

These bowls are "full" (*gemo*, "full to the brim") emphasizes the devastating effect of these judgments. The final phrase, "who lives forever and ever," indicates His eternal nature, which is different from everything and everyone in heaven, and indicates that He alone has the power to put an end to sin so that it cannot exist again in His presence.

This is the purpose of time and history. God has patiently withheld His judgment in grace (2 Pet 3:8-9), but now His grace has reached its end. Man has failed to respond in trust; rather has rejected God's offer of grace, refusing to believe that wrath would ever come.

The millennium and eternity are different stories of an entirely new existence and relationship with God. Everything now is preparatory for that time. Jesus knows about the outpouring of the wrath of God and He detested the thought of having to suffer it, even sweat drops of blood contemplating it (Luke 22:44), but He suffered it once and for all so that repentant sinners would never have to be condemned to live forever under His wrath.

Now the wrath of God is about to be poured out on sinners because of what they did and have done to Jesus and His own. Sinners have been constantly warned throughout the Tribulation period, they have seen miraculous people (144,000 and the two witnesses) demonstrate God's power; yet for all that, they will harden their hearts and reap the consequences (Prov 28:14).

Reflection: Have you known people that refuse to listen to the gospel or would not consider trusting in Christ? (See John 3:19)

B. THE REACTION OF THE PRESENCE OF GOD (15:8)

15:8

The temple was filled with smoke from the glory of God and from His power, and no one was able to enter the temple till the seven plagues of the seven angels were completed.

15:8 As God set in motion these final judgments the "smoke from the glory of God and from His power" filled the temple prohibiting entry into the temple area. The smoke illustrates the absolute holiness of God, impossible to see or be associated with wickedness. "Your eyes are too pure to approve evil and You cannot look on wickedness" (Hab 1:13).

No sooner had the tabernacle opened than the angels appeared, and the tabernacle filled with smoke, as it did with Moses (Ex 40:34-35) when he finished the construction of the tabernacle until it was time for Israel to journey. It is as though even the worship was suspended until this final act of history was complete. Mercy now is past history. Intercession is paused as nothing now can delay the outpouring of wrath. This is the beginning of the end.

God is totally committed to anger and justice in these final days of the Tribulation. Everything else ceases. The Psalmist wrote, "You, even You are to be feared; and who may stand in Your presence when once You are angry."

Reflection: How do people behave when they do not believe they will ever be caught or found out? If someone has never been punished for wrong doing in their life, has he learned that he is not bad or evil, and thus any sudden punishment seems unjust or unfair? How does such a person tend to respond to the one who punishes them? (Prov 14:16).

CHAPTER 16

SEVEN BOWLS

"These judgments are greater, more intense, more global and more severe than any comparable event in human history."

This is the third and final set of judgments revealed against all of sinful mankind. The seal judgments (6:1-8:5), followed by the trumpet judgments (8:6-11:19) and finally the bowl judgments (16:1-21) conclude God's wrath against evil. The Seven Bowls occur in the last year or possibly in the last six months of the Tribulation period. These are global judgments, whereas earlier judgments were more localized. The first four bowls (as well as the first four trumpets) affect all the earth, sea, inland waters, and the sky; the last three bowls affect all humanity.

The differences between the trumpets and the bowls are:
(1) the bowl judgments are complete and global, whereas the trumpets are partial or limited (i.e. 1/3 of the earth);
(2) the trumpet judgments continue to give unbelievers the offer to repent and believe, but the bowl judgments do not;
(3) mankind is indirectly affected by the trumpet judgments, but directly affected by the bowl judgments, and painfully so.

The bowl judgments are a parallel or reenactment of the Egyptian plagues (Exodus 7-12). The result of these judgments brings absolute conviction that God is all-powerful over all creation. Simultaneously, as the bowl judgments are being poured out, Daniel describes a World War that will occur, culminating with the global battle of Armageddon (11:36-45).

I. THE ORDER FOR THE BOWL JUDGMENTS TO BEGIN (16:1)

16:1

Then I heard a loud voice from the temple saying to the seven angels, "Go and pour out the bowls of the wrath of God on the earth,

16:1 The scene continues from the front of the heavenly temple (as chapter 15), where the seven angels appear (15:5-8), each of which has been given a bowl filled with the wrath of God (15:7). A "loud" voice (*megales*, "large, great, huge or loud" from which we have the word megaphone). This word is used 11 times in this chapter!

The voice shouts from the Temple now and after the last bowl is poured out (16:17). The voice must be that of God since no one else is in the temple (15:8). The adjective is used to describe the intense heat (v. 9), the great river Euphrates (v. 12), the great day of

God Almighty (v. 14), a severe earthquake (v. 18), the great city and Babylon the Great (v. 19), huge hailstones (v. 21) and a terrible plague (v. 21). These judgments are greater, more intense, more global, and more severe than any comparable event in human history.

They can not begin until the order is given. This will be the time that all heaven has waited for. There is a similarity between the bowl judgments and the trumpet judgments, but the differences indicate that they are separate judgments, not simultaneous. For example, the trumpet judgment dealt with a third of the world population, but the bowl judgment affected the entire population of the world. Therefore, it is best to understand these events as sequential chronologically, with only one pause to reiterate that the judgments are just and righteous (vvs. 5-7).

It should be remembered that there are three destructive elements occurring simultaneously:
(1) Judgments from God,
(2) The Antichrist's attacks and killings, and
(3) The unrelenting attacks from the full number of demons that exist (those that were thrown out of heaven, the "normal" group of demons that have been operating on the earthly scene throughout history, and the recently released group of demons from the abyss. The voice commanded them to "Go your ways and empty out the seven bowls of God's wrath on earth."

Reflection: Do you think that a person can cross a line and must be judged, or should mercy be given even if caught in the act, when the guilty person says he is sorry?

1) THE FIRST BOWL JUDGMENT (16:2) -- PAINFUL SORES

16:2

So the first went and poured out his bowl upon the earth, and a foul and loathsome sore came upon the men who had the mark of the beast and those who worshiped his image. .

16:2 With immediate response, these angels begin "pouring" out their judgments on the whole earth. These "foul"(*kakos*, "injurious, troublesome, destructive") and "loathsome," (*poneros*, "annoyance, hardship, causing pain, diseased") or ugly "sours" (*helkos*, "wound producing discharge pus, ulcer) is an inflamed, oozing, ulcerous and painful sore on nearly everyone. These sores are specifically targeted on everyone who had accepted the mark of the beast (13:16-17) and worshipped the image of the Antichrist (13:12), who had ignored the warnings of the first angel (Rev. 14:6-7). There will be sores associated with the fifth bowl as well (vv. 10-11). This is the same word used in the Septuagint to translate the Hebrew word for "boils" inflicted on the Egyptians in the sixth boil-plague in Egypt (Ex 9:8-12; see also Deut 28:27,35 for promised sore-judgments). It is possible that the sores do not go away, but become cumulative, one piling on top of the other.

By the time of the fifth bowl judgment the people are still in pain from the first judgment. Rather than stopping to reflect on what will be happening to them they continue to rebel and lust after their evil deeds (9:20-21). This characteristic will only get worse with each judgment. It is hard to imagine the global population suffering from painful sores that nothing can cure, especially the beast.

Generally, people in such conditions do not get along with others and become irritable. This may be what Zechariah saw in his vision: "Now this will be the plague with which the Lord will strike all the peoples who have gone to war against Jerusalem; their flesh will rot while they stand on their feet, and their flesh will rot while they stand on their feet, and the eyes will rot in their sockets, and their tongue will rot in their mouth" (Zech 14:12). Have you ever had carbuncles, boils or chicken pox? The author once had 32 boils all over his body at one time from a blood infection in the Colombian jungle. It was miserable.

Reflection: Can you imagine everyone suffering from the same thing?

(2) THE SECOND BOWL JUDGMENT (16:3) – SEA LIFE DESTROYED

16:3

Then the second angel poured out his bowl on the sea, and it became blood as of a dead man; and every living creature in the sea died.

16:3 Every living creature in the sea dies as the water changes from a deadly toxic substance to a blood-like appearance. The second trumpet (8:8-9) turned a third of the sea to a similar blood-like substance, killing a third of the creatures. It is interesting that the first plague in Egypt was the turning of the Nile into blood (Ex 7:14-25), killing everything in the river and causing a horrible stench. The oceans cover about 70 percent of the earth's surface, which now is transformed into a death trap for all living creatures.

This may be similar to the phenomenon of the "Red Tide," which occurred in Florida in 1949. Where this occurs all sea animals and plants die and will poison anyone who might eat them. Much of the food supply of the world is dependent upon the sea. Nothing has ever compared to the vastness of the pollution of this second bowl.

Reflection: Have you ever been around a lot of dead fish on the shoreline? Can you imagine this scene?

(3) THE THIRD BOWL JUDGMENT (16:4-7) -- RIVERS POLLUTED

16:4

Then the third angel poured out his bowl on the rivers and springs of water, and they became blood

16:4 The third bowl now extends the second bowl judgment from the oceans to the fresh water rivers and springs, which likewise became as blood. The third trumpet made a third of the inland waters to become bitter and poisoned as wormwood (8:10-11).

In addition to this, the two witnesses "have the power to shut up the sky, so that rain will not fall during the days of their prophesying (that is, the last 3 ½ hears of the Tribulation); and they have power over the waters to turn them into blood" (11:6). With the temporary restraining of the earth's winds (7:1) there is not cycling of evaporation and condensation, causing droughts and the end of the hydrological cycle.

Now all sea and water creatures die and all the fresh water sources become putrefied, except what will be stored. Perhaps well water is the only exception, but few of us use wells today. The more than 55% of the world's population that live in urban cities are in for difficulties.

The amount of suffering, hardships, and starvation cannot be imagined. No water to drink or in which to bathe. With oozing sores from the first bowl judgment and scorching heat from the fourth bowl judgment to come, life is unbearable. The many earthquakes will make every city look like a bombed out war zone and power plants will be inoperable, leaving populations mostly without electricity. Camping can be enjoyable for a while, only if fresh water is accessible.

Reflection: Have you ever been in a situation where water or other drinks were not available? Did you turn to the Lord for help?

Before it really gets bad, there is a pause to reflect on how a God of compassion, mercy and love could send such horrible judgments on mankind. This next angel speaks to all observers in defense of God's character and justification for the Tribulation.

RIGHTEOUS JUSTIFICATION OF JUDGMENTS

16:5

And I heard the angel of the waters saying: "You are righteous, O Lord, The One who is and who was and who is to be, Because You have judged these things."

16:5 After the horrors of the first four bowls, we need a reiteration of the reasoning and justice of God in all these judgments. Many people have a problem accepting the severity of the judgment of God in these descriptions (as in the severity of the conquest of Canaan).

The answer lies in the character and justice of God. His wrath can be terrifying and final, but it is always just and appropriate according to the individual's rejection of Christ's messenger. His principle is that the way you treat others is the way you will be treated.

In the title of the Author of these judgments there is a change: "Holy One, who is and who always was…" This passage does not add the earlier description, "and who is still to come" (Rev 1:4, 8; 4:8). The point is that, at this time, it is not that He "is to come," but that He is now coming in victory. He is the One who has "judged" these things.

No one who knows the situation of the Tribulation will be able to say that the destruction is unjust. Our glimpses into this future time are enough to know that these judgments are merited by the entire rebellious and wicked population.

SEVEN BOWLS

Reflection: What do these verses teach about God's judgments?

Gen 18:25

Psa 19:9

Psa 119:75

Rom 2:5

Rev 19:1-2

GOLDEN RULE

16:6

For they have shed the blood of saints and prophets, And You have given them blood to drink. For it is their just due.

16:6 Unbelievers' treatment of believers and prophets/messengers through the ages and, now in the present Tribulation experience, will now be returned back to them. These populations will have had multiple opportunities to hear and understand the gospel throughout the Tribulation, which is apparent because of the hundreds of thousands or millions that believe and are killed, as in the fifth seal (Rev 6:9-11), the heavenly martyrs (7:9, 14) and the martyred two witnesses (11:7).

The nations will become enraged in their aggression against the believers, such that they will be "drunk with the blood of the saints, and with the blood of the witnesses of Jesus" (17:6). These apostate and rebellious people have shamelessly slaughtered countless millions of believers, so these murderers will receive a just punishment. They have been bloodthirsty, now that is all they can drink.

These judgments are all part of the last minute preparation before He comes, although the judgments are gruesome and terrifying. Pharaoh tried to drown the Jewish baby boys, but his whole army was later drowned in the Red Sea. Such are the ways of God. God's justice in all these horrible events is exalted (v. 7 and 15:3). As devastating as the judgments are, if this is just, then one can only imagine how the world has been treating the believers.

Reflection: Have you ever been bold enough to provoke a criticism or unjust persecution for your faith?

IN THE MIDST OF JUDGMENT GOD IS JUST

16:7

"And I heard another from the altar saying, "Even so, Lord God Almighty, true and righteous are Your judgments."

16:7 The personification of the altar or the voice(s) "from the altar" may refer to the souls of the martyred saints (6:9-11) who were waiting for their just vengeance.

These all confirm what the angel will announce (16:5). The angel will proclaim the justice in the wrath of God being poured out on the leaders and their followers in their revolt against all that is God's.

Most people build a false image of God in their minds, that He is a grandfather-type, always fair and kind, overlooking evil and never punishing wrong. They imagine that He will always bestow benefits on the undeserving without discrimination of any kind. Man's view of justice stems from a humanistic worldview of an idealistic reality with man at the beneficial center, rather than God. Man thinks God must play by man's rules if man deems to allow God be God. However, God sets His own standards of justice and righteousness. His decrees are just and holy, even if we do not understand it or like it. Those who choose to reject God's person, are not rejecting a mere lifestyle option; they are rejecting truth and justice itself.

Reflection: Have you struggled with understanding the horrible treatment that the world will receive in the Tribulation? Why?

(4) THE FOURTH BOWL (16:8-9) – SCORCHING HEAT

16:8-9

Then the fourth angel poured out his bowl on the sun, and power was given to him to scorch men with fire. 9 And men were scorched with great heat, and they blasphemed the name of God who has power over these plagues; and they did not repent and give Him glory.

16:8-9 The first three angels have poured out their bowls of wrath on the earth, while the fourth poured out his judgment on the sun. Since the 4th day of creation, the sun has been the source of life on earth, but now becomes a deadly tool for God's 4th judgment. The fourth trumpet (8:12) darkened the sun, moon and star's illumination for a 1/3 of the day, which will have created freezing temperatures.

Now he 4th bowl judgment the sun scorches the earth with heat. One of the last prophecies of the OT described this horrible heat in Mal 4:1. The sun can emit bursts of energy or solar explosions to any level that could literally burn any part of the earth's surface to any degree. The sun's rays will penetrate everything and the pain will be unbearable.

The phrase "to scorch men with fire" does not translate the article, which should read "to scorch the men..." The use of the article implies that "the men" refer to a specific group of men, i.e. probably the ones with the mark of the beast. Surviving believers will not be affected.

No one doubts that these unprecedented catastrophic events are, in fact, judgments from God. No matter how moderate or severe the experiences of the survivors in the Tribulation, they continued to refuse to acknowledge God or repent and believe. They are so influenced by demonic seducing spirits that they increasingly hate God and perpetually blaspheme His name. They had reached a point of no return when they took the mark of the beast.

Reflection: Have you ever met someone who appeared to hate God?

What a warning to everyone! How blind and hard can man become? Anyone who becomes bitter towards God, grows indifferent to His Word and ignores the convicting work of the Spirit, becomes more callused, indifferent and hardened against God.

Reflection: What do these verses teach us about becoming hardened?

Heb 3:7-19

1 Cor 10:10

What was the promise for the believer in Rev 7:14, 16?

How will they become increasingly like the Beast they worship according to 13:6 and 9:20-21?

(5) THE FIFTH BOWL (16:10-11) – DARKNESS

16:10

Then the fifth angel poured out his bowl on the throne of the beast, and his kingdom became full of darkness; and they gnawed their tongues because of the pain.

16:10a The fifth through the seventh bowl judgments are part of the Armageddon development. After the universal scorching, the fifth bowl is poured out selectively on the throne of the beast, which brings darkness on the administration of the Antichrist's empire and his worldwide kingdom, and painful sores continue on all people.

Whether this "throne" or headquarters is the rebuilt Babylon, Jerusalem or Rome, it will be very apparent that this judgment is targeting specifically the Antichrist. The darkness will only add to their terror and inability to escape the judgments, because there is nothing they can do to alleviate the darkness.

Joel described this time as "a day of darkness and gloom, a day of clouds and thick darkness...Multitudes, multitudes in the valley of decision! For the day of the Lord is near in the valley of decision. The sun and moon grow dark and the stars lose their brightness" (Joel 2:2; 3:14-15).

Zephaniah saw the same event, "a day of darkness and gloom, a day of clouds and thick darkness" (Zeph 1:15). Luke described this time as well, "The sun will be changed to darkness and the moon to blood before the great and glorious day of the Lord comes, and then everyone who calls on the name of the Lord will be saved" (Acts 2:20-21). Is this a foretaste of the "outer darkness"? (Matt 5:0; 22:13; 8:12).

God is communicating to the world that the domain of the Antichrist is the kingdom of darkness. God never gives up. He still hopes some will repent.

Reflection: Have you ever been really mad at someone? How easy was it to ask forgiveness and be reconciled to them? ... or have you yet to be reconciled?

16:l0b The judgment we are seeing is designed to discredit the Antichrist, who will pretend to control the earth. One author mentions

SEVEN BOWLS

that this is the last reference to a failure to repent (2:21; 9:21; 16:9). Now we see that people are becoming more obstinate and aggressive against all that is God. This is similar to the fifth trumpet (9:1-11), which was partial darkness (1/3 of the day), and the ninth plague (Ex 10:21-23). Moses wrote of that plague that was so dark that "during that time people scarcely moved, for they could not see" (Ex 10:23).

They will probably still be suffering from the sores or boils from the first bowl (16:2) and the burns from the 4th bowl (16:8). Men are unable to see to find any alleviation from their sores and burns so they "gnawed" (present tense, continually kept on gnawing") their tongues out of agony."

Reflection: What does it take to break the will of a person?

REBELLION PROVOKES BLASPHEMY

16:11

They blasphemed the God of heaven because of their pains and their sores, and did not repent of their deeds.

16:11 But they will not repent. Now they are confirmed in their rebellion and unbelief. They do not care at all. They can only think of how much they hate God. They have become like their master, Satan.

The final two judgments are the most severe of all and are poured out on hardened, hating, hurting slaves of Satan. Where is the throne of the "beast"? His image is in the temple at Jerusalem, so that may be the headquarters of his empire. However, he could be ruling from Rome, in cooperation with the apostate church and the false prophet (Rev. 17).

If "Babylon" is to be taken literally, then he is ruling from Iraq. These Tribulation survivors are not atheists. They know God exists, but they will choose to hate Him as the God of the Jews and Christians. They initially recognize that the circumstances they are suffering are from the hand of Jewish God (as all insurance policies state about calamites), but they refuse to want to trust Him, repent or worship Him.

Instead of an awakening and a turning to God, it produces a self-pity and a bitter self-centeredness that rages against anything that discredits their importance or that they cannot control. As circumstances get worse universally they become convinced that the Judeo/Christian God must be destroyed to have any relief. Therefore all remaining

Christians and Jews must be killed. It will behoove them to see how David took his anger to God and found that he could still trust God.

Reflection: Can you see any help for anger in these Psalms?

Psa 10

Psa 13

Psa 38

Psa 68

Their rage will lead them to think irrationally and to easily be persuaded by demonic influence to launch an all out attack on Israel.

(6) THE SIXTH BOWL (16:12-16) – THE EUPHRATES DRIES UP ALLOWING EASTERN ARMIES TO INVADE ISRAEL

16:12

Then the sixth angel poured out his bowl on the great river Euphrates, and its water was dried up, so that the way of the kings from the east might be prepared.

16:12 The sixth bowl will dry up the Euphrates River, opening the avenue for the kings of the East to invade the Middle East. It is the longest river in the Middle East, being 1,800 miles long from Mt Ararat (modern Turkey) down to the Persian Gulf. Today the only thing that separates Iran and Iraq is the Euphrates River, but originally, it was the Eastern boundary of the land promised to Abraham (Gen 15:18; Deut 1:7; 11:24; Josh 1:4), thus any invader crossing this river was technically entering the Promise Land. It was also the Eastern boundary of the Roman Empire.

This river was also the scene of the sixth trumpet (Rev 9:13ff), which unleashed an army of 200 million demonic horsemen. After the scorching heat of the 4th bowl, the snow on Mt Ararat will be melting sending torrents of water downstream, probably washing out all the bridges and spreading out beyond its banks. Now an army from the nations of the world will have gathered for the great battle of Armageddon.

Who are the "kings from the East?" This question has been answered by over fifty interpretations of their identities. The one thing that is clear is that they come from the Orient or East of Israel, where a majority of the world's population live, most of which already hold strong anti-Judeo/Christian views. The political or ideological motivation for this attack is only explained by the next verses.

The Euphrates is the basic geographical boundary that separates the Middle East from the Orient, including the people of Iran (Persia), Afghanistan, Pakistan, India, and China. Already dams have been built across the Euphrates River in the latter 20th century for irrigation leaving little water in the Euphrates. The drying up of this river is prophesied in Isa 11:15.

Reflection: What do you think would motivate the Eastern armies to march against Israel? Do any countries today to the north and east of Israel hate the Jews?

THREE DEMONS

16:13

And I saw three unclean spirits like frogs coming out of the mouth of the dragon, out of the mouth of the beast, and out of the mouth of the false prophet.

16:13-14 God's plan is to deal with all the world nations in judgment in the land of Israel. The rage and hatred against Israel and her God will need to be inculcated into the minds of millions of Easterners.

Three demons that looked like frogs (unclean animals to the Jews – Lev 11:10-11, 41) came out of the mouths of Satan (the dragon—12:3-9), the Antichrist (13:1-10) and the false prophet (13:11-18). These are Satan's counterfeit trinity.

These demons will perform miraculous signs to convince the world to gather at the plain of Megiddo in Central Israel. Jesus warned that "false Christ's and false prophets ... will show signs and wonders, in order to lead astray, if possible, the elect" (Mark 13:22; also 2 Thes 2:9-10).

The "spirit of antichrist" is that doctrine that rejects the Jesus Christ is the Son of God (1 Jn 4:3), which is an innate characteristic of demonic influence. This rejection is the core doctrine of Islam. To call Jesus the "Son of God" is the most offensive term a Muslim can hear and it drives them into a frenzy of murder, even if their own family member expresses it. The insanity of this hatred and fanaticism is a demonic influence that will become global in the Tribulation.

SEDUCING SPIRIT GATHER THE LAST REBELLION

16:14

For they are spirits of demons, performing signs, which go out to the kings of the earth and of the whole world, to gather them to the battle of that great day of God Almighty.

16:14 These demon seducers will convince the world that their only relief is to destroy everything that has to do with the God of the Jews/Christians. All this rebellious activity will perfectly fulfill the will of God and His revealed purposes (Rev 17:17). The battle will go on for a brief period of time and include ravaging the city of Jerusalem (Zech 14:1-3), since many of the Jews will not bow down to the image.

God has decided "enough is enough." Now is the time to end all rebellion and evil on earth once and for all. This will fulfill the prophecy: "Why do the nations rebel? Why are the countries devising plots that will fail? The kings of the earth form a united front, the rulers collaborating against the Lord and his anointed king... The one enthroned in heaven laughs in disgust; the Lord taunts them" (Ps 2:1-4).

Reflection: Why do these nations come to Israel?

Zech 14:2-3

Joel 3:2

Joel 3:9-13

FINAL WARNING FROM JESUS DIRECTLY TO BELIEVERS

16:15

Behold, I am coming as a thief. Blessed is he who watches, and keeps his garments, lest he walk naked and they see his shame.

16:15 This parenthetical verse is written to the believing remnant who have survived, to give them comfort and hope, as well as warning of the quickness of Christ's return. The suddenness of Christ's coming is compared to a thief who attacks when one is least aware. People will gather in Jerusalem and be insane in their lust for blood because of their initial successes, never dreaming that tragedy is about to hit them.

Just as Christians in the time of the Church are not to be surprised by the Rapture (1 Thes 5:4), so the believers in the Tribulation should not be taken by surprise, but rather, they should be anticipating His coming. Having seen the signs of the bowl judgments they should know that the end is imminent.

The metaphor of the garments refers to the garment or robe of righteousness, which God provides by faith.

The sixth trumpet (Rev 9:14) a short time before had dried up the Euphrates, but now the armies are much larger than the 200 million. The time between the sixth and seventh judgments may be relatively short.

The Lord Jesus Himself speaks these words of encouragement. The suddenness of His return is also mentioned in Rev 3:3. His enemies will fear these words, but His surviving people will take encouragement: "Please come, Lord Jesus."

The believers are to do two things:
(1) "Stay awake" (*gregoreo*, present tense, "continually… give attention to") means keeping the right priorities and life focus.
(2) The believer is to "keep his garments," which refer to the practical result of the Christian behavior, or the Christ-likeness.

In an age of horrible persecution there will be a terrible price to pay to maintain this character. The imagery is of a soldier's need to stay awake with his clothes on to be prepared for the battle whenever it will occur. It will be so sudden that there will be no time to get dressed. The shame is of a soldier being derelict in his duty and not prepared for the battle. In a similar way the believer today is to be ready at all times for the rapture. But this is more specific. They will know that the end is soon when the see the bowl judgments taking place as predicted.

Reflection: How did John describe the readiness of the believer today in 1 John 2:28?

GATHERING AT ARMAGEDDON

16:16

And they gathered them together to the place called in Hebrew, Armageddon.

16:16 After a brief encouragement the battle begins. However, the real battle will take place north of Jerusalem in the valley of Esdraelon or Jezreel, near the city of Megiddo. It is about 14 miles wide and 20 miles long. The battle of "Armageddon" transliterates the Hebrew words for "mount of Megiddo" (*harmagedon*, "place of troops or slaughter") (v. 16). The Aramaic meaning of the word is "mount of the assembly," and may refer to the assembly of the kings who come to fight. There is no mountain by this name, so it could refer to the hill or tell on which the city of Megiddo is located.

More than 200 battles have been fought in this region. This was the plain where Barak defeated the armies of Canaan (Jud 5:19) and Gideon met the Midianites (Jud 7).

The slaughter of the Antichrist's armies will be beyond description, leaving few, if any, survivors. The blood will splatter 4-5 feet high and will run in streams for nearly 200 miles (14:20). The sixth bowl sets the stage for the final bowl, the battle of Armageddon that will finally end it all, which is described in chapter 19.

(7) THE SEVENTH BOWL (16:17-21) – WIDESPREAD DESTRUCTION

16:17

Then the seventh angel poured out his bowl into the air, and a loud voice came out of the temple of heaven, from the throne, saying, "It is done!"

16:17 The seventh bowl is a devastating series of quick, global and massive destruction on earth. It primarily targets the air, the primary domain of devil, "the prince of the power of the air" (Eph 2:2), but the immediate result of the instability of the atmosphere is metrological, resulting in convulsions in the air.

There was a similar reaction after the seventh seal (8:5) and the seventh trumpet (11:15-19), when there were voices in heaven shouting

SEVEN BOWLS

Christ's kingdom had come (11:15), then lightning, thunder, a hailstorm, and an earthquake (11:19). But these earlier metrological demonstrations were not comparable to this final bowl judgment. This is the worse judgment of all. In a few words, there is the description of the most destructive event in human history.

With the conclusion of the seventh bowl the time is up. A massive voice shouts out: "It is done" (*gegonen*, perfect tense, "it has come to pass"). There are no more judgments to come. Each had been designed to allow the afflicted to repent, but now the judgments are over.

One cannot but compare this declaration with that of Christ on the cross, where God's wrath was poured out on the Son, "It is finished" (John 19:30). The history of mankind will end here. From now on will be the beginning of the millennial kingdom. The world will rush into a conflict, which they think is their last hope, but it is their doom. Their egos and false ideology will lead them into a direct conflict with Christ in His second coming. There will be no survivors of this conflict.

GREATEST EARTHQUAKE

16:18

And there were noises and thunderings and lightnings; and there was a great earthquake, such a mighty and great earthquake as had not occurred since men were on the earth.

16:18 This final bowl judgment will be followed by thunders and lightening and a unparalleled global earthquake. There had been other horrible earthquakes in 8:5 and 11:19, but this one will be global, except for Israel.

Haggai prophesied, "In just a little while I will once again shake the sky and the earth, the sea and the dry ground. I will also shake up all the nations..." (2:6-7a). The phrase "once again" is translated in Hebrews 12:26-27 as "once more," which indicates that at a time in the past there was a comparable "shaking." This must refer back to the geological "shaking" or moving of the earth's surface to form the present continents. According to vs. 20, the entire geology of the earth's surface will be flattened, probably back to a pre-flood state. Everything will be different. Nearly everything constructed will be destroyed.

Reflection: How do people feel when all their possessions are destroyed? What causes this feeling?

THE DESTRUCTION OF BABYLON

16:19-20

Now the great city was divided into three parts, and the cities of the nations fell. And great Babylon was remembered before God, to give her the cup of the wine of the fierceness of His wrath. 20 Then every island fled away, and the mountains were not found.

16:19-20 The "great city" refers to the destruction of Jerusalem, which was divided into three parts by the geological upheavals of the great earthquake (v. 18). Zechariah 14:4-10 describes these geological shifts in detail.

According to 11:8 the "great city" is Jerusalem, "the great city... where the Lord was crucified." At the same time the "cities of the nations fell." These cities are a distinct group from the "great city."

This mega-earthquake will reduce to rubble all the Gentile cities of the world, and the geological catastrophe may occur simultaneously with the defeat of the Antichrist (see 17:12-14). Can you imagine the total collapse of every city such as New York, Chicago, Mexico City, London, Tokyo, Sao Paulo, Beijing, New Deli, Paris, and Sydney, all at the same time?

Scholars are divided about the meaning of "Babylon," except that it becomes the capital of the Antichrist's empire. God has not forgotten her idolatry, cruelty and religious confusion for centuries. Babylon had seduced the nations (17:2) into her false idolatry.

This will result in enormous loss of life and the collapse of the world empire of the Antichrist. The earthquake will be so universal that all islands will disappear and mountains will be flattened, probably stretching out the landmasses, raising the global sea level and causing tsunamis on every coastline. Isaiah describe this geological upheaval in Isa 40:4. The mega-earthquake will complete the process begun in the 6th seal (6:12-14).

These judgments will be the massive topographical preparation for the millennial kingdom. There will be no more uninhabitable mountain ranges, desert wastelands or ice caps. This will be the restoration of the antediluvian (pre-flood) topography and climate. Jerusalem will become the highest point on earth and the center of the globe.

Reflection: What is the reason Jer 3:17 gives for this focus?

GIGANTIC GLOBAL HAIL STORM
16:21

"And great hail from heaven fell upon men, each hailstone about the weight of a talent. Men blasphemed God because of the plague of the hail, since that plague was exceedingly great."

16:21 To make matters worse, with all the earthquakes and now meteorological storms, there will be enormous hailstorms, with hail weighing up to 125 lbs. bombarding humans all over the world, destroying any building left standing and any exposed people. The heaviest hailstone recorded weighed about 2 lbs.

This final judgment is similar to seventh plague in Egypt (Ex 9:22-26). Just as Pharaoh and the Egyptian army did not repent, so the Tribulation survivors will still not repent; in fact, they will blaspheme God in disgust.

In the OT, blasphemers were supposed to be stoned to death (Lev. 24:16). Yet unrepentant and increasingly bitter man will not be broken, rather "men blasphemed God" because the judgment will be "exceedingly great."

The eternal punishment of man is hard for some to accept, but the best answer is that men in hell are eternally unrepentant. They are described as "weeping and gnashing of teeth" (Matt 8:12), with no remorse for not believing and having bitter hatred for their sentence. We cannot imagine how horrible either the earthly judgment will be or the eternal torment of hell, but free men get what they choose. They have sold their souls to Satan and they are bound to his same destiny.

Reflection: These eschatological events are inevitable. Nothing can prevent them from happening (Isa 43:13); however, there is only one way of escape from the final doom of the Antichrist. God has promised that those who by faith put their total trust in Christ as their Savior and Lord will escape both the "end time" wrath to come (Rev 3:10) and His eternal wrath (1 Thess 1:10). Since Christ suffered the wrath of God, because He took the condemnation for our sins, being made sin for us (2 Cor 5:21), so we can be forgiven and freely given the righteousness of God. We are no longer "children of wrath" (Eph 2:3), and now we are promised to be "delivered ... from the wrath to come" (1 Thes 1:10). We owe Jesus Christ everything for our future and eternity (1

Pet 2:24). Do I hear an "Amen!"?

Reflection: Every generation of Christians can identify to a degree with the saints of the Tribulation. There has always been a "beast" or demonic leader who has oppressed God's people and a false prophet religious leader of controlling religions that has led nations astray. But nothing has compared to the days of the Tribulation. Another parenthesis is now written to bring the reader more data on the significance of "Babylon" that suffered these final judgments.

CHAPTER 17

BABYLON, THE WHORE RELIGION

"Babylon appears more than 300 times in the Bible. It is the origin and symbol of the Satanic religious system that imitates the true faith and deceives millions who fail to seek the truth or discern error of its system."

While the judgments of God are taking place, the Antichrist is building his kingdom to entrap the people of the world in a false religion, which ultimately will worship him, along with the global political/economic system that obligates total submission of the United Nations to his government. This long task began in ancient Babylon, the site of the first major human rebellion against God (Gen 11:1-9), which became the source of major pagan religions opposing Israel and the true faith throughout the ages.

Man was created as a relational being, especially desirous of a relationship with his Creator, thus he longs to feel religious or "spiritual." Demonic sources sought to satisfy man's religious tendency without allowing him to come under God's authority or understanding of God's Word ("blinded their minds" – 2 Cor 4:4).

Satan works to "seduce" mankind into believing "doctrines of demons" (1 Tim 4:1). "Babylon" appears more than 300 times in the Bible. It is the origin and symbol of the satanic religious system that imitates the true faith and deceives millions who fail to seek the truth or discern the error of its system. The ultimate Babylon will be the Antichrist's political power base.

This chapter begins another parenthesis in the chronology of the Tribulation. The events have to overlap and fit somewhere among the seals, trumpets and bowls. Chapter 17 unveils the religious Babylon of the Antichrist's empire as a world religion, which seems to fit the first half of the Tribulation period. Only a religion with the appearance of the supernatural that can reach beyond the physical, historical, geographical and cultural barriers will be able to accomplish world unity.

The Babylon described in chapter 18 appears to be a commercial/political center and the seat of the global empire of the Antichrist, which will dominate the second half of the Tribulation, enduring until the Second Advent of Christ.

These two chapters describe the world system under the leadership of Satan, the Antichrist and the false prophet. They eventually gain full global control of all aspects of life to deceive and destroy mankind. Every move they make only confirms the justice of the horrific judgments that God pours out on the earth. As the severity of the seal, trumpet and bowl judgments increase and accelerate, it becomes apparent that the Antichrist is powerless to alleviate the situation, so he skillfully turns the table and makes the enemy to be God. Instead of giving up and turning to God, man increases his hatred for God as it is inspired by the Antichrist, whose demonic deceit has successfully worked for millennia.

The Antichrist along with the false prophet will establish a mandatory world religion as a means to unify the peoples of the world (chap 17), "BABYLON THE GREAT, THE MOTHER OF HARLOTS AND OF THE ABOMINATIONS OF THE EARTH." Then jealousy or paranoia will lead the Antichrist to assume the leadership and focus of this world religion. Why is this future world religion referred to as "Babylon?"

After the flood Noah's descendents migrated East from Mt. Ararat to the plains of Babylon where they decided to "make for [themselves] a name" (Gen 11:4). This refusal to continue to spread out and repopulate the globe had religious implications. They built brick towers, today known as ziggurats, to reach to the gods. On the top they inscribed the sign of the zodiac, which was used by pagan priests to categorize the stars in supposed influential forces on earth.

This gave them the "power" to discern the future: a human effort to supplant any need of the true God and become omniscient. The "name" they built for themselves became human-like gods often of their ancestors. Nimrod, Noah's great-grandson, was a powerful leader who built the empire of Babel with cities in the land of Shinar to Assyria (Iran and Iraq). His name may be the root of the Hebrew word "to rebel," thus becoming a forerunner of the Antichrist.

When God judged the rebellion by confusing the language, He destroyed their ability to unite and forced them to spread out. They carried with them the notions of the false religions begun in Babel. Babylon remained an idolatrous center of contagious false worship. Even Israel became enraptured with the idol worship of Ishtar, the goddess of fertility, whose title was the "Queen of Heaven." Jeremiah wrote to the remnant of Judah who fled to Egypt, that their deterioration as a nation was caused by their Babylonian idolatry. Jeremiah 44:15-19 describes how all of Israel from the wives to the kings and princes in all the cities worshipped Ishtar, the "Queen of Heaven." Then God told Jeremiah to pronounce judgment on the Jewish nation for their defiant and addictive adherence to the Ishtar cult in (Jer 44:20-27). The goddesses, gods and priesthood developed in Babylon would spread both east and west mutating into various religious forms, then infiltrating into Judaism and Christianity. This final world religion described as a "harlot" is exposed and destroyed in chapter 17

I. RELIGIOUS BABYLON EXPOSED (17:1-6)

17:1

Then one of the seven angels who had the seven bowls came and talked with me, saying to me, "Come, I will show you the judgment of the great harlot who sits on many waters.

AUTHORITY OF THE HARLOT

17:1 One of the angels who had one of the bowl judgments exposes the "great harlot" and invites John to witness her judgment as well. As John is told the meaning of the metaphors he tells us the answers: the harlot is "the great city that has sovereignty over the kings of the earth" (17:18).

This harlot-city sits on "many waters," which is explained in v. 15 as a symbol for "peoples, multitudes, nations and languages." The idea of "sitting" has the meaning of a position of authority over the global populations. The harlot will not only be a seducer, but also will dominate and rule all the peoples of the earth. This delegated authority given to the Harlot was described in 13:7, "The beast was permitted to go to war against the saints and conquer them. He was given ruling authority over every tribe, people, language, and nation." The false prophet ("the beast from the earth") "exercised all the ruling authority of the first beast on his behalf..." (13:12).

The entire world will be forced to submit to the false worship of a Babylonian system, rather than the true God. Later the focus will change to the idol worship of the Antichrist, but the system of idolatrous religious worship is already set in place.

Reflection: What is the largest religious groups today and how many people do they dominate?

ALLIANCES OF THE HARLOT
17:2

with whom the kings of the earth committed fornication, and the inhabitants of the earth were made drunk with the wine of her fornication.

17:2 The kings of the earth had "committed adultery" with the harlot, leading their people to be "drunk" in her "fornication." They are addicted to and dependent upon what she offers and unthinkingly follow her dictates. The historical way to control people is through their leaders, especially in a day of kings and nobles. The language of the text appears to indicate a system that transcended the political Roman Empire of John's day, yet is related to ancient Rome, and is called Babylon. Is there a religion that grew out of Babylon and is associated with Rome with a global foundation?

The interaction of the "kings of the earth" and "all the inhabitants of the earth" with this harlot is called "fornication" (*porneuo*, "sexual immorality" of any kind). In the OT the association with false religions is considered "spiritual adultery," which describes Israel's apostasy with false religions, most of which originated in Babylon (Ezek 16, 23). The term expresses God's distain with false religions.

Rulers from around the world will become intimately allied with the future Babylonian Harlot religion, deceived by the Antichrist and the false prophet. This is not a description of an alcoholic drunkenness with "wine of fornication" or immorality with an actual prostitute, though such immorality may happen and was part of the Babylonian religions. This is a metaphoric description of the world's intoxication with the Antichrist's idolatrous false religion.

Jeremiah saw this future global Babylonian religion when he wrote, "Babylon has been a golden cup in the hand of the Lord, intoxicating all the earth. The nations have drunk of her wine; therefore the nations are going mad." This Harlot religion is described in the next passage.

It is difficult to show unbelievers how their sin is repugnant in God's sight and that He will judge sin. He gives people a free will and patiently waits to allow them time to repent before experiencing the consequences of their sins. God does not take pleasure in punishing sin, but eventually it becomes an imperative. Paul wrote, "But no, you won't listen. So you are storing up terrible punishment for yourself because of your stubbornness in refusing to turn from your sin. For there is going to come a day of judgment when God, the just judge of all the world, will judge all people according to what they have done" (Rom 2:5-6^{NLT}).

Reflection: Do you think people see how God is discussed with man's sin or they do not think God should judge sin?

APPEARANCE OF THE HARLOT

17:3

So he carried me away in the Spirit into the wilderness. And I saw a woman sitting on a scarlet beast, which was full of names of blasphemy, having seven heads and ten horns.

17:3 John now "carried away in [his] spirit" (i.e. in a vision, not physically, as 1:10; 4:2; 17:3; 21:10) to a "wilderness" (*eremos*, "deserted, desolate wasteland" – similar to where Babylon is located) where he sees the "woman" (the harlot of 17:1) sitting on a "scarlet beast." As she rides the beast, she takes advantage of him to giver her ascendency to world dominion.

The beast had seven heads and ten horns with names of blasphemy. This description identifies the beast as the Antichrist (13:1, 4; 14:9; 16:10). In Rev 13:1 Satan is seen as a "great red dragon," but here the "scarlet" signifies regal status, and likewise is the color of sin (Isa 1:18). The beast is full of "names of blasphemy" on each of its seven heads (13:1). The arrogance and self-deification of the Antichrist will lead him to assume names that belong to God. The Antichrist "will speak out against the Most High. ... and will speak monstrous things against the God of gods" (Dan 7:25; 11:36).

The Scriptures give the interpretation of the symbols of the seven heads in vss. 9-10 to be "seven mountains on which the woman sits, and they are seven kings; five have fallen, one is, the other has not yet come; and when he comes, he must remain a little while."

The seven heads are seven governments, past, present, and future upon which the Antichrist's kingdom will build, "for a little while." The "ten horns" are ten kings (v. 12), who will eventually form the federation kingdom of the Antichrist. Once again, church and state will be united as throughout the Dark Ages, but now in a universal unity without parallel in history. It will unite every culture and nation from king to peon to worship one religion.

Reflection: Do you see any efforts today to unite all religions, or to unite governments under a group of major leaders or to unite the world economy? Is there any need to do so?

RELIGIOUS WEALTH FROM EXTORTION

17:4

The woman was arrayed in purple and scarlet, and adorned with gold and precious stones and pearls, having in her hand a golden cup full of abominations and the filthiness of her fornication.

17:4 This harlot will be adorned in royalty and luxury; "purple and scarlet clothing and beautiful jewelry made of gold and precious gems and pearls." Through her religious immorality she has acquired the status of royalty, prosperity, nobility and wealth. "Scarlet" is likewise the dress of successful prostitutes (Prov 7:10). Likewise, her adornment is all too similar to the dress of ritualistic religions today.

In her hand she will hold "a golden cup full of abominations and of the unclean things of her immorality." It is like uncovering the inner self of a prostitute that appears so attractive on the outside, but is corrupt and rebellious on the inside. It is hard to imagine a religion that fits this description, because we only see the external and want to see the best in religions.

When truth is prostituted for gain and twisted for manipulative control, a religious system can become very much like a prostitute. When spiritual benefits can be purchased, they are prostituted and worthless. As John was visually taken into a desert place to see the reality of the façade of a false religion, perhaps we need to examine our lives not from the appearance we attempt to project, but the reality of whom we are inside.

Reflection: Do we fall into the same trap of hiding internal corruption, while appearing religious and spiritual on the outside?

WHO IS BABYLON?

17:5

And on her forehead a name was written: MYSTERY, BABYLON THE GREAT, THE MOTHER OF HARLOTS AND OF THE ABOMINATIONS OF THE EARTH.

17:5 The identity of this harlot is further revealed by her title. The first word, "mystery," is probably not part of the title, but describes the title. The word "mystery" implies that we are not talking about the geographical location, but a previously unknown truth that now is revealed and will become more evident in the course of history and especially in the end times.

"Babylon the Great, Mother of Prostitutes and of the abominations of the earth" is an awful description of anything, but more so of a religion. Adultery and fornication are often symbols of idolatry and false religion in Scripture (Judg 2:17; 8:27, 33; 1 Chron 5:25; 2 Chron 21:11; Jer 3:6, 8-9; Ezek 16:30-31, 36), so Babylon is the source that birthed the false religions that corrupted the global populations, and will do so again. Since the false religion of the tower of Babel (Gen 10-11) about 3,000 years before Christ, she has lived up to the meaning of her title, "Confusion."

The founder of Babylon, Nimrod, had a wife named Semiramis, who founded the secret religious rites of the Babylonian mystery religion. Semiramis had a son, who was "miraculously" conceived, which was a counterfeit fulfillment of Gen 3:15, centuries before Moses wrote Genesis by revelation. His name was Tammuz, but he was later killed by a wild animal, then restored to life, as an early Satanic imitation of the Messiah's resurrection. The worship of Baal is an adaptation of the worship of Tammuz.

The corruption of these false religions is evident in the perversion that pervaded the land of Canaan at the time of Joshua. After a period of decline, Babylon rose to prominence again under Nebuchadnezzar, 600 years before Christ. When the Persians took over Babylon in 539 BC they discouraged the mystery religions of the former empire Babylon. History reveals that the priesthood of Babylon migrated west to Pergamum (Pergamos) and is referred to in one of the seven churches of Asia Minor (2:12-17) as "Satan's seat." In the *Bible Knowledge Commentary*, John Walvoord writes:

> Crowns in the shape of a fish were worn by the chief priests of the Babylonian cult to honor the fish god. The crowns bore the words "Keeper of the Bridge," symbolic of the "bridge" between man and Satan. This handle was adopted by the Roman emperors, who used the Latin title *Pontifex Maximus*, which means "Major Keeper of the Bridge." The pope today is often called the pontiff, which comes from *pontifex*. When the teachers of the Babylonian mystery religions later moved from Pergamum to Rome, they were influential in paganizing Christianity and were the source of many

so-called religious rites which have crept into ritualistic churches. Babylon then is the symbol of apostasy and blasphemous substitution of idol-worship for the worship of God in Christ. In this passage Babylon comes to its final judgment. (John F. Walvoord, Roy B. Zuck and Dallas Theological Seminary, "Revelation," *The Bible Knowledge Commentary : An Exposition of the Scriptures* (Wheaton, IL: Victor Books, 1983-c1985), 2:971.)

Reflection: What do you know about the Roman Catholic Church?

ASSASSINATIONS OF THE HARLOT

17:6

I saw the woman, drunk with the blood of the saints and with the blood of the martyrs of Jesus. And when I saw her, I marveled with great amazement.

17:6 The "woman" religious system was "drunk with the blood of the saints and with the blood of the martyrs of Jesus." Killing Christians was the pastime entertainment in the city of Rome and the cult worship. Rome lived to hurt and to slaughter the people of God.

The killing of Christians associated with the harlot religion is the primary reference to religious persecution, not the political persecution that was common throughout history. The false religion of the harlot is a murderous system. An example of religious persecution is seen in the massacre of an estimated more than 50 million evangelical believers brutally killed in religious purges by the Roman Catholic religion throughout the history of the church.   This does not include the persecution against Christians from political movements (i.e. communism and Islam). It seems apparent that the apostate religious system of the first half of the seven years of Tribulation will virtually eliminate all true believers worldwide. The believers already in heaven (Rev 7:9-17) were slaughtered in the first 3 ½ years of the Tribulation by this religious system. John was shocked at this revelation.

Reflection: Can you ever imagine a global holocaust of evangelical believers? How many are killed today in China? How many evangelicals are killed in Muslim lands for being Christians?

David Hunt quotes Will Durant saying, "Compared with the Persecution of heresy in Europe from 1227 to 1492, the persecution of Christians

REVELATION 17

by Romans in the first three centuries after Christ was a mild and humane procedure." (David Hunt, *A Woman Rides the Beast*, pp. 243-244).

II. THE EXPLANATIONS OF THE BEAST (17:7-8)

17:7

But the angel said to me, "Why did you marvel? I will tell you the mystery of the woman and of the beast that carries her, which has the seven heads and the ten horns.

17:7 The angel questioned John's astonishment ("Why did you marvel?") at these massacres and symbols as though John should have recognized what was happening.

For clarity, the angel promised to interpret the symbols of the vision, "I will tell you the mystery..." In Rev 13:4, 8, 12 John had seen that a massive religious system would coordinate a global worship of the Antichrist, that will take place in the second half of the Tribulation. This is the harlot woman riding on the beast in her rise to global authority in the first half of the Tribulation.

Mysteries in Scripture are explained somewhere in Scriptures as Paul wrote, "comparing spiritual things with spiritual" (1 Cor 2:13). Each of the elements of the "mystery" will be explained later on. The rest of chapter 17 explains this mystery of the beast and the harlot; then, chapter 18 explains more about the Babylonian system.

IMITATION OF CHRIST

17:8

The beast that you saw was, and is not, and will ascend out of the bottomless pit and go to perdition. And those who dwell on the earth will marvel, whose names are not written in the Book of Life from the foundation of the world, when they see the beast that was, and is not, and yet is.

17:8 First, John is told the identity of the harlot and of the beast, which John had already seen. The angel wanted to make sure that John (and all his readers) would know the identity of these two cohorts.

Mysteries are explained for all who will search the Scriptures. This understanding is not acquired by mystical or special revelation.

John was given the answers by revelation so that he could record them by inspiration for us to discover in his writings. The beast is identified as the Antichrist (17:3), with his power source from Satan himself. The reference to the Beast that "was, and is not, and shall ascend out of the bottomless pit and go into perdition." This fits the description of the Beast in 13:3, "And I saw one of his heads as if it had been mortally wounded, and his deadly wound was healed. And all the world marveled and followed the beast."

The false prophet will use fake miracles to convince the world to worship the Antichrist. When he is resuscitated, he is possessed with the spirit of a powerful demon "out of the abyss." Those whose names are not recorded in the "Book of Life" will be deceived since they cannot know the Word of God (1 Cor 2:14) or possess the Holy Spirit to guide them in truth (Jn 16:13). Those "who dwell on earth" (a phrase that describes unbelievers in the Tribulation – 17:2; 3:10; 6:10; 8:13; 11:10; 13:8, 12, 14; 14:6) will be amazed by the Antichrist and deceived into worshipping him as a god come in the flesh. Only the elect will not be deceived (Matt 24:24).

Reflection: Do people today tend to follow anyone who can perform "miracles," regardless of their doctrines?

III. THE DESCRIPTION OF THE HARLOT (17:9-11)

17:9-10

Here is the mind which has wisdom: The seven heads are seven mountains on which the woman sits. 10 "There are also seven kings. Five have fallen, one is, and the other has not yet come. And when he comes, he must continue a short time.

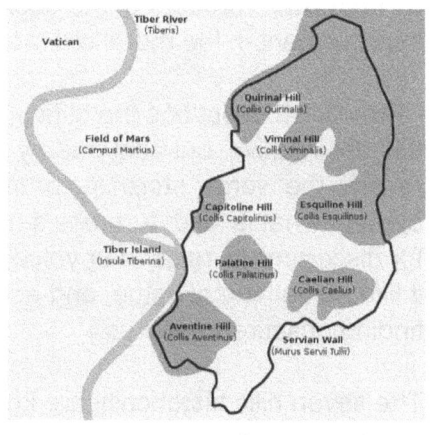

17:9-10 The angel states that "wisdom" is required to understand the meaning (as 13:18); that is, it requires spiritual insight to understand. Wisdom is not common sense, but is acquired investigative knowledge

REVELATION 17

applied to practical situations.

Historically, there have been many interpretations of these passages, effectively illustrating their difficulty. The "seven heads" of the beast are symbols of "seven mountains," the foundation of the harlot religion. The challenge to apply "wisdom" in conjunction with the interpretation of the seven mountains must mean that this is not obviously a geographical interpretation.

The earliest commentary on Revelation described these seven mountains as the "city of seven hills," that is, Rome. However, taking the passage as a whole, the seven mountains are "also seven kings." Thus the interpretation of the city being Rome is a little dubious.

"Five have fallen, one is, and the other has not yet come." When taken from John's first century perspective, we see that five major Gentile empires had fallen (Egypt, Assyria, Babylon, Medo-Persia, and Greece). The sixth kingdom ("that is") that existed at John's writing was Rome. The seventh empire was yet to come; the Antichrist's final world empire. All seven of these empires were centers of the idolatrous Babylonian pantheon of the Harlot. The seventh empire coming to unite the world in a 10-kingdom Federation will only "continue a short time." This probably refers to 3 ½ years or the last half of the Tribulation. The Antichrist's doom is sure, though he is fighting to annul God's judgment.

Reflection: Throughout the course of history has there been an improvement in the moral character of nations?

(Prov 2:1-5 describes the difficulty and challenge of acquiring wisdom. It is not intuitive, but acquired by an 8-fold diligence investigation: receive the words; store up commands, make one's ears attentive or open to what is said; turn one's heart to understand; call out in prayer for discernment; raise your voice (asking others?); seek or investigate it like something of value; and accept the demanding requirements of finding obscure treasures.)

The seven hills historically are known as Palatine, Aventine, Caelian, Equiline, Viminal, Quirimal, and Capitoline. However, as the city expanded it included two other hills Janiculum and Pincian.

THE DOOMED BEAST LAST TRY

17:7

And the beast that was, and is not, is himself also the eighth, and is of the seven, and is going to perdition.

17:11 Out of the seventh empire comes the Beast, "the eighth" king, who is wounded mortally, but amazingly is resuscitated. When the Antichrist is possessed of a demonic spirit from the Abyss at the mid-point of the Tribulation, he becomes essentially Satan incarnate.

If the seventh king (kingdom) is yet future, then it refers to the initial ten-kingdom Federation of the Antichrist, which will be set up at the beginning of the first half of the 7-year Tribulation and bring initial peace to the world.

At the mid-point of the Tribulation a crisis is reached, (after the six seals) when the Antichrist will destroy the global religious Harlot system (to be described later in this chapter) and supplant three of the ten kingdoms. This action will leave seven kings in the global federation who will submit to the Antichrist's assumption of absolute divine authority, both politically and religiously, over the entire world for the last 3 ½ years of the Tribulation.

Daniel likewise saw a ten-nation federation under the Antichrist:
> "The ten horns are ten kings who shall arise from this kingdom. And another shall rise after them; He [Antichrist] shall be different from the first ones, And shall subdue three kings. :25 He shall speak pompous words against the Most High, shall persecute the saints of the Most High, And shall intend to change times and law. Then the saints shall be given into his hand for a time and times and half a time" [or 3 ½ years]. (Daniel 7:24-25)

No matter how powerful the Antichrist may appear to be, his doom is fixed and he cannot avoid God's final judgment. The only question is how many deceived and unwitting humans can he drag down with him. The alliance with the Harlot's apostate world church will obligate a bond with the Antichrist that will doom their souls along with Satan.

Reflection: Why are nations attempting to unite in regional political blocks today? i.e., Andean group, European Group, N. American group, N. African group, S. African group, Muslim groups, India Group,

REVELATION 17

Chinese, Soviet republic groups and SE Asia group. Do these groups exist today to unite their economies, trade laws, etc.?

Reflection: If what is being described in Rev 17 is not far from what exists today. Does this motivate us to live godly and evangelize?

IV. THE TEN NATION FEDERATION (17:12-14)

17:12

The ten horns which you saw are ten kings who have received no kingdom as yet, but they receive authority for one hour as kings with the beast.

17:12 The "ten horns" (17:3) were the "ten kings" who will rule the ten nations of the Antichrist's empire. They have not received their kingdoms yet, but will be given authority as kings. All ten of these "kings" are contemporary in the Tribulation Period that will form a vast global Federation. The ten kings will have special "authority," (*exousia*, "the power of rule or government") probably a demonic power, granted to them for "one hour," which is a figure of speech that indicates a brief time.

Reflection: How similar is this story to that of the classic German legend "Faust?"

POWER OF UNITY (GOOD OR EVIL)

17:13

These are of one mind, and they will give their power and authority to the beast.

17:13 They are "of one mind," which sounds like a similar characteristic at the tower of Babel: "the people are one and they have one language...now nothing that they propose to do will be withheld from them" (Gen 11:6). These kings will give unquestioned loyalty and submission to the Antichrist. This Middle-East ruler who will emerge at the beginning of the Tribulation is so dynamic and convincing, even while the global situation is becoming chaotic, that these rulers give unquestioned total submission to the Antichrist.

Reflection: Is leadership defined as being able to get people to give the leader absolute blind authority in their lives?

COMMITMENT TO WAR WITH CHRIST

17:14

These will make war with the Lamb, and the Lamb will overcome them, for He is Lord of lords and King of kings; and those who are with Him are called, chosen, and faithful.

17:14 The agenda of the ten kings and the Antichrist is to destroy any notion of God and His people throughout the seven years of Tribulation. They are extremely effective in wiping out nearly all believers in the first half of the Tribulation. Then by the end of the seven-year period they will attack Israel and Jerusalem to destroy the last vestige of the God of the Bible. However bleak the situation may look for them at that time, the persecution of the Antichrist will fail and everyone associated with him will be doomed.

The Lamb [the Lord Jesus Christ] cannot be defeated; He is the "Lord of lords and King of kings." He is not an enemy to provoke, because He will defeat the Antichrist's army in total destruction as described in Rev 19. He is the only real authority. How foolish to go against God!

When He returns, "with him will be his called, chosen and faithful followers." When this confrontation occurs at Armageddon, all the believers of the Church Age will have been in heaven and now will return with Him, implying that the Rapture will have occurred long before this return (7 years before).

Since the ultimate battle with Satan is sure, we can win the battle over demonic temptations every day. He has no power, but to tempt and to suggest false ideas or teachings. By knowing the Word of God we will not be deceived and by committing to His will in Scripture, we can resist the lusts and temptations that Satan can use to destroy a life.

Reflection: Describe how you overcome temptation today.

V. REBELLION OF THE "WATERS" UNDER THE HARLOT (17:15-17)

17:15

Then he said to me, "The waters which you saw, where the harlot sits, are peoples, multitudes, nations, and tongues.

17:15 In 17:1 the Harlot "sits on many waters." These "waters" are now interpreted to mean "peoples, multitudes, nations, and tongues." The harlot religion will be a global, inclusive and possessing religion. The image of "sitting" on the people of the world, suggests suppression, domination, and authority.

Since she is riding on the back of the beast, this false religion has the authority of the beast to demand absolute submission with the consequence being to suffer capital punishment. This was a similar case when the Catholic Church was declared the sole state religion (AD 380), obligating everyone to become Roman Catholic or be considered a traitor to the empire and eventually suffer the death penalty for rebelling. So now the world will be obligated to join the false worship of the Babylonian system, abandoning any other religion, much less a biblical faith.

As was the case with the Roman Catholic Church's rise to power (AD 500-1000), the political powers despised the leaders of the Catholic Church because they "interfered" and assumed authority over the "sovereign" rulers of the land. One can only imagine what would provoke the hatred of the Antichrist (17:16) against this harlot religion. The Anabaptists in the 16th century and the First Amendment to the Constitution of the United States were the first to establish the separation of church and state as an official policy of government, which sought to eliminate these abuses of power in the church.

Reflection: Why do you think people today are so afraid of the power of churches that are involved with politics and law?

(This authority was based on the worldview that the only hope for salvation was through the Roman Catholic Church. Any rebellion from what the pope or a bishop declared would mean excommunication. If this was an insufficient threat, the pope could declare that every person in the nation or realm of the rebellious king or noble would likewise be excommunicated and have no hope of ever going to heaven.)

THE DESTRUCTION OF THE HARLOT RELIGION

17:16

And the ten horns which you saw on the beast, these will hate the harlot, make her desolate and naked, eat her flesh and burn her with fire.

17:16 The Antichrist's love affair or mutual admiration with the Babylonian cult religion will probably end around the mid-Tribulation point, when the "abomination of desolation" occurs (Dan 9:27; Matt 24:15).

The Antichrist and the Harlot will have used each other to rise to absolute power over the entire world, but there is only room for one at the top. Paranoia and distrust are common symptoms of powerful leaders who believe that they alone should lead and others are seen as competitors.

As the survivors of the first six seals see how powerless is the Harlot Babylonian church to protect them, so the Antichrist and the 10-nation Federation decide to rid themselves of this molesting religion. They take matters into their own hands and set up the religion and worship of the Antichrist. Anyone who does not worship him will be killed (Dan 11:36-38; 2 Thes 2:4; Rev 13:8, 15). The church of the Harlot will be a necessary evil to gain power over the world, but the Antichrist will not trust her.

The four-fold means of destroying the Harlot religious system sounds like the Inquisition with some hyperboles ("eat her flesh"). She will be stripped of all her beauty, power, wealth, authority and made illegal to congregate. "Desolate" may indicate her isolation (imprisonment?), "naked" may indicate the stripping of all her possessions, "eat her flesh" (as with Jezebel, Elijah prophesied that dogs would eat her flesh (2 Ki 9:36) could mean that the Harlot's leaders will be mercilessly killed and left for animals to eat, and "burn her with fire" may indicate the burning of all her churches to the ground or possibly a return to burning dissidents at the stake. It is not a pretty picture whatever John is describing. To fall into disfavor of the Antichrist is fatal.

Reflection: Have you witnessed how destructive selfish ambition for power and prestige can be?

GOD'S INVOLVEMENT IN THE FALL OF THE BEAST

17:17

For God has put it into their hearts to fulfill His purpose, to be of one mind, and to give their kingdom to the beast, until the words of God are fulfilled.

17:17 Of the 23 verses that speak of God putting ideas into the hearts of men, only two have a negative consequence: God gave Judas the idea to betray Jesus (Jn 13:2) and this text where kings get the idea

REVELATION 17

to give their kingdoms to the Antichrist. Both are key events in the fulfillment of prophecy. The word "purpose" is *gnome*, "that which is thought or known, resolve, or decreed." By doing this, the kings will act exactly as the prophecies predicted.

There is nothing that Satan would rather do than to annul one of the prophecies or purposes of God's Word. God puts it in their hearts, but they still consciously make the choice to join ranks with the Antichrist and abandon the Harlot religion.

As Satan overruns the world and finally destroys his kingdom and followers, he is doing exactly what God knew he would do. Ironically, the self-serving, egotistical, get-on-the-winning-side choice of the kings of the earth to serve the Antichrist fit perfectly into the prophetic plan of God for the eventual destruction of Satan's world government.

At last all of mankind is united in a one-world government, fulfilling the dream of the humanist, but it will only bring about the doom of the world. The last phrase is a key concept: "until the words of God will be fulfilled." Satan thinks he is ruling, but he is only doing what God said he would do. Nothing can stop the destruction of the Harlot's religion, which will carry out God's final judgment against all who have rejected His offer of salvation.

Reflection: Why is God so harsh on false religions according to Isa 42:8?

REIGNING CITY

17:18

And the woman whom you saw is that great city which reigns over the kings of the earth.

17:18 The answer to the question, "Who is that Harlot woman?," (17:1, 3) is given in vs. 18. She is that "great city that rules over the kings of the earth." John's readers and the Early Church identified this city as Rome, the capital of the known world at the writing of Revelation (AD 95). Both as a political empire and later as a twisted form of Christianity, Rome has persecuted Bible believers without mercy for 1600 years. Is there a link to Babylon?

After the destruction of Babylon by the Persians, the Babylonian priesthood migrated to Pergamum (Rev 2:13). Then the priesthood migrated to Rome as the Roman College of Pontiffs [*Collegium Pontificum*]

BABYLON, THE WHORE RELIGION

of the ancient Roman pagan religions. To gain political power, the emperor Augustus (BC 63 to AD 14) was made the first *Pontiex Maximus* of the Babylonian/Roman priesthood. This pagan religious office became an inseparable part of the Imperial office.

When Constantine declared Christianity legal (AD 313) he was the *Pontifex Maximus* of the Roman pantheon. To make Christianity on a par with the pagan religions, the emperor became the head of the Catholic Church. Constantine presided at the early Church Councils with this same title, *Pontifex Maximus,* as the official head of the Church to give authority to the Church's decisions.

Later, with the emperor residing in Constantinople, by the edict of Theodosius in February 380, Christianity was declared the only legal religion and Damasus I, bishop of Rome (366-384), was named the *Pontifex Maximus* to enforce the imperial decree. Emperors were no longer titled as *Pontifex Maximus*.

It was the same decrees of Theodosius that gave legal grounds for the Inquisitions 600 years later to begin persecuting any dissenters. The Roman Catholic Church has made all the popes since Damasus I the *Pontifex Maximus* with full civil and religious authority, as well as the infallible Vicar (representative) of Christ.

At the Rapture, any who are genuine believers in the Roman Catholic Church will be taken away, leaving a vast global infrastructure filled with unbelievers easily deceived by the Antichrist's logic and persuasion. She will ride his rise to global power destroying or subjugating all religions until they alone control the destiny of mankind, only to be betrayed and destroyed by the same Antichrist 3 ½ years later who can stand no other authority to question his decisions.

Babylon and Rome were the foundation of this vast religious system that will be more cruel and merciless than anyone can imagine. In the end her cruelties will pale in comparison to the Antichrist's religion of self-deification in the last 3 ½ years of the Tribulation.

Reflection: What do you know about the "Persecuted Church" today? Is it comparable?

CHAPTER 18

THE FALL OF BABYLON

"This chapter details the destruction of the Antichrist's global commercial control and self-worship system and how it will affect the inhabitants of the world."

Chapter 17 reveals the "great harlot" called "Babylon the Great" (17:5) and why she will be destroyed (17:1): she represents an immoral and wicked religious system whose chief purposes will be to murder believers in the Tribulation. But her destruction (chap. 17) will only set up a far worse religious/political/commercial enterprise that will bleed the world of its diminishing resources for the profit of the Antichrist and his enterprise. This chapter details the destruction of the Antichrist's global commercial control and self-worship system, and how it will affect the inhabitants of the world.

I. THE ANNOUNCEMENT OF THE JUDGMENT ON THE GREAT CITY (18:1-8)

18:1

After these things I saw another angel coming down from heaven, having great authority, and the earth was illuminated with his glory.

18:1 "After these things," that is, the next sequence of events will be after the destruction of the Harlot religion (chapter 17) at the mid-point of the Tribulation and the establishment of the Antichrist's self-worship and global commercial take-over.

"Another" (*allos*) angel, not one of the "seven angels" of 17:1, nor does this refer to a manifestation of Christ; however, by the presence and majesty of this angel "the earth was illuminated with his glory (or "splendor" NIV, NLT)." The different ranking and authority of the angels probably are evident by their likeness to the splendor of Christ. This angel will have "great" (*megas*) "authority," in comparison to the angels of the bowl judgments who will be capable of generating a global catastrophe.

The resplendent glory or brightness emanating from this angel appears to reflect the very glory of God Himself, indicating that he may have just come from His presence. This will be the final message of destruction on the corrupt world system of the Antichrist. This angel not only brings the message, but will carry out the judgment as well.

Reflection: Do we believe that if we are rebellious and disobedient that God becomes our enemy or our chastiser (Heb 12:5-8) to teach us the hard way to be obedient?

GREAT CITY IS FALLEN

18:2

And he cried mightily with a loud voice, saying, "Babylon the great is fallen, is fallen, and has become a dwelling place of demons, a prison for every foul spirit, and a cage for every unclean and hated bird!

18:2 He shouted "mightily," "Fallen! Fallen is Babylon the Great!" Is this the same destruction described in 17:16-17? A comparison reveals that these are separate events. The Harlot of chapter 17 "sat upon" or was associated with the political power of the beast, but was not that same political power as is described in this chapter.

The description of this new vast global religion is interlaced with a vast economic system like no other in history. The metaphorical use of "Babylon" describes an evil, corrupt world power that is going to be difficult to identify this side of the Tribulation. With certain elements in place a total world take-over could occur in a matter of months, then, after 3 ½ years of development, this Messianic global dictatorial one-world economy and leader worship will have in place a Babylon-like global infrastructure.

When the events of the 7-year period begin they will accelerate rapidly. This destruction crashes the political and economic powers of the world at the end of the seven years. The catastrophe describe here is not from the beast or the ten-king Federation, but from an earthquake, which sounds like what was described in 16:19-21 in the seventh bowl judgment.

Babylon had become a "dwelling place of demons, a prison for every foul spirit, a cage for every unclean and hated bird! (*orneon*, "bird"). The type of bird is the "unclean and hated" thus some translations use "buzzard" or "vulture."

The enormous concentration of demon resources (all of the fallen angels in the bottomless pit (9:1-2), plus the fallen angels who fell from heaven with Satan (12:4), and the permanent activity of demons on earth throughout the ages) makes this a most unholy place. The pervasive demonic influence will be overwhelming.

Reflection: Have you ever sensed a demon's presence or recognized a demonic influence in your life?

BUSINESS WITH BABYLON MAKES MILLIONAIRES

18:3

For all the nations have drunk of the wine of the wrath of her fornication, the kings of the earth have committed fornication with her, and the merchants of the earth have become rich through the abundance of her luxury.

18:3 For all the nations have "drunk" (*pino*, "drink, absorb, soak up") of the wine of the wrath of her adulteries and her luxurious living (*strenos*, "excessive strength, eager desire, sensuality, wantonness" or "a way of life characterized by headstrong pride" Friberg). The word for "drunk" is used metaphorically by Jesus: "drink the water I shall give" (Jn 4:14) which results in eternal life; but here, the notion is negative.

The first accusation is against the "nations" (*ethnos*, human race or individual people groups) who have committed the act of absorbing all that the Antichrist offers, yielding to him their souls and delighting in his temptations of lust and evil on a global scale causes a bonding of their souls to the Antichrist. The reason for the fall of Babylon is that this false religion drives people into maddening vices and addictions, while the "merchants" become rich. Babylon personifies everything that is evil: sexual immorality, idolatry, greed, addictions, power and oppression.

The second accusation is against the rulers of the world who have committed adultery with her; that is, they have joined the Babylonian system in her shameful greed, seeking the feelings and experiences of all self-gratifying passions. The term "adultery" can refer to shameful alliances for political advantage and/or a total abandoning of biblical morality.

The third accusation is how the merchants around the world have grown rich in "Babylon's" luxurious living. Businesses were seduced by the enormous wealth gained by associating with her. Not that there will be any choice in the matter, because the global economy and the Antichrist have no competition. Their prosperity motivated their pride and self-sufficiency: this is spiritual adultery. They are on the inside of the system making themselves rich without regard to any moral scruples. This prosperity will be the result of a total monopoly of the world economy through the enforcement of the exclusive buying/selling with the mark of the beast. The nations submitted to it, the leaders enforced it and the merchants prospered from it.

Reflection: Can you see any comparisons with contemporary socialist governments?

WARNING TO THE INHABITANTS

18:4

And I heard another voice from heaven saying, "Come out of her, my people, lest you share in her sins, and lest you receive of her plagues.

18:4 "Another" (*allos*) voice, evidently from God Himself, warns the people of God ("my people") to abandon the city so they can escape its judgment or "plagues." To the very end, God warns His own to deliver themselves from the coming catastrophe as He did with Noah (Gen 6:13-22) and Lot (Gen 19:12-22).

Evidently there will continue to be a constant influx of new believers to the end. True believers must always separate from the ungodliness of evil systems. This is the same manner Abraham was commanded to separate himself from the paganism of Ur of the province of Babylon (Gen 12:1).

Jeremiah had seen this same dilemma for surviving believers, "Flee from Babylon! Save yourselves! Don't get trapped in her punishment! It is the Lord's time for vengeance; he will fully repay her" (Jer 51:6; see also Jer 51:45). There is collateral damage when God's judgment falls. If believers are too close, it is because they want to be that close to evil. They are forewarned. An earthquake cannot be selective. When one associates with fools, a fool's destruction shall be shared (Prov 13:20). The command "come out" (*exerchomai*, aorist imperative, "immediately, urgently... separate yourself").

John gives two reason why God's people are to separate from this demonic system:
(1) First, they are to avoid the pollution and corruption from associating with them or becoming "partakers of her sins" (18:4; see also 1 Tim 5:22; Eph 5:11). Believers are not supposed to share in society's sins lest they share in its judgment, which will be inevitable.

This means both physical separation as well as spiritual, mental, and emotional separation from the sins that destroy a society. The shame of believers is when they enjoy the same sins as the corrupt society, secretly, if not publicly, mixed up in the commercializing of sin. Merchants learn how to exploit the sinful pleasures of people who believe they "need" certain things to be happy, satisfied, fulfilled, successful, etc. Christians are to model the life of Christ in serving, giving, self-sacrificing, living in obedience, holiness and truth.

(2) Second, believers are not to be present when God judges Babylon, as He surely will. Any association with this corrupt system will result in suffering its coming judgment.

Reflection: What sinful practices would these words warn you personally to flee or to disassociate from lest you be judged with wrong-doers? Do you do anything or go anywhere that would be an embarrassment to you if Christ were to suddenly come and find you there?

SINS LEAVE PERMANENT MARKS

18:5

For her sins have reached to heaven, and God has remembered her iniquities.

18:5 The impact of Babylon's sins (spiritual adulteries with gross false worship and lustful sensual living – 18:4) has "reached to heaven" (*ekollēthēsan*, aorist passive, "cling to, come in close contact with," as piling up on top of each other).

Ancient Babylon built high towers (ziggurats) to reach their gods (Gen 11:4), but what was effective in reaching the true God's attention was their sinfulness, of which He never missed a single deed, and each would have its just recompense. The phrase "God has remembered" does not imply that He could forget, but rather that "their sins" have now become such an offense that they become a priority and now they must be dealt with once and for all.

God never forgets the offense of sin unless it is paid for by a just punishment. For the believer, the promise is the opposite. He says "I will not remember your sins...I will forgive your iniquities and their sin, I will remember no more (Isa 42:25; Jer 31:34).

Reflection: If God punishes a sinner for his sin, is this a "just" recompense? Why must it last forever? What is the 2-fold nature of God's judgment on sin in 1 Tim 5:24?

Reflection: What do we learn about God in our text (18:5) and 1 Tim 5:27?

GOLDEN RULE

18:6

Render to her just as she rendered to you, and repay her double according to her works; in the cup which she has mixed, mix double for her.

18:6 However Babylon has treated or "rendered" (*apodidomi*, aorist, "pay off, return what is due, or recompense") to "you"(this direct object is omitted in the Greek when the object is obvious from the context as "you" or "others"), she, Bablylon, will receive a double portion in return. The object "you" refers back to the "souls under the altar" (6:9-10) who will have been slain in the first half of the Tribulation. God is constantly encouraging those in heaven with what is happening on the earth.

This retribution would have been understood under the Roman law, lex talionis, which required that a person's punishment should match his crime, except here the angel asked God to give her a double penalty for all Babylon's evil deeds. Recompense in the Mosaic law was to be doubled (Ex 21:23-25). Notice the principle taught in 1 Cor 6:6-7. She had given terror (making war against all believers and Jews spilling their blood – 13:7; 17:6) so she should receive twice as much for the evil done. The powerful never believe that they will be forced to give account for any injustice or sinfulness they may have committed, believing that they have always been and will always be the exception to the rule.

Reflection: Do you ever think that you can sin with immunity, that no one will ever know? Do you ever think there is not any harm in sinning in secret?

It must be noted that however cruel the torture of the Antichrist or any enemy against believers, we must never seek vengeance (Rom 12:14, 17, 19-21). See also 1 Thes 5:15; 1 Pet 3:9 for other commands regarding vengeance seeking. If Israel, God's elected people, received double for her sins (Isa 40:1-2; Jer 16:18), how much more will God's enemies receive double for their defiance of His will?

PROPORTIONATE AND JUST

18:7

In the measure that she glorified herself and lived luxuriously, in the same measure give her torment and sorrow; for she says in her heart, 'I sit as queen, and am no widow, and will not see sorrow.'

18:7 This Antichrist Babylonian system will live in luxury and pleasure, which will be matched with torments and suffering. This was Jeremiah's prayer against ancient Babylon in Jer 51:34-35. The extent that she "glorified (*doxazo*, aorist, "praise, magnify, honor, make renown") herself and lived luxuriously" (*streniao*, aorist, "be wanton, indulge, revel") to this same extent she will be given "torment and sorrow."

The sentence is given because she thinks or "says in her heart," "I sit as queen, and am no widow, and will not see sorrow." She believes that she is exempt from the judgments of the Tribulation, and may fake her exemption by covering her sores, etc., pretending to be like the 144,000 and the two witnesses were exempt.

Babylon's sins will be her godlessness, pride, self-security and her glorification of her wealth and luxury, seeking to exalt herself. She will not believe until it is too late that she is doomed. God will be her judge as surely as He was of ancient Babylon (Isa 47:9-11).

Three sins demand Babylon's punishment: (1) she is proud. God said "I will not give my glory to another" (Isa 42:8). He hates pride (Prov 6:16-1; James 4:6); (2) she pursued sensual, selfish, self-gratification. Paul called such "to be dead even while they live" (1 Tim 5:6); (3) she is guilty of self-sufficiency and presumption of power to never "see sorrow" or "grief" which is a reflection on the pride of ancient Babylon who said, "I will be a queen forever...I will not sit as a widow, nor know loss of children" (Isa 47:7,8).

But just as Isaiah prophesied of ancient Babylon, "Both of these will come upon you suddenly, in one day! You will lose your children and be widowed. You will be overwhelmed by these tragedies, despite your many incantations and your numerous amulets" (Isa 47:9).

Reflection: Is it natural to think that bad things will not happen to us? Do we sometimes get presumptuous, that is, presuming on God? Have you ever been jolted back from your egotism to a humbling reality of utter dependence on His providence regardless of the outcome? It is better to be chastened than doomed!

HOW THE MIGHTY ARE FALLEN

18:8

Therefore her plagues will come in one day-- death and mourning and famine. And she will be utterly burned with fire, for strong is the Lord God who judges her.

18:8 "Therefore" (*dia touto*, "through this") means "for the reasons mentioned" her punishment will be just. Her "plagues" or judgment will come in "one day," (literal or representing a very short time; i.e. "one hour" in 17:12) that will include "death, and mourning and famine."

In the same manner that ancient and mighty Babylon fell in one night (Dan 5:30) so it will occur again. Evidently for the most part, Babylon had been able to avoid many of the serious consequences of the Tribulation, but no more. For all her pride, pomp and prestige, she will be brought down to humiliating chaos and destruction. The most evil city in human history will be destroyed as surely as Sodom and Gomorrah. She shall be "utterly burned with fire."

The seventh bowl judgment will bring unparalleled destruction to "Babylon" (16:17-21) then she will be burn with fire. Jeremiah had given a similar prophecy of ancient Babylon (at the peak of her power), "The wide walls of Babylon will be leveled to the ground, and her high gates will be burned. The builders from many lands have worked in vain, for their work will be destroyed by fire!" (Jer 51:58 [NLT]).

What should have been obvious to everyone and provoked a broken sense of repentance is the phrase "Strong is the Lord God who judges her." No one can change or stop God's plans or keep Him from accomplishing His will. Job said it this way, "I know that You can do all things, and that no purpose of Yours can be thwarted" (Job 42:2). See also Isa 14: 27; 43:13; 46:10; Dan 4:35 for similar assurances of God's purposes.

Reflection: Is it easy for believers to forget that God will chasten all disobedience? Do we really believe that He will punish our disobediences? God is so patient that careless men begin to presume that God does not mean what He says. If believers are careless, how much more the rebellious and unregenerate will face their inevitable judgment.

II. THE RULERS OF THE WORLD LAMENT THE DESTRUCTION OF THE CITY (18:9-10)

18:9

The kings of the earth who committed fornication and lived luxuriously with her will weep and lament for her, when they see the smoke of her burning,

18:9 The absent kings, addicted to her "fornication and lived luxuriously with her," will be able to escape her destruction, but not the consequences of her collapse. Their "lament" is for the loss of income and pleasure, "when they see the smoke of her burning."

They will never be sorry for their sins, but will cry for their loss of pleasure, prestige and power. This "lament" quickly turns to resentment, then bitterness then in desperation to retaliation and vengeance, when the world will gather to destroy the last vestige of the Judeo/Christian God.

Verses 9-20 are a funeral sentiment for the fall of Babylon as sung by three different groups: (1) rulers of the world (18:9-10), (2) the merchants (18:11-16), and (3) the ship owners – transporters (18:17-20). All of these groups will have grown rich through the exclusive and mandatory business deals obligated by the mark of the beast.

All who associate with the Antichrist will prosper enormously, feeding the resentment against any impediment to this prosperity, such as those not receiving the mark of the beast who try to negotiate illegally and against the Judeo/Christian God who will be blamed for destroying the entire global economy and environment.

These are the ten kings of the federation and regional vassal kings under them all of whom "committed acts of immorality and lived sensually with her (Babylon)" (v. 3). First, these "kings of the earth" will "weep and lament for her" – well, for their personal loss of wealth, prestige and power. All are dissolved in a few hours. How fickle is power and prestige!

The lament is as much for themselves (if not more so), as for Babylon. Selfish living leaves little concern for others. So if they have to aid in causing horrible affliction to some in order to gain a better deal for the masses (and themselves of course!), then their conscience is annulled. They will be emotionally distraught for their losses. In economic collapse many wealthy can loose their fortunes in a matter of hours and wake up penniless.

Reflection: How should a believer respond to these kinds of circumstances? Do you know anyone who has suffered such losses?

AVOIDANCE OF THE FALLEN

18:10

standing at a distance for fear of her torment, saying,` Alas, alas, that great city Babylon, that mighty city! For in one hour your judgment has come.'

18:10 The kings will not want to get too close to this city for "fear of her torment," but rather, will witness it from a distance via the media. The word for "Alas" is *oiai*, translated "woe," an interjection of grief used in special cases for a horrible judgment (8:13). They will declare with shock, "For in one hour your judgment has come," a judgment that they thought would never come.

The sense of immortality makes people careless: the it-will-never-happen-to-me syndrome. This city/system has survived the judgments of the Tribulation until now. Their despair is rooted in their selfish values being destroyed: now they too are nothing, powerless, and broken.

They may fear retaliation from those whom they will have abused in their power/business dealings. All their wealth will evaporate and their power base will be destroyed, leaving them defenseless. How many today give their lives for a company's product line, that goes broke just before the workers is about to retire and the employee looses everything including his job and pension?

Reflection: Far worse is the sad story of many believers who spend their lives building a retirement, home and an enjoyable life (cars, stuff, vacations, etc.) paying off unending debt, but have invested minimal if any in any significant contribution to the kingdom of God.

III. THE MERCHANTS WHO BECAME RICH THROUGH TRADE (18:11-16)

18:11-13

And the merchants of the earth will weep and mourn over her,

for no one buys their merchandise anymore: 12 "merchandise of gold and silver, precious stones and pearls, fine linen and purple, silk and scarlet, every kind of citron wood, every kind of object of ivory, every kind of object of most precious wood, bronze, iron, and marble; 13 "and cinnamon and incense, fragrant oil and frankincense, wine and oil, fine flour and wheat, cattle and sheep, horses and chariots, and bodies and souls of men.

18:11-13 The next group of desperate people (after the destruction of the city/system of Babylon and her kings or leaders) will be the merchants. Huge economic losses will bring the wealthiest magnates to their knees in tears.

Whatever this city is commercializing because of the global devastation of the Tribulation, will be no more, "no one buys their merchandise anymore." Their materialistic fantasies will fade away. Does this mean that the required mark of the beast is no longer valid?

For a brief period people will do what they want. The list of 28 products or categories of products from gold to human lives comes from every part of the world; from China, India to N. Africa and probably the rest of the world as well.

In the midst of horrible chaos and catastrophes of the seals, trumpets and bowl judgments, the people will become even more self-indulgent, pleasure seeking and status building and will be willing to do anything to satisfy their lusts. The list of items includes a long list of luxurious products and "every kind of object," then the angel ends the list with the phrase, "and bodies and souls of men." Probably because of debts and calamities, people will have no choice but to give themselves, or be taken, into slavery.

The list described in this text reads like the luxurious commodities of the ancient Babylonia Empire of the sixth century BC and the Roman Empire in the first century. When the wealthy loose everything they are attached to for personal value or self-worth, they feel worthless, and incapacitated of power, authority and resources to make things happen and pay creditors. Desperate times lead to desperate measures.

When a true believer dies, he takes everything that he valued in life with him, but when the non-believer dies, he looses everything he valued in life and has nothing to show for his journey though life. When a person finds his satisfaction in the things of this world, then those substances, or stuff, become his god, filling the place that God would fill if He were allowed to be integrated into his life.

Reflection: Have you seen, heard of or experienced anything similar to this economic collapse?

EMPTY DREAMS

18:14

The fruit that your soul longed for has gone from you, and all the things which are rich and splendid have gone from you, and you shall find them no more at all.

18:14 The "fruit that your soul longed for" and "all the things which are rich and splendid" will no longer satisfy your lusts. The secret to success is to find what men desire for gratification and appearance, buy it cheap and sell it for much more.

The luxuries and pleasures of this world can never satisfy the soul, only lure it on to more dissatisfaction and disillusionment. This breeds the false notion that more indulgence will bring more satisfaction, but saturation cannot bring more satisfaction, only false hope.

Now there is no hope of acquiring any satisfaction through this commercialization. Despair and frustration mount to enormous proportions in people's minds. Believers are not exempt from these temptations to substitute finding fulfillment alone in God's fellowship. Many people seek to be important before men or divert their attention from personal misery around them by indulging in lust and pleasure.

Reflection: How many pleasures does a person need, how many clothes, cars, etc.? Put limits on yourself, your budget, and your desire to have the best, latest or most pleasing. The test comes when you lose something, does it hurt deeply?

Give everything to the Lord and if He takes it away, it was His anyway, you just got to borrow it for a while. Make sure you use it to honor Him and that it never takes His place of importance in your heart. He sees your heart.

Reflection: How would you feel if today a storm or fire destroyed your home and all you owned? – and you did not have insurance?

VANITY OF MATERIALISM

18:15-16

The merchants of these things, who became rich by her, will stand at a distance for fear of her torment, weeping and wailing, 16 "and saying, `Alas, alas, that great city that was clothed in fine linen, purple, and scarlet, and adorned with gold and precious stones and pearls!

18:15-16 The merchants will lose their prime or exclusive source of income. Theirs will not be a sadness of sympathy because of Babylon's destruction, but because of their bankrupts and losses. Their monopoly on commercial enterprises through the mandatory use of the mark of the beast will end. They will echo the agony of the leaders and kings, who also will lose their share in the commercialism as well as their political power and position.

This weeping will last for eternity! (Matt 8:12; 13:43, 50; 22:13; 24:51; 25:30). Everyone is on his own from now on. No one could believe that such a global enterprise could collapse so suddenly. Now everyone is interested in survival and has little interest in the luxuries of these merchants. Their commodities will now have little to no value.

Reflection: These greedy consciousless merchants are illustrative of all who sell their souls for things (Mark 8:36). Does this seem foolish to you?

IV. THE SHIP OWNERS, AND CAPTAINS OF THE MERCHANT SHIPS (18:18-20)

LOST EXPECTATIONS BRING FRUSTRATION

18:17

For in one hour such great riches came to nothing.' Every shipmaster, all who travel by ship, sailors, and as many as trade on the sea, stood at a distance

18:17 All the wealth of world trade "came to nothing." Economic collapse always has ripple effects. All the employees and alliance companies affiliated with the global economy will likewise be without a job overnight. All pension plans, savings and bank accounts are destroyed.

Reflection: Have you ever known someone who quickly lost everything, all his investments and perhaps all of the reserves of his company? We never believed such losses would be possible in the world market today, but thousands have lost everything in the recession of 2009. Yet this is nothing in comparison.

LOST HOPE BRINGS DESPAIR

18:18

and cried out when they saw the smoke of her burning, saying, `What is like this great city?' 19 "They threw dust on their heads and cried out, weeping and wailing, and saying, `Alas, alas, that great city, in which all who had ships on the sea became rich by her wealth! For in one hour she is made desolate.

18:18-19 Here we see lament over the "great city" which will be utterly and irrecoverably destroyed. People will not believe what they are witnessing. The third group down the chain will be the transporters and seamen, shipmasters and sailors. The wealth of this system has brought luxuries from distant lands. Now wealth means nothing when survival is the issue.

Ezekiel saw this same destruction when he wrote, "All the oarsmen abandon their ships; the sailors and helmsmen come to stand on the shore. They weep bitterly as they throw dust on their heads and roll in ashes" (Ezek 27:29-30). Their ships are useless. Their risky investments have become valueless. The monetary system will collapse.

Nothing will sell, because there are no buyers with means of payment. They throw "dust on the heads" (as Josh 7:6; 1 Sam 4:12; 2 Sam 1:2; 15:32; Job 2:12; Lam 2:10; Ezek 27:30). Then will not be able to believe that this vast, powerful and global system is destroyed so quickly.

Reflection: What are the best and worse examples that you have heard about when men and companies loose everything? Can you imagine how this experience at the end of the Tribulation will leave men devastated?

REACTION IN HEAVEN TO THE FALL OF BABYLON

18:20

"Rejoice over her, O heaven, and you holy apostles and prophets, for God has avenged you on her!"

18:20 On the other hand, the saints in heaven are told to "rejoice" (*euphraino*, present tense, "be continually, being gladdened, delighted in a thing"), "for God has avenged you on her!" This is the beginning of the final end of the long-promised justice to the murderers of the Tribulation saints (6:9-10). This rejoicing will not be over the damnation of sinners, but because of the victory of justice, the elimination of all the enemy system and soon coming climax of the Tribulation (ch. 19).

Those who will have special interest in this rejoicing will be those who have suffered severely at the hands of the "Babylonian" system of Rome and/or the Antichrist's adaptation of they global system. The "O heaven" is a general term for all believers of all ages, and the "apostles and prophets," that is, the founders of the Christian Church (Eph 2:20; 4:11).

This is the only mention of the "apostles and prophets in Revelation. For Christians today who know little to nothing of persecution for their faith, this vengeance for harm done to believers will not have the same significance.

Reflection: Do you know of any injustice to Christians or yourself that merits the judgments of the Tribulation?

V. THE VIOLENT OVERTHROW OF BABYLON (18:21-24)

VIOLENCE OR QUICK DESTRUCTION

18:21

Then a mighty angel took up a stone like a great millstone and threw it into the sea, saying, "Thus with violence the great city Babylon shall be thrown down, and shall not be found anymore.

18:21 "A mighty angel" (*ischuros*, "strong") will give an illustration of the destruction of Babylon as the casting of a "great millstone" into the sea. To pick up and cast such a millstone is no meager feat (4-5 ft in diameter, 1 ft thick of solid stone). To describe the horrible destruction the

THE FALL OF BABYLON

author merely adds, "with violence" the city-system will be destroyed. Without warning and with "violence" the city will be overthrown. Just as quickly as the millstone strikes the sea and disappears, so will Babylon be quickly destroyed. The added phrase, "shall not be found anymore," gives the impression of utter destruction in a brief time.

Jeremiah saw this utter destruction, "so shall Babylon sink down and not rise again because of the calamity that I am going to bring upon her; and they will become exhausted" (Jer 51:61-64).

Reflection: To put one's hope on a political system, no matter how powerful, is foolish. God raises up and brings to nothing whatever fits His purpose. Wisdom says to trust in the Almighty, not in the earthly powers.

NO MORE MUSIC, BUILDING, OR BAKERIES
(Other prophets saw this same destruction: Isa 13:19-22; 14:22-23; Jer 50:13, 39; 51:37).)

18:22

The sound of harpists, musicians, flutists, and trumpeters shall not be heard in you anymore. No craftsman of any craft shall be found in you anymore, and the sound of a millstone shall not be heard in you anymore.

18:22 A characteristic of the corrupt city is the "sound of harpists, musicians, flutists, and trumpeters," thus Babylon will be a music dominated society. There will be no sound of craftsmen manufacturing the goods to be sold around the world, or construction of building in order to house the leaders of the global government/commercial center or the "sound of a millstone," used for making flour for bread and pastries.

Reflection: Can you imagine the bitter silence in the rubble of this city's vast destruction?

NO MORE ELECTRICITY OR WEDDINGS

18:23

The light of a lamp shall not shine in you anymore, and the voice of bridegroom and bride shall not be heard in you anymore. For your merchants were the great men of the earth, for by your sor-

cery all the nations were deceived.

18:23 There shall be no more "brides" or "bridegrooms," nor any wedding sounds. No one has a future, no jobs are left, no economy, no security, only fear and attempts to survive another day. "For" introduces a reason for a certain action: what follows is a series of three reasons for Babylon's judgments.

First, the abuse of the commercial system. The merchants that sold the products of the Great Babylon become the "great men of the earth." James asked the question, "Is it not the rich who oppress you are personally drag you into court?" (James 2:6; see also James 5:4-6).

Second, the means used to deceive "all the nations" will be by her "sorcery" (*pharmakeia*, refers to magic and occult practices, as 9:21; Gal 5:20), which can refer to her occult practices or drug use. With all the tragedies occurring around the world, the temptation to alleviate the suffering via drugs could be overwhelming. It appears Babylon will keep the world in drug addition, enslaved to her supply of "medicinal drugs." Once addicted, people will do anything for additional drugs.

Reflection: Why do you think people allow themselves to become addicted to drugs?

GUILTY OF KILLING THE SAINTS

18:24

And in her was found the blood of prophets and saints, and of all who were slain on the earth.

18:24a *Third,* the wanton and indiscriminate killing of all believers. Babylon is guilty of the merciless slaughter of countless believers: "in her was found the blood of prophets and saints, and of all who were slain on the earth" (6:10; 11:7; 13:7, 15; 16:6; 17:6). This condemnation appears to go beyond the Tribulation period, but the passage has special reference the persecution in the Tribulation.

In the Tribulation Period no one will be able to buy or sell without the mark of the beast, which Babylon must have been the guardian of the mark to control the economy. They will have full license to kill anyone without the mark who would attempt to buy or sell. This would imply that the entire economy of the world will be controlled by the government of *Babylon* and everything bought and sold only through state controlled bank/credit card, etc. This may imply the transformation of a cash society to a global credit society or an internet cyber economy managed by government officials in order to control the negotiations and maximize the profits, supposedly for the benefit of the masses.

Reflection: What does this commercial system sound like to you?

18:24b To what contemporary city does "Babylon the Great" refer? Is it the Roman Catholic system based in Rome or the Muslim capital of ancient Babylon on the Euphrates River? This would demand a major modification not only of the city, but of the river to enable the predicted navigation.

The events of Revelation 17 will occur at the mid-point of the Tribulation, whereas Revelation 18 will occur near the end of the Tribulation, immediately before the Second Coming of Christ. The total destruction of the world religion and the global economy and as well as the major cities of the world, including Babylon the Great and simultaneously, the unprecedented global earthquakes and huge hailstorms, will all be cause for great hatred toward the God of the Jews and Christians.

The stage is set for the rage of man to vainly explode against the omnipotent God of the universe. Man will discover, however, that he is dead wrong and will be ushered into his folly and doom in the great Battle of Armageddon in chapter 19.

CHAPTER 19

WEDDING OF THE LAMB AND BATTLE OF ARMAGEDDON

"The different multitudes in heaven shout the praise of God's final victor over evil. The judgment on the earthly corrupt system and its participants is only beginning, since 'her smoke rises up for ever and ever.'"

Till now we have been studying the events of the Tribulation Period (Rev. 4-18), and are seeing the final days of the Tribulation on earth. This brief time is filled with misery, disillusionment, frustration, hatred and bitter resentment against God, which will culminate in a angry global mob army attempting to destroy anything related to the Judeo/Christian God. Meanwhile, in heaven, the reader is introduced to the greatest celebration since creation.

I. PRAISE AND WORSHIP IN HEAVEN (19:1-10)

HALLELUJAH FROM THE MULTITUDES IN HEAVEN (19:1-3)

19:1

After these things I heard a loud voice of a great multitude in heaven, saying, "Alleluia! Salvation and glory and honor and power belong to the Lord our God!

19:1 "After these things" (*meta tauta*, "after these," a direct reference to chapter 18) means that these events are sequential. John is drawn to a "loud voice" (*phonen*, "sound or roar") described as "loud" (*megalen*, "great") shouting "Alleluia! Salvation and glory and honor and power belong to the Lord our God!"

The word "*alleluia*" is a transliterated word from the Greek, *hallelouia*, and is used four times in the NT, all of them in Revelation 19 (vss. 1, 3, 4 and 6). The word is a combination of Hebrew words *halal* and *Jah*, meaning "Praise *Yahweh* or God." Then the word is again transliterated into Greek and transliterated into English and other languages. Psalms 113-118 use "hallelujah" so frequently they are known as the Hallelujah Psalms.

Reflection: What are some things that you can praise the Lord for today? Is there a similarity in meaning between "Thank you, Lord" and "Praise the Lord?" Can you describe why there would be such rejoicing in heaven at this time?

EVIL IS FINALLY BROKEN

19:2-3

For true and righteous are His judgments, because He has judged the great harlot who corrupted the earth with her fornication; and He has avenged on her the blood of His servants shed by her." 3 Again they said, "Alleluia! Her smoke rises up forever and ever!

19:2-3 The motive of the praise is the proclamation that His judgments are "true and righteous" or "just" (See 15:3; 16:5, 7 for the same emphasis). They are perfectly just for the offense. He will be praised for avenging the murder of the Tribulation saints.

The two-fold reason for the destruction of the "great harlot" is because
(1) she "corrupted the earth with her fornication." This corruption is so pervasive that people become consumed with their lusts, greed and addictions, which she uses to manipulate people and keep them disinterested or despising the true God.
(2) She shed "the blood of His servants," especially during the seven years of Tribulation. Earlier the Harlot was described as being "drunk with the blood of God's holy people who were witnesses for Jesus" (17:6 NLT).

Again and again the different multitudes in heaven shout the praise of God's final victory over evil. The judgment on this earthly corrupt system and its participants is only beginning since "her smoke rises up forever and ever!" (See 9:2; 14:11; 18:9, 18). The destruction of the city and her inhabitants will carry with them the fire and smoke of Hades and the Lake of fire.

This passage makes it clear that there is no annihilation of the unsaved, or second chance to reconsider. Choices we make have permanent and eternal consequences. We choose to be deceived because we reject or do not want the truth and prefer to believe lies about reality. People think that if they are sincere about their beliefs, even if they are wrong, God will understand and still accept them.

Reflection: Can you describe how men prefer secular humanism and arguments for sensual, immoral satisfaction more than the choice to trust God's revelation in His Word?

HALLELUJAH FROM THE 24 ELDERS (19:4-5)

19:4-5

And the twenty-four elders and the four living creatures fell down and worshiped God who sat on the throne, saying, "Amen! Alleluia!" 5 Then a voice came from the throne, saying, "Praise our God, all you His servants and those who fear Him, both small and great!"

19:4 Not only is this a praise time for the retribution of the Tribulation saints ("a great multitude" vs. 1), but also they are joined by all of the saints of heaven in the singing of praise as represented by the twenty-four elders and the angelic body represented by the "four living creatures," or cherubim, the high-ranking angels nearest to the presence of God. The shout of "amen" means, "we agree," or "so be it," that is, a solemn agreement. They are saying, "Your will be done."

Reflection: Does your praise include a submissive attitude to His will in your daily life?

19:5

19:5 "A voice from the throne," is probably from one of the "four living creatures" (vs. 4 who constantly are praising God – 4:6-8) or another angel, since it uses the phrase, "our God." With an extremely powerful voice this angel will declare, "Praise (*aineo*, present tense imperative, "continually be... extolling, allowing, recommending, honoring") our God, all you His servants and those who fear Him, both small and great."

This command is directed toward the "bond-servants" who are the redeemed believers in heaven, and all those "who fear Him." The description is further broadened to include "the small and great" (as 11:18). This scope goes beyond all categories and distinctions to include everyone.

It is similar to the Psalmist, "Praise the Lord! Yes, give praise, O servants of the Lord. Praise the name of the Lord!" (Psa 113:1) "From east to west the Lord's name is deserving of praise" (Psa 113:3). "He will bless his loyal followers, both young and old" (Psa 115:13). Here is an overarching command for all ages, all nations, all times and forever more to praise and thank the Lord for His dealings with you personally. However, now is a special time. The world of evil has been completely destroyed.

Reflection: Can you wholeheartedly join in this chorus? Do you harbor

WEDDING OF THE LAMB AND BATTLE OF ARMAGEDDON

resentments, an unforgiving spirit towards others, a rejection of how God has made you or disillusionment with the circumstances of your life and people around you?

If you cannot see the wisdom and hand of God in your life and accept whatever it may be, then your heart can never be free to fully praise God.

PRAISE BECAUSE CHRIST IS REIGNING (19:6)

19:6

And I heard, as it were, the voice of a great multitude, as the sound of many waters and as the sound of mighty thunderings, saying, "Alleluia! For the Lord God Omnipotent reigns!

19:6 The fourth and final hallelujah sounded like a "great multitude" as the "sound of many waters and as the sound of mighty thunderings." Everyone is united. They see the reality of how necessary it is to destroy sin and its demonic influences. The celebration explodes from the heavenly scene because "the Lord God Omnipotent reigns." The term "Omnipotent" (*pantokrator*, "all powerful, almighty") translated the Hebrew, "God of hosts." This word is used ten times in the NT, nine of which are in the Revelation.

Through all the events of the Tribulation an all-powerful God will be accomplishing His will. But now the focus changes from the past to the future. Now He is coming to reign in person and to share this coming kingdom with His loyal followers, His "wife," the Church.

Reflection: It is not what God has done in His just judgments, but what He is about to do in honor of those who have been faithful to Him. How different do you think your life will be when Christ in person is reigning on earth?

PRAISE FOR THE COMING WEDDING OF THE LAMB (19:6-9)

19:7

Let us be glad and rejoice and give Him glory, for the marriage of the Lamb has come, and His wife has made herself ready.

19:7 The "marriage of the Lamb" is about to begin. The "bride has made herself ready." Weddings are traditionally the biggest social event in the Jewish culture. Typically a wedding could be years in preparation. A betrothal agreement could be signed when the children are barely teenagers, years before the ceremony. Only a divorce proceeding (as in the case of Mary and Joseph in Matt 1:18-19) could break this agreement.

A wedding typically consisted of three parts:
(1) The legal consummation of the marriage by the parents of the bride and groom, usually with the payment of a dowry;
(2) The bridegroom coming to claim his bride or the presentation of the bride, sometimes several years later, which is reflective of the rapture and our presentation before the Father (2 Cor 4:14; Eph 5:27; Col 1:22; Jude 24);
(3) The actual ceremony and wedding supper (as in John 2:1-11), which was a feast that could last several days. This passage is introducing the actual "wedding supper" or phase 3.

The marriage symbolism of *Phase 1* appears to reflect the Church Age in which individuals are being saved and incorporated into the Body of Christ and into a personal relationship with Christ.

Paul wrote about this "betrothal" period in 2 Cor 11:2, "For I am jealous for you with a godly jealousy; for I betrothed you to one husband, so that to Christ I might present you as a pure virgin." This marriage contract was signed before creation when our names were written in the Book of Life. This is reiterated in Eph 5:25-27 further describing this waiting period before the marriage.

Phase 2 is the presentation of the Bride to the Bridegroom, is reflected in the Rapture of the Church, when Christ comes to take His bride to His Father's home that He has prepared in heaven (Jn 14:1-3).

Phase 3 takes place at the beginning of the millennium occurring as the wedding supper and marriage of the Lamb. The term "bride" (*gyne*, "betrothed or married woman") implies that the Phase 2 of the wedding has already occurred leaving only the wedding feast or reception. Now she has "made herself ready" during the 7 year period between the rapture and the Second Advent. This is the time period of the Judgment Seat of Christ, which concludes with everyone being praised and rewarded according to their lifetime contribution to the kingdom of God.

Reflection: What does 1 Cor 4:5 say will be the outcome of this judgment seat? Does this sound like a husband talking to his wife to be?

THE FINE LINEN OF THE SAINTS

19:8

And to her it was granted to be arrayed in fine linen, clean and bright, for the fine linen is the righteous acts of the saints.

19:8 "It was granted (*didomi*, aorist passive, "once was given") to be arrayed" (*periballo*, "throw around, put on or cloth one's self") "in fine linen," described as "clean" (*katharos*, "pure," metaphorically: "free from corruption of desire, sin and guilt") and "bright" (*lampros*, "shining, brilliant, splendid") which is used to describe angels (15:6) and the clothing of the armies of heaven, both the Church, "his servants" and the angels when Christ returns to earth (19:14). This linen is explained as representing "the righteous acts of the saints" (19:8).

From the moment of personal faith in Christ and His Word and forever thereafter, the believer is covered in perfect righteousness (Rom 3:21-24; 4:5; 5:19; 1 Cor 1:30; 2 Cor 5:21; Phil 3:8-9).

Upon this flawless foundation of perfect righteousness, the believer is to build his own godly lifestyle and his labor of love, for which he will be eternally rewarded (1 Cor 3:12-15). This décor follows the Judgment Seat of Christ where the saints are honored for their contributions to the advancement of the Gospel and the kingdom of God during their life's journey. Ultimately when He appears "we will be like Him, because we will see Him just as He is" (Rom 8:19-21).

Reflection: How do these verses describe this final preparation?

Matt 5:12

Matt 6:4

Matt 10:41

Matt 10:42

Matt 16:27

Luke 6:35

Heb 11:26

THE INVITED GUESTS TO THE WEDDING

19:9

Then he said to me, "Write: 'Blessed are those who are called to the marriage supper of the Lamb!'" And he said to me, "These are the true sayings of God."

19:9 Once again John is commanded to write (see 14:13) a message to the believers, "Blessed are those who are called to the marriage supper of the Lamb!" It seems apparent that this does not refer to the "bride" but to the invited guests. Are there different groups in heaven? Are the Old Testament saints going to fulfill a purpose distinct from the purpose of the Church, as well as a distinct group from the Tribulation period?

According to Matt 8:11, "I tell you this, that many Gentiles will come from all over the world and sit down with Abraham, Isaac, and Jacob at the feast in the Kingdom of Heaven." All the people of faith from Hebrews 11 (OT saints) will be there as invited guests.

Likewise, John the Baptist, who was known as the greatest of all OT believers (Matt 11:11), described himself as "the friend of the bridegroom" (John 3:29), that is, he will be one of the invited guests. This inclusion of believing Israel demonstrates God's gracious promise to restore her, even though, as a nation, she went into apostasy as an unfaithful wife and rejected the Messiah as described in Hosea 14:4, "I will heal their apostasy, I will love them freely, for My anger has turned away from them."

By grace Israel will have a prominent place in the New Jerusalem as described in Revelation 21:10-14. The twelve patriarchs are named the 12 gates and the twelve apostles are the foundation stones (Eph 2:20) of the walls of the New Jerusalem.

Henry Morris writes concerning the different groups for the different ages who will enjoy the full glories of eternity together:

> Whatever distinctions may exist between the saints of the pre-Abrahamic period, the saints in Israel before Christ, the saints among the Gentiles from Abraham to Christ, the saints of the tribulation, and the saints in the churches from Christ to the rapture ... such distinctions are secondary to the great primary truth that all will be there by virtue of the saving work of Christ and their personal trust in the true Creator God and His provision of salvation.

Many invitations will be extended to the wedding supper, repeated in Rev 22:17. Of all the created beings since the beginning of time, God has finally gathered all those who freely chose to honor and worship Him. This is the group for whom He has prepared eternity. So solemn is this declaration that it is punctuated by the expression, "These are the true words of God."

To the exiled Apostle and the millions who have suffered the worse kind of ridicule and persecution, this special assurance was given that God's kingdom would eventually triumph. Nothing can stop this moment from happening. All believers of all times will be there together. This is the celebration moment that God and the heavenly host have been waiting for since the beginning of time.

Reflection: Can you see why Paul wrote that "there should be no schism in the body, but that the members should have the same care one for another" (1 Cor 12:25)?

COMMAND TO WORSHIP GOD (19:10)

19:10

And I fell at his feet to worship him. But he said to me, "See that you do not do that! I am your fellow servant, and of your brethren who have the testimony of Jesus. Worship God! For the testimony of Jesus is the spirit of prophecy."

19:10 John was so overwhelmed at this scene, the four powerful hallelujahs and the announcement of the wedding feast, that he could not help himself, but fall on his face in worship. The angel was quick to terminate any such admiration or worship with the prohibition, "See that you do not do that!"

The angel is only another fellow-servant of the Most High God, albeit much more powerful and glorious than man. Angels remain only another form of created beings made by our Creator, thus it is absurd to worship any of them as though they were divine. This episode demonstrates the attitude in heaven when humans bow down to saints and angels. It is never allowed! It is a form of idolatry.

The imperative, "Worship God" is not an option. Indeed, believers have been redeemed for this purpose (John 4:23) and it will be our activity throughout eternity. The angel adds, "For the testimony of Jesus is the spirit of prophecy." The nature of prophecy is to reveal the character and person of Jesus Christ and bring Him glory. The central theme of the OT prophecy and NT preaching is the Lord Jesus Christ.

The entire book of Revelation reveals how Christ will exercise His power and authority and His second coming as the Judge of the wicked and the launching of His kingdom that He will share with all believers.

Paul wrote, "For after all, it is only just for God to repay with affliction those who afflict you, and to give relief to you who are afflicted and to us as well when the Lord Jesus will be revealed from heaven with His mighty angels in flaming fire, dealing out retribution to those who do not know God and to those who do not obey the gospel of our Lord Jesus" (2 Thess 1:6-8).

Reflection: What are two characteristics of true believers in these verses?

> 2 Tim 4:8
>
> Phil 3:20

II. THE SECOND COMING OF CHRIST (19:11-21)

John now shifts his vision, just as we will one day, from heaven to the most powerful, majestic and awe inspiring moment in the history of the world: the Second Coming of Christ. Any literal, grammatical, linguistic understanding of the text points to a future event. Just as He came literally the first time, so He will come again the second time.

The major issue is when the "rapture" occurs that is described in 1 Thess 4:13-18 and 1 Cor 15:51-58. The pretribulational view is that the rapture occurred at the beginning of the Tribulation or 7 years previous to the Second Advent of Christ. Though there are some similarities between the rapture and the Second Advent, the major difference is that the rapture occurs in the air or clouds (1 Thes 4:17), whereas the Second Advent occurs on earth (Rev 19:11-21).

In the entire passage of Revelation 19-20 there is no mention of the living, believers being transformed into their incorruptible, resurrected state (as in the Rapture), rather the emphasis is on the surviving believers who remain on earth to enter alive into the millennial kingdom and to populate it in their natural bodies.

Naturally, if there were a rapture at the Second Advent, there would be no living believers on earth to populate the new millennium. Although the possibility of the Rapture is an argument from silence, since there is no mention or hint of a rapture connected with the Second Advent, and it would create the problem of launching the millennium with only unbelieving survivors of the Tribulation (since all remaining believers would have been taken away), it makes better sense to see the rapture as an earlier pre-tribulation event.

This narration begins the Return of Christ to earth to set up a thousand year reign with the believing survivors of the Tribulation. This is the monumental revelation of the power and majesty of the conquering Messiah-Savior-Lord of lords, Jesus Christ in all His glory… and we will be there with Him.

A. THE REVELATION OF THE RIDER ON THE WHITE HORSE (19:11-13)

19:11

Now I saw heaven opened, and behold, a white horse. And He who sat on him was called Faithful and True, and in righteousness He judges and makes war.

19:11 John now is viewing the scene from the earth's perspective as he sees "heaven open" and Christ comes charging out on "a white horse." In 4:1 the heavens opened to let John in, but here the door opens to let Jesus out. This is the fulfillment of Matt 24:27-31.

This Rider is distinct from the white-horse rider in 6:2 who becomes the ruler of the Great Tribulation. This Rider comes from heaven, not earth, and all the saints of the ages who are in heaven come with Him. In the first coming of the Messiah, Jesus is portrayed in prophecy in humiliation as "humble, and mounted on a donkey, even on a colt, the foal of a donkey" (Zech 9:9), but now He is seen riding a white horse, as was the Roman custom for a conquering general to parade on the *Via Sacra*, the main road through Rome, followed by evidences of His victory in the form of booty and captives.

Symbolic language emphasizes real actions or aspects of the events such as white horse, the crowns (v. 12), the sharp sword (v. 15), the rod of iron (v. 15) and the wine press (v. 15).

This Rider is called, "Faithful and True," as in 3:14, "the faithful and true

Witness," thus He is the same Person. He is faithful to keep all His promises (2 Cor 1:20) and whatever He speaks is always true (John 8:45-46; Titus 1:2).

The rider of the first "white horse" will be the great deceiver and liar (Rev 12:9). This title is applied to the description that follows, "with justice He judges and makes war." His holy and righteous nature demands a just reaction to sin and evil. The fierceness of His response only demonstrates the offensiveness and wickedness of sin.

To those who see sin as "mistakes" or "unfortunate character flaws," the harshness of His judgment seems unfair, because sinners do not see how repugnant their own sin is to a holy God. He cannot ignore sin in anyone's life. Now He also goes forth to "make war" against all evil and the ones who have twisted and corrupted His creation. The outcome is never in question, but He will not let sin prevail indefinitely, neither in the Tribulation nor in our personal lives.

Reflection: If He will not let sin in the lives of believers go unpunished, how much more will He deal with wicked unbelievers? What do these verses show concerning God's treatment of just chastisement to believers?

Heb 12:6-9

Rev 3:19

THE FEARSOME IMAGE OF THE KING

19:12-13

His eyes were like a flame of fire, and on His head were many crowns. He had a name written that no one knew except Himself. 13 He was clothed with a robe dipped in blood, and His name is called The Word of God.

19:12-13 This Rider is described as having "eyes... like a flame of fire" (Rev 1:14). This is not a corrective action, but a final destruction of all evil. The enemy is defiant and confirmed in his rebellion against anything related to God. God's scourges and judgments to break his stubbornness has only hardened the rebellion (9:20-21; 16:9, 11). His unquestioned authority to rule and judge is evident by "many crowns" (*diadema*, "ruler's crown" as in 12:3; 13:1).

Conquering kings displayed the crowns of the vanquished rulers. This illustrates that the "kingdoms of this world has become the kingdom of our Lord and of His Christ; and He will reign forever and ever" (Rev 11:115).

Jesus will have a "name written that no one knew except Himself," suggesting the inability to describe and know everything about Him. It is possible that we are seeing here a reference to a name that He will show us when He establishes His reign.

As John sees him, His robe is "dipped in blood" as coming from the scene of a bloody battle (Isa 63:2-3; Rev 14:20). War is never pretty, and ultimate, final judgment against evil is horrible.

This One called "Faithful and True" is also titled, "The Word of God" (*logos* as in John 1:1, 14; 1 John 1:1), that is, He is the "radiance of His glory and the exact representation of His nature" (Heb 1:3).

In Rev 19:16 another of His names is written on His robe and thigh (so it could be seen at eye-level as He sat on horseback) that name is the "King of kings and Lord of lords" (1 Tim 6:15; Rev 17:14). There can be no doubt that this Rider is none other than Jesus Christ.

Reflection: Do these descriptions provoke a level of fear of our God and Savior Jesus Christ? When the exhortation to believers to "conduct yourselves throughout the time of your stay here in fear" (1 Pet 1:17), what does this mean?

B. THE COMING KING AND HIS ARMIES OF HEAVEN (19:14-16)

19:14

And the armies in heaven, clothed in fine linen, white and clean, followed Him on white horses. .

19:14 Accompanying the Coming King is the vast host of the "armies of heaven" who likewise are "on white horses," but their dress is "fine linen, white and clean," whereas the King is bloodied from battle. The bride of the Lamb (the Church) has just been described as wearing "fine linen, white and clean" (19:7-8). The "armies in heaven" appear to include:
(1) the bride of the lamb or the church,
(2) the Tribulation believers likewise are dressed in white robes (7:9),
(3) the OT saints are resurrected at the end of the Tribulation (Dan 12:1-2), and
(4) the powerful angels will accompany Christ (Matt 25:31). The "white

horses" are symbolic of some form of transportation, as was the means of mobilization of demonic armies in 9:7 and 16, which "looked like horses." In this vast "army" only One is armed, the rest are unarmed. Only Christ will destroy His enemies. The saints will come to reign with Christ, not to fight with Him. It is ultimately His battle.

Reflection: : What does 1 Cor 6:2 indicate about our ultimate responsibility in the millennium?

THE RULE OF THE CONQUERING KING

19:15

Now out of His mouth goes a sharp sword, that with it He should strike the nations. And He Himself will rule them with a rod of iron. He Himself treads the winepress of the fierceness and wrath of Almighty God.

19:15 The King is armed with "a sharp sword, that with it He should strike the nations." The word "sword" (*rhomphaia*) refers to a long sword that can be used as a spear. John had seen this sword earlier (1:16 and 2:12) when He used it to defend the church against the attacks of demons. The sword comes out of His mouth to visualize the power of His spoken words. He can speak words of life and comfort or of death and condemnation. His objective is to "strike the nations" (*patasso*, "cut down, kill, slay") who have chosen to attempt to destroy any semblance of His memory on earth.

This battle against Israel will have been taking place for weeks or months, with armies marching throughout the land of Israel. On the day of the return of Christ, armies will have invaded Jerusalem in house-to-house fighting (Zech 14:2). Satan will have filled these armies with hate, bitterness, and who knows what kind of lies, to motivate a last ditch effort to destroy everything that pertains to God (16:12-16).

During the battle and afterwards "He Himself will rule them with a rod of iron" (Psa 2:9; Rev 2:27), that is, over the global survivors. This will undoubtedly strike fear in the heart of anyone in the millennium who might doubt that He will do what He says. The Psalmist wrote of the Messiah "You will break [the nations] with an iron rod and smash them like clay pots" (Psa 2:9 NLT).

Earlier Jesus had promised that believers would rule with Him in the kingdom: "He who overcomes, and he who keeps My deeds until the end to him I will give authority over the nations; and he shall rule them with a rod of iron, as the vessels of the potter are broken to pieces, as I also have received authority from My Father" (Rev 2:26-2).

Furthermore, He is seen as the One who "treads the winepress of the fierceness and wrath of Almighty God" (imagery from 14:19-20), describing God's great wrath against those who reject Him. This final strike against the rebellious surviving nations will be witnessed by people throughout the (possibly through means of the modern media). Instead of grapes Christ is, as it were, stomping on people, splattering blood (as grape juice) also described by Joel 3:12-14.

The remaining unbelievers around the world will be gathered, judged and executed at the Judgment of the Sheep and Goats (Matt 25: 31-46) following Christ's return, but before the millennium begins. Sometimes it is hard to imagine Jesus Christ in such a wrathful mode, because it is hard for sinners to understand how horrible (our) sin is to a holy God.

Reflection: How often have we confessed our sins to God or are we even conscious of specific sins? How broken hearted are we for how we have offended Christ by our sins? Are we conscious of how we hurt God when we merely contemplate sinning?

Or worse yet, do we believe that we are really a pretty good person who rarely sins? If our sins do not bother us very much, it is hard to understand how they could offend God to such an extent. We have much to learn about our God.

THE TITLE OF THE KING

19:16

And He has on His robe and on His thigh a name written: KING OF KINGS AND LORD OF LORDS

19:16 The world's army will be following the Antichrist, whom they believe has all power. Then suddenly Christ appears and they are cut to pieces. From the ground, the thigh of a rider is at eye-level. The last sight they will see will be the title of the conquering king: "King of kings and Lord of lords." They will understand the truth, but too late.

This title of Christ's sovereignty (King of kings and Lord of lords") is used in several other Scriptures as well (Rev 17:14; Deut 10:17; Dan

2:47; 1 Tim 6:15). Why is it so hard for believers to let Christ become the King and Lord of every aspect of our lives? Most believers do not trust Him enough to say, "Lord, be the King of my life; I yield to Your every instruction in Your Word; I give up my right to my life and surrender it totally and fully to my King."

Reflection: : Can you say this prayer sincerely and freely?

C. THE DESTRUCTION OF THE ANTICHRIST'S ARMY (19:17-21)

19:17-18

Then I saw an angel standing in the sun; and he cried with a loud voice, saying to all the birds that fly in the midst of heaven, "Come and gather together for the supper of the great God, 18 "that you may eat the flesh of kings, the flesh of captains, the flesh of mighty men, the flesh of horses and of those who sit on them, and the flesh of all people, free and slave, both small and great."

19:17-18 No matter what kind of sophisticated weaponry they may have, the armies of the world cannot stand their ground against the armies of heaven.

An angel appears in front of the brightness of the sun and calls for all the birds "that fly in the midst of heaven," that is, the sky, as they search for animal carcasses. These are eagles and vultures. They are to gather in Israel to eat the carcasses of "kings" and "generals" and "mighty men," "horses" and their riders along with their followers who have all been killed without mercy.

Demonic power, even Satanic power, is mighty, but it fails to compare to the power of Christ. This will be the greatest single carnage in the history of the world. Since there will be no one to bury the dead, the flesh will be left for the birds to eat, at the "great supper of God." Likewise, this animal feast was described by the prophet Ezekiel (39:17-20). There will be millions of dead bodies spread out over this valley of Jezreel or Megiddo for 200 miles (14:20).

Even after the birds have had their fill, it will take seven months to bury the remaining corpses (Ezek 39:12). The birds are called to do their duty even before the great battle begins. The greatest of mankind becomes nothing but bird food. What a waste! Living apart from, or worse, in opposition to God is the end of a fool's life.

THE BATTLE ITSELF

19:19

And I saw the beast, the kings of the earth, and their armies, gathered together to make war against Him who sat on the horse and against His army.

19:19 The "beast" (Rev. 13 – the Antichrist) along with the "kings of the earth" (the "ten horns" and their surrogate kings) and their armies were manipulated by the Antichrist and his demons, as described in the sixth bowl of God's wrath where, "miracle-working demons, caused all the rulers of the world to gather for battle against the Lord ... to a place called Armageddon" (16:14-16 NLT).

This massive battle is called "the battle on the great day of God Almighty" in 16:14. This army has gathered to finally destroy every vestige of Israel and the "Holy Lands" and Christianity. The battle has been raging for some time throughout Israel before the appearance of Jesus, which will result in two-thirds of Israel having been killed before the arrival of Jesus.

As Jesus appears, every force is concentrated on the destruction of this single Rider. Their presumption and pride, as well as their bitterness and hatred against God, led them to "gather together to make war against Him who sat on the horse and against His army" to their own destruction. They could not believe that they would loose.

Reflection: Do people today find it easy to oppose God and make His truth to be a laughing stock?

THE CONCLUSION OF THE BATTLE FOR THE ANTICHRIST AND THE FALSE PROPHET

19:20

Then the beast was captured, and with him the false prophet who worked signs in his presence, by which he deceived those who received the mark of the beast and those who worshiped his image. These two were cast alive into the lake of fire burning with brimstone.

19:20 Within seconds of the beginning of the battle, it will all be over. During the battle the "beast" and "false prophet who worked signs" will be captured. These two leaders of the New World Order will find that their miraculous demonic power and great authority will be stripped from them and they will be thrown alive into the "lake of fire burning with brimstone" (or sulfur).

The False Prophet is the Great Manipulator who "deceived those who received the mark of the beast and those who worshiped his image" (described in 13:11-18). At this point in time all the unsaved of the history of mankind are condemned to a place called Hades (Luke 16:23).

But the destiny of the Antichrist and the False Prophet is the "lake of fire," which is a distinct place of torment, that has been prepared for the "devil and his angels" (Mat 25:41) and will not be inhabited by humans until after the millennium (Rev 20:14-15). This is the first mention of the Lake of Fire in Scriptures. Eventually, Satan himself, the Dragon and all the occupants of Hades (Matt 25:41), will be thrown into that lake of fire (20:10). This will be a place of "weeping and gnashing of teeth" (Matt 13:42) and the "smoke of their torment goes up forever and ever; they have no rest day and night" (Rev 14:11). These two men are (evidently) transformed into their immortal state as they are cast into the Lake of Fire, as they are still living a thousand years later when Satan joins them (20:10).

Following the devastating defeat at the battle of Armageddon Satan is cast into the "bottomless pit" for a thousand years alone. He will be released at the end of the millennium to give sin one final opportunity to deceive men on earth. When this final rebellion is over, Satan is cast into the Lake of Fire to join the Antichrist and the False Prophet who are still alive and in perpetual suffering.

The fact that the Antichrist and False Prophet are alive a thousand years later disproves any validity of annihilation. Their torment will never end. Satan is well aware of this prophecy, but he does not believe it! He is convinced he can alter the end game's outcome.

Reflection: Why is it easy to deceive the unsaved? How would you describe his strategy?

THE CONCLUSION OF THE BATTLE FOR THE DECEIVED ARMIES

19:21

And the rest were killed with the sword, which proceeded from the mouth of Him who sat on the horse. And all the birds were filled with their flesh.

19:21 The only survivors of the Battle of Armageddon will be the beast and his false prophet. Everyone else will be slaughtered by Christ's sword (Rev. 1:16; 2:12, 16; 19:15) and sent to Hades, until the end of the millennium. The number that will be killed will be so great that the vultures will not be able to eat their corpses fast enough.

The global survivors of this horrible battle scene will be summoned to appear before the Judgment of Nations (Matt 25) and the unsaved will be destroyed and cast into the fires of Hades to await the Great White Throne Judgment at the end of the millennium (20:12-13). When the sentence is given from this judgment all the inhabitants of "death and hell" will be cast into the lake of fire (20:14).

This description of such a bloody war motivates some who want to doubt the validity of Scriptures to point to the contradiction in God's character. Liberals tend to ignore the judgment passages seeking to emphasize only the love of God. "How could God do this?" This is so gruesome that the liberals want to spiritualize this narration to mean something entirely different from what it says.

This is the final judgment that awaits the rebellious unbeliever. Walvoord wrote, "The Second Coming of Christ is the occasion for a worldwide judgment unparalleled in Scriptures since the time of Noah's flood." Indeed, the knowledge of such events as these should motivate us to godly living (2 Peter 3:11).

Paul described the believer's response to knowing what is going to happen in the future in these verses: "The night is almost gone, and the day is near. Therefore let us lay aside the deeds of darkness and put on the armor of light. Let us behave properly as in the day, not in carousing and drunkenness, not in sexual promiscuity and sensuality, not in strife and jealousy. But put on the Lord Jesus Christ, and make no provision for the flesh in regard to its lusts" (Rom. 13:12–14).

Reflection: How does the knowledge of these future events help you overcome sin and temptation in your life now?

CHAPTER 20

MILLENNIAL REIGN OF CHRIST

"According to our text Satan is not bound until the end of the Tribulation Period at the beginning of the millennium. He will be chained in the Abyss alone for a thousand years."

Though there are a variety of views on this chapter, a simple reading of the text, taking it for what is says as true and literal, as has been done throughout this study, is the most consistent way to discover its meaning. Whatever the text states in the chronological sequence in which it is written, is the view we will take. Furthermore, chapters 21-22 were written in chronological sequence and will be taken as written.

I. THE BINDING OF SATAN (20:1-3)

KEY TO BOTTOMLESS PIT

20:1

Then I saw an angel coming down from heaven, having the key to the bottomless pit and a great chain in his hand.

20:1 "Then" begins this chapter suggesting a sequence of events after chapter 19, which likewise begins with "after this." In chapter 19 the original text has "and" at the beginning of 15 verses, and continues in chapter 20 beginning every verse (except vs. 5), which grammatically indicates that these events proceed in sequence, thus chapter 20 must occur after the Second Advent.

In addition, chapter 19 gives cause to the events of chapter 20, that is, the casting of the beast and the false prophet into the lake of fire and the destruction of the entire army of the Antichrist, leaving Satan himself as the primary protagonist causing the global rebellion. He will now be dealt with in judgment.

Once again "an angel" comes "from heaven" with the "key to the bottomless pit and a great chain in his hand." In 9:1-12 an angel came with this key to release the demonic locust/scorpions in the fifth trumpet judgment from the bottomless pit (Abyss). It appears that the bottomless pit is vacated after the fifth trumpet judgment, awaiting its new resident. Either this angel is amazingly powerful, or Satan has now been stripped of all his former powers.

Reflection: Do you think any human could have the authority and power to bind Satan and cast him into the pit? If so, why has it not been done before now?

(The different millennial views include the following main views:
(1) The *amillennial view* (a- means "no," so "no millennium") of the reign of Christ is an earthly reign of peace or a spiritual reign in the hearts of God's people throughout the Church Age. This view denies the literal seven years of Tribulation at the end of the Church Age, seeing these events throughout the Church Age. This view does believe that in the end the Antichrist will increase the persecution of believers until Jesus returns to judge the world in one final Judgment and the His eternal state.
(2) The *postmillennial view* sees the thousand years representative of the triumph of the gospel through the gospel ministries previous to the second coming of Christ, thus the millennium will be established by Christians who will prepare the world for Christ's return. The resurgence of this view is called the Kingdom Now theology.
(3) The *premillennialism views* the coming of Christ before the millennium as the conquering King of kings to establish a literal kingdom as seen in this study.)

CHAINED FOR A THOUSAND YEARS

20:2

He laid hold of the dragon, that serpent of old, who is the Devil and Satan, and bound him for a thousand years;

20:2-3 This same angel "laid hold of" (*krateo*, "to have power, get possession of, become master of, seize") the "dragon, that serpent of old, who is the Devil and Satan." The grammatical chronology of these events indicates that this event occurs after the second coming of Christ.

For some naive believers to say that they can bind Satan to make him ineffective today is presumptuous, to say the least. He can be resisted and he will flee (James 4:7)… to somewhere else, but he is not bound from the earth by this action. Until this future event, Satan exerts great destructive power in the world and especially against the Jews and true Christians. It takes a lot of imagination to deny the work of Satan today.

Reflection: Describe what Satan does or can do in this present age:

Luke 22:3

Acts 5:3

1 Cor 5:5

1 Cor 7:5

2 Cor 2:11

2 Cor 4:4

2 Cor 11:14

2 Cor 12:

Eph 2:2

1 Thess 2:18

1 Tim 1:20

2 Tim 2:26

1 Peter 5:8

There is no question that Satan is presently limited by the power of God (e.g., Job), but he can destroy any unwary believer ignorant of his strategies (2 Cor 2:11 and characteristics. In the Tribulation it appears that Satan is cast out of heaven and remains unrestrained on earth to destroy and corrupt the world for seven years, probably hoping to change the outcome prophesied in Scripture.

But, according to our text, Satan is not bound until the end of the Tribulation at the beginning of the millennium. He will be chained in the Abyss alone for a thousand years. The demon of the locusts will have been there for thousands of years until they are released in the fifth trumpet. Then the worse of the demons, Satan himself, will be isolated from God's creation for a thousand years.

Reflection: What would it be like to not have satanic deception today? (This is the first of six references to a thousand years in this chapter (20:2, 3, 4, 5, 6, 7).)

THE THOUSAND YEARS IMPRISONMENT

20:3

and he cast him into the bottomless pit, and shut him up, and set a seal on him, so that he should deceive the nations no more till the thousand years were finished. But after these things he must be released for a little while.

MILLENNIAL REIGN OF CHRIST

20:3 The same period of the imprisonment of Satan in the bottomless pit is the thousand-year reign of Christ (20:4-6). The chief activity of Satan throughout history has been to "deceive the nations" to do his destructive bidding, which he will no longer have the power to do.

Paul wrote that the spiritual struggle is against "powers, against the rulers of the darkness of this age, against spiritual hosts of wickedness in the heavenly places" (Eph 6:12). But Paul pictures our present struggle as a defensive posture to stand against demonic attacks, not an offensive confrontation. The heavenly battles are between angelic beings.

At the beginning of the Tribulation he will have been cast out of heaven ("heavenly places") to manipulate the world leaders to hate God, but now that global evil seductive influence (1 Tim 4:1) will be no more for a thousand years. Evidently God's plan is to test all humanity one more time: would mankind trust in God's truth after a thousand years of the reign of Christ on earth?

At the conclusion of the thousand years Satan "must be released for a little while." Not all who enter the millennium will be believers who survived the Tribulation. The Judgment of Nations in Matt 25 for entrance into the beginning of the millennium is on the basis of how the nations treated the Jews and believers during the Tribulation. Many will be converted and come to Zion or Jerusalem seeking the truth, but not everyone. Before eternity begins, every last unconverted person on earth must be made evident and weeded out.

Satan will be allowed to wield his tempting lies and deceit to provoke one final rebellion against God. As foolish as this seems it clearly indicates the powerful deceitfulness of Satan. Earlier John wrote, "You are of your father the devil, and the desires of your father you want to do. He was a murderer from the beginning, and does not stand in the truth, because there is no truth in him. When he speaks a lie, he speaks from his own resources, for he is a liar and the father of it" (John 8:44).

The evil intents of the unsaved will be dampened by Christ's "rule of iron," but external pressure never changes the heart of man. When given the opportunity to believe a lie or to get away with sin, evil men will jump at the chance. This will prove the depravity of the unsaved as they join forces for one final rebellion. For this reason Satan is not cast into the Lake of Fire with the beast and the false prophet until the end of the thousand years when this final futile rebellion fails.

Reflection: Why is it easier for man to believe a lie than to accept the truth?

II. THE RESURRECTION AND REWARD OF THE TRIBULATION MARTYRS (20:4-6)

20:4

And I saw thrones, and they sat on them, and judgment was committed to them. Then I saw the souls of those who had been beheaded for their witness to Jesus and for the word of God, who had not worshiped the beast or his image, and had not received his mark on their foreheads or on their hands. And they lived and reigned with Christ for a thousand years.

20:4 John sees two groups of people: (1) people sitting on thrones with authority to judge others; (2) martyrs of the Antichrist's cruel regime during the Tribulation. The first group is not identified, but several promises of ruling/judging authority were made to the 12 disciples who would judge from twelve thrones (Matt 19:28; Luke 22:29-30) and a passing suggestion was given to the Church that they would "judge the world" in 1 Cor 6:2-3 as motivation to resolve internal church problems without going to the civil courts.

The second scene John saw was the vast number of martyrs as embodied "souls." That is, they had visible intermediate bodies awaiting the resurrection.

The first group were those "who had been beheaded (*pelekizo*, "cut off with an axe") for their witness to Jesus and the word of God" (the group under the alter in Rev 6:9-11). The Antichrist will attempt to erase all remnants of believers. The translation next says "who" which translates *kai oitives*, ("and whoever"), which could refer to the same group or another group who will not be martyred, but "had not worshiped the beast or his image, and had not received his mark on their foreheads or on their hands," thus, they will be contemporaries with the reign of the Antichrist.

This could be a separate group of believers killed in the wars, famines, plagues and judgments affecting the globe, but not be directly sentenced to death by beheading. Whether two groups or one, these "lived (*zao*, aorist tense, "came to life, began to enjoy real life," and is used to describe a physical, bodily resurrection – Rev 1:18; 2:8; 13:14; 20:5; Matt 9:18; 27:63; Mark 5:23; Luke 24:23; John 11:25; Acts 1:3, 9:41; Rom 14:9; 2 Cor 13:4) and reigned with Christ for a thousand years."

Will this be a special reward for their faithfulness to Christ? All the saints of all the ages have been promised to reign with Christ in His kingdom: OT saints (Dan 7:27); the apostles (Matt 19:28); NT saints (1 Cor 6:2; 2 Tim 2:12; Rev 2:26; 3:21; 5:10).

The almost identical sentence is found in 5:10 but adds the phrase "reign upon the earth." This is not a reference to a spiritual or heavenly kingdom but a physical, earthly kingdom. All believers from the church age will join the Tribulation saints in a joint reign with Christ (2 Tim 2:12).

Reflection: If faithfulness and usefulness now will have a determining factor in this time of reigning with Christ and who knows what responsibilities in eternity, how should we live our lives?

FIRST RESURRECTION

20:5

But the rest of the dead did not live again until the thousand years were finished. This is the first resurrection.

20:5 The unsaved dead, "the rest of the dead," from all the previous ages, but especially the unsaved from the Tribulation will remain in the grave for a thousand years. The word "again" implies that this whole group of Tribulation population will have recently died.

It is estimated that perhaps 90% of the population of the globe will have died in the judgments against humanity. "This is the first resurrection," which ushers its participants into a glorified, eternal state with unusual powers and bodies and will capacitate the believer to reign with Christ in their immortal bodies.

First of all, if there is a "first resurrection" there must be a "second." The first is comprised of all the believers in all of the previous ages. There is a separation of at least 1,000 years between the first and second resurrections.

Reflection: If there are two resurrections separated by a 1000 years, what is the purpose of the first resurrection? What does it prepare us to do with Christ?

BENEFIT OF FIRST RESURRECTION

20:6
Blessed and holy is he who has part in the first resurrection. Over such the second death has no power, but they shall be priests of God and of Christ, and shall reign with Him a thousand years.

20:6 The believers in general of all ages will be part of the "first resurrection," (1 Cor 15:51-53). It is the "first" resurrection in the sense that it is before the "second" resurrection and "second death" (20:6, 14). The second resurrection is of the unsaved, wicked dead at the end of the millennium. Thus the "first resurrection" includes all those previously resurrected before the millennium. All these believers are "blessed and holy."

If the church had not been raptured before the Tribulation, the resurrection of only the saints of the seven-year period, not the whole church age, is partial and preferential. There is no hint here of the resurrection of the entire church. However, since the church will have been raptured before the Tribulation begins, it makes sense that this is the completion of the resurrection of all believers, which now would include the believers who will die or be killed in the seven-year Tribulation period.

The believers are "blessed" in this passage because of two promises and are "holy" because "He has reconciled you to himself through the death of Christ in his physical body. As a result, he has brought you into his own presence, and you are holy and blameless as you stand before him without a single fault" (Col 1:21-22^{NLT}). This is the fifth of seven "blessed" passages (1:3; 14:13; 16:15; 19:9; 22.7, 14).

The first reason for being "blessed" is that following their resurrection, these believers likewise are promised that the "second death has no power" over them. The second death is defined in 20:14 as the "lake of fire," or eternal hell, the habitation of the unsaved forever. This freedom from the second death is true of all believers of all ages.

Paul wrote, "we shall be saved from the wrath of God through Him" (Rom 5:9). The Thessalonians believers were promised, "Jesus, who delivers us from the wrath to come...For God did not appoint us to wrath, but to obtain salvation through our Lord Jesus Christ" (1 Thess 1:10; 5:9).

The second reason for being "blessed" is that they will be able to "be priests of God and of Christ and will reign with him for a thousand years." This was also promised to the believers of the church age (1:5; 5:10). Believers have always served as a "royal priesthood" being called to "proclaim the excellencies of Him who has called [them] out of darkness into His marvelous light" (1 Peter 2:9).

A priest is a worshipper, intercessor, guide who leads others to God and the Savior and teaches the truths of God's Word: the tasks of all believers of all ages. Not only will believers always be priests, but "will reign with him" along with the surviving believers of the Tribulation as the fulfillment of Psa 2:6-8 and Isa 11:3-5 as we build a global kingdom from the rubble of the Tribulation judgments.

This will be a time when the surviving remnant of Israel is converted to their Messiah (Jer 30:5-8; Rom 11:26) and Israel is restored to the land promised to Abraham (Gen 15:18). The Gentile nations will worship the King (Isa 11:9; Mic 4:2; Zech 14:16). The kingdom will bring peace and security to the world (Isa 32:17) and, great joy (Isa 12:3-4). During this time the curse of the Garden of Eden will be lifted or modified (Isa 11:7-9; 30:23-24; 35:1-2, 7), food will be abundant (Joel 2:21-27). There will be universal physical health (Isa 33:24; 35:5-6) and a return to the long lives of the pre-flood age (Isa 65:20).

Reflection: Whatever regional part a believer plays in the global reign of Christ will be determined by our faithfulness and usefulness to Christ in the preparation of the kingdom. Today is the training and testing grounds for the kingdom to come. He is equipping us as we equip others for a strategic role with Him in His kingdom to come.

This first resurrection includes the resurrection of Moses (Jude 9); Elijah (2 Kings 2:11); some near the scene of Jesus' resurrection (Matt 27:52-53); the raptured church (1 Thess 4:13-18); the two witnesses (Rev 11:3, 11); then the believers killed in the Great Tribulation soon after the return of Christ to earth (20:4-5); and likely at this time the resurrection of the OT saints occurs (Isa 26:19-21; Ezek 37:12-14; Dan 12:2-3).

III. THE DOOM OF SATAN (20:7-10)

20:7-8

Now when the thousand years have expired, Satan will be released from his prison 8 and will go out to deceive the nations

which are in the four corners of the earth, Gog and Magog, to gather them together to battle, whose number is as the sand of the sea.

20:7-8 Without any more explanation of the millennium, the text jumps to the end of the thousand years. We learn more of the promises of the millennium from the OT prophets than from the NT prophecies. The nature of God is to put man to the test time and again. He wants sin, evil and false notions to be exposed for what they are. People who want to believe a lie, will be given a lie to believe and be deceived thereby.

After a thousand years of being confined in the bottomless pit "Satan will be released from his prison [the "Abyss"] and will go out to deceive the nations." When the millennium begins there are few or no unsaved people alive who enter the kingdom. Only the saved among the Jews (Rev 12:6, 13-17; Isa 60:21; Rom 11:26), and Gentiles surviving believers (most of whom were killed – 7:9-17) will begin the new global families.

The perfect social and environmental conditions of the millennium coupled with the lengthened life spans of those in their physical bodies (Isa 65:20), children will proliferate. If women are restored to their pre-curse physical condition, then they can have children without pain (Gen 3:16).

Humans at the beginning of the millennium are primarily all saved, though they are still sinners. After a thousand years of multiple generations in a perfect environment, children born to these families will come into the world with a sinful nature requiring regeneration and a personal salvation encounter with Christ; however, many will love their sins and reject the Lord (Rom 8:7). They will not have experienced the mighty hand of God, so will have to believe by faith.

Sadly human corruption will ruin even the most perfect conditions. As humanity began in a perfect environment yet selfish human depravity refused to trust God. Now in the end of human history, once again in a global Garden of Eden, sinners born of the believing parents will be easily deceived and choose to love their sin (John 3:19) rather than the King of kings.

Those who rebel during the millennium will face a swift judgment (as in 2:2; 12:5; 19:15; Ps 2:9), but there will be an abundance of the unrepentant who are alive when Satan is released that a worldwide rebellion will occur. Not only will Satan never repent, he will find humans who will resent Christ's rule and their superficial fake Christianity will be an easy prey for the Master Liar. The deceived will come from "the four corners of the earth" (7:1; Isa 11:12), that is the four points of the compass (north, south, east, west).

The reference to "Gog and Magog" refers to a war in Ezekiel 38-39, where Gog was a ruler and Magog was the people who were both in rebellion against God and were enemies of Israel. This battle at the end of the millennium is distinct from the battle referred to in Ezekiel 38-39, though there are some similarities. Ezekiel refers to a few nations, but Revelation 20 refers to all nations; Ezekiel shows the armies coming from the north, but in Revelation 20 the nations come from all directions. The Ezekiel passage refers to a battle that will occur with the end-time events before the millennium (Rev 19:17-18).

John's reference of the infamous battle of Gog and Magog is similar to the symbolic use of "Waterloo" to refer to the defeat of Napoleon at battle of Waterloo in Belgium, but is used metaphorically to refer to any personal or national disaster. The "number [of the rebels] is as the sand of the sea," a hyperbole describing a huge innumerable mass of people who will gather to destroy God's people.

Reflection: Sadly the beginning and end of humanity demonstrate the same story; sinful humans are depraved and committed to their sins, ignoring their Savior, preferring to obey and follow the Father of lies, Satan, himself. What does this tell us about God? What precautions does anyone need to avoid being deceived by Satan?

Other verses describe this judgment:
Dan 7:9-10 ("The Ancient One sat down to judge...and the books were opened");
Matt 16:27 ("I, the Son of Man... will judge all people according to their deeds");
Rom 2:5-6 ("For there is going to come a day of judgment when God, the just judge of all the world, will judge all people according to what they have done");
Rom 2:16 ("The day will surely come when God, by Jesus Christ, will judge everyone's secret life");
2 Tim 4:1 ("Christ Jesus ... will someday judge the living and the dead when he appears to set up his Kingdom");
2 Peter 3:7 ("And God has also commanded that the heavens and the earth will be consumed by fire on the day of judgment, when ungodly

people will perish");
Jude 14-15 ("Look, the Lord is coming with thousands of his holy ones. He will bring the people of the world to judgment. He will convict the ungodly of all the evil things they have done in rebellion."
The Book of Life is the record of those who are saved (Rev 3:5; 13:8; 17:8; 20:15; 21:27).)

SITE OF THE FINAL BATTLE

20:9

They went up on the breadth of the earth and surrounded the camp of the saints and the beloved city. And fire came down from God out of heaven and devoured them.

20:9 This vast multitude of rebels gathers on a vast plain, "breadth of the earth," which probably was created in the geological transformation of the earth's surface in Rev 16:20 (also Zech 14:4, 9-11), which flattened the mountains leaving the earth's surface a vast plain as before the flood. The rebels "surrounded the camp of the saints and the beloved city [the city He loves]," which refers to Jerusalem.

Here we see an amazing display of ignorance, arrogance, audacity, ambition and anger precipitated by the lies and bitterness of the great Dragon, Satan, who has been plotting this final effort for a thousand years. The "camp" (*parembole*, "the camp of Israel in the desert, barracks of the Roman soldiers") is located around Jerusalem, where Christ's throne is the center of the millennial kingdom (Isa 24:23; Ezek 38:12; 43:7; Mic 4:7; Zech 14:9-11) in "majestic splendor" (Isa 24:23).

No sooner does this threatening army congregate around the city than "fire came down from God out of heaven and devoured them." Satan's forces will be executed and their souls will pass into the temporary punishment of Hades, awaiting the final judgment of the Great White throne to occur shortly (20:11-15). The "folly of fools is deceit/deception" (Prov 14:8), that is they are easily deceived. Likewise the "fool rages and is self-confident" (Prov 14:16).

These two enormous battles (Armageddon and Gog and Magog) are only given two verses to describe each battle (Antichrist's defeat in 19:20-21; Satan's final defeat in 20:9-10). There is absolute assurance of victory with Christ. Never doubt it or have second thoughts about whether it is worth it or if you have chosen the right side. God allows sin to manifest itself in all of its awfulness and pride, only to suddenly destroy it.

Fire from heaven is a common method of divine judgment (Gen 19:24; Ex 9:23-24; Lev 9:24; 10:2; Num 11:1; 16:35; 26:10; 1 Kings 18:38; 2 Kings 1:10, 12, 14; 1 Chron 21:26; 2 Chron 7:1, 3; Psa 11:6).

Reflection: Do you ever have thoughts of rebellion, secret pride or presumptuous sins that you think you can avoid disclosing?

God tends to allow time for men to recognize their folly and repent, but at some point He intervenes bringing punishment, justice and righteousness. Have you seen this happen in someone's life? (Prov 19:25)

POPULATION OF LAKE OF FIRE GROWS BY ONE

20:10

The devil, who deceived them, was cast into the lake of fire and brimstone where the beast and the false prophet are. And they will be tormented day and night forever and ever.

20:10 The leader of this grand deception is quickly judged and condemned forever to the Lake of fire from which he will never again be free. He joins the only other inhabitants of this vast Lake of fire, the "beast [Antichrist] and the false prophet" who are still alive in this place after a thousand years (19:20).

This verse destroys the notion of annihilation (The belief that the wicked are utterly obliterated and consumed, thus cease to exist). People continue to live forever in bodies that cannot be destroyed, never becoming numb to torment and pain. This is a place of mental agony (Dan 12:2 - "disgrace" or "shame and everlasting contempt"; Matt 8:12; 13:42, 50; 22:13; 24:51; 25:30; Luke 13:28 - "weeping and gnashing of teeth"), as well as physical torment (Rev 14:10, "...tormented with fire and brimstone[sulfur]"; Matt 25:41, "eternal fire;" Mark 9:43-44, "unquenchable fire;" Luke 16:23-24, "anguish in this fire").

Those sentenced to this habitation "will be tormented day and night forever and ever." This is probably the most ominous statement ever made. Only a fool would risk this destiny. "The smoke of their torment goes up forever and ever; they have no rest day and night" (Rev 14:10-11). The punishment of the wicked is as eternal as heaven is eternal for the saved (Matt 25:46). Paul wrote, "They will be punished with eternal destruction, forever separated from the Lord and from his glorious power" (2 Thess 1:9^{NLT}).

Reflection: What good does it do us to know what will happen to the unsaved? On the other hand what do these verses teach the believer about his secure relationship and destiny?

Phil 3:20

Col 1:13

1 Thess 2:12

1 Pet 1:4

IV. THE GREAT WHITE THRONE JUDGMENT (20:11-15)

These final five verses describe the end of human earthly history and the beginning of the eternal state.

A. THE RESURRECTION AND JUDGMENT OF THE UNSAVED DEAD (20:11-13)

20:11

Then I saw a great white throne and Him who sat on it, from whose face the earth and the heaven fled away. And there was found no place for them.

20:11 The "great white throne" judgment follows the thousand years, referred to six times in 20:1-6. This throne is distinct from the "throne" mentioned 30 times in Revelation (e.g. 4:2). "Him who sat on it [the throne]" refers to Jesus as "the Father leaves all judgment to his Son" (John 5:22) and the fact that "we must all stand before Christ to be judged" (2 Cor 5:10).

This is the last judgment that will ever occur for all eternity. The planet earth and the vast universe "fled away" (*pheugo*, aorist tense, "shun, avoid by flight something abhorrent, vanish") as described in Matt 24:35; Mark 13:31; Luke 16:17; and 21:33.

This dissolving of all the original creation is described 2 Peter 3:10[NET], "the heavens will disappear with a horrific noise, and the celestial bodies will melt away in a blaze, and the earth and every deed done on it will be laid bare."

The whole purpose of time and space from the beginning of creation until the return of eternity, is to find created beings who willingly choose to know and love God against all pressures to the contrary so that inhabitants of eternity would never again be flawed by sin.

Once sin is finally dealt with, a new purpose of existence begins for all eternity (See Isa 51:6). The new heavens and new earth in Rev 21 are totally different from anything in the present creation.

Reflection: Does this give you a sense of destiny, hope and gracious privilege that we have a part in this eternal new world?

THE PRISONER'S JUSTICE

20:12

And I saw the dead, small and great, standing before God, and books were opened. And another book was opened, which is the Book of Life. And the dead were judged according to their works, by the things which were written in the books.

20:12 The scene is vast and the multitudes of the "dead, small and great, standing before God" will include the ones recently destroyed in the end of the millennium as well as the wicked dead from the Tribulation and all human history who were told they would not be resurrected until after the thousand years, since they had no part in the "first resurrection" a thousand years earlier (20:5).

This is a sentencing court scene. The verdict is in, and these all have been found guilty. The evidence is contained in the "books" and whether their names in the "Book of Life." Any verdict that will be passed down from this judgment seat will be just, because He, the Judge, is just. Deut 32:4 declares about God: "His work is perfect, for all His ways are just; a God of faithfulness and without injustice, righteous and upright is He." God is always absolutely just and right in all He does. Justice is His nature.

Sinners have all wronged and offended God's justice, but God's justice has not wronged or been unjust to them, for it cannot be. There will never be grounds for a complaint about the verdict and sentence at the

Judgment Seat. Jesus warned the world, "You will die in your sins; for unless you believe that I am He, you will die in your sins" (John 8:24).

All believers are inscribed by name in the Book of Life and everyone's life works are recorded in the books (plural) of works in an accurate life history of every individual. Everyone will be ultimately measured by their works. Even the unsaved will be sentenced and punished according to their works and their response to the knowledge of truth.

Jesus warned Capernaum, who witnessed years of Jesus' teaching and miracles, yet rejected His message, "I say to you that it shall be more tolerable for the land of Sodom in the Day of Judgment than for you" (Mat 11:24). Sins are horrible, but rejecting truth is far worse in God's values.

Every unsaved person from history "great and the small" without exception, will stand before God, who has these characteristics: "no partiality" (Rom 2:11); "unbiased and takes no bribe" (Deut 10:17); "does not take note of the rich more than the poor" (Job 34:19); "no favoritism with him" (Eph 6:9); "there are no exceptions" (Col 3:25); and "Father the one who impartially judges" (1 Pet 1:17).

This judgment does not determine whether a person has merited an entrance into heaven, since no one ever could merit such acceptance by his own works before a Holy God. This judgment is only to determine the degree of eternal unavoidable punishment. John Phillips described this day:

> There is a terrible fellowship there.... The dead, small and great, stand before God. Dead souls are united to dead bodies in a fellowship of horror and despair. Little men and paltry women whose lives were filled with pettiness, selfishness, and nasty little sins will be there. Those whose lives amounted to nothing will be there, whose very sins were drab and dowdy, mean, spiteful, peevish, groveling, vulgar, common, and cheap. The great will be there, men who sinned with a high hand, with dash, and courage and flair. Men like Alexander and Napoleon, Hitler and Stalin will be present, men who went in for wickedness on a grand scale with the world for their stage and who died unrepentant at last. Now one and all are arraigned and on their way to be damned: a horrible fellowship congregated together for the first and last time. (John Philips, *Exploring Revelation*, rev. ed. [Chicago: Moody, 1987; reprint, Neptune, N.J.: Loizeaux, 1991], pp. 242–243).

Another amazing book in heaven is described in Psalms 139:15-16 where it is recorded how every man was "made in secret" and "sewed together"[NET] or "woven together"[NIV-NLT] or "skillfully wrought"[NKJ] in the "dark part of the womb"[NLT], which seem to describe the record of our DNA.

Reflection: Does it make any difference whether they never heard the gospel or not? Should I attempt to do anything to get the gospel to the unreached as well as the unevangelized?

No one is forgotten or overlooked.

20:13

The sea gave up the dead who were in it, and Death and Hades delivered up the dead who were in them. And they were judged, each one according to his works.

20:13a As the scene unfolds the soul of every unsaved person has been summoned from its temporary state in Hades. As soon as a person dies he/she immediately faces a decisive judgment: "Just as each person is destined to die once and after that comes judgment" (Heb 9:27).

For the unsaved this will mean a temporary confinement in Hades, awaiting this final Day of Judgment. The bodies of the dead who perished in "the sea" and the bodies that were laid in "death" in the earth will be united with their souls coming from Hades. This will be the resurrection of the spiritually dead, that is, the lost.

Hades is used 10 times in the NT, always as a place of punishment (cf. Luke 16:23) where the lost are kept until their final sentencing to the Lake of Fire at the Great White Throne Judgment.

The "Sea," "Death and Hades" are emptied of their bodies and united with their souls to live forever in an indestructible body and to experience unending torment. Death is defined as the separation of the body and soul, which will never again occur. "The last enemy to be destroyed is death" (1 Cor 15:26).

John exclaimed that in heaven, "there will be no more death" (21:4). By this time every human being who will have ever lived and died will be reunited, body and soul, and will be, henceforth, an immortal being. In the resurrection, both of the saved and the unsaved, "this corruptible has put on incorruption, and this mortal has put on immortality..." (1 Cor 15:54).

Reflection: Now with an indestructible and more sensitive body, rather than merely a soul, will the torment of hell be worse or the same?

The "unreached" technically refer to those whose people group or language group does not have a viable functioning group of disciples yet. The "unevangelized" refers to people who already have functioning groups of disciples or churches, but many in that group have still not heard the gospel.

The believers will have been resurrected into their immortal, eternal bodies at the Rapture, before the Tribulation Period began (1 Thess 4:17).

20:13b As stated in vs. 12, so here is repeated: they "were judged, each one according to his works." The books contain every thought, word, and deed of every unsaved person who ever lived. God's omniscience never overlooks a single offence. Every sinner's wickedness will be measured against the holiness of God (Rom 3:23), only to find that no one can measure up to His sinlessness.

Paul wrote, " For as many as are of the works of the Law are under a curse; for it is written, 'Cursed is everyone who does not abide by all things written in the book of the law, to perform them'" (Gal 3:10).

James amplified this truth saying, "For whoever keeps the whole law and yet stumbles in one point, he has become guilty of all" (James 2:10). No one will presume to think or say here that they are innocent or they are "not that bad."

Jesus warned, "The Son of Man is going to come in the glory of His Father with His angels, and will then repay every man according to his deeds" (Matt 16:27). Attempting to claim ignorance of God's standards will not be an acceptable excuse, because both creation (Rom 1:20) and every human conscience (Rom 2:14-15), reveals God's perfection, flawlessness and righteousness.

Those without the biblical revelation of God's law (i.e. Ten Commandments), will be judged equitably according to the knowledge they do have (Rom 2:12). However varied the punishment, it will intolerable, indescribable and unending, without any hope of reprieve, and all this happens because of each person's own choice.

The writer of Hebrews wrote, "How much severer punishment do you think he will deserve who has trampled under foot the Son of God, and has regarded as unclean the blood of the covenant by which he was sanctified, and has insulted the Sprit of grace?" (Heb 10:29).

Some will be deceived by their religiosity and attempts at being spiritual only to discover in horror that they where never genuinely saved, "Lord, Lord, did we not prophesy in Your name, and in Your name cast out demons, and in Your name perform many miracles?" (Matt 7:22), but they will hear the most frightening words ever to be spoken, "I never knew you; depart from me, you who practice lawlessness" (Matt 7:23).

Those who seek to establish their own righteousness ignoring their own sins without confessing their sinfulness. They are unwilling to depend on the substitutionary work of Christ, preferring to attempt to be "good enough," but will find themselves condemned forever.

Reflection: What does it mean to genuinely "know Christ?"

    John 17:3

    1 Cor 2:2

    2 Cor 13:5

    2 Thess 1:8

    1 Jn 5:20

Verses that indicate a variation in the individual eternal punishment in hell are indicated in these verses: Matt 10:14-15; 11:21-24; Mark 12:38-40; Luke 12:47-48; Heb 10:29.

B. THE LAKE OF FIRE (20:14-15)

20:14-15

Then Death and Hades were cast into the lake of fire. This is the second death. 15 And anyone not found written in the Book of Life was cast into the lake of fire.

20:14-15 There is no acceptable excuse , no appeal, no second chance, no extension of grace beyond the grave, and no exceptions. "Anyone not found written in the Book of Life…," Those who choose by conscious rejection of the message of Christ or because they never heard the message of Christ's death for their sins, their names were never written in the Book of Life as believers in Jesus Christ.

All of these, without exception or excuse, will be "cast into the lake of fire." For a thousand years the beast [Antichrist] and the false prophet will have been tormented there (19:20), and only just previous to this White Throne Judgment, the Dragon, Satan, will have been cast into the lake of fire (20:10).

As the sentence is pronounced the condemned are cast into the fires of hell never to be heard from again. There is nothing more painful than fire. If this is symbolic language describing something perhaps outside of the existing universe, which is soon to be destroyed, then whatever it represents must be even more horrific.

The descriptions of this place include a place of total darkness, which will result in total isolation of every person (Matt 8:12; 22:13; 25:30; 2 Pet 2:17; Jude 13). Likewise, it is a place where even the "worm does not die" (Mark 9:44, 46, 48), and a place of unending bitter sorrow and rabid hatred as "weeping and gnashing of teeth" (Matt 8:12; 13:42, 50; 22:13; 24:51; 25:30; Luke 13:28).

The only way anyone on earth can avoid this terrifying end of human existence is to have heard the gospel of the grace of God, allowing the sacrificial death of Christ to be sufficient substitute for his sins. This applies to any and all persons willing to trust with all their heart in the death-payment on the cross of Christ and who will invite Him into their lives as Savior and Lord.

Reflection: What then, becomes our life-long task of the believers toward those who have never heard or cannot yet hear the good news of the gospel?

CHAPTER 21

NEW HEAVEN, NEW EARTH & NEW JERUSALEM

"This is an entirely new world never before seen or imagined by mortals... Life in eternity will be radically different."

This is an entirely new world never before seen or imagined by mortals. This new creation was prophesied in Isaiah 65:17, "For behold, I create new heavens and a new earth; and the former things will not be remembered or come to mind." Later Isaiah wrote, "just as the new heavens and the new earth which I make will endure before Me... so your offspring and your name will endure."

I. CREATION OF NEW HEAVEN AND NEW EARTH (21:1)

21:1

Now I saw a new heaven and a new earth, for the first heaven and the first earth had passed away. Also there was no more sea.

21:1 Following the White Throne Judgment and the end of the millennium John describes the creation of the "new heaven and the new earth." The word "new" (*kainos*, "recently made something superior to what it succeeds, unused, new kind") does not refer to chronologically new, but new in the sense of quality. The old world and universe "will disappear with a horrific noise, and the celestial bodies will melt away in a blaze, and the earth and every deed done on it will be laid bare. All these things are to melt away in this manner..." (2 Pet 3:10-11).

The original creation was corrupted by the entrance of sin, which required God's judgmental destruction (20:11). This pollution included the present universe according to Job 15:15, "the heavens are not pure in His sight." All creation yearns or groans for this day when the universal curse will be removed (Rom 8:20-22), but first "Heaven and earth will pass away" (Luke 21:33).

The most unusual characteristic of this new earth is that "there was no more sea." Although the present life is based on water with 70% of the earth's surface being covered in water in five major ocean basins. The Pacific Ocean covers 1/3 of the earth's surface, all, of which, will disappear in the new earth.

Life in eternity will be radically different with no hydrological cycle of evaporation and rain. This new world will not have sun or moon, and apparently stars. Thus there is no comparison with the millennium; it is an entirely new form of life and planetary system. This world is only temporary.

Reflection: There is no sense in wasting our lives living for things, stuff, real estate, or possessions, which will all be destroyed and brought to nothing. Does this make sense? How then should we live?

II. THE NEW JERUSALEM (21:2-8)

21:2

Then I, John, saw the holy city, New Jerusalem, coming down out of heaven from God, prepared as a bride adorned for her husband.

21:2 John's vision becomes focused on the most unique feature of the new earth, the capital city of eternity, "the holy city, New Jerusalem, coming down out of heaven from God." This New Jerusalem is called "the holy city" as contrasted with the old Jerusalem, which was called Sodom in 11:8. To live in this city has been the hope of all believers through the ages (Rev. 3:12; Heb 11:10; 12:22-24; 13:14).

This is the special future for those who have chosen to walk in fellowship with God, refusing the attractions of sin, reasonings and lies of human philosophies. We will believe and love the God of the Bible, and each other.

The city is "holy," (*hagios*) in the sense that it is "set apart" exclusively for God's purposes. Everyone who participates in this city is likewise "holy," since "blessed and holy is the one who has a part in the first resurrection" (20:6). John sees this holy city come down out of heaven where its "architect and builder" is God (Heb 11:10).

This is the home of all believers now in heaven according to Heb 12:22-23, "You have come to Mount Zion and to the city of the living God, the heavenly Jerusalem, and to myriads of angels, to the general assembly and church of the firstborn who are enrolled in heaven, and to God, the Judge of all, and to the spirits of the righteous made perfect."

This "heavenly Jerusalem" is where believers go when they die, where Jesus went "to prepare a place" for them (John 14:1-3). When the new heaven and new earth are created, the "New Jerusalem" will descend to this new earth. The city is described as a "bride" because it contains all the redeemed and its character describes the beauty of the Body of Christ.

The first stage is the betrothal of the Lord's bride, which took place in eternity past (Eph 1) when God pledged His Son to a redeemed people.

The second stage of the wedding will be the presentation of the bride at the Rapture of the church, when believers bodies are united to their souls and brought to the His heavenly home.

The third stage of the wedding will begin at the marriage supper of the Lamb (19:7-9) and will last throughout the millennium.
The final stage of the marriage, the consummation, is the eternal state. She is "'adorned' for her husband" (*kosmeo*, perfect passive, "has been – made beautiful or attractive"). This will include all of the believers since creation. Nothing in this world could ever compare to this moment in time.

Reflection: No wonder Paul exhorted us to set our affection on things above (Col 3:1). How can you practically set your affections on things above? (Col 3:1)

GOD WILL DWELL WITH HIS PEOPLE

21:3-4

And I heard a loud voice from heaven saying, "Behold, the tabernacle of God is with men, and He will dwell with them, and they shall be His people. God Himself will be with them and be their God. 4 "And God will wipe away every tear from their eyes; there shall be no more death, nor sorrow, nor crying. There shall be no more pain, for the former things have passed away.

21:3-4 The "loud voice from heaven" was probably that of an angel (God speaks in vs. 5) as on various other occasions (5:2; 7:2; 14:9, 15, 18; 19:17). This is the last of twenty times "a loud voice" is used in Revelation between Rev 5-22. The announcement concerned the "tabernacle of God" which will be "among men." "Tabernacle" (*skene*) means "tent" or "dwelling place:" God has "pitched His tent" or tabernacled "among men."

This is the same concept as John 1, "He dwelt among us." God will no longer be transcendent and distant, but close and intimate. This is the fulfillment of the John 17 prayer, "Father, I desire that they also, whom You have given Me, be with Me where I am, so that they my see My glory which You have given me" (John 14:1-3). However, there will be "no temple in [heaven], for the Lord God the Almighty and the Lamb are its temple" (21:22). The glory of the Lord will fill all of heaven and will not be limited to one place.

This concept is repeated in three different forms: (1) "God is with men;"

(2) "He will dwell with them;" and (3) "God Himself will dwell with them." Such reiteration implies the importance of the truth. The intimacy and proximity of God's glorious presence will be incomparable to the greatest bond of fellowship experienced during our sin-limited relationship in our physical lifetime.

An additional benefit to this time is stated in 1 John 3:2, "We know that when He appears, we will be like Him, because we will see Him just as He is." No one has seen the fullness of His glory for He "dwells in unapproachable light" (1 Tim 6:16), yet Jesus promised that in heaven, "the pure in heart...shall see God" (Matt 5:8). No mortal man has seen God in the fullness of His glory and survived (Ex 33:20).

Nothing in this world begins to compare with this experience, which is why Paul wrote, "the desire to depart and be with Christ, for that is very much better" (Phil 1:23). Every view of heaven describes the redeemed in acts of worship (4:10; 5:14; 7:11; 11:1, 16; 19:4).

All of this will be in the context of a purposeful service: "they serve [God] day and night in His temple" (7:15). This service will reflect our faithfulness during our earthly life (2 Tim 2:12). As a consequence, five experiences of human life will never again exist: tears and death (Isa 25:8), sorrow, crying, and pain. All these "former things have passed away" (*aperchomai*, aorist, "go away"), just as the "first heaven and the first earth are passed away" (21:1); here it is the same word.

Reflection: Where would these sentiments come from? Chronologically, it follows the conclusion of the millennium with its final rebellion of mankind and the Great White Throne Judgment of the lost throughout history. Is there a relationship? How will you feel?

INAUGURATION OF THE ETERNAL WORLD ORDER

21:5

Then He who sat on the throne said, "Behold, I make all things new." And He said to me, "Write, for these words are true and faithful." 6 And He said to me, "It is done! I am the Alpha and the Omega, the Beginning and the End. ...

21:5-6a The announcement concerns the radical change in the new world order with an entirely new universe and new earth. Old human experiences typical in a fallen, sinful creation are gone forever. This is a new creation: "I make all things new." The One making this announcement is the same One "from whose presence earth and heaven fled away, and no place was found for them" (20:11). God brings John back to the present with the command, "Write, for these words are true and faithful," just as the One who is revealing them is "faithful and true" (3:14;19:11).

Even though the present "heaven and earth will pass away," yet God's "words will not pass away" (Luke 21:33). As surely as there is a God these events will occur precisely as they are described. Then He declares, "It is done!" (*ginomai*, perfect voice, "have come into existence or have begun to be") as a completed action, not one in progress. This is the fulfillment of 1 Cor 15:24-28:

Then comes the end, when He hands over the kingdom to the God and Father, when He has abolished all rule and all authority and power. For He must reign until He has put all His enemies under His feet. The last enemy that will be abolished is death. For He has put all things in subjection under His feet. But when He says, "All things are put in subjection," it is evident that He is excepted who put all things in subjection to Him. When all things are subjected to Him, then the Son Himself also will be subjected to the One who subjected all things to Him, so that God may be all in all.

This the completion of the redemption, which began when Jesus said, "It is finished!" (John 19:20) on the cross. A loud voice cried from the heavenly temple when the judgment on Babylon and sinful man was complete, "It is done" (Rev 16:17).

Jesus redeemed and will safely bring all the redeemed of the ages to this new creation. God is "the Alpha and the Omega" (1:8, 17-18; 22:13, 16; the first and last letters of the Greek alphabet), "the beginning and the end" (Isa 44:6; 48:12-13).

God wrote the history of man and earth before it began, and it occurred precisely as planned. This same descriptive phrase is applied to the Lord Jesus Christ in 22:13, proving that His full deity is completely equal with the Father. The inauguration of eternity will be even more dramatic than the inauguration of the millennial kingdom.

Reflection: Will it be worth anything we might have to suffer now just to be present at this time?

ONLY FOR THIRSTY OVERCOMERS

21:6-8

I will give of the fountain of the water of life freely to him who thirsts. 7 He who overcomes shall inherit all things, and I will be his God and he shall be My son.

21:6-8 John turns his focus to the participants of this eternal new earth who are promised "the fountain of the water of life [given] freely to him who thirsts." This promise was made twice by Jesus (John 4:10, 14; 7:37). He characterized believers as ones who recognize their desperate spiritual need, who "hunger and thirst for righteousness" (Matt 5:6).

The redeemed are dissatisfied with the sinfulness they know they cannot undo, and crave for cleansing and acceptance before God. David put it this way, "As the deer pants for the water brooks, so my soul pants for You, O God. My soul thirsts for God, for the living God; when shall I come and appear before God?" (Ps 42:1-2).

The promise of this verse is that earnest seekers of God will find through Christ their deepest thirst fully satisfied. Jesus said on a great feast day, "If anyone is thirsty, let him come to Me and drink. He who believes in Me, as the Scripture said, 'Form his innermost being will flow rivers of living water'" (John 7:37-38).

And the final invitation to the readers in Revelation 22:17, "Come. And let the one who is thirsty come; let the one who wishes to take the water of life without cost." The water here is the symbol of eternal life. Those who thirst for and passionately seek salvation are the ones who will share in its blessings and be filled with the eternal delights of heaven.

Likewise, the phrase, "He who overcomes" is the same promise used by Jesus to the seven churches (2:7, 11, 17, 26; 3:5, 12, 21). John defined this term in 1 John 5:4-5, "For everyone born of God overcomes the world. This is the victory that has overcome the world, even our faith. Who is it that overcomes the world? Only he who believes that Jesus is the Son of God."

Three incredible promises are given to the believers:
(1) They "will inherit these things," which Peter described as "an inheritance, which is imperishable and undefiled and will not fade away, reserved in heaven for [them]" (1 Pet 1:4). This does not refer to the

millennial earth, which will be dissolved. Heaven is the topic of 237 verses in the NT. Beyond a doubt this moment is the dream of all the redeemed, to begin the eternal heavenly relations in the new earth.
(2) "I will be their God" in the most personal, intimate and proximate of relationships.
(3) The overcomers "will be My son." Now we are adopted sons by faith (John 1:12; Rom 8:14-17; 2 Cor 6:18; Gal 4:5; Eph 1:5; Heb 12:5-9; 1 John 3:1), but in the new earth this adoption is fully realized as anticipated by Paul, "we ourselves also, who have the firstfruits of the Spirit, even we ourselves groan within ourselves, eagerly waiting for the adoption, the redemption of our body" (Rom 8:23).

Reflection: Have you meditated and contemplated the greatness of this moment when everything is changed and prepared for the new eternity?

(This phrase is promised throughout Scriptures (Gen 17:7-8; Ex 6:7; 29:45; Lev 26:12; Deut 29:13; 2 Sam 7:24; Jer 7:23; 11:4; 24:7; 30:22; Ezek 11:20; 34:24; 35:28; 37:23, 27; Zech 8:8).)

THE EXCLUDED IN THE SECOND DEATH

21:8

But the cowardly, unbelieving, abominable, murderers, sexually immoral, sorcerers, idolaters, and all liars shall have their part in the lake which burns with fire and brimstone, which is the second death.

21:8 The discussion on the eternal new heaven and new earth ends with a warning for all time that all unforgiven and unrepentant sinners are forever excluded from the blessings of heaven. This list includes

(1) The "cowardly" (*deilos*, "timid, fearful") who turn away from God when challenged because their faith was not genuine. Jesus described them in the parable of the soils: "The one on whom seed was sown on the rocky places, this is the man who hears the word and immediately receives it with joy; yet he has no firm root in himself, but is only temporary, and when affliction or persecution arises because of the word, immediately he falls away" (Matt 13:20-21). Jesus described true believers as those who continue in His Word regardless (John 8:31);
(2) The "unbelieving" (*apistos*, "no+faith") who lack saving faith or are faithless. Jesus said "He that believes in Him is not condemned;

NEW HEAVEN, NEW EARTH AND NEW JERUSALEM

but he who does not believe is condemned already, because he has not believed in the name of the only begotten Son of God" (John 3:18);
(3) The "abominable" (*bdelosso*, perfect passive, "have been rendered foul, abhorred, to turn away from on account of the stench") are "detestable, wholly caught up in wickedness and evil;"
(4) The "murderers" (*phoneus*, "homicide") which violates the sixth commandment;
(5) The "immoral persons" (*pornos*, "a person who prostitutes his/her body to another's lust for hire") which violates the seventh commandment;
(6) The "sorcerers" (*pharmakeus*, "one who uses magical remedies;" from pharmakon, "drugs or mind-altering or spell-casting potion");
(7) The "idolaters" (*eidololatres*, "worshipper of false gods, a covetous man as a worshipper of Mammon"), which violates the 2nd commandment; and
(8) "All liars" (*pseudes*, "false, deceitful"), which violates the 9th commandment. All whose lives are characterized by these traits have never been saved and will never enter the heavenly city. James declared that "whoever keeps the whole law and yet stumble in one point, he is guilty of all" (James 2:10), because a sinner is always a sinner who is unacceptable in heaven.

Lists of lost sinners who know nothing of the grace of God include: Rev 22:15; Rom 1:28-32; 1 Cor 6:9-10; Gal 5:19-21; and 2 Tim 3:2-5.

The big issue is that human sinners have little appreciation for how despicable sin is to a holy God. Their inheritance will be "their part... in the lake that burns with fire and brimstone, which is the second death." The only hope for any sinner is to trust in the grace of God who freely grants the righteousness of God to be credited to the repentant believer, thus covering his sins with God's righteousness.

There could be no greater stark contrast: unimaginable eternal bless heaven in the presence of God; whereas, unbelievers will eternally reside in a terrifying place of unimaginable torment and unrelieved misery, in isolation separated forever from the presence of God (2 Thess 1:9). This statement repeats the declaration that entrance into the lake of fire is the "second death" from which there is no escape or relief forever.

Reflection: Do you believe these are the only two options for mankind? What responsibility do we have to help unbelievers understand and accept the gospel?

III. New Jerusalem as the Bride (21:9-11)

The remainder of the chapter is a description of the New Jerusalem. However, symbolic this description may be, it is evident that the believer's eternal home cannot easily be described. There will be no disappointment here. Jesus told His disciples on the eve of His own death, "Do not let your heart be troubled; believe in God, believe also in Me. In My Father's house are many dwelling places; if it were not so, I would have told you; for I go to prepare a place for you. If I go and prepare a place for you, I will come again and receive you to Myself, that where I am, there you may be also" (John 14:1-3). This is now where the believer goes immediately when he/she dies. This city in heaven will descend to the New Earth in the eternal state, where it becomes the capital city of the New Heavens and the New Earth.

THE LAMB'S WIFE

21:9

Then one of the seven angels who had the seven bowls filled with the seven last plagues came to me and talked with me, saying, "Come, I will show you the bride, the Lamb's wife.

21:9 One of the angels who brought one of the last destructive bowl judgments to earth a thousand years earlier (15:1), now comes to show John the Bride of Christ. One of those same seven angels had told John earlier, "Come, I will show you the judgment of the great harlot" (17:1), now John is shown the bride. As the great harlot represented the world system of evil and those who rebelled against God, so now the bride symbolizes those who know and are faithful to the living God and Savior, Jesus Christ.

In chapter 17 John is "carried...away into the wilderness" (17:3), but now is carried away to a great and high mountain (v.10). The "Lamb's wife" is a magnificent resplendent city, which John saw earlier (v. 2) as adorned as a bride.

The attire of the bride John sees as having the glory of God (v. 11). The city is inhabited by the church (19:7) and all the redeemed from history, who will live here forever.

The "bride" is clarified as the "Lamb's wife," because the marriage has taken place (19:7). As eternity begins the dazzling character of the city is designed to reflect the radiance of it inhabitants. Malachi 3:16-17 describes those who fear the Lord and meditate on His name, "'They shall be Mine,' says the Lord of hosts, 'on the day that I make them my jewels.'" For every inhabitant of this city Christ will "transform our lowly body that it may be conformed to His glorious body, according to the working by which He is able even to subdue all things to Himself" (Phil 3:21). Whatever this means, we will become the Bride that fills this "great city."

Reflection: How does 1 John 3:2-3 describe what our response to this great hope now should be?

THE DESCENDING CITY

And he carried me away in the Spirit to a great and high mountain, and showed me the great city, the holy Jerusalem, descending out of heaven from God, 11 having the glory of God. Her light was like a most precious stone, like a jasper stone, clear as crystal.

21:10-11 John is "carried... away in the Spirit" to "a great and high mountain" in this new earth. Being "carried away in the Spirit" is not merely a dream. It is important to note that John's visions are not fantasy or imaginary dreams, but spiritual realities, similar to Paul's experience when he was taken to the third heaven (2 Cor 12:2-4).

John was allowed to see and observe what only God knows and sees. To Him the future is as real as the present, and in these moments of revelation, John is allowed to experience the future as though it were the present. In time, John's experience will be ours.

Of note is a topological difference of a thousand years earlier during the outpouring of the seventh bowl, "all the mountains were leveled" (16:20^{NLT}), which may have lasted throughout the millennium. In the new earth there will be mountains.

From this elevated position John could see the "holy Jerusalem, descending out of heaven from God." This is the city, "whose architect and builder is God" (Heb 11:10). During the millennial reign of Christ the New Jerusalem will be suspended over the earth's surface.

In the destruction of the old earth and new creation the new earth and new heaven, the city is located in the heavenly scene until the creation of the new earth, at which point the New Jerusalem descends to the earth's surface. The uniqueness of this city is "the glory of God" that will radiate from the full manifestation of God's glorious presence such that "the city has no need of the sun or of the moon to shine on it, for the glory of God has illuminated it, and its lamp is the Lamb" (v. 23).

Isaiah described this new environment: "No longer will you have the sun for light by day...but you will have the Lord for an everlasting light, and your God for your glory" (Isa 60:19). Jesus' prayer was that believers could see the full glory of Christ as before the creation of the world (John 17:24).

This radiance is like "a most precious stone, lake a jasper stone, clear as crystal." The modern stone of this name is opaque. This is merely the transliteration of *iaspis*, which means a translucent stone, which some think refers to a diamond (THAYER). The refraction of the light of the *Shekinah* glory radiating from this city illuminates the entire new heavens and new earth. As the sun is the center of our world, so this New Jerusalem will be the center of the new earth.

Reflection: Can you see why we should be motivated to live pure lives and reflect the principles of Jesus Christ?

IV. NEW JERUSALEM AS A CITY (21:12-27)

THE EXTERIOR DESIGN

21:12-13

Also she had a great and high wall with twelve gates, and twelve angels at the gates, and names written on them, which are the names of the twelve tribes of the children of Israel: 13 three gates on the east, three gates on the north, three gates on the south, and three gates on the west.

21:12-13 It was a near impossibility for a first century man (or modern man) to adequately describe the magnificence of the believer's eternal home. What John describes over the next 9 verses are beyond our imagination and given only to build our expectation and hope. This is a physical, concrete facility that can be measured and quantified.

NEW HEAVEN, NEW EARTH AND NEW JERUSALEM

There is a "high wall and twelve gates…" with "twelve angels" standing at the gates. The "names of the twelve tribes of the children of Israel" were written over each of the gates, perhaps in the same order as in the desert, "there were three gates on the east and three gates on the north and three gates on the south and three gates on the west" for a total of twelve gates. These names may be reflective of the tribal camp around the tabernacle in the desert (Num 2) or the tribal land around the millennial temple (Ezek 48). For all eternity God will celebrate the covenant relationship that He promised to Abraham and his descendants who were used to bring to mankind the promises, the Scriptures and the Messiah. God never forgets loyalty to Him and His purpose.

Reflection: How can we be loyal to His purpose in our day since God has called us to Himself in salvation?

The number 12 is referred to throughout the description of the city: 12 gates, 12 angels, and 12 tribes of Israel (v. 12); 12 foundations and 12 apostles (v. 14); 12 pearls (v. 21); 12 kinds of fruit (22:2); dimension of the wall 144 cubits (12 x 12) (21:17) and the height, width, and length is 12,000 stadia or furlongs (21:16).

The millennial gates are describe in Ezekiel 48:31-34 (north side: Levi, Judah, and Reuben); (west side: Naphtali, Asher and Gad); (south side: Simeon, Issachar, and Zebulun); and (east side: Joseph, Benjamin, and Dan).

THE FOUNDATION AND THE MEASURE OF THE WALL

21:14-16

Now the wall of the city had twelve foundations, and on them were the names of the twelve apostles of the Lamb. ¹⁵ And he who talked with me had a gold reed to measure the city, its gates, and its wall. ¹⁶ The city is laid out as a square; its length is as great as its breadth. And he measured the city with the reed: twelve thousand furlongs. Its length, breadth, and height are equal.

21:14 Between each of the 12 gates there are 12 walls, which "had twelve foundations, an on them were the names of the twelve apostles of the Lamb." These foundation stones were each inscribed with the name of one of the apostles.

In the NT the church was built upon the foundational ministry and revelations of the "apostles and prophets" (Eph 2:20). When the representatives of the OT saints (v. 12) and the apostles of the NT believers (v. 14) are linked as co-residence of the New Jerusalem, yet they are still considered as distinct groups even in the eternal city.

This is the city that Abraham saw: "the city which has foundations, whose builder and maker is God" (Heb 11:10).

John watched as the angel took a ten-foot "measuring rod of gold" and measured "the city, its gates and its wall." The dimension of the city was 12,000 furlongs or stadia in length and width and depth, or approximately a 1,400-mile square, which is either a cube or pyramid. Paganism tends to prefer pyramid structures, whereas the temple construction was cubical, which best fits this description.

Morris calculates that the approximate believing population since creation would result in every person's "cube" to be approximately 75-acres on each side. To put the size of the city in perspective in the US geography, it would stretch from the Canadian border to the Gulf of Mexico, from Colorado to the Atlantic coast. God not only made provision for the salvation of all men on the cross, he made provision for men in the heavenly city.

A furlong or stadia is about 607 feet long, thus a 12,000 stadia would be about 1,340 miles in each direction. (H. M. Morris, *The Revelation Record,* Tyndale House, pp. 450-451).

Reflection: What are we doing to populate this city with our generation? Should this be a concern of ours?

THE WALL CONSTRUCTION

21:17-18

Then he measured its wall: one hundred and forty-four cubits, according to the measure of a man, that is, of an angel. 18 The construction of its wall was of jasper; and the city was pure gold, like clear glass.

21:17-18 The measure of the wall was 144 cubits, 72 yards or 216 feet thick, "according to the measure of a man," that is the angel is using human dimensions, but it is the same as angelic dimensions. The wall construction "was of jasper" – the same clear, diamond-like element used in vs. 11.

Not only was the wall translucent, but the city itself "was pure gold, like clear glass." This enables the resplendent glory to radiate everywhere, but precluded any privacy, which is not necessary in heaven. John is using a descriptive language for how the wall and city appeared, not necessarily a description of these metals as they are known today.

Reflection: Does this communicate wealth and riches or construction elements for practical purposes? Why?

THE WALL, GATES, AND STREETS OF THE CITY

21:19-20

The foundations of the wall of the city were adorned with all kinds of precious stones: the first foundation was jasper, the second sapphire, the third chalcedony, the fourth emerald, 20 the fifth sardonyx, the sixth sardius, the seventh chrysolite, the eighth beryl, the ninth topaz, the tenth chrysoprase, the eleventh jacinth, and the twelfth amethyst.

21:19-21 John then turns his attention to the decorations of the "foundation stones of the city wall," which are named after the 12 apostles. They are 12 stones of different colors. The first foundation stone is jasper. Its color is not indicated, but appears to be clear as diamond. The second stone is sapphire which is probably blue; the third stone is chalcedony, which can be in a wide range of colors, but commonly is gray or grayish-blue to brown; The fourth stone is emerald, which is a bright green; the fifth stone is sardonyx, which is red and white; the sixth stone is sardius, which is ruby red; the seventh stone is chrysolite, which is a golden color; the eighth stone is beryl, which is a sea green; the ninth stone is topaz, which is a transparent yellow-green; the tenth stone is chrysoprase, which is also a green; the eleventh stone is jacinth, which is violet color; and the twelfth stone is amethyst, which is purple. Together these stones reflected a brilliant rainbow of colors from the New Jerusalem throughout the New Earth.

Reflection: Do you think God enjoys the gems and beautiful elements of His creation?

THE GATES

21:21

The twelve gates were twelve pearls: each individual gate was of one pearl. And the street of the city was pure gold, like transparent glass.

The next aspect of the New Jerusalem John noticed was "the twelve gates, which were twelve pearls." As today, pearls were greatly prized in the 1st century, but there has never been a pearl the size of these gates. This is the only gem that is formed by a living organism, an oyster. As a grain of sand penetrates and hurts or irritates the oyster, its mechanism builds up layers of beautiful pearl to cover the irritation, permitting the irritation to exist inside the oyster without pain.

Our God is like the oyster in that He also is irritated at the offense or wound of the sinner, so He covers it (him) with the beautiful pearl of His righteousness, so that the sinner's offenses do not irritate His holiness and thus allows a perfect co-habitation. We cannot imagine a gate, perhaps 1,400 miles tall of one stone, but what a beauty and what a symbol of God's mercy and covering for sinners.

Lastly, "the streets of the city was pure gold, like transparent glass." The transparency indicates that there are no impurities in the material, but there is no transparent gold in this creation. This is something new that helps to magnify and radiate the glory of God.

Reflection: Does this indicate how much God wants to be evident in the world today as well? How is the glory of the nature of God evident today? Do these verses help?

    Rom 3:23 (negatively)

    Rom 4:20

    Rom 15:7

    1 Cor 10:31

    2 Cor 4:6

    2 Cor 4:15

    Phil 1:11

    Phil 2:11

INSIDE THE CITY: NO TEMPLE OR LIGHTS AND OPEN GATES

21:22

But I saw no temple in it, for the Lord God Almighty and the Lamb are its temple.

21:22 Apparently surprised, John saw no temple in the New Jerusalem, "for the Lord God Almighty and the Lamb are its temple." All through the church age, the Tribulation and the millennium there has been a temple in heaven (see 7:15; 11:19; 14:15, 17; 15:5-8; 16:1, 17), but now there is no need of a special place to worship in heaven.

The proximity and bond of the believer to Christ is such that worship is as natural as breathing from anywhere and worship will be like living itself. These are the true worshippers that God has always sought (John 4:23).

21:23

The city had no need of the sun or of the moon to shine in it, for the glory of God illuminated it. The Lamb is its light.

21:23 As seen earlier, the splendor of God's radiance and glory is such that the "city had no need of the sun or of the moon to shine in it, for the glory of God illuminated it." With the absence of any natural light source in the new heaven, anything outside of the light of the glory of God (*Shekinah* glory) remains in absolute outer darkness. Where the Lord Jesus resides is perfect light in abundance.

The new earth will be very different. Our earth presently depends on cycles of day and night, tides caused by the moon, and annual seasons. With no seas, no sun or moon. The new earth will need only the resplendent glory of God to illuminate it. Likewise this is a different type of light, which does not originate from burning a fuel source that consumes its source and generates heat. In eternity the light source is God himself who is an infinite energy source. He is the "light of the world" spiritually now, and also physically in eternity.

Reflection: We don't know all the answers, but life will always be dependent on God. Do you like to be totally dependent on God for everything?

THE NATIONS IN ETERNITY

21:24

And the nations of those who are saved shall walk in its light, and the kings of the earth bring their glory and honor into it.

21:24 "The nations (*ethnos*, "people, Gentiles") of those who are saved" and the "kings of the earth" represent those from "every tongue, tribe, and nation," may sound like a millennial description, but the introductory "and" (*kai*) is used to introduce a chronological sequence.

There will be living human beings in the millennium, but physical life as we know it, will be impossible in the environment of the New Earth for eternity. These are glorified redeemed people equipped to live in the eternal state. The "kings of the earth bring their glory and honor into it" to indicate that there are no social or class structure.

Everyone surrenders their earthly or millennial prestige in order to be equal with every other believer before the only King of kings.

21:25-26

Its gates shall not be shut at all by day (there shall be no night there). 26 And they shall bring the glory and the honor of the nations into it.

21:25-26 "The gates shall not be shut" since there will be no restrictions to entry for the redeemed, nor obviously any threat in existence. "There shall be no night there," since the glory of God will never fade. All the "glory and the honor of the nations" will be left in New Jerusalem and dissolved. It will mean nothing in eternity. This is the implication of the statements of twenty-four elders who "cast their crowns before the throne" (4:10).

Reflection: That kind of self-glory is foreign to eternity. Can you handle not being anyone special in eternity?

A FINAL WARNING AND CLARIFICATION

21:27

But there shall by no means enter it anything that defiles, or causes an abomination or a lie, but only those who are written in the Lamb's Book of Life.

21:27 Just to make it clear, nothing or no one "that defiles, or causes an abomination or a lie" will be able to enter the New Jerusalem. They will have long since been dealt with, and no one or thing will slip by His final judgment. The NIV reads, "Nothing impure will ever enter it, nor will anyone who does what is shameful or deceitful…" Other lists of the excluded are 21:8 and 22:15.

The only ones who can live in this city are "those who are written in the Lamb's Book of Life." Of the six times the "book of life" is mentioned, this is the only reference to the "Lamb's Book of Life" (3:5; 18:8; 17:8; 20:12, 15).

Obviously there are many questions unanswered about the eternal state, but the final chapter will reveal a few more details. Let there be no mistake, however, no unredeemed, unforgiven, or fake believers will ever enter this city. No one could ever be good enough to enter. They must be given the righteousness of God and Christ must have taken their penalty for all their sins, or they would never be allowed to enter this city.

Amazingly, this offer of full forgiveness and absolute cleansing of every sin is freely available to anyone who recognizes their unworthiness and is willing to trust God's Word by accepting Christ as their only hope and personal Savior. To this group, and this group alone, is granted the eternal citizenship in the New Jerusalem.

Reflection: How can you be sure your name is in the Book of Life? (1 Jn 5:13).

CHAPTER 22

NEW WORLD

"As the Bible began in the Garden of Eden, so it ends in the lost Paradise."

A few new details of the eternal city are added before bringing this amazing book to conclusion. As the Bible began in the Garden of Eden, so it ends in the lost Paradise. John is shown "a pure river of water of life, clear as crystal." Since there is no sea or ocean in the New World (21:1), there could be no hydrologic cycle, thus no rain to flow into the river, nor sea for it to flow into. Either the river is a spring and is totally consumed or the description of the "water of life" is not "water" as we know it. It certainly is symbolic of eternal life (Isa 12:3; John 4:13-14; 7:38), which flows "from the throne of God and of the Lamb." This cannot be confused with the millennial river that flows from the temple and from Jerusalem described in Ezek 47:1, 12 and Zech 14:8.

I. THE RIVER OF THE WATER OF LIFE (22:1-2A)

22:1-2

And he showed me a pure river of water of life, clear as crystal, proceeding from the throne of God and of the Lamb. 2 In the middle of its street, and on either side of the river, was the tree of life, which bore twelve fruits, each tree yielding its fruit every month.

22:1-2 The "river of water of life" is a symbol of a never-ending, pure, unpolluted life-stream from God Himself. The reference in Rev 22 describes water flowing "in the middle of its street." The overarching "tree of life" extends itself "on either side of the river."

This tree of life is the eternal counterpart to the tree of life that appeared in the Garden of Eden (Gen 2:; 3:22-24) which gives provision for the immortals who habitat the city. The "tree of life" is connected to a "blessing" in Prov 3:18; 11:30; 13:12; 15:4, which would indicate that the "tree of life" must indicate the blessing of eternal spiritual life.

The tree produces "twelve fruits, each tree yielding its fruit every month," which indicates the variety of refreshing aspects in the eternal city. The term "month" is an anthropomorphic concept since there is no day or night, or time in eternity, but from our perspective this is how frequently the fruit is produced.

Reflection: Though we only have glimpses of the environment, can

THE NEW WORLD

you imagine such a paradise? Why would we need fruit in eternity? Or is it merely to be enjoyed?

II. THE TREE OF LIFE (22:2b)

22:2b

"The leaves of the tree were for the healing of the nations.

22:2 The "leaves of the tree were for the healing (therapeia) of the nations" seem unnecessary since there is neither sickness nor wounds in eternity. The word has the idea of "life-giving" or "health-giving." Whatever the benefits may be they appear to be central to eternal existence. Though there is no indication that the saints will eat these leaves, it is possible. The Lord Jesus ate fish with His disciples after the resurrection (Luke 24:42-43; Acts 10:41).

Reflection: Could this be one of the enjoyments of heaven?

III. THE THRONE OF GOD (22:3-4)

22:3-4

And there shall be no more curse, but the throne of God and of the Lamb shall be in it, and His servants shall serve Him. 4 They shall see His face, and His name shall be on their foreheads.

22:3 In this amazing New World "there shall be no more curse," which refers back to the Genesis 3 devastating consequence of the first sin that destroyed mankind and all of creation. Thus there will be no more death (Gen 2:17), the most terrifying aspect of the curse. On the contrary, the "throne of God and of the Lamb" (the Lord Jesus Christ) will reign forever.

Our occupation throughout eternity is described in the phrase, "His servants shall serve Him." A mere glimpse at our creation indicates the amazing creativity of our God who will have an infinite variety of tasks to be accomplished. Yes, He could do whatever He wills without assistance, but His nature is to do things with and through His servants even in eternity. But the thrill of eternity will be the privilege to "see His face."

Jesus had promised the "pure in heart for they shall see His face" (Mat 5:8). Sinful man cannot survive this exposure to His blazing, radiance (Ex 33:20). This privilege is amplified by the fact that no mortal has ever seen God in person face to face (John 1:18; 6:46; 1 Tim 6:16; 1 John 4:12). The "name" of God will be "on their foreheads," referring to "servants" (the redeemed of all the ages). This forever will symbolize that we belong to the Lamb, since He "purchased" us with His blood (Rev 5:9).

Reflection: How does it feel to be a "bond-slave" to Jesus? Can you imagine being a slave to anyone else?

IV. THE SAINT'S REIGN WITH GOD (22:5)

22:5

There shall be no night there: They need no lamp nor light of the sun, for the Lord God gives them light. And they shall reign forever and ever.

22:5 As a further description of the heavenly scene John gives reiteration of the environment of eternity that describes what evidently most impressed John as he wrote. "There shall be no night there." Since there is no sun as a light source, or rotating earth's surface in that light source, night and day as we know it has ceased. "They need no lamp nor light of the sun, for the Lord God gives them light." In an amazing display of refracted light from the crystal city of the New Jerusalem the new world will exist in perpetual light (21:22-26). All the conditions of life under the cursed earth require activity-rest and day-night cycles, but not so in eternity.

The final descriptive words to the saints have echoed throughout the ages: "they shall reign forever and ever." Jesus had promise this in the beginning of this book, "He who overcomes, I will grant to him to sit down with Me on My throne, as I also overcame and sat down with My Father on His throne" (Rev 3:21).

Paul likewise told us of the promise, "If we endure, we will also reign with Him" (2 Tim 2:12). Whatever His plans are for eternity, He has chosen to share them with His special people, the ones who were willing to trust His Word, even in the face of persecution, when they could not see any of the amazing experiences awaiting them. He will honor our trusting obedience to Him forever.

Reflection: Can you explain the relationship between trusting Him

THE NEW WORLD

and obeying Him today?

V. THE CERTAINTY OF THE RETURN OF CHRIST (22:6-7)

22:6

Then he said to me, "These words are faithful and true." And the Lord God of the holy prophets sent His angel to show His servants the things which must shortly take place.

22:6-7 John now begins his concluding remarks or his epilogue to this incredible book. From the perspective of eternity, John looks back into time and gives some concluding challenges and remarks. John is told, "These words are faithful and true," to describe the absolute certainty of what he had been told and seen.

John had been told this earlier (21:5), which indicates the reaffirm their reality. Twice before in the Book of Revelation, the Lord Jesus is referred to as the "Faithful and True" One (3:14; 19:11). Just as He is, so are the Words He has revealed to John. Absolutely everything John has described will take place precisely as it was written.

The prophecies of Jesus' First Coming are more than 300 fulfilled prophecies. Here are a few prophecies that were fulfilled in the OT: Israel would go into captivity (Lev 26:33-39); Babylon would be destroyed (Isa 13:1; 14:27; Jer 50:51); Messiah would be born in Bethlehem (Mic 5:2), to a virgin mother (Isa 7:14), only to be killed by sinners (Isa 53:7-10).

Revelation is not a fanciful dream or the vivid imagination of John. On the contrary, John has placed the integrity of God and the accuracy of His angels at risk should these events not take place as described, when he said, "the Lord God of the holy prophets sent His angel to show His servants the things which must shortly take place."

Just as certainly as God spoke through the prophets of the OT and NT, so now He is speaking with the same certainty. John is claiming equal inspiration for the Book of Revelation as with all the other books of revelation.

Reflection: Could God remain true or truth, if His Word failed to be true?

Then since this Book is true, then a number of responses are called for:

RESPONSE 1: OBEY THE BOOK

22:7

Behold, I am coming quickly! Blessed is he who keeps the words of the prophecy of this book.

22:7 The urgency of the Book is emphasized again with the warning that "I am coming quickly!," which means that Jesus will come rapidly or suddenly, with no time to prepare. In light of this hope and warning,

John writes the sixth of seven beatitudes in Revelation: "Blessed is he who keeps (*tereo*, "to hold fast, or guard") the words of the prophecy of this book." This is the word used in 14:12, "the perseverance of the saints who keep the commandments of God and their faith in Jesus." Many Christians do not prize their opportunity to show their obedience to the Lord, rather they claim to live under grace with no interest in commandments for believers. Rather they want to merely follow the Spirit's leadings.

Most Christians can not state the Ten Commandments, much less have any notion of the specific 365 NT commands that they are expected to obey. How can anyone obey His commands when they do not know them? "If you love Me, you will keep My commandments... If you keep My commandments, you will abide in My love; just as I have kept My Father's commandments and abide in His love (John 14:15; 15:10).

John wrote in his epistle, "By this we know that we have come to know Him, if we keep His commandments. The one who says, 'I have come to know Him,' and does not keep His commandments, is a liar, and the truth is not in him" (1 John 2:3,4).

Some only want to be accountable for what the Holy Spirit speaks to them, not the written commands in the Bible, also called the Moral Law of God. They either want a mystical reiteration or a series of special personal commands just for them, but they do not want to take the time to find, remember and apply the commands already revealed in Scripture. If they do not sense such personal commands, then they are free to do whatever they want.

THE NEW WORLD

However, in this text, what are the "words" that the believer is called to obey? There are no specific commands in the Revelation for believers from chapters 4 through 22. There were commands addressed to the churches in chapters 2-3.

The best solutions to heed the Book of Revelation seems to be to live in the light of certainty of coming events, to desire to see Christ reign over all the earth ("thy kingdom come; thy will be done on earth as it is in heaven"), and especially to warn mankind of the end time events and the certainty of a horrible judgment for unbelievers.

The Revelation and study of prophecy is not to satisfy our curiosity about the future, but, when properly understood, becomes the core of our worldview and thus our motivation for holiness and intense evangelistic fervor. If prophecy leads to speculation and schemes of knowing precisely details not clearly revealed. Generally, this leads one away from practical motivation for witnessing the gospel and reaching the unreached peoples of the world.

God has revealed sufficient to keep us on-course as "fishers of men." Peter summed up the proper understanding of end time events saying, "Since all these things are to be destroyed in this way, what sort of people ought you to be in holy conduct and godliness, looking for and hastening the coming of the day of God... Therefore, beloved, since you look for these things, be diligent to be found by Him in peace, spotless and blameless" (2 Pet 3:11-12, 14).

Reflection: How has the study of Revelation changed your life? What decisions have you made for your life because you know what is soon to happen?

RESPONSE 2: SPONTANEOUS WORSHIP (22:8-9)

22:8-9

Now I, John, saw and heard these things. And when I heard and saw, I fell down to worship before the feet of the angel who showed me these things. 9 Then he said to me, "See that you do not do that. For I am your fellow servant, and of your brethren the prophets, and of those who keep the words of this book. Worship God.

22:8 John now testifies that he really "saw and heard these things" that he was writing about. This is the first time since Rev 1:9 when John directly refers to himself. So overwhelmed by his experiences he "fell down to worship before the feet of the angel who showed me these things." His enthusiasm motivated a worship of the wrong object. John knew that angels were not to be worshipped (19:10), nor other celestial beings (from his experience on the Mt. of Transfiguration – Matt 17:6). He could not contain himself in excitement. The angel said to John, "See that you do not do that." It is strictly forbidden to worship, or give adoration to, or pray to, any created being, for any reason.

He continues, "I am your fellow servant, and of your brethren the prophets and of those who keep the words of this book." Angels are great an powerful creatures, but still mere creatures. They are nowhere near worthy of worship. Angels serve God's purpose and God's people at His command.

The author of Hebrews asked a rhetorical question of angels, "Are they not all ministering spirits, sent out to render service for the sake of those who will inherit salvation?" (Heb 1:14).

Succinctly the angel gives the command to John, "Worship God." This is how a proper understanding of Revelation should lead its reader to respond. No one else, even the angels, are ever to be worshipped (Col 2:18), this includes the saints, the Virgin Mary, and certainly any other supposed god, all of which is considered idolatry.

Reflection: How do you understand that you are to worship God? What does God expect from His servants in worship?

(Worship is a often repeated theme in Revelation (4:8-11; 5:8-14; 7:9-12; 15:2-4; 19:1-6).)

RESPONSE 3: PROCLAIM THE PROPHECY OF THE BOOK (22:10-11)

22:10

And he said to me, "Do not seal the words of the prophecy of this book, for the time is at hand.

22:10 Another command follows, "Do not seal the words of the prophecy of this book," that is to say that the message of this prophecy of the end times is not to be a secret guarded by a few, but rather is to become general knowledge of all believers. This must become part of everyone's worldview. They are to understand the words for what they say, not some irrelevant meaning that the interpreter's imagination invented or allegorized for some other purpose. Daniel had been told to seal up his prophecies that dealt with last half of the Tribulation (Dan 8:26), because John's revelation puts all the pieces together describing the major details of end of time and the imminence of Christ's return for every generation since the Apostle John.

Notice the focus is on the "words of the prophecy," not the mystical, or allegorical or varying meanings that can be invented to these passages. It is the clear, obvious, literal, linguistic meaning of the "words" that convey God's meaning. They are not sealed in mystery or mysticism.

Furthermore, to not teach this Book of Revelation is to be disobedient to this command, and miss the enormous benefit of living in the light of His wisdom (1:3). This is also a key part of the "whole counsel [or purpose] of God" (Acts 20:27) that we are not to "hold back" from teaching. All the more so when we see the world setting up for the literal fulfillment of these prophesies, "for the time is at hand."

Reflection: How does the fact that any moment could bring the initiation of these events by the occurrence of the rapture of all believers affect your life's plans, ambitions and lifestyle?

RESPONSE TO TRUTH FIXES ONE'S DESTINY

22:11

He who is unjust, let him be unjust still; he who is filthy, let him be filthy still; he who is righteous, let him be righteous still; he who is holy, let him be holy still.

22:11 Anyone who hears truth and continues to "be unjust" or "be filthy" will only be hardened in his own choices and firmly fixed forever in their eternal destiny in hell. Whereas, those who continue to practice "righteousness" and "keep himself holy" demonstrates that he has chosen to live by faith in His Word. The adverb "still" (*eti*) has the sense of "yet all the more." Thus those who are "unjust" or "filthy" in this life will only be more so in hell; and those who are "righteous" and "holy" will be even more so in their glorified bodies in heaven.

However one responds to truth in this life will not only determine their eternal destiny, but will be amplified in their existence forever. This is why the Scripture warns the reader not to "harden your hearts as in rebellion" (Heb 3:15 quoting Psa 95:7b-8), or later adds, "O, that today you would listen as he speaks! Do not harden your hearts" (Heb 4:7).

There comes a time when God ceases to convict the sinner and "gives them over to the desires of their hearts" (Rom 1:24, 26, 28).

Jesus said, "Let them alone; they are blind guides of the blind" (Matt 15:14). God created man with the freedom to choose and He does not interfere with the unrepentant unbeliever who will not trust His Word to the consequences of their choices.

The Revelation is the final watershed issue: either the reader will take seriously God's Word or he will ignore it to his own destruction. Paul wrote, "For the message about the cross is foolishness to those who are perishing, but to us who are being saved it is the power of God" (1 Cor 1:18).

Reflection: What can we do to persuade men to take seriously what God has said in His Word?

RESPONSE 4: REMAIN FAITHFUL IN SERVING FOR HE IS COMING JUDGMENT AND REWARD (22:12)

22:12

And behold, I am coming quickly, and My reward is with Me, to give to every one according to his work.

22:12 Suddenly Jesus speaks, "Behold, I come quickly." This event could occur at any moment. We are to live in the light or truth that time is short and everything as we know it could change in a moment, with no chance to prepare or change our ways; therefore, we must choose to make His kingdom our priority now while there is time, and be found faithful.

He promises to bring His "reward" and to "give to everyone according to his work." Whatever this "reward" will be is not clarified, except to say that it is "great" (?). This will not be a prideful or selfish reward but rather an increased capacity to serve God.

Our faithfulness now will determine our opportunities to serve the King in His Kingdom and in eternity (Matt 25:14-30). This is why John exhorted the believers to "Watch for yourselves, that you do not lose what we have accomplished, but that you may receive a full reward" (2 John 8).

Reflection: If reward is based on faithfulness, then how will you live if His coming appears to be sooner rather than later? What specifically

VI. THE ETERNAL CHRIST (22:13)

22:13

I am the Alpha and the Omega, the Beginning and the End, the First and the Last.

22:13 God was the same in the beginning as He has now revealed Himself to be in the end of time. He has not changed in His original purpose in creating earth and man, and His eternal purpose will be fulfilled. As He was in the beginning of history, so He is in the end of history.

All of time and history has been but a blink in eternity, but in that brief span when time existed He will have bought with His own blood a people made in His image who chose to love Him and be like Him and who long with all their heart to spend eternity in His presence even more than life itself.

All three of these titles (Alpha and Omega- Rev 1:8; Beginning and the End – Rev 21:6; First and the Last – Isa 41:4; 48:12) are all titles are applied to God yet here they are applied to Jesus Christ to clarify forever His deity. Now we know so much more about the eternal God and Savior who is revealed in this "Revelation" of Himself.

Reflection: Does this revelation make you love Him more? Does it give clarity and understanding about how to relate to this One who is from eternity?

VII. THE STARK CONTRAST IN HUMANITY (22:14-15)

22:14-15

Blessed are those who do His commandments, that they may have the right to the tree of life, and may enter through the gates into the city. 15 But outside are dogs and sorcerers and sexually immoral and murderers and idolaters, and whoever loves and practices a lie.

22:14-15 The seven beatitudes of the Revelation (1:3; 14:13; 16:15;

19:9; 20:6; 22:7, 14). The last of the seven beatitudes in Revelation, which are all introduced by the purpose of God for His followers, that is, they will be "blessed."

A number of Bible versions have different renderings of this verse. In the manuscripts of the KJV and NJV the expression "those who do His commandments" is hallmark of the saved which gives them "the right to the tree of life," because they want to become like God. Whichever the case, both describe the righteous. These are the ones that give purpose and reason to all of time and history.

By contrast, created beings in the image of God with immortal souls have chosen to live like "dogs" using "sorcerers" (*pharmakos*, the root of "pharmaceuticals" or drugs – Rev 9:21; 18:23; 21:8) to live in a drug induced fantasy world rather than take responsibility for their own reality, and to become "sexually immoral (*pornos*, root of English "pornography") and murderers (excluded in 21:8; 9:21 and Rom 1:29) and idolaters"(worshipers of false gods- Rev 21:8).In Deut 23:18 the Hebrew term is applied to male homosexual prostitutes.

How unlike God could they choose to become? And probably the worse of the descriptions that make them totally incompatible with God are those who "loves and practices a lie." It is not those who have ever lied (lest no one ever could be admitted to heaven- 1 Cor 6:11), but those who choose to believe in and love to practice lying refusing to come to repentance and the truth.

A similar description of the lost of mankind is found in 21:8, 27, which is here reiterated to make it clear forever that unrepentant sinners who refuse to come to Christ for cleansing and the gift of righteousness by faith will have no part with God in eternity. They will have their wish to live forever without Him in isolation and torment "outside" the New Jerusalem in the lake of fire (20:15; 21:8).

Reflection: At life's end one's eternal destiny is sealed forever. May this final warning keep us faithful!

VIII. THE INVITATION OF THE SPIRIT AND THE BRIDE (22:16-17)

22:16

I, Jesus, have sent My angel to testify to you these things in the churches. I am the Root and the Offspring of David, the Bright and Morning Star."

22:16 Christ Himself delivered the entire book to John meticulously through His "angel" for the benefit "of the churches." Jesus further reveals Himself as the "Root and the Offspring of David" and "the Bright and Morning Star," both which have great Jewish significance. "A star shall come forth from Jacob, a scepter shall rise from Israel" (Num 24:17).

Then Jesus promised the overcomers in the church of Thyatira that they would receive the "morning star" (2:28), which refers to Jesus Himself. In history (time and space) Christ came as a descendent of David (Matt 1:1; Isa 11:11; Rev 5:5). His coming was like the morning star that appears just before daybreak (a new day is dawning, when this star is seen).

THE FINAL INVITATION

22:17

And the Spirit and the bride say, "Come!" And let him who hears say, "Come!" And let him who thirsts come. Whoever desires, let him take the water of life freely.

22:17 The "Spirit and the bride" join together to extend the invitation to all and any who "thirsts" to "come." "Whoever desires, let him take the water of life freely." This gracious and benevolent invitation is extended to every generation and to all people as long as they are alive in this world to choose life and walk away from death, deception and deceit of sin and falsehood.

How can believers consciously keep this a hidden secret from those who desperately need to hear it? It has always been a heart issue: "whoever desires." He promised, "Come to Me, all who are weary and heavy laden and I will give you rest" (Matt 11:28), and "The one who comes to Me I will certainly not cast out" (John 6:37).

Do you truly want Christ in every aspect of your life now and do you want to be in every aspect of His life forever? This is not a rite or ceremony or repeating a prayer or being baptized.

Reflection: It is all about accepting and depending on His Word as truth and wanting His partnership in this life more than anything else. Does this describe your testimony?

IX. THE FINAL WARNING (22:18-19)

22:18-20

For I testify to everyone who hears the words of the prophecy of this book: If anyone adds to these things, God will add to him the plagues that are written in this book; 19 and if anyone takes away from the words of the book of this prophecy, God shall take away his part from the Book of Life, from the holy city, and from the things which are written in this book.

22:18 Jesus personally gives this final warning concerning the "words of the prophecy of this book" that they are a serious matter. The certainty of the doom of sinners and the reward of the saints will all come true. This dual warning against either adding to or subtracting from this book will bring serious consequences. This warning was given in the OT (Deut 4:2; 12:32; Prov 30:5-6) and now in the conclusion of the NT. Inspiration and revelation of God's words to mankind are extremely serious and only given to a few individuals in history. It is not a perpetual, on-going revelation.

The canon of Scripture was closed at the end of the first century. Anyone pretending to add to these Holy Scriptures, or cut inconvenient passages from the texts or minimize the value of the first century documents stating that contemporary revelations are more valuable, are in serious jeopardy of incurring His wrath.

From the beginning of the church false prophets have pretended to add new revelations (Montanists, Joseph Smith, Mary Baker Eddy and many false prophets in modern times). Rejecting or depreciating the revealed Word of God is to reject God Himself and such persons will receive His judgment and have no participation in "the tree of life" nor have access to "the holy city" of eternity (22:14).

No true believer would ever tamper with revealed Scripture. Their love for His Word as well as this warning would keep them from falsifying or misrepresenting an addition to this finished revelation. Some today attempt to sell "special revelations from God" for profit which Paul warned, "we are not like so many others, hucksters who peddle the word of God for profit..." (2 Cor 2:17).

The true believers will value what God has revealed, guard its precepts, learn to live by its commands, and take every word as though delivered to them to take very seriously.

Reflection: What would give you the motivation to study His Word daily and commit to living its plan? Has anyone ever asked you what you learned from the Word today? Lets exhort one another daily.

X. THE FINAL PRAYER AND PROMISE (22:20-21)

22:20

He who testifies to these things says, "Surely I am coming quickly." Amen. Even so, come, Lord Jesus! The grace of our Lord Jesus Christ be with you all. Amen."

22:20-21 Jesus personally give His final words, "Surely I am coming quickly" to which John prays to Jesus, "Amen. Even so, come, Lord Jesus!" Sounds like John loved to see His return (2 Tim 4:8).

There is only one reason why He has delayed His return: "he does not wish for any to perish but for all to come to repentance," especially the last people group ("this gospel of the kingdom will be preached throughout the whole inhabited earth as a testimony to all the nations from *ethnos* or ethnic people groups. When this task is accomplished the end will come" (Matt 24:14).

Then John adds a benediction for all the readers: "the grace of our Lord Jesus Christ be with you all. Amen." This common benediction now brings finality to the revelations of the NT. No book in the Bible is clearer about what happens to man after death and will happen in the future of this world and the world to come after the millennium.

No one who knows these words will ever see life the same. Until the end-time clock begins with the rapture of the church before the Tribulation Period begins, may we commit ourselves to world evangelism and finally bring about the fulfillment of the Great Commission to build a functioning group of disciples among every last tribe, language and ethnic people group.

Reflection: His grace is sufficient to enable His church to accomplish His mission before He returns. May we ever be about His business till we see Him face to face.

Bibliography

Aune, David E. Vol. 52A, *Revelation 1–5. Word Biblical Commentary*. Dallas: Word, Incorporated, 1998.

Barton, Bruce B. *Revelation*. Edited by Osborne, Grant R. Life Application Bible Commentary. Wheaton, IL: Tyndale House Publishers, 2000.

Beale, G. K. *The Book of Revelation: A Commentary on the Greek Text. New International Greek Testament Commentary*. Grand Rapids, MI; Carlisle, Cumbria: W.B. Eerdmans; Paternoster Press, 1999.

Biblical Studies Press. *The NET Bible First Edition Notes,* Biblical Studies Press, 2006.

Bratcher, Robert G. and Howard Hatton. *A Handbook on the Revelation to John.* UBS Handbook Series. New York: United Bible Societies, 1993.

Brunk, M. J., "The Seven Chruches of Revelation Two and Three," *Bibliotheca Sacra* Volume 126. Dallas, TX: Dallas Theological Seminary, July,1969.

Cabal, Ted, Chad Owen Brand, E. Ray Clendenen et al. *The Apologetics Study Bible: Real Questions, Straight Answers, Stronger Faith.* Nashville, TN: Holman Bible Publishers, 2007.

DeBruyn, Lawrence A. "Preterism and 'This Generation,'" *Bibliotheca Sacra* Volume 167. Dallas, TX: Dallas Theological Seminary, 2010.

Deere, Jack S., "Premillennialism in Revelation 20:4-6," *Bibliotheca Sacra* Volume 135. Dallas, TX: Dallas Theological Seminary, (Jan 1978).

Dyer, Charles H., "The Identity of Babylon in Revelation 17-18: Part 1," *Bibliotheca Sacra* Volume 144. Dallas, TX: Dallas Theological Seminary, (July 1987).

Easley, Kendell H. Vol. 12, *Revelation. Holman New Testament Commentary.* Nashville, TN: Broadman & Holman Publishers, 1998.

Gregg, Steve. *Revelation, Four Views: A Parallel Commentary.* Nashville, TN: T. Nelson Publishers, 1997.

Holman Concise Bible Commentary. Edited by Dockery, David S. Nashville, TN: Broadman & Holman Publishers, 1998.

Hughes, Robert B. and J. Carl Laney. *Tyndale Concise Bible Commentary. The Tyndale reference library*. Wheaton, IL: Tyndale House Publishers, 2001.

Ironside, H. A. *Lectures on the Book of Revelation.* Neptune, N. J.: Loizeaux Brothers, 1920.

Jamieson, Robert, A. R. Fausset and David Brown. *Commentary Critical and Explanatory on the Whole Bible.* Oak Harbor, WA: Logos Research Systems, Inc., 1997.

Kistemaker, Simon J. and William Hendriksen. Vol. 20, *Exposition of the Book of Revelation. New Testament Commentary.* Grand Rapids: Baker Book House, 1953-2001.

KJV Bible Commentary. Edited by Hindson, Edward E. and Woodrow Michael Kroll. Nashville: Thomas Nelson, 1994.

Lukaszewski, Albert L. and Mark Dubis. *The Lexham Syntactic Greek New Testament: Expansions and Annotations*, Logos Bible Software, 2009.

MacArthur, John F., Jr. *Revelation 1–11. MacArthur New Testament Commentary*. Chicago: Moody Press, 1999.

MacDonald, William. Believer's Bible Commentary: Old and New Testaments. Edited by Farstad, Arthur. Nashville: Thomas Nelson, 1995.

MacLeod, David J., "The Second "Last Thing"; The Defeat of Antichrist (Rev 19:17-21)," *Bibliotheca Sacra* Volume 156. Dallas, TX: Dallas Theological Seminary, (July 1999).

McGee, J. Vernon. *Thru the Bible Commentary*. electronic ed. Nashville: Thomas Nelson, 1997.

Metzger, Bruce Manning and United Bible Societies. *A Textual Commentary on the Greek New Testament,* Second Edition a Companion Volume to the United Bible Societies' Greek New Testament (4th Rev. Ed.). London; New York: United Bible Societies, 1994.

Nakhro, Mazie, "The Meaning of Worship according to the Book of Revelation," *Bibliotheca Sacra* Volume 158. Dallas, TX: Dallas Theological Seminary, (Jan 2001).

New Bible Commentary: 21st Century Edition. Edited by Carson, D. A., R. T. France, J. A. Motyer and G. J. Wenham. 4th ed. Leicester, England; Downers Grove, IL: Inter-Varsity Press, 1994.

Osborne, Grant R. *Revelation.* Baker Exegetical Commentary on the New Testament. Grand Rapids, MI: Baker Academic, 2002.

Radmacher, Earl D., Ronald Barclay Allen and H. Wayne House. *Nelson's New Illustrated Bible Commentary.* Nashville: T. Nelson Publishers, 1999.

Radmacher, Earl D., Ronald Barclay Allen and H. Wayne House. *The Nelson Study Bible: New King James Version.* Nashville: T. Nelson Publishers, 1997.

Revelation. Edited by Spence-Jones, H. D. M. The Pulpit Commentary. London; New York: Funk & Wagnalls Company, 1909.

Richards, Lawrence O. *The Bible Reader's Companion*. electronic ed. Wheaton: Victor Books, 1991.

The Ante-Nicene Fathers, Volume VII: Fathers of the Third and Fourth Centuries: Lactantius, Venantius, Asterius, Victorinus, Dionysius, Apostolic Teaching and Constitutions, Homily, and Liturgies. Edited by Roberts, Alexander, James Donaldson and A. Cleveland Coxe. Buffalo, NY: Christian Literature Company, 1886.

The Apocalypse of St. John. Edited by Swete, Henry Barclay. 2d. ed. Classic Commentaries on the Greek New Testament. New York: The Macmillan Company, 1906.

The Revelation of John: Volume 1. Edited by Barclay, William. The Daily Study Bible Series. Philadelphia: The Westminster John Knox Press, 1976.

The Teacher's Bible Commentary. Edited by Paschall, Franklin H. and Herschel H. Hobbs. Nashville: Broadman and Holman Publishers, 1972.

Thiessen, Henry Clarence, "Will the Church Pass Through the Tribulation?" *Bibliotheca Sacra* Volume 92. Dallas, TX: Dallas Theological Seminary, (Apr 1935).

Thomas, Robert L., "The Chronological Interpretation of Revelation 2-3," *Bibliotheca Sacra* Volume 124. Dallas, TX: Dallas Theological Seminary, (Oct 1967).

Utley, Robert James. Vol. Volume 12, "Hope in Hard Times - The Final Curtain:" *Revelation. Study Guide Commentary Series*. Marshall, TX: Bible Lessons International, 2001.

Walvoord, John F., Roy B. Zuck and Dallas Theological Seminary. *The Bible Knowledge Commentary: An Exposition of the Scriptures*. Wheaton, IL: Victor Books, 1985.

Wiersbe, Warren W. *The Bible Exposition Commentary*. Wheaton, IL: Victor Books, 1996.

Willmington, H. L. *Willmington's Bible Handbook*. Wheaton, IL: Tyndale House Publishers, 1997.

Wong, Daniel K. K., "The First Horseman of Revelation 6," *Bibliotheca Sacra* Volume 153. Dallas, TX: Dallas Theological Seminary, (Apr 1996).

Wong, Daniel K. K., "The Two Witnesses in Revelation 11," *Bibliotheca Sacra* Volume 154. Dallas, TX: Dallas Theological Seminary, (July 1997).

Wuest, Kenneth S., "The Rapture—Precisely When?" *Bibliotheca Sacra* Volume 114. Dallas, TX: Dallas Theological Seminary, (Jan 1957).

Yates, Richard Shalom, "The Resurrection of the Tribulation Saints," *Bibliotheca Sacra* Volume 163:652. Dallas, TX: Dallas Theological Seminary, (Oct-Dec 2006).

_____, "The Rewards of the Tribulation Saints," *Bibliotheca Sacra* Volume 163. Dallas, TX: Dallas Theological Seminary, (July-Sept 2006).

Yeatts, John R. *Revelation*. Believers Church Bible Commentary. Scottdale, PA: Herald Press, 2003.